Practical Machine Learning for Computer Vision

End-to-End Machine Learning for Images

Valliappa Lakshmanan, Martin Görner,
and Ryan Gillard

Beijing · Boston · Farnham · Sebastopol · Tokyo

Practical Machine Learning for Computer Vision

by Valliappa Lakshmanan, Martin Görner, and Ryan Gillard

Copyright © 2021 Valliappa Lakshmanan, Martin Görner, and Ryan Gillard. All rights reserved.

Published by O'Reilly Media, Inc., 1005 Gravenstein Highway North, Sebastopol, CA 95472.

O'Reilly books may be purchased for educational, business, or sales promotional use. Online editions are also available for most titles (*http://oreilly.com*). For more information, contact our corporate/institutional sales department: 800-998-9938 or *corporate@oreilly.com*.

Acquisition Editor: Rebecca Novack
Development Editor: Amelia Blevins and Shira Evans
Production Editor: Katherine Tozer
Copyeditor: Rachel Head
Proofreader: Piper Editorial Consulting, LLC

Indexer: Ellen Troutman-Zaig
Interior Designer: David Futato
Cover Designer: Karen Montgomery
Illustrator: Robert Romano

July 2021: First Edition

Revision History for the First Edition
2021-07-21: First Release
2021-10-01: Second Release

See *http://oreilly.com/catalog/errata.csp?isbn=9781098102364* for release details.

The O'Reilly logo is a registered trademark of O'Reilly Media, Inc. *Practical Machine Learning for Computer Vision*, the cover image, and related trade dress are trademarks of O'Reilly Media, Inc.

The views expressed in this work are those of the authors, and do not represent the publisher's views. While the publisher and the authors have used good faith efforts to ensure that the information and instructions contained in this work are accurate, the publisher and the authors disclaim all responsibility for errors or omissions, including without limitation responsibility for damages resulting from the use of or reliance on this work. Use of the information and instructions contained in this work is at your own risk. If any code samples or other technology this work contains or describes is subject to open source licenses or the intellectual property rights of others, it is your responsibility to ensure that your use thereof complies with such licenses and/or rights.

978-1-098-10236-4
[LSI]

Table of Contents

Preface

Machine learning on images is revolutionizing healthcare, manufacturing, retail, and many other sectors. Many previously difficult problems can now be solved by training machine learning (ML) models to identify objects in images. Our aim in this book is to provide intuitive explanations of the ML architectures that underpin this fast-advancing field, and to provide practical code to employ these ML models to solve problems involving classification, measurement, detection, segmentation, representation, generation, counting, and more.

Image classification is the "hello world" of deep learning. Therefore, this book also provides a practical end-to-end introduction to deep learning. It can serve as a stepping stone to other deep learning domains, such as natural language processing.

You will learn how to design ML architectures for computer vision tasks and carry out model training using popular, well-tested prebuilt models written in TensorFlow and Keras. You will also learn techniques to improve accuracy and explainability. Finally, this book will teach you how to design, implement, and tune end-to-end ML pipelines for image understanding tasks.

Who Is This Book For?

The primary audience for this book is software developers who want to do machine learning on images. It is meant for developers who will use TensorFlow and Keras to solve common computer vision use cases.

The methods discussed in the book are accompanied by code samples available at *https://github.com/GoogleCloudPlatform/practical-ml-vision-book*. Most of this book involves open source TensorFlow and Keras and will work regardless of whether you run the code on premises, in Google Cloud, or in some other cloud.

Developers who wish to use PyTorch will find the textual explanations useful, but will probably have to look elsewhere for practical code snippets. We do welcome contributions of PyTorch equivalents of our code samples; please make a pull request to our GitHub repository.

How to Use This Book

We recommend that you read this book in order. Make sure to read, understand, and run the accompanying notebooks in the book's GitHub repository (*https://github.com/ GoogleCloudPlatform/practical-ml-vision-book*)—you can run them in either Google Colab or Google Cloud's Vertex Notebooks. We suggest that after reading each section of the text you try out the code to be sure you fully understand the concepts and techniques that are introduced. We strongly recommend completing the notebooks in each chapter before moving on to the next chapter.

Google Colab is free and will suffice to run most of the notebooks in this book; Vertex Notebooks is more powerful and so will help you run through the notebooks faster. The more complex models and larger datasets of Chapters 3, 4, 11, and 12 will benefit from the use of Google Cloud TPUs. Because all the code in this book is written using open source APIs, the code *should* also work in any other Jupyter environment where you have the latest version of TensorFlow installed, whether it's your laptop, or Amazon Web Services (AWS) Sagemaker, or Azure ML. However, we haven't tested it in those environments. If you find that you have to make any changes to get the code to work in some other environment, please do submit a pull request in order to help other readers.

The code in this book is made available to you under an Apache open source license. It is meant primarily as a teaching tool, but can serve as a starting point for your production models.

Organization of the Book

The remainder of this book is organized as follows:

- In Chapter 2, we introduce machine learning, how to read in images, and how to train, evaluate, and predict with ML models. The models we cover in Chapter 2 are generic and thus don't work particularly well on images, but the concepts introduced in this chapter are essential for the rest of the book.

- In Chapter 3, we introduce some machine learning models that do work well on images. We start with transfer learning and fine-tuning, and then introduce a variety of convolutional models that increase in sophistication as we get further and further into the chapter.

- In Chapter 4, we explore the use of computer vision to address object detection and image segmentation problems. Any of the backbone architectures introduced in Chapter 3 can be used in Chapter 4.

- In Chapters 5 through 9, we delve into the details of creating production computer vision machine learning models. We go though the standard ML pipeline stage by stage, looking at dataset creation in Chapter 5, preprocessing in Chapter 6, training in Chapter 7, monitoring and evaluation in Chapter 8, and deployment in Chapter 9. The methods discussed in these chapters are applicable to any of the model architectures and use cases discussed in Chapters 3 and 4.

- In Chapter 10, we address three up-and-coming trends. We connect all the steps covered in Chapters 5 through 9 into an end-to-end, containerized ML pipeline, then we try out a no-code image classification system that can serve for quick prototyping and as a benchmark for more custom models. Finally, we show how to build explainability into image model predictions.

- In Chapters 11 and 12, we demonstrate how the basic building blocks of computer vision are used to solve a variety of problems, including image generation, counting, pose detection, and more. Implementations are provided for these advanced use cases as well.

Conventions Used in This Book

The following typographical conventions are used in this book:

Italic
: Indicates new terms, URLs, email addresses, filenames, and file extensions.

`Constant width`
: Used for program listings, as well as within paragraphs to refer to program elements such as variable or function names, data types, environment variables, statements, and keywords.

`Constant width bold`
: Used for emphasis in code snippets, and to show command or other text that should be typed literally by the user.

`Constant width italic`
: Shows text that should be replaced with user-supplied values or by values determined by context.

 This element signifies a tip or suggestion.

This element signifies a general note.

This element signifies a warning.

Using Code Examples

Supplemental material (code examples, exercises, etc.) is available for download at *https://github.com/GoogleCloudPlatform/practical-ml-vision-book*.

If you have a technical question or a problem using the code examples, please send email to *bookquestions@oreilly.com*.

This book is here to help you get your job done. In general, if example code is offered with this book, you may use it in your programs and documentation. You do not need to contact us for permission unless you're reproducing a significant portion of the code. For example, writing a program that uses several chunks of code from this book does not require permission. Selling or distributing a CD-ROM of examples from O'Reilly books does require permission. Answering a question by citing this book and quoting example code does not require permission. Incorporating a significant amount of example code from this book into your product's documentation does require permission.

We appreciate, but do not require, attribution. An attribution usually includes the title, author, publisher, and ISBN. For example: "*Practical Machine Learning for Computer Vision*, by Valliappa Lakshmanan, Martin Görner, and Ryan Gillard. Copyright 2021 Valliappa Lakshmanan, Martin Görner, and Ryan Gillard, 978-1-098-10236-4."

If you feel your use of code examples falls outside fair use or the permission given above, feel free to contact us at *permissions@oreilly.com*.

O'Reilly Online Learning

For more than 40 years, O'Reilly Media has provided technology and business training, knowledge, and insight to help companies succeed.

Our unique network of experts and innovators share their knowledge and expertise through books, articles, and our online learning platform. O'Reilly's online learning platform gives you on-demand access to live training courses, in-depth learning paths, interactive coding environments, and a vast collection of text and video from O'Reilly and 200+ other publishers. For more information, visit *http://oreilly.com*.

How to Contact Us

Please address comments and questions concerning this book to the publisher:

O'Reilly Media, Inc.
1005 Gravenstein Highway North
Sebastopol, CA 95472
800-998-9938 (in the United States or Canada)
707-829-0515 (international or local)
707-829-0104 (fax)

We have a web page for this book, where we list errata, examples, and any additional information. You can access this page at *https://oreil.ly/practical-ml-4-computer-vision*.

Email *bookquestions@oreilly.com* to comment or ask technical questions about this book.

For news and information about our books and courses, visit *http://www.oreilly.com*.

Find us on Facebook: *http://facebook.com/oreilly*

Follow us on Twitter: *http://twitter.com/oreillymedia*

Watch us on YouTube: *http://www.youtube.com/oreillymedia*

Acknowledgments

We are very thankful to Salem Haykal and Filipe Gracio, our superstar reviewers who reviewed every chapter in this book—their eye for detail can be felt throughout. Thanks also to the O'Reilly technical reviewers Vishwesh Ravi Shrimali and Sanyam Singhal for suggesting the reordering that improved the organization of the book. In addition, we would like to thank Rajesh Thallam, Mike Bernico, Elvin Zhu, Yuefeng Zhou, Sara Robinson, Jiri Simsa, Sandeep Gupta, and Michael Munn for reviewing chapters that aligned with their areas of expertise. Any remaining errors are ours, of course.

We would like to thank Google Cloud users, our teammates, and many of the cohorts of the Google Cloud Advanced Solutions Lab for pushing us to make our explanations crisper. Thanks also to the TensorFlow, Keras, and Google Cloud AI engineering teams for being thoughtful partners.

Our O'Reilly team provided critical feedback and suggestions. Rebecca Novack suggested updating an earlier O'Reilly book on this topic, and was open to our recommendation that a practical computer vision book would now involve machine learning and so the book would require a complete rewrite. Amelia Blevins, our editor at O'Reilly, kept us chugging along. Rachel Head, our copyeditor, and Katherine Tozer, our production editor, greatly improved the clarity of our writing.

Finally, and most importantly, thanks also to our respective families for their support.

— *Valliappa Lakshmanan, Bellevue, WA*
Martin Görner, Bellevue, WA
Ryan Gillard, Pleasanton, CA

## CHAPTER 1

Machine Learning for Computer Vision

Imagine that you are sitting in a garden, observing what's going on around you. There are two systems in your body that are at work: your eyes are acting as sensors and creating representations of the scene, while your cognitive system is making sense of what your eyes are seeing. Thus, you might see a bird, a worm, and some movement and realize that the bird has walked down the path and is eating a worm (see Figure 1-1).

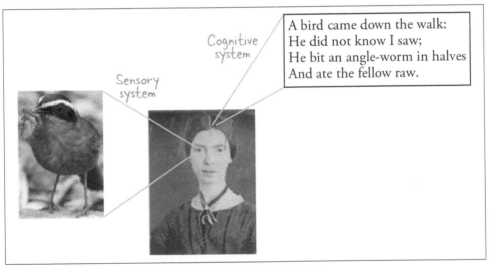

Cognitive system

Sensory system

A bird came down the walk:
He did not know I saw;
He bit an angle-worm in halves
And ate the fellow raw.

Figure 1-1. Human vision involves our sensory and cognitive systems.

Computer vision tries to imitate human vision capabilities by providing methods for image formation (mimicking the human *sensory* system) and machine perception (mimicking the human *cognitive* system). Imitation of the human sensory system is focused on hardware and on the design and placement of sensors such as cameras.

The modern approach to imitating the human cognitive system consists of machine learning (ML) methods that are used to extract information from images. It is these methods that we cover in this book.

When we see a photograph of a daisy, for example, our human cognitive system is able to recognize it as a daisy (see Figure 1-2). The machine learning models for image classification that we build in this book imitate this human capability by starting from photographs of daisies.

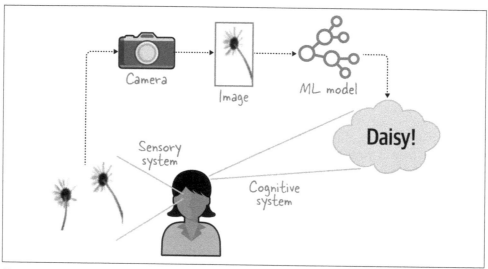

Figure 1-2. An image classification machine learning model imitates the human cognitive system.

Machine Learning

If you were reading a book on computer vision in the early 2010s, the methods used to extract information from photographs would not have involved machine learning. Instead, you would have been learning about denoising, edge finding, texture detection, and morphological (shape-based) operations. With advancements in artificial intelligence (more specifically, advances in machine learning), this has changed.

Artificial intelligence (AI) explores methods by which computers can mimic human capabilities. *Machine learning* is a subfield of AI that teaches computers to do this by showing them a large amount of data and instructing them to learn from it. *Expert systems* is another subfield of AI—expert systems teach computers to mimic human capabilities by programming the computers to follow human logic. Prior to the 2010s, computer vision tasks like image classification were commonly done by building bespoke image filters to implement the logic laid out by experts. Nowadays, image classification is achieved through convolutional networks, a form of deep learning (see Figure 1-3).

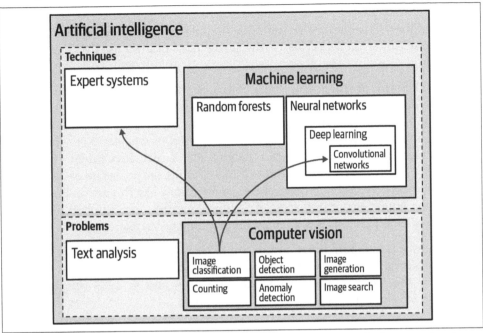

Figure 1-3. Computer vision is a subfield of AI that tries to mimic the human visual system; while it used to rely on an expert systems approach, today it's done with machine learning.

Take, for example, the image of the daisy in Figure 1-2. A machine learning approach teaches a computer to recognize the type of flower in an image by showing the computer lots of images along with their *labels* (or correct answers). So, we'd show the computer lots of images of daisies, lots of images of tulips, and so on. Based on such a *labeled training dataset,* the computer learns how to classify an image that it has not encountered before. How this happens is discussed in Chapters 2 and 3.

In an expert system approach, on the other hand, we would start by interviewing a human botanist on how they classify flowers. If the botanist explained that *bellis perennis* (the scientific name for a daisy) consists of white elongated petals around a yellow center and green, rounded leaves, we would attempt to devise image processing filters to match these criteria. For example, we'd look for the prevalence of white, yellow, and green in the image. Then we'd devise edge filters to identify the borders of the leaves and matched morphological filters to see if they match the expected rounded shape. We might smooth the image in HSV (hue, saturation, value) space to determine the color of the center of the flower as compared to the color of the petals. Based on these criteria, we might come up with a score for an image that rates the likelihood that it is a daisy. Similarly, we'd design and apply different sets of rules for roses, tulips, sunflowers, and so on. To classify a new image, we'd pick the category whose score is highest for that image.

This description illustrates the considerable bespoke work that was needed to create image classification models. This is why image classification used to have limited applicability.

That all changed in 2012 with the publication of the AlexNet paper (*https:// dl.acm.org/doi/10.1145/3065386*). The authors—Alex Krizhevsky, Ilya Sutskever, and Geoffrey E. Hinton—were able to greatly outperform any existing image classification method by applying convolutional networks (covered in Chapter 3) to the benchmark dataset used in the ImageNet Large-Scale Visual Recognition Challenge (ILSVRC). They achieved a top-5[1] error of 15.3%, while the error rate of the runner-up was over 26%. Typical improvements in competitions like this are on the order of 0.1%, so the improvement that AlexNet demonstrated was one hundred times what most people expected! This was an attention-grabbing performance.

Neural networks had been around since the 1970s (*https://oreil.ly/IRHqY*), and convolutional neural networks (CNNs) themselves had been around for more than two decades by that point—Yann LeCun introduced the idea in 1989 (*https://oreil.ly/ EqY3a*). So what was new about AlexNet? Four things:

Graphics processing units (GPUs)
> Convolutional neural networks are a great idea, but they are computationally very expensive. The authors of AlexNet implemented a convolutional network on top of the graphics rendering libraries provided by special-purpose chips called GPUs. GPUs were, at the time, being used primarily for high-end visualization and gaming. The paper grouped the convolutions to fit the model across two GPUs. GPUs made convolutional networks feasible to train (we'll talk about distributing model training across GPUs in Chapter 7).

Rectified linear unit (ReLU) activation
> AlexNet's creators used a non-saturating activation function called ReLU in their neural network. We'll talk more about neural networks and activation functions in Chapter 2; for now, it's sufficient to know that using a piecewise linear non-saturating activation function enabled their model to converge much faster.

---

1 *Top-5 accuracy* means that we consider the model to be correct if it returns the correct label for an image within its top five results.

Regularization

The problem with ReLUs—and the reason they hadn't been used much until 2012—was that, because they didn't saturate, the neural network's weights became numerically unstable. The authors of AlexNet used a regularization technique to keep the weights from becoming too large. We'll discuss regularization in Chapter 2 too.

Depth

With the ability to train faster, they were able to train a more complex model that had more neural network layers. We say a model with more layers is *deeper*; the importance of depth will be discussed in Chapter 3.

It is worth recognizing that it was the increased depth of the neural network (allowed by the combination of the first three ideas) that made AlexNet world-beating. That CNNs could be sped up using GPUs had been proven in 2006 (*https://oreil.ly/9p3Ba*). The ReLU activation function itself wasn't new, and regularization was a well-known statistical technique. Ultimately, the model's exceptional performance was due to the authors' insight that they could combine all of these to train a deeper convolutional neural network than had been done before.

Depth is so important to the resurging interest in neural networks that the whole field has come to be referred to as *deep learning*.

Deep Learning Use Cases

Deep learning is a branch of machine learning that uses neural networks with many layers. Deep learning outperformed the previously existing methods for computer vision, and has now been successfully applied to many other forms of unstructured data: video, audio, natural language text, and so on.

Deep learning gives us the ability to extract information from images without having to create bespoke image processing filters or code up human logic. When doing image classification using deep learning, we need hundreds or thousands or even millions of images (the more, the better), for which we know the correct label (like "tulip" or "daisy"). These labeled images can be used to train an image classification deep learning model.

As long as you can formulate a task in terms of learning from data, it is possible to use computer vision machine learning methods to address the problem. For example, consider the problem of optical character recognition (OCR)—taking a scanned image and extracting the text from it. The earliest approaches to OCR involved teaching the computer to do pattern matching against what individual letters look like. This turns out to be a challenging approach, for various reasons. For example:

- There are many fonts, so a single letter can be written in many ways.
- Letters come in different sizes, so the pattern matching has to be scale-invariant.
- Bound books cannot be laid flat, so the scanned letters are distorted.
- It is not enough to recognize individual letters; we need to extract the entire text. The rules of what forms a word, a line, or a paragraph are complex (see Figure 1-4).

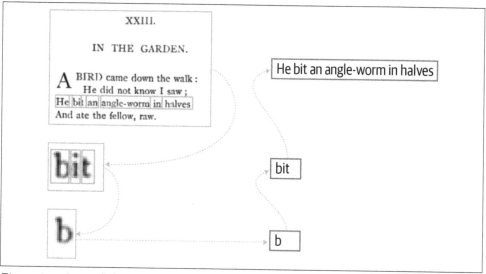

Figure 1-4. Optical character recognition based on rules requires identifying lines, breaking them into words, and then identifying the component letters of each word.

On the other hand, with the use of deep learning, OCR can be quite easily formulated as an image classification system. There are many books that have already been digitized, and it's possible to train the model by showing it a scanned image from a book and using the digitized text as a label.

Computer vision methods provide solutions for a variety of real-world problems. Besides OCR, computer vision methods have been successfully applied to medical diagnosis (using images such as X-rays and MRIs), automating retail operations (such as reading QR codes, recognizing empty shelves, checking the quality of vegetables, etc.), surveillance (monitoring crop yield from satellite images, monitoring wildlife cameras, intruder detection, etc.), fingerprint recognition, and automotive safety (following cars at a safe distance, identifying changes in speed limits from road signs, self-parking cars, self-driving cars, etc.).

Computer vision has found use in many industries. In government, it has been used for monitoring satellite images, in building smart cities, and in customs and security inspections. In healthcare, it has been used to identify eye disease and to find early signs of cancer from mammograms. In agriculture, it has been used to spot malfunctioning irrigation pumps, assess crop yields, and identify leaf disease. In manufacturing, it finds a use on factory floors for quality control and visual inspection. In insurance, it has been used to automatically assess damage to vehicles after an accident.

Summary

Computer vision helps computers understand the content of digital images such as photographs. Starting with a seminal paper in 2012, deep learning approaches to computer vision have become wildly successful. Nowadays, we find successful uses of computer vision across a large number of industries.

We'll start our journey in Chapter 2 by creating our first machine learning models.

ML Models for Vision

In this chapter, you will learn how to represent images and train basic machine learning models to classify images. You will discover that the performance of linear and fully connected neural networks is poor on images. However, along the way, you will learn how to use the Keras API to implement ML primitives and train ML models.

 The code for this chapter is in the *02_ml_models* folder of the book's GitHub repository (*https://github.com/GoogleCloudPlatform/practical-ml-vision-book*). We will provide file names for code samples and notebooks where applicable.

A Dataset for Machine Perception

For the purposes of this book, it will be helpful if we take a single practical problem and build a variety of machine learning models to solve it. Assume that we have collected and labeled a dataset of nearly four thousand photographs of flowers. There are five types of flowers in the *5-flowers* dataset (see Figure 2-1), and each image in the dataset has already been labeled with the type of flower it depicts.

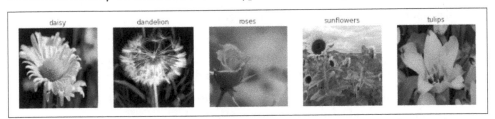

Figure 2-1. The photographs in the 5-flowers dataset are of five types of flowers: daisies, dandelions, roses, sunflowers, and tulips.

Suppose we want to create a computer program that will, when provided an image, tell us what type of flower is in the image. We are asking the machine learning model to learn to perceive what's in the image, so you might see this type of task called *machine perception*. Specifically, the type of perception is analogous to human sight, so the problem is termed *computer vision*, and in this case we will solve it through image classification.

5-Flowers Dataset

The 5-flowers dataset was created by Google and placed in the public domain with a Creative Commons license. It is published as a TensorFlow dataset (*https://oreil.ly/ tqwFi*) and available in a public Google Cloud Storage bucket (`gs://cloud-ml-data/`) in the form of JPEG files. This makes the dataset both realistic (it consists of JPEG photographs of the sort collected by off-the-shelf cameras) and readily accessible. Therefore, we will use it as an ongoing example in this book.

An Example, but Not a Template

The 5-flowers dataset is a great dataset to learn with, but you should not use it as the template for how you create a training dataset. There are several factors that make the 5-flowers dataset subpar from the perspective of serving as a template:

Quantity
> To train ML models from scratch, you'll typically need to collect millions of images. There are alternative approaches that work with fewer images, but you should attempt to collect the largest dataset that is practical (and ethical!).

Data format
> Storing the images as individual JPEG files is very inefficient because most of your model training time will be spent waiting for data to be read. It is better to use TensorFlow Record format.

Content
> The dataset itself consists of *found* data—images that were not explicitly collected for the classification task. You should, if your problem domain allows, collect data more purposefully. More on this shortly.

Labeling
> The labeling of images is a topic in and of itself. This dataset was manually labeled. This can become impractical for larger datasets.

> We will discuss these factors and provide best practices for how to design, collect, organize, store, and label data throughout the book.

In Figure 2-2, you can see several of the tulip photographs. Note that they range from close-up photographs to photographs of fields of tulips. All of these are photographs that a human would have no problem labeling as tulips, but it's a difficult problem for us to capture using simple rules—if we were to say a tulip is an elongated flower, for example, only the first and fourth images would qualify.

Figure 2-2. These five photographs of tulips vary widely in terms of zoom, color of the tulips, and what's in the frame.

Standardize Image Collection

We are choosing to address a hard problem where the flower images are all collected in real-world conditions. However, in practice, you can often make a machine perception problem easier by standardizing how the images are collected. For example, you could specify that your images have to be collected in controlled conditions, with flat lighting, and at a consistent zoom. This is common in the manufacturing industry—factory conditions can be precisely specified. It is also common to design the scanner in such a way that an object can be placed in only one orientation. As a machine learning practitioner, you should be on the lookout for ways to make machine perception problems easier. This is not cheating—it's the smart thing to do to set yourself up for success.

Keep in mind, however, that your training dataset has to reflect the conditions under which your model will be required to make predictions. If your model is trained only on photographs of flowers taken by professional photographers, it will probably do poorly on photographs taken by amateurs whose lighting, zoom, and framing choices are likely to be different.

Reading Image Data

To train image models, we need to read image data into our programs. There are four steps to reading an image in a standard format like JPEG or PNG and getting it ready to train machine learning models with it (the complete code is available in *02a_machine_perception.ipynb* in the GitHub repository for the book):

```
import tensorflow as tf
def read_and_decode(filename, reshape_dims):
    # 1. Read the file.
    img = tf.io.read_file(filename)
    # 2. Convert the compressed string to a 3D uint8 tensor.
    img = tf.image.decode_jpeg(img, channels=3)
    # 3. Convert 3D uint8 to floats in the [0,1] range.
    img = tf.image.convert_image_dtype(img, tf.float32)
    # 4. Resize the image to the desired size.
    return tf.image.resize(img, reshape_dims)
```

We first read the image data from persistent storage into memory as a sequence of bytes:

```
img = tf.io.read_file(filename)
```

The variable img here is a tensor (see "What's a Tensor?" on page 13) that contains an array of bytes. We parse these bytes to convert them into the pixel data—this is also called *decoding* the data because image formats like JPEG require you to decode the pixel values from lookup tables:

```
img = tf.image.decode_jpeg(img, channels=3)
```

Here, we specify that we want only the three color channels (red, green, and blue) from the JPEG image and not the opacity, which is the fourth channel. The channels you have available depend on the file itself. Grayscale images may have only one channel.

The pixels will consist of RGB values that are of type uint8 and are in the range [0,255]. So, in the third step, we convert them to floats and scale the values to lie in the range [0,1]. This is because machine learning optimizers are tuned to work well with small numbers:

```
img = tf.image.convert_image_dtype(img, tf.float32)
```

Finally, we resize the image to the desired size. Machine learning models are built to work with inputs of known sizes. Since images in the real world are likely to come in arbitrary sizes, you might have to shrink, crop, or expand them to fit your desired size. For example, to resize the image to be 256 pixels wide and 128 pixels tall, we'd specify:

```
tf.image.resize(img,[256, 128])
```

In Chapter 6, we'll see that this method does not preserve the aspect ratio and we'll look at other options to resize images.

What's a Tensor?

In mathematics, a 1D array is called a vector, and a 2D array is called a matrix. A *tensor* is an array that could have any number of dimensions (the number of dimensions is called the *rank*). A matrix with 12 rows and 18 columns is said to have a *shape* of (12, 18) and a rank of 2. So, a tensor can have arbitrary shape.

The common array math library in Python is called numpy. You can use this library to create *n*-dimensional arrays, but the problem is that they are not hardware-accelerated. For example, this is a 1D array whose shape is (4):

```
x = np.array([2.0, 3.0, 1.0, 0.0])
```

whereas this is a 5D array of zeros (note that there are five numbers in the shape):

```
x5d = np.zeros(shape=(4, 3, 7, 8, 3))
```

To obtain hardware acceleration using TensorFlow, you can convert either numpy array into a tensor, which is how TensorFlow represents arrays, using:

```
tx = tf.convert_to_tensor(x, dtype=tf.float32)
```

And you can convert a tensor back into a numpy array using:

```
x = tx.numpy()
```

Mathematically, numpy arrays and TensorFlow tensors are the same thing. However, there is an important practical difference—all numpy arithmetic is done on the CPU, while the TensorFlow code runs on a GPU if one is available. Thus, doing:

```
x = x * 0.3
```

will typically be less efficient than:

```
tx = tx * 0.3
```

In general, the more you can do using TensorFlow operations, the more efficient your program will be. It is also more efficient if you *vectorize* your code (to process batches of images) so that you are carrying out a single in-place tensor operation instead of a bunch of tiny little scalar operations.

These steps are not set in stone. If your input data consists of remotely sensed images from a satellite that are provided in a band interleaved format or brain scan images provided in Digital Imaging and Communications in Medicine (DICOM) format, you obviously wouldn't decode those using decode_jpeg(). Similarly, you may not always resize the data. In some instances, you might choose to crop the data to the desired size or pad it with zeros. In other cases, you might resize, keeping the aspect ratio constant, and then pad the remaining pixels. These preprocessing operations are discussed in Chapter 6.

Visualizing Image Data

Always visualize a few of the images to ensure that you are reading the data correctly —a common mistake is to read the data in such a way that the images are rotated or mirrored. Visualizing the images is also useful to get a sense of how challenging a machine perception problem is.

We can use Matplotlib's imshow() function to visualize an image, but in order to do so we must first convert the image, which is a TensorFlow tensor, into a numpy array using the numpy() function.

```
def show_image(filename):
    img = read_and_decode(filename, [IMG_HEIGHT, IMG_WIDTH])
    plt.imshow(img.numpy());
```

Trying it out on one of our daisy images, we get what's shown in Figure 2-3.

Figure 2-3. Make sure to visualize the data to ensure that you are reading it correctly.

Notice from Figure 2-3 that the filename contains the type of flower (daisy). This means we can use wildcard matching with TensorFlow's glob() function to get, say, all the tulip images:

```
tulips = tf.io.gfile.glob(
    "gs://cloud-ml-data/img/flower_photos/tulips/*.jpg")
```

The result of running this code and visualizing a panel of five tulip photographs was shown in Figure 2-2.

Reading the Dataset File

We now know how to read an image. In order to train a machine model, though, we need to read many images. We also have to obtain the labels for each of the images. We could obtain a list of all the images by carrying out a wildcard match using glob():

```
tf.io.gfile.glob("gs://cloud-ml-data/img/flower_photos/*/*.jpg")
```

Then, knowing that the images in our dataset have a naming convention, we could take a filename and extract the label using string operations. For example, we can remove the prefix using:

```
basename = tf.strings.regex_replace(
    filename,
    "gs://cloud-ml-data/img/flower_photos/", "")
```

and get the category name using:

```
label = tf.strings.split(basename, '/')[0]
```

As usual, please refer to the GitHub repository for this book for the full code.

However, for reasons of generalization and reproducibility (explained further in Chapter 5), it is better to set aside in advance the images that we will retain for evaluation. That has already been done in the 5-flowers dataset, and the images to use for training and evaluation are listed in two files in the same Cloud Storage bucket as the images:

```
gs://cloud-ml-data/img/flower_photos/train_set.csv
gs://cloud-ml-data/img/flower_photos/eval_set.csv
```

These are comma-separated values (CSV) files where each line contains a filename followed by the label.

One way to read a CSV file is to read in text lines using `TextLineDataset`, passing in a function to handle each line as it is read through the `map()` function:

```
dataset = (tf.data.TextLineDataset(
    "gs://cloud-ml-data/img/flower_photos/train_set.csv").
    map(parse_csvline))
```

We are using the `tf.data` API, which makes it possible to handle large amounts of data (even if it doesn't all fit into memory) by reading only a handful of data elements at a time, and performing transformations as we are reading the data. It does this by using an abstraction called `tf.data.Dataset` to represent a sequence of elements. In our pipeline, each element is a training example that contains two tensors. The first tensor is the image and the second is the label. Many types of `Datasets` correspond to many different file formats. We're using `TextLineDataset`, which reads text files and assumes that each line is a different element.

`parse_csvline()` is a function that we supply in order to parse the line, extract the filename of the image, read the image, and return the image and its label:

```
def parse_csvline(csv_row):
    record_defaults = ["path", "flower"]
    filename, label = tf.io.decode_csv(csv_row, record_defaults)
    img = read_and_decode(filename, [IMG_HEIGHT, IMG_WIDTH])
    return img, label
```

The record_defaults that are passed into the parse_csvline() function specify what TensorFlow needs to replace in order to handle a line where one or more values are missing.

To verify that this code works, we can print out the average pixel value for each channel of the first three images in the training dataset:

```
for img, label in dataset.take(3):
    avg = tf.math.reduce_mean(img, axis=[0, 1])
    print(label, avg)
```

In this code snippet, the take() method truncates the dataset to three items. Notice that because decode_csv() returns a tuple (img, label), that's what we obtain when we iterate through the dataset. Printing out the entire image is a terrible idea, so we are printing out the average pixel value in the image using tf.reduce_mean().

The first line of the result is (with line breaks added for readability):

```
tf.Tensor(b'daisy', shape=(), dtype=string)
tf.Tensor([0.3588961  0.36257887 0.26933077],
          shape=(3,), dtype=float32)
```

Note that the label is a string tensor and the average is a 1D tensor of length 3. Why did we get a 1D tensor? That's because we passed in an axis parameter to reduce_mean():

```
avg = tf.math.reduce_mean(img, axis=[0, 1])
```

Had we not supplied an axis, then TensorFlow would have computed the mean along all the dimensions and returned a scalar value. Recall that the shape of the image is [IMG_HEIGHT, IMG_WIDTH, NUM_CHANNELS]. Therefore, by providing axis=[0, 1], we are asking TensorFlow to compute the average of all columns (axis=0) and all rows (axis=1), but not to average the RGB values (see Figure 2-4).

Printing out statistics of the image like this is helpful for another reason. If your input data is corrupt and there is unrepresentable floating-point data (technically called NaN (*https://oreil.ly/E0xc2*)) in your images, the mean will itself be NaN. This is a handy way to ensure that you haven't made a mistake when reading data.

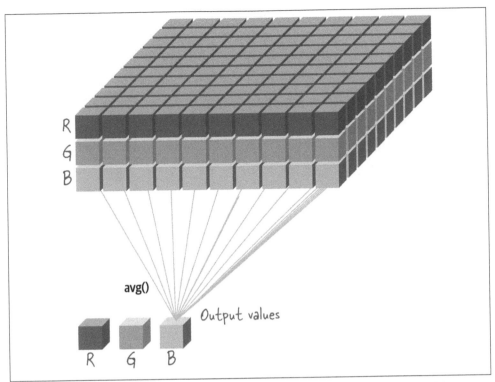

Figure 2-4. We compute the `reduce_mean()` *along the row and column axes of the image.*

A Linear Model Using Keras

As Figure 2-4 demonstrates, the `reduce_mean()` function weights each pixel value in the image the same. What if we were to apply a different weight to each of the width * height * 3 pixel-channel points in the image?

Given a new image, we can compute the weighted average of all its pixel values. We can then use this value to choose between the five types of flowers. Therefore, we will compute five such weighted averages (so that we are actually learning width * height * 3 * 5 weight values; see Figure 2-5), and choose the flower type based on which output is the largest.

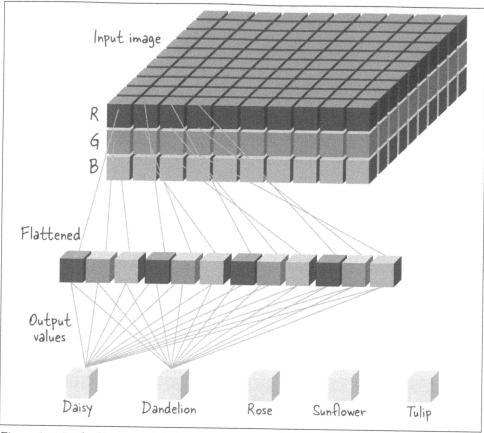

Figure 2-5. In the linear model, there are five outputs, one for each category; each of the output values is a weighted sum of the input pixel values.

In practice, a constant term called a *bias* is also added, so that we can represent each output value as:

$$Y_j = b_j + \sum_{rows} \sum_{columns} \sum_{channels} \left(w_i * x_i \right)$$

Without the bias, we'd be forcing the output to be zero if all the pixels are black.

Keras Model

Rather than write the preceding equation using low-level TensorFlow functions, it will be more convenient to use a higher-level abstraction. TensorFlow 1.1 shipped with one such abstraction, the Estimator API, and Estimators are still supported for backward compatibility. However, the Keras API has been part of TensorFlow since TensorFlow 2.0, and it's what we recommend that you use.

A linear model can be represented in Keras as follows:

```
model = tf.keras.Sequential([
    tf.keras.layers.Flatten(input_shape=(IMG_HEIGHT, IMG_WIDTH, 3)),
    tf.keras.layers.Dense(len(CLASS_NAMES))
])
```

A *Sequential model* consists of *layers* that are connected such that the output of one layer is the input to the next. A layer is a Keras component that takes a tensor as input, applies some TensorFlow operations to that input, and outputs a tensor.

The first layer, which is implicit, is the input layer, which asks for a 3D image tensor. The second layer (the Flatten layer) takes a 3D image tensor as input and reshapes it to be a 1D tensor with the same number of values. The Flatten layer is connected to a Dense layer with one output node for each class of flower. The name Dense means that every output is a weighted sum of every input and no weights are shared. We will encounter other common types of layers later in this chapter.

To use the Keras model defined here, we need to call model.fit() with the training dataset and model.predict() with each image we want to classify. To train the model, we need to tell Keras how to optimize the weights based on the training dataset. The way to do this is to *compile* the model, specifying an *optimizer* to use, the *loss* to minimize, and *metrics* to report. For example:

```
model.compile(
    optimizer='adam',
    loss=tf.keras.losses.SparseCategoricalCrossentropy(from_logits=True),
    metrics=['accuracy'])
```

The Keras predict() function will do the model computation on the image. The parameters to the compile() function make more sense if we look at the prediction code first, so let's start there.

Prediction function

Because the model has the trained set of weights in its internal state, we can compute the predicted value for an image by calling model.predict() and passing in the image:

```
pred = model.predict(tf.reshape(img,
    [1, IMG_HEIGHT, IMG_WIDTH, NUM_CHANNELS]))
```

The reason for the reshape() is that predict() expects a batch of images, so we reshape the img tensor as a batch consisting of one image.

What does the `pred` tensor that is output from `model.predict()` look like? Recall that the final layer of the model was a `Dense` layer with five outputs, so the shape of `pred` is (5)—that is, it consists of five numbers corresponding to the five flower types. The first output is the model's confidence that the image in question is a daisy, the second output is the model's confidence that the image is a dandelion, and so on. The predicted confidence values are called *logits* and are in the range –infinity to +infinity.

The model's prediction is the label in which it has the highest confidence:

```
pred_label_index = tf.math.argmax(pred)
pred_label = CLASS_NAMES[pred_label_index]
```

We can convert the logits to probabilities by applying a function called the *softmax* function to them. So, the probability corresponding to the predicted label is:

```
prob = tf.math.softmax(pred)[pred_label_index]
```

Probability, Odds, Logits, Sigmoid, and Softmax

The output of a classification model is a *probability*—the likelihood that an event will occur over many trials. Therefore, when building classification models, it is important to understand several concepts related to probabilities. For example, if you are building a model that classifies a machine part as being defective or non-defective, the model does not provide a Boolean (true or false) output. Instead, it outputs the probability that the part is defective.

Suppose you have an event that can happen with a probability p. Then, the probability that it will *not* happen is $1 - p$. The *odds* that it will happen in any given trial is the probability of the event occurring divided by the probability of it not occurring, or $p / (1 - p)$. For example, if $p=0.25$, then the odds of the event happening are 0.25 / 0.75 = 1:3. On the other hand, if $p=0.75$, then the odds of it happening are 0.75 / 0.25 = 3:1.

The *logit* is the natural logarithm of the odds of the event happening. Thus, for an event with $p=0.25$, the logit is log(0.25 / 0.75), or –1.098. For an event with $p=0.75$, the logit is 1.098. As the probability approaches 0 the logit approaches –infinity, and as the probability approaches 1 the logit approaches +infinity. Therefore, the logit occupies the entire space of real numbers, as shown in Figure 2-6.

The *sigmoid* is the inverse of the logit function. Thus, the sigmoid of 1.098 is 0.75. Mathematically, the sigmoid is given by:

$$\sigma(Y) = \frac{1}{1 + e^{-Y}}$$

The sigmoid is in the range 0–1. If we have a `Dense` layer in Keras with one output node, by applying the sigmoid to it we can obtain a binary classifier that outputs a valid probability.

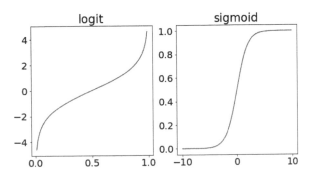

Figure 2-6. The logit and sigmoid functions are inverses of each other (the x-axis in the first graph and the y-axis in the second are the probability).

The *softmax* is the multiclass counterpart of the sigmoid. If you have N mutually exclusive events, and their logits are given by Y_j, then softmax(Y_j) provides the probability of the jth event. Mathematically, the softmax is given by:

$$S\left(Y_j\right) = \frac{e^{-Y_j}}{\sum\limits_{j} e^{-Y_j}}$$

The softmax function is nonlinear and has the effect of squashing low values and boosting the maximum, as shown in Figure 2-7. Note that the sum of the probabilities in both instances adds up to 1.0. This property is useful because we can have a `Dense` layer in Keras with five output nodes, and by applying the softmax to it, we can obtain a sound probability distribution.

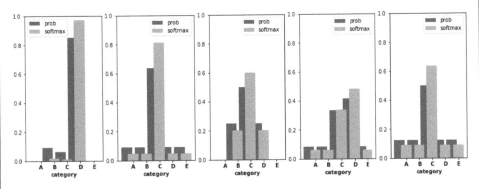

Figure 2-7. The softmax function squashes low values and boosts the maximum value.

Activation function

It is not sufficient to simply call `model.predict()`, because `model.predict()` returns a weighted sum that is unbounded. We can treat this weighted sum as logits and apply either the sigmoid or the softmax function (depending on whether we have a binary classification problem or a multiclass one) to obtain the probability:

```
pred = model.predict(tf.reshape(img,
                      [1, IMG_HEIGHT, IMG_WIDTH, NUM_CHANNELS]))
prob = tf.math.softmax(pred)[pred_label_index]
```

We can make things more convenient for end users if we add an *activation function* to the last layer of the model:

```
model = tf.keras.Sequential([
    tf.keras.layers.Flatten(input_shape=(IMG_HEIGHT, IMG_WIDTH, 3)),
    tf.keras.layers.Dense(len(CLASS_NAMES), activation='softmax')
])
```

If we do this, then `model.predict()` will return five probabilities (not logits), one for each class. There is no need for the client code to call `softmax()`.

Any layer in Keras can have an activation function applied to its output. Supported activation functions include `linear`, `sigmoid`, and `softmax`. We'll look at other activation functions later in this chapter.

Optimizer

Keras allows us to choose the optimizer that we wish to use to tune the weights based on the training dataset. Available optimizers include:

Stochastic gradient descent (SGD)
    The most basic optimizer.

Adagrad (adaptive gradients) and Adam
    Improve upon the basic optimizer by adding features that allow for faster convergence.

Ftrl
    An optimizer that tends to work well on extremely sparse datasets with many categorical features.

Adam is the tried-and-proven choice for deep learning models. We recommend using Adam as your optimizer for computer vision problems unless you have a strong reason not to.

SGD and all its variants, including Adam, rely on receiving mini-batches (often just called *batches*) of data. For each batch of data, we feed forward through the model and calculate the error and the *gradient*, or how much each weight contributed to the error; then the optimizer updates the weights with this information, ready for the next batch of data. Therefore, when we read the training dataset, we have to also batch it:

```
train_dataset = (tf.data.TextLineDataset(
    "gs://cloud-ml-data/img/flower_photos/train_set.csv").
    map(decode_csv)).batch(10)
```

Gradient Descent

Training the neural network actually means using training images and labels to adjust weights and biases so as to minimize the cross-entropy loss. The cross-entropy is a function of the model's weights and biases, the pixels of the training image, and its known class.

If we compute the extent to which the cross-entropy changes when we adjust each of the weights independently, we get the *partial derivative* of the cross-entropy. We can compute the gradient in different directions from the partial derivative computed for a given image, label, and current weights and biases. The mathematical property of a gradient is that it points "up" if, by moving in that direction, the loss increases. Since we want to go where the cross-entropy is low, we go in the direction where the gradient decreases the most. To do this, we update the weights and biases by a fraction of the gradient. We then do the same thing again and again using the next batches of training images and labels, in a training loop. The training process is depicted in Figure 2-8. The hope is that this will converge to a place where the cross-entropy is minimal, although nothing guarantees that this minimum is unique or even that it is the global minimum.

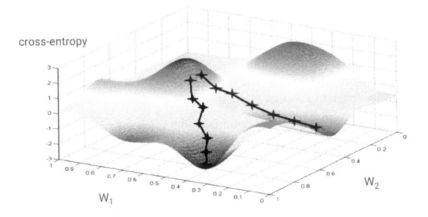

Figure 2-8. The training process involves taking small steps in the direction where the loss decreases the most.

Note that you cannot update your weights and biases by the whole length of the gradient at each iteration—you would be jumping from one side of the valley to the other. To get to the bottom, you need to do smaller steps by using only a fraction of the gradient, typically in the 1/1,000 range. This fraction is called the learning rate; we'll discuss it in more detail later in this chapter.

You can compute your gradient on just one example image and update the weights and biases immediately, but doing so on a batch of, say, 128 images gives a gradient that better represents the constraints imposed by different example images and is therefore likely to converge toward the solution faster. The size of the mini-batch is an adjustable parameter.

This technique is called *stochastic gradient descent*. It has another, more pragmatic benefit: working with batches also means working with larger matrices, and these are usually easier to optimize on GPUs and TPUs (tensor processing units, which are specialized hardware to accelerate machine learning operations).

Training loss

The optimizer tries to choose the weights that minimize the model's error on the training dataset. For classification problems, there are strong mathematical reasons to choose cross-entropy as the error to be minimized. To calculate the cross-entropy, we compare the output probability (p_j for the jth class) of the model against the true label for that class (L_j) and sum this up over all the classes using the formula:

$$\sum_j - L_j \log(p_j)$$

In other words, we take the logarithm of the probability for predicting the correct label. If the model gets it exactly correct, this probability will be 1; log(1) is 0, and so the loss is 0. If the model gets it exactly wrong, this probability will be 0; log(0) is – infinity, and so the loss is +infinity, the worst possible loss. Using cross-entropy as our error measure allows us to tune the weights based on small improvements in the probability assigned to the correct label.

In order to compute the loss, the optimizer will need to compare the label (returned by the `parse_csvline()` function) with the output of `model.predict()`. The specific loss you use will depend on how you are representing the label and what the last layer of your model returns.

If your labels are one-hot encoded (e.g., if the label is encoded as [1 0 0 0 0] for daisy images), then, you should use *categorical cross-entropy* as your loss function. This will show up in your `decode_csv()` as follows:

```
def parse_csvline(csv_row):
    record_defaults = ["path", "flower"]
    filename, label_string = tf.io.decode_csv(csv_row, record_defaults)
    img = read_and_decode(filename, [IMG_HEIGHT, IMG_WIDTH])
```

```
label = tf.math.equal(CLASS_NAMES, label_string)
return img, label
```

Because CLASS_NAMES is an array of strings, comparing to a single label will return a one-hot-encoded array where the Boolean value is 1 in the corresponding position. You will specify the loss as follows:

```
tf.keras.losses.CategoricalCrossentropy(from_logits=False)
```

Note that the constructor takes a parameter which specifies whether the last layer of the model returns logits of probabilities, or whether you have done a softmax.

On the other hand, if your labels will be represented as integer indices (e.g., 4 indicates tulips), then your decode_csv() will represent the label by the position of the correct class:

```
label = tf.argmax(tf.math.equal(CLASS_NAMES, label_string))
```

And the loss will be specified as:

```
tf.keras.losses.SparseCategoricalCrossentropy(from_logits=False)
```

Again, take care to specify the value of from_logits appropriately.

Why Have Two Ways to Represent the Label?

When we do one-hot encoding, we represent a flower that is a daisy as [1 0 0 0 0] and a flower that is a tulip as [0 0 0 0 1]. The length of the one-hot-encoded vector is the number of classes. The sparse representation would be 0 for daisy and 4 for tulip. The sparse representation takes up less space (especially if there are hundreds or thousands of possible classes) and is therefore much more efficient.

Why, then, does Keras support two ways to represent labels?

The sparse representation will not work if the problem is a multilabel multiclass problem. If an image can contain both daisies and tulips, it is quite straightforward to encode this using the one-hot-encoded representation: [1 0 0 0 1]. With the sparse representation, there is no way to represent this scenario unless you are willing to create separate categories for each possible combination of categories.

Therefore, we recommend you use the sparse representation for most problems; but remember that one-hot encoding the labels and using the CategoricalCrossen tropy() loss function will help you handle multilabel multiclass situations.

Error metrics

While we can use the cross-entropy loss to minimize the error on the training dataset, business users will typically want a more understandable error metric. The most common error metric that is used for this purpose is *accuracy*, which is simply the fraction of instances that are classified correctly.

However, the accuracy metric fails when one of the classes is very rare. Suppose you are trying to identify fake ID cards, and your model has the following performance characteristics:

	Card identified as fake	Card identified as genuine
Actual fake ID cards	8 (TP)	2 (FN)
Actual genuine ID cards	140 (FP)	850 (TN)

The dataset has 990 genuine ID cards and 10 fake ID cards—there is a *class imbalance*. Of the fake ID cards, 8 were correctly identified as fake. These are the true positives (TP). The accuracy on this dataset would thus be (850 + 8) / 1,000, or 0.858. It can be immediately seen that because fake ID cards are so rare, the model's performance on this class has very little impact on its overall accuracy score—even if the model correctly identified only 2 of the 10 fake ID cards, the accuracy would remain nearly the same: 0.852. Indeed, the model can achieve an accuracy of 0.99 simply by identifying all cards as being valid! In such cases, it is common to report two other metrics:

Precision
> The fraction of true positives in the set of identified positives: TP / (TP + FP). Here, the model has identified 8 true positives and 140 false positives, so the precision is only 8/148. This model is very imprecise.

Recall
> The fraction of true positives identified among all the positives in the dataset: TP / (TP + FN). Here, there are 10 positives in the full dataset and the model has identified 8 of them, so the recall is 0.8.

In addition to the precision and recall, it is also common to report the F1 score, which is the harmonic mean of the two numbers:

$$F1 = 2/\left[\frac{1}{precision} + \frac{1}{recall}\right]$$

In a binary classification problem such as the one we're considering here (identifying fake ID cards), the accuracy, precision, and recall all rely on the probability threshold we choose to determine whether to classify an instance in one category or the other. By varying the probability threshold, we can obtain different trade-offs in terms of precision and recall. The resulting curve is called the *precision-recall curve* (see Figure 2-9). Another variant of this curve, where the true positive rate is plotted against the false positive rate, is called the *receiver operating characteristic* (ROC) curve. The area under the ROC curve (commonly shortened as *AUC*) is also often used as an aggregate measure of performance.

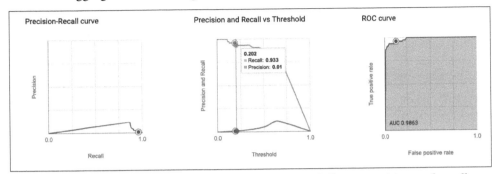

Figure 2-9. By varying the threshold, it is possible to get different precision and recall measures.

We normally want to report these metrics not on the training dataset, but on an independent evaluation dataset. This is to verify that the model hasn't simply memorized the answers for the training dataset.

Training the Model

Let's now put all the concepts that we covered in the previous section together to create and train a Keras model.

Creating the datasets

To train a linear model, we need a training dataset. Actually, we want two datasets—a training dataset and an evaluation dataset—to verify whether the trained model *generalizes*, or works on data that it has not seen during training.

So, we first obtain the training and evaluation datasets:

```
train_dataset = (tf.data.TextLineDataset(
    "gs://cloud-ml-data/img/flower_photos/train_set.csv").
    map(decode_csv)).batch(10)

eval_dataset = (tf.data.TextLineDataset(
    "gs://cloud-ml-data/img/flower_photos/eval_set.csv").
    map(decode_csv)).batch(10)
```

where decode_csv() reads and decodes JPEG images:

```
def decode_csv(csv_row):
    record_defaults = ["path", "flower"]
    filename, label_string = tf.io.decode_csv(csv_row, record_defaults)
    img = read_and_decode(filename, [IMG_HEIGHT, IMG_WIDTH])
    label = tf.argmax(tf.math.equal(CLASS_NAMES, label_string))
    return img, label
```

The `label` that is returned in this code is the sparse representation—i.e., the number 4 for tulips, that class's index—and not the one-hot-encoded one. We batch the training dataset because the optimizer class expects batches. We also batch the evaluation dataset to avoid creating two versions of all our methods (one that operates on batches, and another that requires one image at a time).

Creating and viewing the model

Now that the datasets have been created, we need to create the Keras model that is to be trained using those datasets:

```
model = tf.keras.Sequential([
    tf.keras.layers.Flatten(input_shape=(IMG_HEIGHT, IMG_WIDTH, 3)),
    tf.keras.layers.Dense(len(CLASS_NAMES), activation='softmax')
])
model.compile(optimizer='adam',
    loss=tf.keras.losses.SparseCategoricalCrossentropy(from_logits=False),
    metrics=['accuracy'])
```

We can view the model using:

```
tf.keras.utils.plot_model(model, show_shapes=True, show_layer_names=False)
```

This yields the diagram in Figure 2-10. Note that the input layer takes a batch (that's the ?) of [224, 224, 3] images. The question mark indicates that the size of this dimension is undefined until runtime; this way, the model can dynamically adapt to any batch size. The Flatten layer takes this input and returns a batch of 224 * 224 * 3 = 150,528 numbers that are then connected to five outputs in the Dense layer.

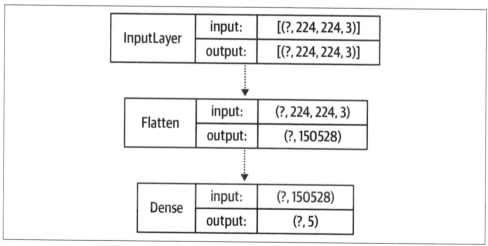

Figure 2-10. A Keras linear model to classify flowers.

We can verify that the `Flatten` operation does not need any trainable weights, but the Dense layer has 150,528 * 5 = 752,645 weights that need to be trained by using `model.summary()`, which yields:

```
Model: "sequential_1"
```

Layer (type)	Output Shape	Param #
flatten_1 (Flatten)	(None, 150528)	0
dense_1 (Dense)	(None, 5)	752645

```
Total params: 752,645
Trainable params: 752,645
Non-trainable params: 0
```

Fitting the model

Next, we train the model using `model.fit()` and pass in the training and validation datasets:

```
history = model.fit(train_dataset,
                    validation_data=eval_dataset, epochs=10)
```

Note that we are passing in the training dataset to train on, and the validation dataset to report accuracy metrics on. We are asking the optimizer to go through the training data 10 times (an *epoch* is a full pass through the dataset). We hope that 10 epochs will be sufficient for the loss to converge, but we should verify this by plotting the history of the loss and error metrics. We can do that by looking at what the history has been tracking:

```
history.history.keys()
```

We obtain the following list:

```
['loss', 'accuracy', 'val_loss', 'val_accuracy']
```

We can then plot the loss and validation loss using:

```
plt.plot(history.history['val_loss'], ls='dashed');
```

This yields the graph shown in the lefthand panel of Figure 2-11. Note that the loss does not go down smoothly; instead, it is quite choppy. This is an indication that our choices of batch size and optimizer settings can be improved—unfortunately, this part of the ML process is trial and error. The validation loss goes down, and then starts to increase. This is an indication that *overfitting* is starting to happen: the network has started to memorize details of the training dataset (such details are called *noise*) that do not occur in the validation dataset. Either 10 epochs is too long, or we need to add regularization. Overfitting and regularization are topics that we will address in more detail in the next section.

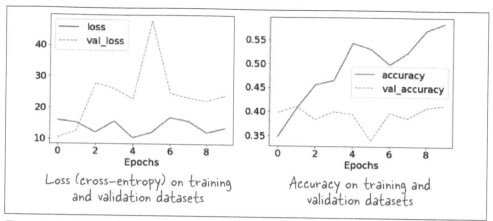

Figure 2-11. Loss and accuracy curves on the training (solid) and validation (dashed) sets.

It is also possible to plot the accuracy on the training dataset and the validation dataset using:

```
training_plot('accuracy', history)
```

The resulting graph is shown in the righthand panel of Figure 2-11. Notice that the accuracy on the training dataset goes on increasing the longer we train, while the accuracy on the validation dataset plateaus.

These lines are also choppy, providing us with the same insights we got from the loss curves. However, the accuracy that we have obtained (0.4) on the evaluation dataset is better than what we would have gotten from random chance (0.2). This indicates the model has been able to learn and become somewhat skillful at the task.

Plotting predictions

We can look at what the model has learned by plotting its predictions on a few images from the training dataset:

```
batch_image = tf.reshape(img, [1, IMG_HEIGHT, IMG_WIDTH, IMG_CHANNELS])
batch_pred = model.predict(batch_image)
pred = batch_pred[0]
```

Note that we need to take the single image that we have and make it a batch, because that's what the model was trained on and what it expects. Fortunately, we don't need to pass in exactly 10 images (our batch size was 10 during training) because the model was designed to take any batch size (recall that the first dimension in Figure 2-10 was a ?).

The first few predictions from the training and evaluation datasets are shown in Figure 2-12.

Figure 2-12. The first few images from the training (top row) and evaluation (bottom row) datasets—the first image, which is actually a daisy, has been wrongly classified as a dandelion with a probability of 0.74.

Image Regression

So far we've been focusing on the task of image classification. Another computer vision problem that you might encounter, though it's far less common, is image *regression*. One reason we might want to do this is because we want to measure something within the image. The problem here isn't counting the number of a certain type of object, which is solved another way that we will discuss in Chapter 11, but instead measuring a more real-valued property like height, length, volume, etc.

For instance, we may want to predict the rainfall amount from aerial images of cloud cover over the region of interest. By training an image regression model with tiles of the cloud images as input (see Figure 2-13, where two tiles are marked) and the precipitation amounts on the ground as our labels, we'd be able to learn the mapping from cloud images to precipitation.

Since we are measuring precipitation amounts in millimeters (mm), our labels are continuous, real numbers. We could of course reframe this as a classification problem by bucketing certain amounts of precipitation into categories such as low, medium, and high, but that may not be relevant for this specific use case.

Fortunately, regression isn't more complicated than image classification. We merely have to change our final neural network layer, the `Dense` output layer, from having a `sigmoid` or `softmax` activation to `None`, and change the number of `units` to the number of regression predictions we want to make from this one image (in this hypothetical case, just one).

 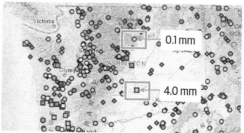

Satellite cloud cover (input)   Ground rain gauge observations (label)

Figure 2-13. Image regression to learn to predict rainfall amount—tiles of the cloud cover image on the left are treated as input, and the labels are measurements of precipitation on the ground (measured by a rain gauge at the center of the tile). Images courtesy of NOAA (left) and USGS (right).

The code would look like this:

```
tf.keras.layers.Dense(units=1, activation=None)
```

In addition, since this is now a regression problem, we should use a regression loss function, such as mean squared error (MSE):

```
tf.keras.losses.MeanSquaredError()
```

Once our model is trained, at inference time we can provide the model with images of clouds and it will return predictions for the amount of precipitation on the ground.

A Neural Network Using Keras

In the linear model that we covered in the previous section, we wrote the Keras model as:

```
model = tf.keras.Sequential([
    tf.keras.layers.Flatten(input_shape=(IMG_HEIGHT, IMG_WIDTH, 3)),
    tf.keras.layers.Dense(len(CLASS_NAMES), activation='softmax')
])
```

The output is the softmax of the weighted average of the flattened input pixel values:

$$Y = \text{softmax}\left(B + \sum_{pixels} W_i X_i\right)$$

B is the bias tensor, W the weights tensor, X the input tensor, and Y the output tensor. This is usually written in matrix form as (using $ to represent the softmax):

$$Y = \$(B + WX)$$

As shown in Figure 2-10, and in the following model summary, there is only one trainable layer, the `Dense` one. The `Flatten` operation is a reshaping operation and does not contain any trainable weights:

```
Layer (type)              Output Shape            Param #
=================================================================
flatten_1 (Flatten)       (None, 150528)          0
_____
dense_1 (Dense)           (None, 5)               752645
=================================================================
```

Linear models are great, but they are limited in what they can model. How do we obtain more complex models?

Neural Networks

One way to get a more complex model is to interpose one or more `Dense` layers in between the input and output layers. This results in a machine learning model called a *neural network*, for reasons that we will explain shortly.

Hidden layers

Suppose that we interpose one more `Dense` layer using:

```
model = tf.keras.Sequential([
    tf.keras.layers.Flatten(input_shape=(IMG_HEIGHT, IMG_WIDTH, 3)),
    tf.keras.layers.Dense(128),
    tf.keras.layers.Dense(len(CLASS_NAMES), activation='softmax')
])
```

The model now has three layers (see Figure 2-14). A layer with trainable weights, such as the one we added that is neither the input nor the output layer, is called a *hidden* layer.

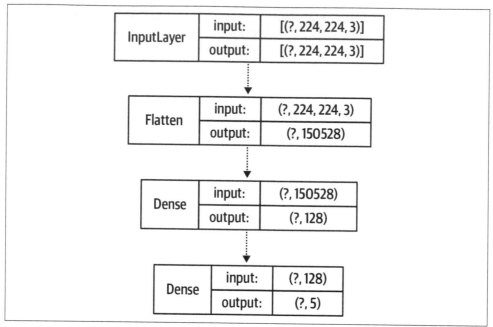

Figure 2-14. A neural network with one hidden layer.

Mathematically, the output is now:

$$Y = \S(B_2 + W_2(B_1 + W_1X))$$

Simply wrapping multiple layers like this is pointless, since we might as well have multiplied the second layer's weight (W_2) into the equation—the model remains a linear model. However, if we add a nonlinear *activation* function $A(x)$ to transform the output of the hidden layer:

$$Y = \S(B_2 + W_2A(B_1 + W_1X))$$

then the output becomes capable of representing more complex relationships than a simple linear function.

In Keras, we introduce the activation function as follows:

```
model = tf.keras.Sequential([
    tf.keras.layers.Flatten(input_shape=(IMG_HEIGHT, IMG_WIDTH, 3)),
    tf.keras.layers.Dense(128, activation='relu'),
    tf.keras.layers.Dense(len(CLASS_NAMES), activation='softmax')
])
```

The rectified linear unit (ReLU) is the most commonly used activation function for hidden layers (see Figure 2-15). Other commonly used activation functions include *sigmoid*, *tanh*, and *elu*.

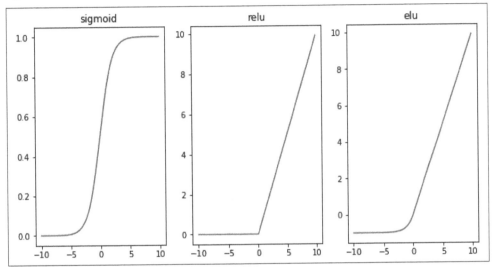

Figure 2-15. A few nonlinear activation functions.

All three of the activation functions shown in Figure 2-15 are loosely based on how neurons in the human brain fire if the input from the dendrites together exceeds some minimum threshold (see Figure 2-16). Thus, a model that has a hidden layer with a nonlinear activation function is called a "neural network."

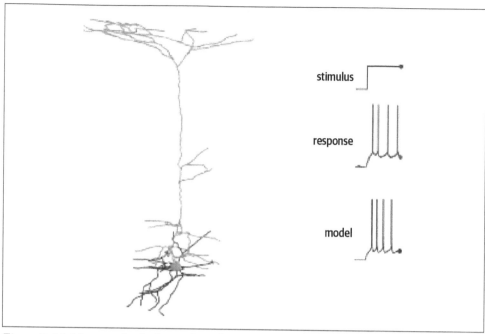

Figure 2-16. Neurons in the brain fire when the sum of the inputs exceeds some minimum threshold. Image credit: Allen Institute for Brain Science, Allen Human Brain Atlas, available from human.brain-map.org.

The sigmoid is a continuous function that behaves most similarly to how brain neurons work—the output saturates at both extremes. However, the sigmoid function suffers from slow convergence because the weight update at each step is proportional to the gradient, and the gradient near the extremes is very small. The ReLU is more often used so that the weight updates remain the same size in the active part of the function. In a `Dense` layer with a ReLU activation function, the activation function "fires" if the weighted sum of the inputs is greater than $-b$, where b is the bias. The strength of the firing is proportional to the weighted sum of the inputs. The issue with a ReLU is that it is zero for half its domain. This leads to a problem called *dead ReLUs*, where no weight update ever happens. The elu activation function (see Figure 2-15) solves this problem by having a small exponential negative value instead of zero. It is, however, expensive to compute because of the exponential. Therefore, some ML practitioners instead use the Leaky ReLU, which uses a small negative slope.

Training the neural network

Training the neural network is similar to training the linear model. We compile the model, passing in the optimizer, the loss, and the metrics. Then we call `model.fit()`, passing in the datasets:

```
model.compile(optimizer='adam',
              loss=tf.keras.losses.SparseCategoricalCrossentropy(
                  from_logits=False),
              metrics=['accuracy'])
history = model.fit(train_dataset,
                    validation_data=eval_dataset,
                    epochs=10)
```

The result, shown in Figure 2-17, reveals that the best validation accuracy that we have obtained (0.45) is similar to what we obtained with a linear model. The curves are also not smooth.

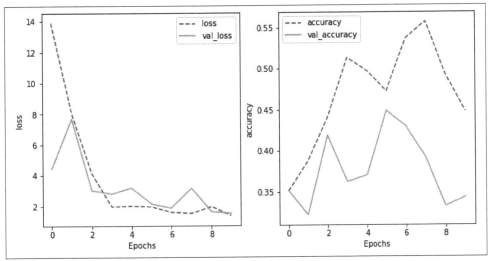

Figure 2-17. Loss and accuracy on the training and validation datasets when training a neural network.

We would normally expect that adding layers to a model will improve the ability of the model to fit the training data, and thus lower the loss. That is, indeed, the case—whereas the cross-entropy loss for the linear model is on the order of 10, it is on the order of 2 for the neural network. However, the accuracies are pretty similar, indicating that much of the improvement is obtained by the model driving probabilities like 0.7 to be closer to 1.0 than by getting items misclassified by the linear model correct.

There are still some improvements that we can try, though. For example, we can change the learning rate and the loss function, and make better use of the validation dataset. We'll look at these next.

Learning rate

A gradient descent optimizer works by looking in all directions at each point and picking the direction where the error function is decreasing the most rapidly. Then it makes a step in that direction and tries again. For example, in Figure 2-18, starting at the first point (the circle marked 1), the optimizer looks in two directions (actually 2^N directions, where N is the dimension of the weight tensor to be optimized) and chooses direction 2, because it is the direction in which the loss function decreases the fastest. Then, the optimizer updates the weight value by making a *step* in that direction, as indicated by the dashed curved line. The size of this step for every weight value is proportional to a model hyperparameter called the *learning rate*.

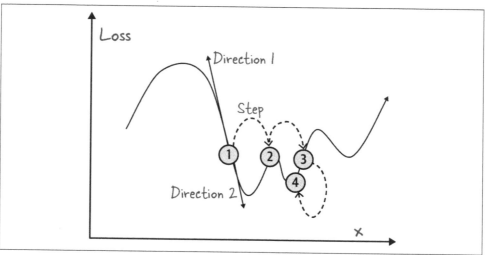

Figure 2-18. How a gradient descent optimizer works.

As you can see, if the learning rate is too high, the optimizer might skip over the minima completely. After this step (denoted by the circle marked 2 in the figure), the optimizer again looks in two directions and then continues to the third point, because the loss curve is dropping faster in that direction. After this step, the gradient is evaluated again. Now the direction points backward, and the optimizer manages to find the local minimum in between the second and third points. The global minimum which was between the first and second steps has, however, been missed.

In order to not skip over minima, we should use a small value for the learning rate. But if the learning rate is too small, the model will get stuck in a local minimum. Also, the smaller the value of the learning rate, the slower the model will converge. Thus, there's a trade-off between not missing minima and getting the model to converge quickly.

The default learning rate for the Adam optimizer is 0.001. We can change it by changing the optimizer passed into the compile() function:

```
model.compile(optimizer=tf.keras.optimizers.Adam(learning_rate=0.0001),
              loss=..., metrics=...)
```

Repeating the training with this lower training rate, we get the same end result in terms of accuracy, but the curves are noticeably less choppy (see Figure 2-19).

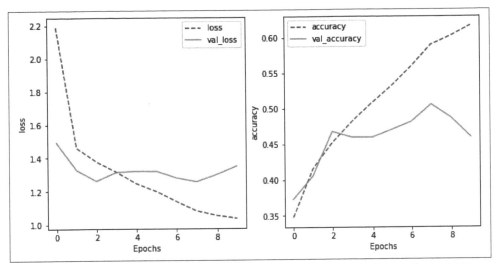

Figure 2-19. The loss and accuracy curves when the learning rate is lowered to 0.0001.

Regularization

It is also worth noting that the number of trainable parameters in the neural network is 128 times the number of trainable parameters in the linear model (19 million versus 750,000). Yet, we have only about 3,700 images. The more complex model might perform better, but we'd probably need much more data—on the order of hundreds of thousands of images. Later in this book, we will look at data augmentation techniques to make the most out of the data that we do have.

Given that we have a relatively small dataset for the complexity of the model that we are using, it is possible that the model will start to use individual trainable weights to "memorize" the classification answers for individual images in the training dataset—this is the overfitting that we can see happening in Figure 2-19 (the loss on the validation set started to increase even though the training accuracy was still decreasing). When this happens, the weight values start to become highly tuned to very specific pixel values and attain very high values.[1] Therefore, we can reduce the incidence of overfitting by changing the loss to apply a penalty on the weight values themselves. This sort of penalty applied to the loss function is called *regularization*.

Two common forms are:

$$loss = cross\!-\!entropy + \sum_i |w_i|$$

---

[1] A good non-mathematical explanation of this phenomenon can be found at DataCamp.com (*https://oreil.ly/N2qH5*).

and:

$$loss = cross-entropy + \sum_i w_i^2$$

The first type of penalty is called an *L1 regularization term,* and the second is called an *L2 regularization term.* Either penalty will cause the optimizer to prefer smaller weight values. L1 regularization drives many of the weight values to zero but is more tolerant of individual large weight values than L2 regularization, which tends to drive all the weights to small but nonzero values. The mathematical reasons why this is the case are beyond the scope of this book, but it's useful to understand that we use L1 if we want a compact model (because we can prune zero weights), whereas we use L2 if we want to limit overfitting to the maximum possible.

This is how we apply a regularization term to the Dense layers:

```
regularizer = tf.keras.regularizers.l1_l2(0, 0.001)
model = tf.keras.Sequential([
    tf.keras.layers.Flatten(input_shape=(
                    IMG_HEIGHT, IMG_WIDTH, IMG_CHANNELS)),
    tf.keras.layers.Dense(num_hidden,
                    kernel_regularizer=regularizer,
                    activation=tf.keras.activations.relu),
    tf.keras.layers.Dense(len(CLASS_NAMES),
                    kernel_regularizer=regularizer,
                    activation='softmax')
])
```

With L2 regularization turned on, we see from Figure 2-20 that the loss values are higher (because they include the penalty term). However, it is clear that overfitting is still happening after epoch 6. This indicates that we need to increase the regularization amount. Again, this is trial and error.

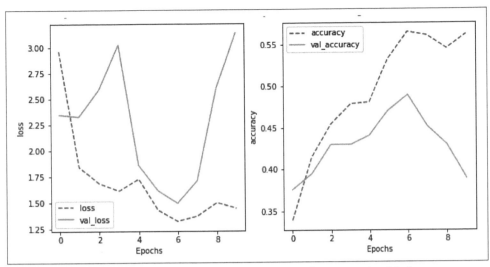

Figure 2-20. The loss and accuracy curves when L2 regularization is added.

Early stopping

Look carefully at the righthand panel in Figure 2-20. Both the training and validation set accuracies increase smoothly until the sixth epoch. After that, even though the training set accuracy continues to increase, the validation accuracy starts to drop. This is a classic sign that the model has stopped generalizing to unseen data, and is now starting to fit noise in the training dataset.

It would be good if we could stop the training once the validation accuracy stops increasing. In order to do that, we pass in a callback to the `model.fit()` function:

```
history = model.fit(train_dataset,
    validation_data=eval_dataset,
    epochs=10,
    callbacks=[tf.keras.callbacks.EarlyStopping(patience=1)]
)
```

Because convergence can be a bit bumpy, the `patience` parameter allows us to configure the number of epochs for which we want the validation accuracy to not decrease before training is stopped.

 Add in the `EarlyStopping()` callback only after you have tuned the learning rate and regularization to get smooth, well-behaved training curves. If your training curves are choppy, it is possible that you will miss out on obtaining better performance by stopping early.

Hyperparameter tuning

We chose a number of parameters for our model: the number of hidden nodes, the learning rate, the L2 regularization, and so on. How do we know that these are optimal? We don't. We need to *tune* these hyperparameters.

One way to do this is to use the Keras Tuner. To use the Keras Tuner, we implement the model-building function to use hyperparameters (the full code is in a *02_ml_models/02b_neural_network.ipynb* on GitHub):

```
import kerastuner as kt

# parameterize to the values in the previous cell
def build_model(hp):
    lrate = hp.Float('lrate', 1e-4, 1e-1, sampling='log')
    l1 = 0
    l2 = hp.Choice('l2', values=[0.0, 1e-1, 1e-2, 1e-3, 1e-4])
    num_hidden = hp.Int('num_hidden', 32, 256, 32)

    regularizer = tf.keras.regularizers.l1_l2(l1, l2)

    # NN with one hidden layer
    model = tf.keras.Sequential([
        tf.keras.layers.Flatten(
            input_shape=(IMG_HEIGHT, IMG_WIDTH, IMG_CHANNELS)),
        tf.keras.layers.Dense(num_hidden,
                        kernel_regularizer=regularizer,
                        activation=tf.keras.activations.relu),
        tf.keras.layers.Dense(len(CLASS_NAMES),
                        kernel_regularizer=regularizer,
                        activation='softmax')
    ])
    model.compile(optimizer=tf.keras.optimizers.Adam(learning_rate=lrate),
                loss=tf.keras.losses.SparseCategoricalCrossentropy(
                        from_logits=False),
                metrics=['accuracy'])
    return model
```

As you can see, we defined the space from which the hyperparameters are drawn. The learning rate (lrate) is a floating-point value between 1e-4 and 1e-1, chosen logarithmically (not linearly). The L2 regularization value is chosen from a set of five predefined values (0.0, 1e-1, 1e-2, 1e-3, and 1e-4). The number of hidden nodes (num_hidden) is an integer chosen from the range 32 to 256 in increments of 32. These values are then used in the model-building code as normal.

We pass the build_model() function into a Keras Tuner optimization algorithm. Several algorithms are supported (*https://keras-team.github.io/keras-tuner/documentation/tuners/*), but Bayesian optimization is an old standby that works well for computer vision problems:

```
tuner = kt.BayesianOptimization(
    build_model,
    objective=kt.Objective('val_accuracy', 'max'),
    max_trials=10,
    num_initial_points=2,
    overwrite=False) # True to start afresh
```

Here, we are specifying that our objective is to maximize the validation accuracy and that we want the Bayesian optimizer to run 10 trials starting from 2 randomly chosen seed points. The tuner can pick up where it left off, and we are asking Keras to do so by telling it to reuse information learned in preexisting trials and not start with a blank slate.

Having created the tuner, we can then run the search:

```
tuner.search(
    train_dataset, validation_data=eval_dataset,
    epochs=5,
    callbacks=[tf.keras.callbacks.EarlyStopping(patience=1)]
)
```

At the end of the run, we can get the top N trials (the ones that ended with the highest validation accuracy) using:

```
topN = 2
for x in range(topN):
    print(tuner.get_best_hyperparameters(topN)[x].values)
    print(tuner.get_best_models(topN)[x].summary())
```

When we did hyperparameter tuning for the 5-flowers problem, we determined that the best set of parameters was:

```
{'lrate': 0.00017013245197465996, 'l2': 0.0, 'num_hidden': 64}
```

The best validation accuracy obtained was 0.46.

Deep Neural Networks

The linear model gave us an accuracy of 0.4. The neural network with one hidden layer gave us an accuracy of 0.46. What if we add more hidden layers?

A *deep neural network* (DNN) is a neural network with more than one hidden layer. Each time we add a layer, the number of trainable parameters increases. Therefore, we will need a larger dataset. We still have only 3,700 flower images, but, as you'll see, there are a few tricks (namely dropout and batch normalization) that we can use to limit the amount of overfitting that happens.

Building a DNN

We can parameterize the creation of a DNN as follows:

```
def train_and_evaluate(batch_size = 32,
                       lrate = 0.0001,
                       l1 = 0,
                       l2 = 0.001,
                       num_hidden = [64, 16]):
    ...

    # NN with multiple hidden layers
    layers = [
            tf.keras.layers.Flatten(
                input_shape=(IMG_HEIGHT, IMG_WIDTH, IMG_CHANNELS),
                name='input_pixels')
    ]
    layers = layers + [
            tf.keras.layers.Dense(nodes,
                    kernel_regularizer=regularizer,
                    activation=tf.keras.activations.relu,
                    name='hidden_dense_{}'.format(hno))
                for hno, nodes in enumerate(num_hidden)
    ]
    layers = layers + [
            tf.keras.layers.Dense(len(CLASS_NAMES),
                    kernel_regularizer=regularizer,
                    activation='softmax',
                    name='flower_prob')
    ]

    model = tf.keras.Sequential(layers, name='flower_classification')
```

Notice that we are providing readable names for the layers. This shows up when we print a summary of the model and is also useful to get a layer by name. For example, here is the model where num_hidden is [64, 16]:

```
Model: "sequential_4"
```

Layer (type)	Output Shape	Param #
input_pixels (Flatten)	(None, 150528)	0
hidden_dense_0 (Dense)	(None, 64)	9633856
hidden_dense_1 (Dense)	(None, 16)	1040
flower_prob (Dense)	(None, 5)	85

```
Total params: 9,634,981
Trainable params: 9,634,981
Non-trainable params: 0
```

The model, once created, is trained just as before. Unfortunately, as shown in Figure 2-21, the resulting validation accuracy is worse than what was obtained with either the linear model or the neural network.

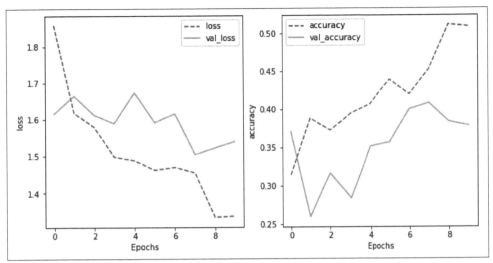

Figure 2-21. The loss and accuracy curves for a deep neural network with two hidden layers.

The 5-flowers dataset is too small for us to take advantage of the additional modeling capability provided by the DNN's extra layer. Recall that we had a similar situation when we started with the neural network. Initially, we did not do better than the linear model, but by adding regularization and lowering the learning rate we were able to get better performance.

Are there some tricks that we can apply to improve the performance of the DNN? Glad you asked! There are two ideas—*dropout layers* and *batch normalization*—that are worth trying.

Dropout

Dropout is one of the oldest regularization techniques in deep learning. At each training iteration, the dropout layer drops random neurons from the network, with a probability p (typically 25% to 50%). In practice, the dropped neurons' outputs are set to zero. The net result is that these neurons will not participate in the loss computation this time around, and they will not get weight updates (see Figure 2-22). Different neurons will be dropped at each training iteration.

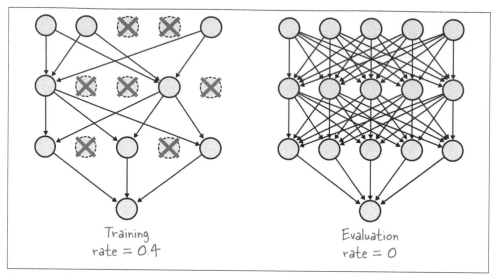

Figure 2-22. Dropout layers are applied during training—here, with a dropout rate of 0.4, 40% of the nodes in the layer are randomly dropped at each step of training.

When testing the performance of the network, all the neurons need to be considered (dropout rate=0). Keras does this automatically, so all you have to do is add a `tf.keras.layers.Dropout` layer. It will automatically have the correct behavior at training and evaluation time: during training, layers are randomly dropped; but during evaluation and prediction, no layers are dropped.

The theory behind dropout is that neural networks have so much freedom between their numerous layers that it is entirely possible for one layer to evolve a bad behavior and for the next layer to compensate for it. This is not an ideal use of neurons. With dropout, there is a high probability that the neurons "fixing" the problem will not be there in a given training round. The bad behavior of the offending layer therefore becomes obvious, and weights evolve toward a better behavior. Dropout also helps spread the information flow throughout the network, giving all weights fairly equal amounts of training, which can help keep the model balanced.

Batch normalization

Our input pixel values are in the range [0, 1], and this is compatible with the dynamic range of the typical activation functions and optimizers. However, once we add a hidden layer, the resulting output values will no longer lie in the dynamic range of the activation function for subsequent layers (see Figure 2-23). When this happens, the neuron's output is zero, and because moving a small amount in either direction makes no difference, the gradient is zero. There is no way for the network to escape from the dead zone.

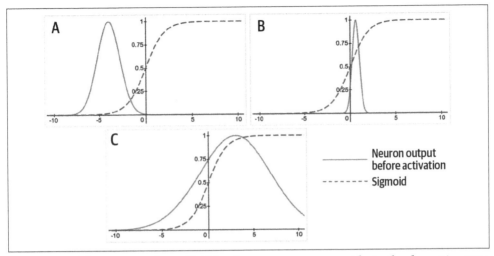

Figure 2-23. The output values of hidden layer neurons may not be in the dynamic range of the activation function. They might be (A) too far to the left (after sigmoid activation, this neuron almost always outputs zero), (B) too narrow (after sigmoid activation, this neuron never outputs a clear 0 or 1), or (C) not too bad (after sigmoid activation, this neuron will output a fair range of outputs between 0 and 1 across a mini-batch).

To fix this, batch normalization normalizes neuron outputs across a training batch of data by subtracting the average and dividing by the standard deviation. However, doing just that could be swinging the pendulum too far in one direction—with a perfectly centered and normally wide distribution everywhere, all neurons would have the same behavior. The trick is to introduce two additional learnable parameters per neuron, called *scale* and *center*, and to normalize the input data to the neuron using these values:

$$normalized = \frac{(input - center)}{scale}$$

This way, the network decides, through machine learning, how much centering and rescaling to apply at each neuron. In Keras, you can selectively use one or the other. For example:

```
tf.keras.layers.BatchNormalization(scale=False, center=True)
```

The problem with batch normalization is that at prediction time you do not have training batches over which you can compute the statistics of your neurons' outputs, but you still need those values. Therefore, during training, neurons' output statistics are computed across a "sufficient" number of batches using a running exponential average. These stats are then used at inference time.

The good news is that in Keras you can use a `tf.keras.layers.BatchNormalization` layer and all this accounting will happen automatically. When using batch normalization, remember that:

- Batch normalization is performed on the output of a layer before the activation function is applied. So, rather than set `activation='relu'` in the `Dense` layer's constructor, we'd omit the activation function there and then add a separate `Activation` layer.

- If you use `center=True` in batch norm, you do not need biases in your layer. The batch norm offset plays the role of a bias.

- If you use an activation function that is scale-invariant (i.e., does not change shape if you zoom in on it), then you can set `scale=False`. ReLu is scale-invariant. Sigmoid is not.

With dropout and batch normalization, the hidden layers now become:

```
for hno, nodes in enumerate(num_hidden):
    layers.extend([
        tf.keras.layers.Dense(nodes,
                        kernel_regularizer=regularizer,
                        name='hidden_dense_{}'.format(hno)),
        tf.keras.layers.BatchNormalization(scale=False, # ReLU
                        center=False, # have bias in Dense
                        name='batchnorm_dense_{}'.format(hno)),
        # move activation to come after batch norm
        tf.keras.layers.Activation('relu',
                            name='relu_dense_{}'.format(hno)),
        tf.keras.layers.Dropout(rate=0.4,
                            name='dropout_dense_{}'.format(hno)),

    ])

layers.append(
    tf.keras.layers.Dense(len(CLASS_NAMES),
                        kernel_regularizer=regularizer,
                        activation='softmax',
                        name='flower_prob')
)
```

Note that we have moved the activation out of the Dense layer and into a separate layer that comes after batch normalization:

hidden_dense_0 (Dense)	(None, 64)	9633856
batchnorm_dense_0 (BatchNorm	**(None, 64)**	**128**
relu_dense_0 (**Activation**)	(None, 64)	0
dropout_dense_0 (Dropout)	(None, 64)	0

The resulting training indicates that these two tricks have improved the ability of the model to generalize and to converge faster, as shown in Figure 2-24. We now get an accuracy of 0.48, as opposed to 0.40 without batch norm and dropout. Fundamentally, though, the DNN is not much better than a linear model (0.48 vs. 0.46), because a dense network is not the correct way to go deeper.

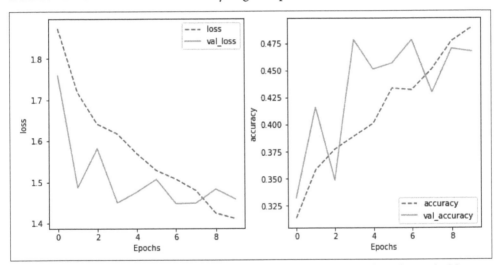

Figure 2-24. The loss and accuracy curves for a deep neural network with two hidden layers with dropout and batch normalization.

The curves are not yet well behaved (note the choppiness of the validation curves). To smooth them out, we will have to experiment with different values of regularization and then do hyperparameter tuning as before. In general, you'll have to experiment with all of these ideas (regularization, early stopping, dropout, batch normalization) for any model you pick. In the rest of the book, we'll simply show the code, but, in practice, model creation will always be followed by a period of experimentation and hyperparameter tuning.

Summary

In this chapter, we explored how to build a simple data pipeline that reads image files and creates 2D floating-point arrays. These arrays were used as inputs into fully connected machine learning models. We started with a linear model, and then added more Dense layers. We discovered that regularization was important to limit overfitting, and that changing the learning rate had an impact on learnability.

The models that we built in this chapter did not take advantage of the special structure of images, where adjacent pixels are highly correlated. That is what we will do in Chapter 3. Nevertheless, the tools that we introduced in this chapter for reading images, visualizing them, creating ML models, and predicting using ML models will remain applicable even as the models themselves become more complex. The techniques that you learned about here—hidden layers, changing the learning rate, regularization, early stopping, hyperparameter tuning, dropout, and batch normalization—are used in all the models we discuss in this book.

This chapter introduced a lot of important terminology. For quick reference, a short glossary of terms follows.

Glossary

Accuracy
> An error metric that measures the fraction of correct predictions in a classification model: (TP + TN) / (TP + FP + TN + FN) where, for example, TP is true positives.

Activation function
> A function applied to the weighted sum of the inputs to a node in a neural network. This is the way that nonlinearity is added to a neural network. Common activation functions include ReLU and sigmoid.

AUC
> Area under the curve of true positive rate plotted against false positive rate. The AUC is a threshold-independent error metric.

Batch or mini-batch
> Training is always performed on batches of training data and labels. Doing so helps the algorithm converge. The batch dimension is typically the first dimension of data tensors. For example, a tensor of shape [100, 192, 192, 3] contains 100 images of 192x192 pixels with three values per pixel (RGB).

Batch normalization
> Adding two additional learnable parameters per neuron to normalize the input data to the neuron during training.

Cross-entropy loss
A special loss function often used in classifiers.

Dense layer
A layer of neurons where each neuron is connected to all the neurons in the previous layer.

Dropout
A regularization technique in deep learning where, during each training iteration, randomly chosen neurons from the network are dropped.

Early stopping
Stopping a training run when the validation set error starts to get worse.

Epoch
A full pass through the training dataset during training.

Error metric
The error function comparing neural network outputs to the correct answers. The error on the evaluation dataset is what is reported. Common error metrics include precision, recall, accuracy, and AUC.

Features
A term used to refer to the inputs of a neural network. In modern image models, the pixel values form the features.

Feature engineering
The art of figuring out which parts of a dataset (or combinations of parts) to feed into a neural network to get good predictions. In modern image models, no feature engineering is required.

Flattening
Converting a multidimensional tensor to a 1D tensor that contains all the values.

Hyperparameter tuning
An "outer" optimization loop where multiple models with different values of model hyperparameters (like learning rate and number of nodes) are trained, and the best of these models chosen. In the "inner" optimization loop, which we call the *training loop*, the model's parameters (weights and biases) are optimized.

Labels
Another name for "classes," or correct answers in a supervised classification problem.

Learning rate
The fraction of the gradient by which weights and biases are updated at each iteration of the training loop.

Logits

The outputs of a layer of neurons before the activation function is applied. The term comes from the *logistic function*, a.k.a. the *sigmoid function*, which used to be the most popular activation function. "Neuron outputs before logistic function" was shortened to "logits."

Loss

The error function comparing neural network outputs to the correct answers.

Neuron

The most basic unit of a neural network, which computes the weighted sum of its inputs, adds a bias, and feeds the result through an activation function. The loss on the training dataset is what is minimized during training.

One-hot encoding

A representation of categorical values as binary vectors. For example, class 3 out of 5 is encoded as a vector of five elements, which are all 0s except the third one, which is a 1: [0 0 1 0 0].

Precision

An error metric that measures the fraction of true positives in the set of identified positives: TP / (TP + FP).

Recall

An error metric that measures the fraction of true positives identified among all the positives in the dataset: TP / (TP + FN).

Regularization

A penalty imposed on weights or model function during training to limit the amount of overfitting. *L1 regularization* drives many of the weight values to zero but is more tolerant of individual large weight values than *L2 regularization*, which tends to drive all the weights to small but nonzero values.

ReLU

Rectified linear unit. A popular activation function for neurons.

Sigmoid

An activation function that acts on an unbounded scalar and converts it into a value that lies between [0,1]. It is used as the last step of a binary classifier.

Softmax

A special activation function that acts on a vector. It increases the difference between the largest component and all others, and also normalizes the vector to have a sum of 1 so that it can be interpreted as a vector of probabilities. Used as the last step in multiclass classifiers.

Tensor
> A tensor is like a matrix but with an arbitrary number of dimensions. A 1D tensor is a vector, a 2D tensor is a matrix, and you can have tensors with three, four, five or more dimensions. In this book, we will use the term tensor to refer to the numerical type that supports GPU-accelerated TensorFlow operations.

Training
> Optimizing the parameters of a machine learning model to attain lower loss on a training dataset.

## CHAPTER 3

Image Vision

In Chapter 2, we looked at machine learning models that treat pixels as being independent inputs. Traditional fully connected neural network layers perform poorly on images because they do not take advantage of the fact that adjacent pixels are highly correlated (see Figure 3-1). Moreover, fully connecting multiple layers does not make any special provisions for the 2D hierarchical nature of images. Pixels close to each other work together to create shapes (such as lines and arcs), and these shapes themselves work together to create recognizable parts of an object (such as the stem and petals of a flower).

In this chapter, we will remedy this by looking at techniques and model architectures that take advantage of the special properties of images.

The code for this chapter is in the *03_image_models* folder of the book's GitHub repository (*https://github.com/GoogleCloudPlatform/ practical-ml-vision-book*). We will provide file names for code samples and notebooks where applicable.

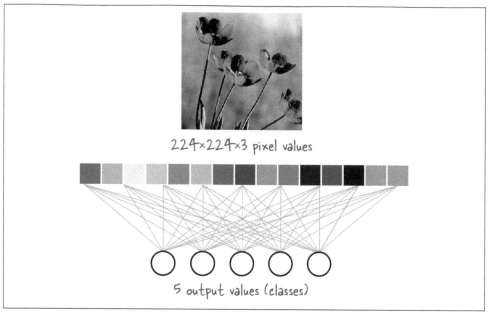

Figure 3-1. Applying a fully connected layer to all the pixels of an image treats the pixels as independent inputs and ignores that images have adjacent pixels working together to create shapes.

Pretrained Embeddings

The deep neural network that we developed in Chapter 2 had two hidden layers, one with 64 nodes and the other with 16 nodes. One way to think about this network architecture is shown in Figure 3-2. In some sense, all the information contained in the input image is being represented by the penultimate layer, whose output consists of 16 numbers. These 16 numbers that provide a representation of the image are called an *embedding*. Of course, earlier layers also capture information from the input image, but those are typically not used as embeddings because they are missing some of the hierarchical information.

In this section, we will discuss how to create an embedding (as distinct from a classification model), and how to use the embedding to train models on different datasets using two different approaches, transfer learning and fine-tuning.

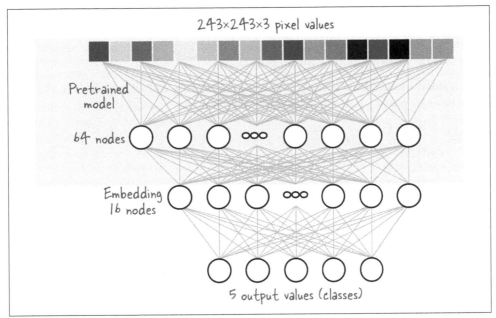

Figure 3-2. The 16 numbers that form the embedding provide a representation of all the information in the entire image.

Pretrained Model

The embedding is created by applying a set of mathematical operations to the input image. Recall that we reiterated in Chapter 2 that the model accuracy that we were getting, on the order of 0.45, was low because our dataset wasn't large enough to support the many millions of trainable weights in our fully connected deep learning model. What if we were to repurpose the embedding creation part from a model that has been trained on a much larger dataset? We can't repurpose the whole model, because that model will not have been trained to classify flowers. However, we can throw away the last layer, or *prediction head*, of that model and replace it with our own. The repurposed part of the model can be *pretrained* from a very large, general-purpose dataset and the knowledge can then be *transferred* to the actual dataset that we want to classify. Looking back to Figure 3-2, we can replace the 64-node layer in the box marked "pretrained model" with the first set of layers of a model that has been trained on a much larger dataset.

Pretrained models are models that are trained on large datasets and made available to be used as a way to create embeddings. For example, the MobileNet model (*https://oreil.ly/JNk0O*) is a model with 1–4 million parameters that was trained on the ImageNet (ILSVRC) dataset (*https://oreil.ly/B9Q85*), which consists of millions of images corresponding to hundreds of categories that were scraped from the web. The resulting embedding therefore has the ability to efficiently compress the information found in a wide variety of images. As long as the images we want to classify are similar in nature to the ones that MobileNet was trained on, the embeddings from MobileNet should give us a great pretrained embedding that we can use as a starting point to train a model on our own smaller dataset.

A pretrained MobileNet is available on TensorFlow Hub, and we can easily load it as a Keras layer by passing in the URL to the trained model:

```
import tensorflow_hub as hub
huburl= "https://tfhub.dev/google/imagenet/\
    mobilenet_v2_100_224/feature_vector/4"
hub.KerasLayer(
    handle=huburl,
    input_shape=(IMG_HEIGHT, IMG_WIDTH, IMG_CHANNELS),
    trainable=False,
    name='mobilenet_embedding')
```

In this code snippet, we imported the package `tensorflow_hub` and created a `hub.KerasLayer`, passing in the URL and the input shape of our images. Critically, we specify that this layer is not trainable, and should be assumed to be pretrained. By doing so, we ensure that its weights will not be modified based on the flowers data; it will be read-only.

Transfer Learning

The rest of the model is similar to the DNN models that we created previously. Here's a model that uses the pretrained model loaded from TensorFlow Hub as its first layer (the full code is available in *03a_transfer_learning.ipynb*):

```
layers = [
    hub.KerasLayer(..., name='mobilenet_embedding'),
    tf.keras.layers.Dense(units=16,
                          activation='relu',
                          name='dense_hidden'),
    tf.keras.layers.Dense(units=len(CLASS_NAMES),
                          activation='softmax',
                          name='flower_prob')
]
model = tf.keras.Sequential(layers, name='flower_classification')
...
```

The resulting model summary is as follows:

```
Model: "flower_classification"
```

Layer (type)	Output Shape	Param #
mobilenet_embedding (KerasLa	(None, 1280)	**2257984**
dense_hidden (Dense)	(None, 16)	20496

```
flower_prob (Dense)            (None, 5)                    85
=================================================================
Total params: 2,278,565
Trainable params: 20,581
Non-trainable params: 2,257,984
```

Note that the first layer, which we called mobilenet_embedding, has 2.26 million parameters, but they are not trainable. Only 20,581 parameters are trainable: 1,280 * 16 weights + 16 biases = 20,496 from the hidden dense layer, plus 16 * 5 weights + 5 biases = 85 from the dense layer to the five output nodes. So despite the 5-flowers dataset not being large enough to train millions of parameters, it is large enough to train just 20K parameters.

This process of training a model by replacing its input layer with an image embedding is called *transfer learning*, because we have transferred the knowledge learned from a much larger dataset by the MobileNet creators to our problem.

Because we are replacing the input layer of our model with the Hub layer, it's important to make sure that our data pipeline provides data in the format expected by the Hub layer. All image models in TensorFlow Hub use a common image format and expect pixel values as floats in the range [0,1]. The image-reading code that we used in Chapter 2 scales the JPEG images to lie within this range, so we're OK.

Pretrained Models in Keras

We've just showed you how to load a pretrained model from TensorFlow Hub. The most popular pretrained models are available directly in Keras. They can be loaded by instantiating the corresponding class in tf.keras.applications.*. For example:

```
pretrained_model = tf.keras.applications.MobileNetV2(
    weights='imagenet',include_top=False,
    input_shape=[IMG_HEIGHT, IMG_WIDTH, 3])
pretrained_model.trainable = False  # For transfer learning
```

The following code uses the pretrained model to build a custom classifier, by attaching a custom classification head to it:

```
model = tf.keras.Sequential([
    # convert image format from int [0,255]
    # to the format expected by this model
    tf.keras.layers.Lambda(
        lambda data: tf.keras.applications.mobilenet.preprocess_input(
            tf.cast(data, tf.float32)),
        input_shape=[IMG_HEIGHT, IMG_WIDTH, 3]),
    pretrained_model,
    tf.keras.layers.GlobalAveragePooling2D(),
    tf.keras.layers.Dense(256, activation='relu'),
    tf.keras.layers.Dense(len(CLASSES),
    activation='softmax')
])
```

Notice how the code snippet handles the pretrained model's expected inputs and outputs:

1. Every model in `tf.keras.applications.*` expects its input images to have pixel values in a specific range, such as [0, 1] or [−1, 1]. A format conversion function named `tf.keras.applications.<MODEL_NAME>.preprocess_input()` is provided for every model. It converts images with pixel values that are floats in the range [0, 255] into the pixel format expected by the pretrained model. If you load images using the `tf.io.decode_image()` operation, which returns pixels with a `uint8` format in the range [0, 255], a cast to float is necessary before applying `preprocess_input()`.

 This is different from the image format convention used in TensorFlow Hub. All the image models in TensorFlow Hub expect pixel values as floats in the range [0, 1]. The easiest way to obtain images in that format is to use `tf.io.decode_image()` followed by `tf.image.con vert_image_dtype(..., tf.float32)`.

2. With the option `include_top=False`, all the models in `tf.keras.applica tions.*` return a 3D feature map. It's the user's responsibility to compute a 1D feature vector from it so that a classification head with dense layers can be appended. You can use `tf.keras.layers.GlobalAveragePooling2D()` or `tf.keras.layers.Flatten()` for this purpose.

 This is again different from the way models in TensorFlow Hub typically return embeddings. All models in TensorFlow Hub that include `feature_vector` in their name already return a 1D feature vector, not a 3D feature map. A dense layer can be added immediately after them to implement a custom classification head.

Training this model is identical to training the DNN in the previous section (see *03a_transfer_learning.ipynb* in the GitHub repository for details). The resulting loss and accuracy curves are shown in Figure 3-3.

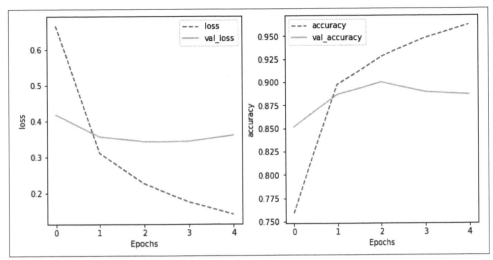

Figure 3-3. The loss and accuracy curves for a deep neural network with two hidden layers with dropout and batch normalization.

Rather impressively, we get an accuracy of 0.9 using transfer learning (see Figure 3-4), whereas we got to only 0.48 when training a fully connected deep neural network from scratch on our data. Transfer learning is what we recommend any time your dataset is relatively small. Only when your dataset starts to exceed about five thousand images *per label* should you start to consider training from scratch. Later in this chapter, we will see techniques and architectures that allow us to get even higher accuracies provided we have a large dataset and can train from scratch.

The probability associated with the daisy prediction for the first image in the second row might come as a surprise. How can the probability be 0.41? Shouldn't it be greater than 0.5? Recall that this is not a binary prediction problem. There are five possible classes, and if the output probabilities are [0.41, 0.39, 0.1, 0.1, 0.1], the arg max will correspond to daisy and the probability will be 0.41.

Figure 3-4. Predictions by the MobileNet transfer learning model on some of the images in the evaluation dataset.

Fine-Tuning

During transfer learning, we took all the layers that comprise MobileNet and used them as is. We did so by making the layers non-trainable. Only the last two dense layers were tuned on the 5-flowers dataset.

In many instances, we might be able to get better results if we allow our training loop to also adapt the pretrained layers. This technique is called *fine-tuning*. The pretrained weights are used as initial values for the weights of the neural network (normally, neural network training starts with the weights initialized to random values).

In theory, all that is needed to switch from transfer learning to fine-tuning is to flip the `trainable` flag from `False` to `True` when loading a pretrained model and train on your data. In practice, however, you will often notice training curves like the one in Figure 3-5 when fine-tuning a pretrained model.

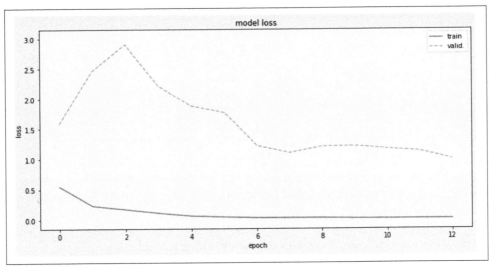

Figure 3-5. The training and validation loss curves when fine-tuning with a badly chosen learning rate schedule.

The training curve here shows that the model mathematically converges. However, its performance on the validation data is poor and initially gets worse before somewhat recovering. With a learning rate set too high, the pretrained weights are being changed in large steps and all the information learned during pretraining is lost. Finding a learning rate that works can be tricky—set the learning rate too low and convergence is very slow, too high and pretrained weights are lost.

There are two techniques that can be used to solve this problem: a learning rate schedule and layer-wise learning rates. The code showcasing both techniques is available in *03b_finetune_MOBILENETV2_flowers5.ipynb*.

Learning rate schedule

The most traditional learning rate schedule when training neural networks is to have the learning rate start high and then decay exponentially throughout the training. When fine-tuning a pretrained model, a warm-up ramp period can be added (see Figure 3-6).

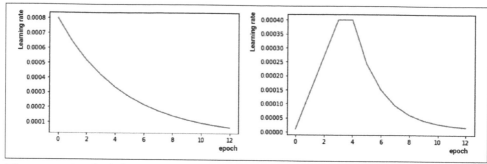

Figure 3-6. On the left, a traditional learning rate schedule with exponential decay; on the right, a learning rate schedule that features a warm-up ramp, which is more appropriate for fine-tuning.

Figure 3-7 shows the loss curves with this new learning rate schedule.

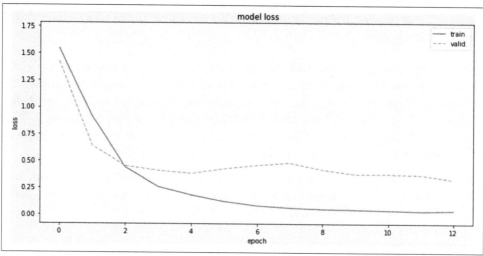

Figure 3-7. Fine-tuning with an adapted learning rate schedule.

Notice that there is still a hiccup on the validation loss curve, but it is nowhere as bad as previously (compare with Figure 3-5). This leads us to the second way to choose learning rates for fine-tuning.

Differential learning rate

Another good trade-off is to apply a *differential learning rate*, whereby we use a low learning rate for the pretrained layers and a normal learning rate for the layers of our custom classification head.

In fact, we can extend the idea of a differential learning rate within the pretrained layers themselves—we can multiply the learning rate by a factor that varies based on layer depth, gradually increasing the per-layer learning rate and finishing with the full learning rate for the classification head.

In order to apply a complex differential learning rate like this in Keras, we need to write a custom optimizer. But fortunately, an open source Python package called AdamW (*https://oreil.ly/z1IfS*) exists that we can use by specifying a learning rate multiplier for different layers (see *03_image_models/03b_finetune_MOBILE-NETV2_flowers5.ipynb* in the GitHub repository for the complete code):

```
mult_by_layer={
    'block1_': 0.1,
    'block2_': 0.15,
    'block3_': 0.2,
    ... # blocks 4 to 11 here
    'block12_': 0.8,
    'block13_': 0.9,
    'block14_': 0.95,
    'flower_prob': 1.0, # for the classification head
}

optimizer = AdamW(lr=LR_MAX, model=model,
                  lr_multipliers=mult_by_layer)
```

 How did we know what the names of the layers in the loaded pretrained model were? We ran the code without any name at first, with `lr_multipliers={}`. The custom optimizer prints the names of all the layers when run. We then found a substring of the layer names that identified the depth of the layer in the network. The custom optimizer matches layer names by the substrings passed to its `lr_multipliers` argument.

With both the per-layer learning rate and a learning rate schedule with a ramp-up, we can push the accuracy of a fine-tuned MobileNetV2 on the `tf_flowers` (5-flowers) dataset to 0.92, versus 0.91 with the ramp-up only and 0.9 with transfer learning only (see the code in *03b_finetune_MOBILENETV2_flowers5.ipynb*).

The gains from fine-tuning here are small because the `tf_flowers` dataset is tiny. We need a more challenging benchmark for the advanced architectures we are about to explore. In the rest of this chapter, we will use the *104 flowers* dataset.

The 104 Flowers Dataset

The 104 flowers dataset has more than 23,000 labeled images of 104 kinds of flowers. It was assembled for the "Petals to the Metal" (*https://oreil.ly/s232c*) competition on Kaggle from various publicly available image datasets. Some samples are shown in Figure 3-8.

Figure 3-8. An excerpt from the 104 flowers dataset.

We will use this dataset for the remainder of this chapter. Being a larger dataset, it also requires more resources to train on. That is why all the examples in the rest of the chapter are set up to run both on GPUs and TPUs (more information on TPUs is provided in Chapter 7). The data is stored in TFRecords, for reasons we explain in Chapter 5.

This dataset is also challenging because it is heavily imbalanced, with thousands of images in some categories and less than a hundred examples in others. This reflects how datasets are found in real life. Accuracy—i.e., the percentage of correctly classified images—is not a good metric for an imbalanced dataset. So, *precision*, *recall*, and *F1* score will be used instead. As you learned in Chapter 2, the precision score for the category "daisy" is the fraction of daisy predictions that are correct, while the recall score is the fraction of daisies in the dataset that are correctly classified. The F1 score is the harmonic mean of the two. The overall precision is the weighted average of the precision of all the categories, weighted by the number of instances in each category. More information about these metrics can be found in Chapter 8.

The GitHub repository contains three notebooks experimenting with these fine-tuning techniques on the larger 104 flowers dataset. The results are presented in Table 3-1. For this task we used Xception, a model with more weights and layers than MobileNet, because the 104 flowers dataset is larger and can support this larger model. As you can see, a learning rate ramp-up or a per-layer differential learning rate is not strictly necessary, but in practice it makes the convergence more stable and makes it easier to find working learning rate parameters.

Table 3-1. Summary of results obtained by a larger model (Xception) fine-tuned on the larger 104 flowers dataset

Notebook name	LR ramp-up	Differential LR	Mean F1 score across five runs	Standard deviation across five runs	Notes
lr_decay_xception	No	No	0.932	0.004	Good, relatively low variance
lr_ramp_xception	Yes	No	0.934	0.007	Very good, high variance
lr_layers_lr_ramp_xception	Yes	Yes	0.936	0.003	Best, nice low variance

So far, we have used MobileNet and Xception for transfer learning and fine-tuning, but these models are black boxes as far as we are concerned. We do not know how many layers they have, or what those layers consist of. In the next section, we will discuss a key concept, *convolution*, that helps these neural networks work well at extracting the semantic information content of an image.

Convolutional Networks

Convolutional layers were designed specifically for images. They operate in two dimensions and can capture shape information; they work by sliding a small window, called a *convolutional filter*, across the image in both directions.

Convolutional Filters

A typical 4x4 filter will have independent filter weights for each of the channels of the image. For color images with red, green, and blue channels, the filter will have 4 * 4 * 3 = 48 learnable weights in total. The filter is applied to a single position in the image by multiplying the pixel values in the neighborhood of that position by filter weights and summing them as shown in Figure 3-9. This operation is called the tensor *dot product*. Computing the dot product at each position in the image by sliding the filter across the image is called a *convolution*.

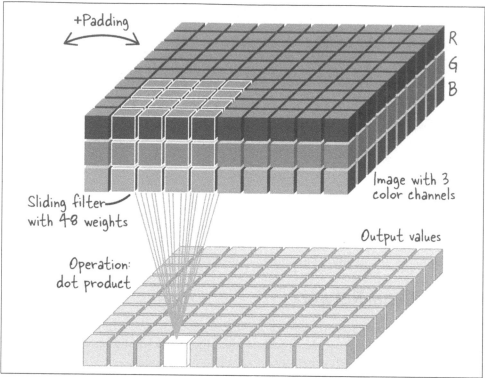

Figure 3-9. Processing an image with a single 4x4 convolutional filter—the filter slides across the image in both directions, producing one output value at each position.

Why Do Convolutional Filters Work?

Convolutional filters have been used in image processing for a long time. They can achieve many different effects. For example, a filter where all the weights are the same is a "smoothing" filter (because each pixel within a window has an equal contribution for the resulting output pixel) and yields the second panel shown in Figure 3-10. Organizing the weights in other specific ways can create edge and intensity detectors (for details, see *03_image_models/diagrams.ipynb* in the GitHub repository).

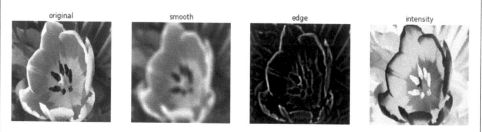

Figure 3-10. The effects of different convolutional filters.

The more interesting filters, like the edge filter in Figure 3-10 (panel 3), use correlations and anti-correlations of adjacent pixels to compute new information about the image. Indeed, adjacent pixels tend to be highly correlated and work together to create what we call *textures* and *edges* at small scales and *shapes* at higher scales. That is where the information of the image is encoded, and that is also what convolutional filters are well equipped to detect.

A convolutional neural network filter, therefore, makes it possible for the machine learning model to learn the arrangement of weights that best picks up pertinent details from the training data. The network will learn whatever combination of weights will minimize the loss.

Another advantage of convolutional filters is that a 5x5x3 filter has only 75 weights, and the same weights are slid across the entire image. Contrast this with a fully connected network layer, where an image that is 200x200x3 will end up with 120K weights *per node* in the next layer! Convolutional filters can therefore help limit the complexity of the neural network. Since the size of the dataset we require for training is related to the number of trainable parameters, using convolutional filters allows us to use our training data more effectively.

A single convolutional filter can process an entire image with very few learnable parameters—so few, in fact, that it will not be able to learn and represent enough of the complexities of the image. Multiple such filters are needed. A convolutional layer typically contains tens or hundreds of similar filters, each with its own independent learnable weights (see Figure 3-11). They are applied to the image in succession, and each produces a *channel* of output values. The output of a convolutional layer is a multichannel set of 2D values. Notice that this output has the same number of dimensions as the input image, which was already a three-channel set of 2D pixel values.

Understanding the structure of a convolutional layer makes it easy to compute its number of learnable weights, as you can see in Figure 3-12. This diagram also introduces the schematic notation of convolutional layers that will be used for the models in this chapter.

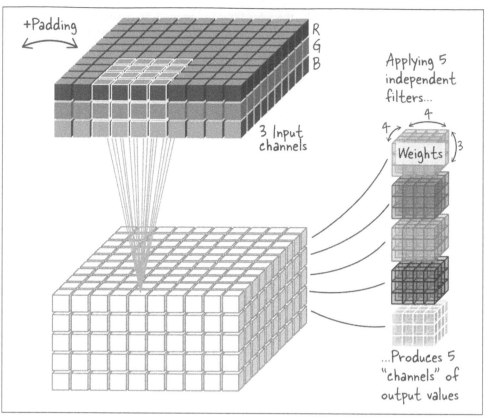

Figure 3-11. Processing an image with a convolutional layer made up of multiple convolutional filters—all filters are of the same size (here, 4x4x3) but have independent learnable weights.

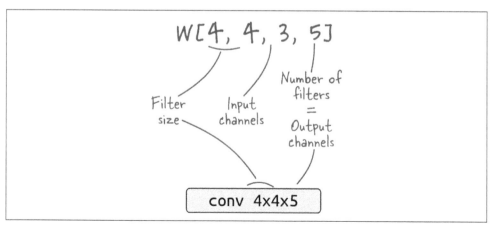

Figure 3-12. W, the weights matrix of a convolutional layer.

In this case, with 5 filters applied, the total number of learnable weights in this convolutional layer is 4 * 4 * 3 * 5 = 240.

Convolutional layers are available in Keras:

```
tf.keras.layers.Conv2D(filters,
                       kernel_size,
                       strides=(1, 1),
                       padding='valid',
                       activation=None)
```

The following is a simplified description of the parameters (see the Keras documentation (*https://oreil.ly/NLRBL*) for full details):

`filters`
> The number of independent filters to apply to the input. This will also be the number of output channels in the output.

`kernel_size`
> The size of each filter. This can be a single number, like 4 for a 4x4 filter, or a pair like (4, 2) for a rectangular 4x2 filter.

`strides`
> The filter slides across the input image in steps. The default step size is 1 pixel in both directions. Using a larger step will skip input pixels and produce fewer output values.

`padding`
> `'valid'` for no padding or `'same'` for zero-padding at the edges. If filters are applied to inputs with `'valid'` padding, convolution is carried out only if all the pixels within the window are valid, so boundary pixels get ignored. Therefore, the output will be slightly smaller in the *x* and *y* directions. The value `'same'` enables zero-padding of the input to make sure that outputs have the same width and height as the input.

`activation`
> Like any neural network layer, a convolutional layer can be followed by an activation (nonlinearity).

The convolutional layer illustrated in Figure 3-11, with five 4x4 filters, input padding, and the default stride of 1 in both directions, can be implemented as follows:

```
tf.keras.layers.Conv2D(filters=5, kernel_size=4, padding='same')
```

4D tensors are expected as inputs and outputs of convolutional layers. The first dimension is the batch size, so the full shape is [batch, height, width, channels]. For example, a batch of 16 color (RGB) images of 512x512 pixels would be represented as a tensor with dimensions [16, 512, 512, 3].

Stacking Convolutional Layers

As described in the previous section, a generic convolutional layer takes a 4D tensor of shape [batch, height, width, channels] as an input and produces another 4D tensor as an output. For simplicity, we will ignore the batch dimension in our diagrams and show what happens to a single 3D image of shape [height, width, channels].

A convolutional layer transforms a "cube" of data into another "cube" of data, which can in turn be consumed by another convolutional layer. Convolutional layers can be stacked as shown in Figure 3-13.

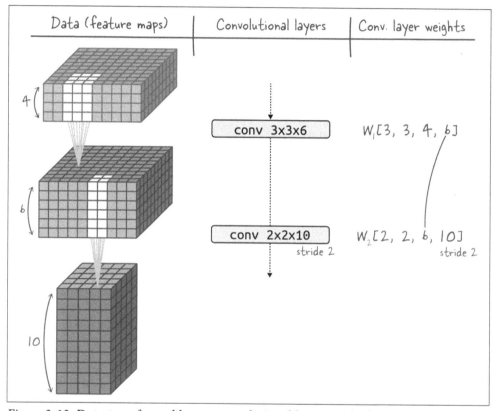

Figure 3-13. Data transformed by two convolutional layers applied in sequence. Learnable weights are shown on the right. The second convolutional layer is applied with a stride of 2 and has six input channels, matching the six output channels of the previous layer.

Figure 3-13 shows how the data is transformed by two convolutional layers. Starting from the top, the first layer is a 3x3 filter applied to an input with four channels of data. The filter is applied to the input six times, each time with different filter weights, resulting in six channels of output values. This in turn is fed into a second convolutional layer using 2x2 filters. Notice that the second convolutional layer uses a stride of 2 (every other pixel) when applying its filters to obtain fewer output values (in the horizontal plane).

Pooling Layers

The number of filters applied in each convolutional layer determines the number of channels in the output. But how can we control the amount of data in each channel? The goal of a neural network is usually to distill information from the input image, consisting of millions of pixels, to a handful of classes. So, we will need layers that can combine or downsample the information in each channel.

The most commonly used downsampling operation is 2x2 *max pooling*. With max pooling, only the maximum value is retained for each group of four input values from a channel (Figure 3-14). *Average pooling* works in a similar way, averaging the four values instead of keeping the max.

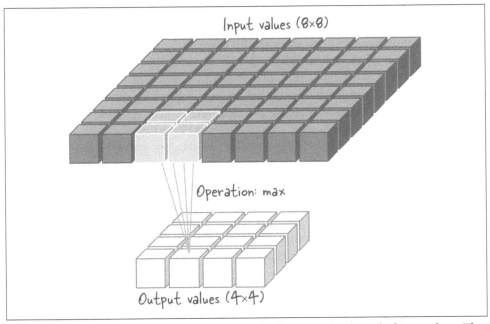

Figure 3-14. A 2x2 max-pooling operation applied to a single channel of input data. The max is taken for every group of 2x2 input values and the operation is repeated every two values in each direction (stride 2).

Note that max-pooling and average-pooling layers do not have any trainable weights. They are purely size adjustment layers.

There is an interesting physical explanation of why max-pooling layers work well with convolutional layers in neural networks. Convolutional layers are series of trainable filters. After training, each filter specializes in matching some specific image feature. The first layer in a convolutional neural network reacts to pixel combinations in the input image, but subsequent layers react to combinations of features from the previous layers. For example, in a neural network trained to recognize cats, the first layer reacts to basic image components like horizontal and vertical lines or the texture of fur. Subsequent layers react to specific combinations of lines and fur to recognize pointy ears, whiskers, or cat eyes. Even later layers detect a combination of pointy ears + whiskers + cat eyes as a cat head. A max-pooling layer only keeps values where some feature X was detected with maximum intensity. If the goal is to reduce the number of values but keep the ones most representative of what was detected, it makes sense.

Pooling layers and convolutional layers also have different effects on the locations of detected features. A convolutional layer returns a feature map with its high values located where its filters detected something significant. Pooling layers, on the other hand, reduce the resolution of the feature maps and make the location information less accurate. Sometimes location or relative location is important, such as eyes usually being located above the nose in a face. Convolutions do produce location information for other layers further along in the network to work with. At other times, however, locating a feature is not the goal—for instance, in a flower classifier, where you want to train the model to recognize flowers in an image wherever they are. In such a case, when training for location invariance, pooling layers help blur the location information to some extent, but not completely. The network will have to be trained on images showing flowers in many different locations if it is to become truly location-agnostic. Data augmentation methods like random crops of the image can be used to force the network to learn this location invariance. Data augmentation is covered in Chapter 6.

A second option for downsampling channel information is to apply convolutions with a stride of 2 or 3 instead of 1. The convolutional filters then slide over the input image by steps of 2 or 3 pixels in each direction. This mechanically produces a certain size of output values, as shown in Figure 3-15.

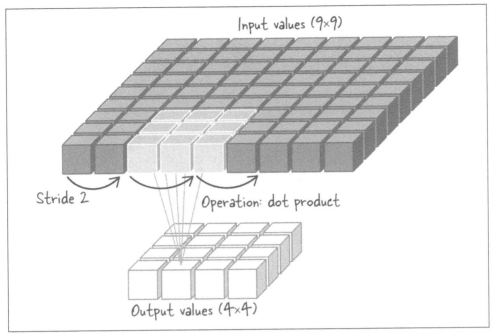

Figure 3-15. A 3x3 filter applied to a single channel of data with a stride of 2 in both directions and without padding. The filter jumps by 2 pixels at a time.

We are now ready to assemble these layers into our first convolutional neural classifier.

AlexNet

The simplest convolutional neural network architecture is a mix of convolutional layers and max-pooling layers. It transforms each input image into a final rectangular prism of values, usually called a *feature map*, which is then fed into a number of fully connected layers and, finally, a softmax layer to compute class probabilities.

AlexNet, introduced in a 2012 paper (*https://oreil.ly/sMlqQ*) by Alex Krizhevsky et al. and shown in Figure 3-16, is such an architecture. It was designed for the ImageNet competition (*https://oreil.ly/G1jfu*), which asked participants to classify images into one thousand categories (car, flower, dog, etc.) based on a training dataset of more than a million images. AlexNet was one of the earliest successes in neural image classification, exhibiting a dramatic improvement in accuracy and proving that deep learning was much better able to address computer vision problems than existing techniques.

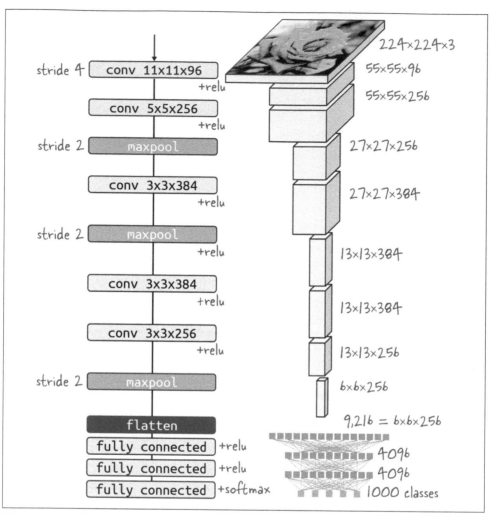

Figure 3-16. The AlexNet architecture: neural network layers are represented on the left. Feature maps (as transformed by the layers) on the right.

In this architecture, convolutional layers change the depth of the data—i.e., the number of channels. Max-pooling layers downsample the data in the height and width directions. The first convolutional layer has a stride of 4, which is why it downsamples the image as well.

AlexNet uses 3x3 max-pooling operations with a stride of 2. A more traditional choice would be 2x2 max pooling with a stride of 2. The AlexNet study claims some advantage for this "overlapping" max pooling, but it does not appear to be significant.

Every convolutional layer is activated by a ReLU activation function. The final four layers form the classification head of AlexNet, taking the last feature map, flattening all of its values into a vector, and feeding it through three fully connected layers. Because AlexNet was designed for a thousand categories, the last layer is activated by a softmax with one thousand outputs that computes the probabilities of the thousand target classes.

All convolutional and fully connected layers use an additive bias. When the ReLU activation function is used, it is customary to initialize the bias to a small positive value before training so that, after activation, all layers start with a nonzero output and a nonzero gradient (remember that the ReLU curve is a flat zero for all negative values).

In Figure 3-16, notice that AlexNet starts with a very large 11x11 convolutional filter. This is costly in terms of learnable weights and probably not something that would be done in more modern architectures. However, one advantage of the large 11x11 filters is that their learned weights can be visualized as 11x11-pixel images. The authors of the AlexNet paper did so; their results are shown in Figure 3-17.

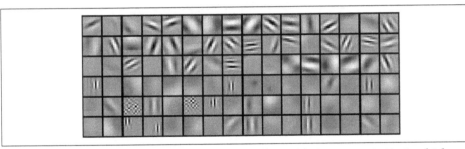

Figure 3-17. All 96 filters from the first AlexNet layer. Their size is 11x11x3, which means they can be visualized as color images. This picture shows their weights after training. Image from Krizhevsky et al., 2012 (https://oreil.ly/X3xRb).

As you can see, the network learned to detect vertical, horizontal and slanted lines of various orientations. Two filters exhibit a checkerboard pattern, which probably reacts to grainy textures in the image. You can also see detectors for single colors or pairs of adjacent colors. All these are basic features that subsequent convolutional layers will assemble into semantically more significant constructs. For example, the neural network will combine textures and lines into shapes like "wheels," "handlebars," and "saddle," and then combine these shapes into a "bicycle."

We chose to present AlexNet here because it was one of the pioneering convolutional architectures. Alternating convolutional and max-pooling layers is still a feature of modern networks. Other choices made in this architecture, however, no longer represent currently recognized best practice. For example, the use of a very large 11x11 filter in the first convolutional layer has since been found to not be the best use of learnable weights (3x3 is better, as we'll see later in this chapter). Also, the three final fully connected layers have more than 26 million learnable weights! This is an order of magnitude more than all the convolutional layers combined (3.7 million). The network is also very shallow, with only eight neural layers. Modern neural networks increase that dramatically, to one hundred layers or more.

One advantage of this very simple model, however, is that it can be implemented quite concisely in Keras (you can see the full example in *03c_fromzero_ALEX-NET_flowers104.ipynb* on GitHub):

```
model = tf.keras.Sequential([
    tf.keras.Input(shape=[IMG_HEIGHT, IMG_WIDTH, 3]),
    tf.keras.layers.Conv2D(filters=96, kernel_size=11, strides=4,
                            activation='relu'),
    tf.keras.layers.Conv2D(filters=256, kernel_size=5,
                            activation='relu'),
    tf.keras.layers.MaxPool2D(pool_size=2, strides=2),
    tf.keras.layers.Conv2D(filters=384, kernel_size=3,
                            activation='relu'),
    tf.keras.layers.MaxPool2D(pool_size=2, strides=2),
    tf.keras.layers.Conv2D(filters=384, kernel_size=3,
                            activation='relu'),
    tf.keras.layers.Conv2D(filters=256, kernel_size=3,
                            activation='relu'),
    tf.keras.layers.MaxPool2D(pool_size=2, strides=2),
    tf.keras.layers.Flatten(),
    tf.keras.layers.Dense(4096, activation='relu'),
    tf.keras.layers.Dense(4096, activation='relu'),
    tf.keras.layers.Dense(len(CLASSES), activation='softmax')
])
```

This model converges on the 104 flowers dataset to an accuracy of 39%, which, while not useful for practical flower recognition, is surprisingly good for such a simple architecture.

AlexNet at a Glance

Architecture
    Alternates convolutional and max-pooling layers

Publication
    Alex Krizhevsky et al.,"ImageNet Classification with Deep Convolutional Neural Networks," NIPS 2012, *https://oreil.ly/X3xRb*.

Code sample
    03c_fromzero_ALEXNET_flowers104.ipynb

Table 3-2. AlexNet at a glance

Model	Parameters (excl. classification head[a])	ImageNet accuracy	104 flowers F1 score[b] (trained from scratch)
AlexNet	3.7M	60%	39% precision: 44%, recall: 38%

[a] Excluding classification head from parameter counts for easier comparisons between architectures. Without the classification head, the number of parameters in the network is resolution-independent. Also, in fine-tuning examples, a different classification head might be used.

[b] For accuracy, precision, recall, and F1 score values, higher is better.

In the remainder of this chapter, we provide intuitive explanations of different network architectures as well as the concepts and building blocks they introduced. Although we showed you the implementation of AlexNet in Keras, you would not typically implement the architectures that we discussed by yourself. Instead, these models are often available directly in Keras as pretrained models ready for transfer learning or fine-tuning. For example, this is how you can instantiate a pretrained ResNet50 model (for more information, see "Pretrained Models in Keras" on page 59):

```
tf.keras.applications.ResNet50(weights='imagenet')
```

If a model is not yet available in `keras.applications`, it can usually be found in TensorFlow Hub. For example, this is how you instantiate the same ResNet50 model from TensorFlow Hub:

```
hub.KerasLayer(
    "https://tfhub.dev/tensorflow/resnet_50/classification/1")
```

So, feel free to skim the rest of this chapter to get an idea of the basic concepts, and then read the final section on how to choose a model architecture for your problem. You don't need to understand all the nuances of the network architectures in this chapter to make sense of the remainder of this book, because it is rare that you will have to implement any of these architectures from scratch or design your own network architecture. Mostly, you will pick one of the architectures we suggest in the final section of this chapter. It is, however, interesting to understand how these architectures are constructed. Understanding the architectures will also help you pick the correct parameters when you instantiate them.

The Quest for Depth

After AlexNet, researchers started increasing the depths of their convolutional networks. They found that adding more layers resulted in better classification accuracy. Several explanations have been offered for this:

The expressivity argument

A single layer is a linear function. It cannot approximate complex nonlinear functions, whatever its number of parameters. Each layer is, however, activated with a nonlinear activation function such as sigmoid or ReLU. Stacking multiple layers results in multiple successive nonlinearities and a better chance of being able to approximate the desired highly complex functionality, such as differentiating between images of cats and dogs.

The generalization argument

Adding parameters to a single layer increases the "memory" of the neural network and allows it to learn more complex things. However, it will tend to learn them by memorizing input examples. This does not generalize well. On the other hand, stacking many layers forces the network to break down its input semantically into a hierarchical structure of features. For example, initial layers will recognize fur and whiskers, and later layers will assemble them to recognize a cat head, then an entire cat. The resulting classifier generalizes better.

The perceptive field argument

If a cat's head covers a significant portion of an image—say, a 128x128-pixel region—a single-layer convolutional network would need 128x128 filters to be able to capture it, which would be prohibitively expensive in term of learnable weights. Stacked layers, on the other hand, can use small 3x3 or 5x5 filters and still be able to "see" any 128x128-pixel region if they are sufficiently deep in the convolutional stack.

In order to design deeper convolutional networks without growing the parameter count uncontrollably, researchers also started designing cheaper convolutional layers. Let's see how.

Filter Factorization

Which one is better: a 5x5 convolutional filter or two 3x3 filters applied in sequence? Both have a receptive area of 5x5 (see Figure 3-18). Although they do not perform the exact same mathematical operation, their effect is likely to be similar. The difference is that two 3x3 filters applied in sequence have a total of 2 * 3 * 3 = 18 learnable parameters, whereas a single 5x5 filter has 5 * 5 = 25 learnable weights. So, two 3x3 filters are cheaper.

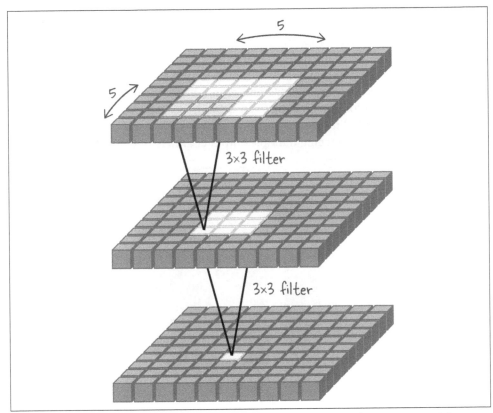

Figure 3-18. Two 3x3 filters applied in sequence. Each output value is computed from a 5x5 receptive field, which is similar to how a 5x5 filter works.

Another advantage is that a pair of 3x3 convolutional layers will involve two applications of the activation function, since each convolutional layer is followed by an activation. A single 5x5 layer has a single activation. The activation function is the only nonlinear part of a neural network and it is probable that the composition of nonlinearities in sequence will be able to express more complex nonlinear representations of the inputs.

In practice, it has been found that two 3x3 layers work better than one 5x5 layer while using fewer learnable weights. That's why you will see 3x3 convolutional layers used extensively in modern convolutional architectures. This is sometimes referred to as *filter factorization*, although it is not exactly a factorization in the mathematical sense.

The other filter size that is popular today is 1x1 convolutions. Let's see why.

1x1 Convolutions

Sliding a single-pixel filter across an image sounds silly. It's multiplying the image by a constant. However, on multichannel inputs, with a different weight for each channel, it actually makes sense. For example, multiplying the three color channels of an RGB image by three learnable weights and then adding them up produces a linear combination of the color channels that can actually be useful. A 1x1 convolutional layer performs multiple linear combinations of this kind, each time with an independent set of weights, producing multiple output channels (Figure 3-19).

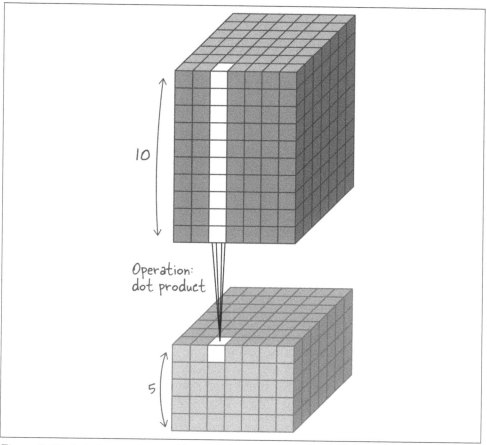

Figure 3-19. A 1x1 convolutional layer. Each filter has 10 parameters because it acts on a 10-channel input. 5 such filters are applied, each with its own learnable parameters (not shown in the figure), resulting in 5 channels of output data.

A 1x1 convolutional layer is a useful tool for adjusting the number of channels of the data. The second advantage is that 1x1 convolutional layers are cheap, in terms of number of learnable parameters, compared to 2x2, 3x3, or larger layers. The tensor of

---

weights representing the 1x1 convolutional layer in the previous illustration is shown in Figure 3-20.

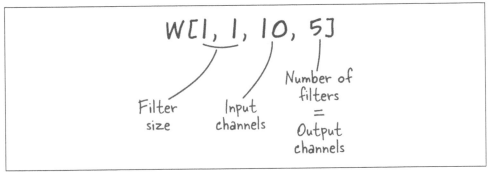

Figure 3-20. The weights matrix of the 1x1 convolutional layer from Figure 3-19.

The number of learnable weights is 1 * 1 * 10 * 5 = 50. A 3x3 layer with the same number of input and output channels would require 3 * 3 * 10 * 5 = 450 weights, an order of magnitude more!

Next, let's look at an architecture that employs these tricks.

VGG19

VGG19, introduced in a 2014 paper (*https://arxiv.org/abs/1409.1556*) by Karen Simonyan and Andrew Zisserman, was one of the first architectures to use 3x3 convolutions exclusively. Figure 3-21 shows what it looks like with 19 layers.

All the neural network layers in this figure use biases and are ReLU-activated, apart from the last layer which uses softmax activation.

VGG19 improves on AlexNet by being much deeper. It has 16 convolutional layers instead of 5. It also uses 3x3 convolutions exclusively without losing accuracy. However, it uses the exact same classification head as AlexNet, with three large fully connected layers accounting for over 120 million weights, while it has only 20 million weights in the convolutional layers. There are cheaper alternatives.

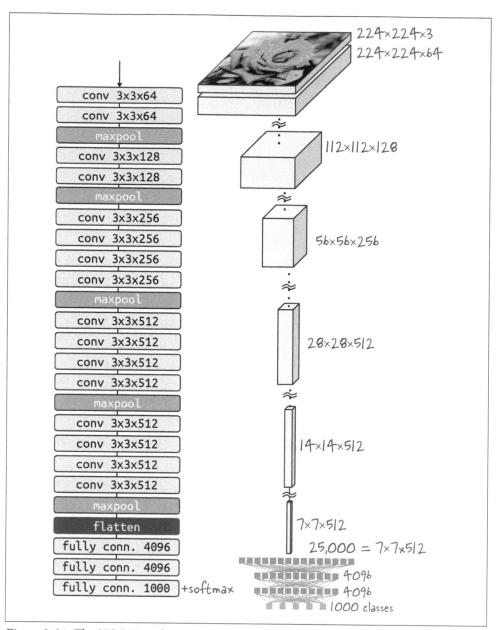

Figure 3-21. The VGG19 architecture with 19 learnable layers (left). The data shapes are shown on the right (not all represented). Notice that all convolutional layers use 3x3 filters.

VGG19 at a Glance

Architecture

Alternates convolutional and max-pooling layers using 3x3 convolutions only

Publication

Karen Simonyan and Andrew Zisserman, "Very Deep Convolutional Networks for Large-Scale Image Recognition," 2014, *https://arxiv.org/abs/1409.1556v6*.

Code sample

03d_finetune_VGG19_flowers104.ipynb

Table 3-3. VGG19 at a glance

Model	Parameters (excl. classif. head[a])	ImageNet accuracy	104 flowers F1 score[b] (fine-tuning)	104 flowers F1 score (trained from scratch)
VGG19	20M	71%	88% precision: 89%, recall: 88%	N/A[c]
Previous best for comparison:				
AlexNet	3.7M	60%		39% precision: 44%, recall: 38%

[a] Excluding classification head from parameter counts for easier comparisons between architectures. Without the classification head, the number of parameters in the network is resolution-independent. Also, in fine-tuning examples, a different classification head might be used.

[b] For accuracy, precision, recall, and F1 score values, higher is better.

[c] We did not bother training VGG16 from scratch on the 104 flowers dataset because the result would be much worse than fine-tuning.

Global Average Pooling

Let's look again at the implementation of the classification head. In both the AlexNet and VGG19 architectures, the feature map output by the last convolutional layer is turned into a vector (flattened) and then fed into one or more fully connected layers (see Figure 3-22). The goal is to end on a softmax-activated fully connected layer with exactly as many neurons as classes in the classification problem at hand—for example, one thousand classes for the ImageNet dataset or five classes for the 5-flowers dataset used in the previous chapter. This fully connected layer has input * outputs weights, which tends to be a lot.

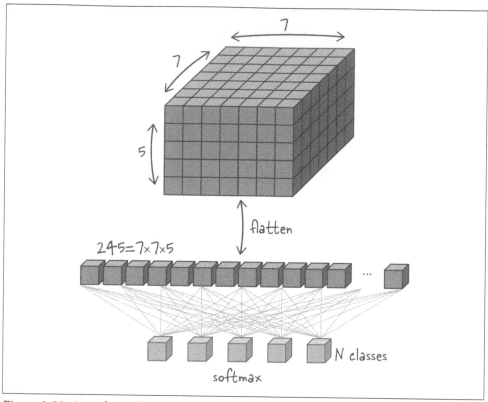

Figure 3-22. A traditional classification head at the end of a convolutional network. The data coming out of convolutional layers is flattened and fed into a fully connected layer. Softmax activation is used to obtain class probabilities.

If the only goal is to obtain N values to feed an N-way softmax function, there is an easy way to achieve that: adjust the convolutional stack so that it ends on a final feature map with exactly N channels and simply average the values in each channel, as shown in Figure 3-23. This is known as *global average pooling*. Global average pooling involves no learnable weights, so from this perspective it's cheap.

Global average pooling can be followed by a softmax activation directly (as in SqueezeNet, shown in Figure 3-26), although in most architectures described in this book it will be followed by a single softmax-activated fully connected layer (for example in a ResNet, as shown in Figure 3-29).

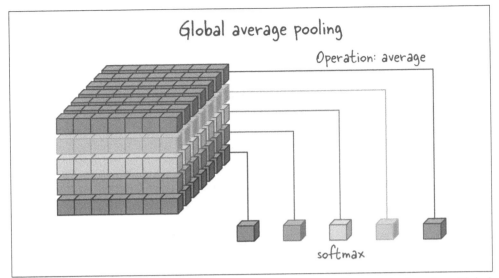

Figure 3-23. Global average pooling. Each channel is averaged into a single value. Global average pooling followed by a softmax function implements a classification head with zero learnable parameters.

 Averaging removes a lot of the positional information present in the channels. That might or might not be a good thing depending on the application. Convolutional filters detect the things they have been trained to detect in a specific location. If the network is classifying, for example, cats versus dogs, the location data (e.g., "cat's whiskers" detected at position x, y in the channel) is probably not useful in the classification head. The only thing of interest is the "dog detected anywhere" signal versus the "cat detected anywhere" signal. For other applications, though, a global average-pooling layer might not be the best choice. For example, in object detection or object counting use cases, the location of detected objects is important and global average pooling should not be used.

Modular Architectures

A straight succession of convolutional and pooling layers is enough to build a basic convolutional neural network. However, to further increase prediction accuracy, researchers designed more complex building blocks, or *modules*, often given arcane names such as "Inception modules," "residual blocks," or "inverted residual bottlenecks," and then assembled them into complete convolutional architectures. Having higher-level building blocks also made it easier to create automated algorithms to search for better architectures, as we will see in the section on neural architecture search. In this section we'll explore several of these modular architectures and the research behind each of them.

Inception

The Inception architecture was named after Christopher Nolan's 2010 movie *Inception*, starring Leonardo DiCaprio. One line from the movie dialog—"We need to go deeper" (*https://oreil.ly/uSwgP*)—became an internet meme. Building deeper and deeper neural networks was one of the main motivations of researchers at that time.

The Inception V3 (*https://arxiv.org/abs/1512.00567v3*) architecture uses 3x3 and 1x1 convolutional filters exclusively, as is now customary in most convolutional architectures. It tries to address another problem, though, with a very original approach. When lining up the convolutional and pooling layers in a neural network, the designer has multiple choices, and the best one is not obvious. Instead of relying on guesswork and experimentation, why not build multiple options into the network itself and let it learn which one is the best? This is the motivation behind Inception's "modules" (see Figure 3-24).

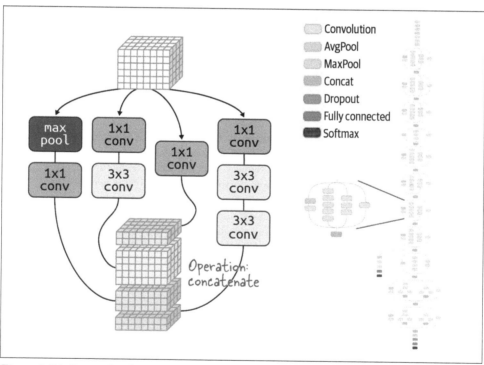

Figure 3-24. Example of an Inception module. The entire Inception V3 architecture (on the right) is made up of many such modules.

Instead of deciding beforehand which sequence of layers is the most appropriate, an Inception module provides several alternatives that the network can choose from, based on data and training. As shown in Figure 3-24, the outputs of the different paths are concatenated into the final feature map.

We will not detail the full InceptionV3 architecture in this book because it is rather complex and has since been superseded by newer and simpler alternatives. A simplified variant, also based on the "module" idea, is presented next.

InceptionV3 at a Glance

Architecture
  Sequence of multipath convolutional modules.

Publication
  Christian Szegedy et al., "Rethinking the Inception Architecture for Computer Vision," 2015, *https://arxiv.org/abs/1512.00567v3*.

Code sample
  03e_finetune_INCEPTIONV3_flowers104.ipynb

Table 3-4. InceptionV3 at a glance

Model	Parameters (excl. classification head[a])	ImageNet accuracy	104 flowers F1 score[b] (fine-tuning)
InceptionV3	22M	78%	95% precision: 95%, recall: 94%
Previous best for comparison:			
VGG19	20M	71%	88% precision: 89%, recall: 88%

[a] Excluding classification head from parameter counts for easier comparisons between architectures. Without the classification head, the number of parameters in the network is resolution-independent. Also, in fine-tuning examples, a different classification head might be used.
[b] For accuracy, precision, recall, and F1 score values, higher is better.

SqueezeNet

The idea of modules was simplified by the SqueezeNet (*https://arxiv.org/abs/1602.07360*) architecture, which kept the basic principle of offering multiple paths for the network to choose from but streamlined the modules themselves into their simplest expression (Figure 3-25). The SqueezeNet paper calls them "fire modules."

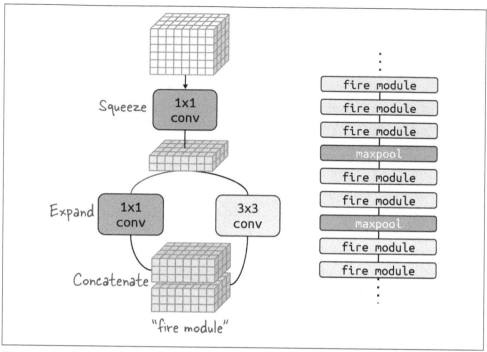

Figure 3-25. A simplified and standardized convolutional module from the SqueezeNet architecture. The architecture, shown on the right, alternates these "fire modules" with max-pooling layers.

The modules used in the SqueezeNet architecture alternate a contraction stage, where the number of channels is reduced by a 1x1 convolution, with an expansion stage where the number of channels is increased again.

To save on weight count, SqueezeNet uses global average pooling for the last layer. Also, two out of the three convolutional layers in each module are 1x1 convolutions, which saves on learnable weights (see Figure 3-26).

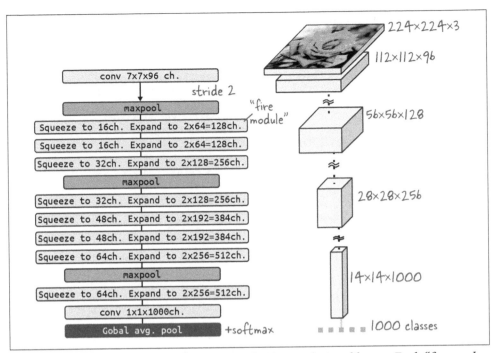

Figure 3-26. The SqueezeNet architecture with 18 convolutional layers. Each "fire module" contains a "squeeze" layer followed by two parallel "expand" layers. The network pictured here contains 1.2M learnable parameters.

In Figure 3-26, "maxpool" is a standard 2x2 max-pooling operation with a stride of 2. Also, every convolutional layer in the architecture is ReLU-activated and uses batch normalization. The thousand-class classification head is implemented by first stretching the number of channels to one thousand with a 1x1 convolution, then averaging the thousand channels (global average pooling) and finally applying softmax activation.

The SqueezeNet architecture aims to be simple and economical (in terms of learnable weights) but still incorporate most of the latest best practices in building convolutional neural networks. Its simplicity makes it a good choice when you want to implement your own convolutional backbone, either for education purposes or because you need to tweak it for your needs. The one architectural element that might not be considered best practice today is the large 7x7 initial convolutional layer, inspired directly by AlexNet.

In order to implement the SqueezeNet model in Keras, we have to use a Keras Functional API model. We can no longer use a Sequential model, because SqueezeNet is not a straight sequence of layers. We first create a helper function that instantiates a fire module (the full code is available in *03f_fromzero_SQUEEZENET24_flowers104.ipynb* on GitHub):

```
def fire(x, squeeze, expand):
    y  = tf.keras.layers.Conv2D(filters=squeeze, kernel_size=1,
                                activation='relu', padding='same')(x)
    y = tf.keras.layers.BatchNormalization()(y)
    y1 = tf.keras.layers.Conv2D(filters=expand//2, kernel_size=1,
                                activation='relu', padding='same')(y)
    y1 = tf.keras.layers.BatchNormalization()(y1)
    y3 = tf.keras.layers.Conv2D(filters=expand//2, kernel_size=3,
                                activation='relu', padding='same')(y)
    y3 = tf.keras.layers.BatchNormalization()(y3)
    return tf.keras.layers.concatenate([y1, y3])
```

As you can see in the first line of the function, using the Keras Functional API, `tf.keras.layers.Conv2D()` instantiates a convolutional layer which is then called with the input x. We can slightly transform the `fire()` function so that it uses the same semantics:

```
def fire_module(squeeze, expand):
    return lambda x: fire(x, squeeze, expand)
```

And here is the implementation of a custom 24-layer SqueezeNet. It performed reasonably well on the 104 flowers dataset, with an F1 score of 76%, which isn't bad considering it was trained from scratch:

```
x = tf.keras.layers.Input(shape=[IMG_HEIGHT, IMG_WIDTH, 3])
y = tf.keras.layers.Conv2D(kernel_size=3, filters=32,
                           padding='same', activation='relu')(x)
y = tf.keras.layers.BatchNormalization()(y)
y = fire_module(16, 32)(y)
y = tf.keras.layers.MaxPooling2D(pool_size=2)(y)
y = fire_module(48, 96)(y)
y = tf.keras.layers.MaxPooling2D(pool_size=2)(y)
y = fire_module(64, 128)(y)
y = fire_module(80, 160)(y)
y = fire_module(96, 192)(y)
y = tf.keras.layers.MaxPooling2D(pool_size=2)(y)
y = fire_module(112, 224)(y)
y = fire_module(128, 256)(y)
y = fire_module(160, 320)(y)
y = tf.keras.layers.MaxPooling2D(pool_size=2)(y)
y = fire_module(192, 384)(y)
y = fire_module(224, 448)(y)
y = tf.keras.layers.MaxPooling2D(pool_size=2)(y)
y = fire_module(256, 512)(y)
y = tf.keras.layers.GlobalAveragePooling2D()(y)
y = tf.keras.layers.Dense(len(CLASSES), activation='softmax')(y)

model = tf.keras.Model(x, y)
```

In the last line, we create the model by passing in the initial input layer and the final output. The model can be used just like a Sequential model, so the rest of the code remains the same.

SqueezeNet at a Glance

Architecture
    Simplified convolutional modules built from parallel 3x3 and 1x1 convolutions

Publication
    Forrest Iandola et al., "SqueezeNet: AlexNet-Level Accuracy with 50x Fewer Parameters," 2016, *https://arxiv.org/abs/1602.07360*.

Code sample
    03f_fromzero_SQUEEZENET24_flowers104.ipynb

Table 3-5. SqueezeNet at a glance

Model	Parameters (excl. classification head[a])	ImageNet accuracy	104 flowers F1 score[b] (trained from scratch)
SqueezeNet, 24 layers	2.7M		76% precision: 77%, recall: 75%
SqueezeNet, 18 layers	1.2M	56%	
Previous best for comparison:			
AlexNet	3.7M	60%	39% prec.: 44%, recall: 38%

[a] Excluding classification head from parameter counts for easier comparisons between architectures. Without the classification head, the number of parameters in the network is resolution-independent. Also, in fine-tuning examples, a different classification head might be used.
[b] For accuracy, precision, recall, and F1 score values, higher is better.

ResNet and Skip Connections

The ResNet architecture, introduced in a 2015 paper (*https://arxiv.org/abs/1512.03385*) by Kaiming He et al., continued the trend of increasing the depth of neural networks but addressed a common challenge with very deep neural networks—they tend to converge badly because of vanishing or exploding gradient problems. During training, a neural network sees what error (or loss) it is making and tries to minimize this error by adjusting its internal weights. It is guided in this by the first derivative (or gradient) of the error. Unfortunately, with many layers, the gradients tend to be spread too thin across all layers and the network converges slowly or not at all.

ResNet tried to remedy this by adding *skip connections* alongside its convolutional layers (Figure 3-27). Skip connections convey the signal as is, then recombine it with the data that has been transformed by one or more convolutional layers. The combining operation is a simple element-by-element addition.

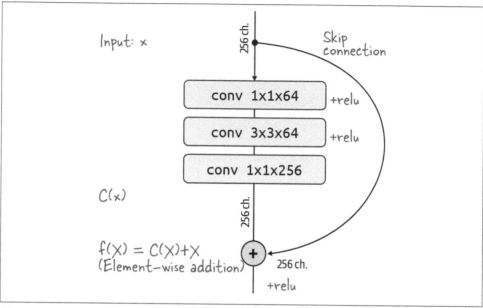

Figure 3-27. A residual block in ResNet.

As can be seen in Figure 3-27, the output of the block $f(x)$ is the sum of the output of the convolutional path $C(x)$ and the skip connection (x). The convolutional path is trained to compute $C(x) = f(x) - x$, the difference between the desired output and the input. The authors of the ResNet paper argue that this "residue" is easier for the network to learn.

An obvious limitation is that the element-wise addition can only work if the dimensions of the data remain unchanged. The sequence of layers that is straddled by a skip connection (called a *residual block*) must preserve the height, the width, and the number of channels of the data.

When size adjustments are needed, a different kind of residual block is used (Figure 3-28). Different numbers of channels can be matched in the skip connection by using a 1x1 convolution instead of an identity. Height and width adjustments are obtained by using a stride of 2 both in the convolutional path and in the skip connection (yes, implementing the skip connection with a 1x1 convolution of stride 2 ignores half of the values in the input, but this does not seem to matter in practice).

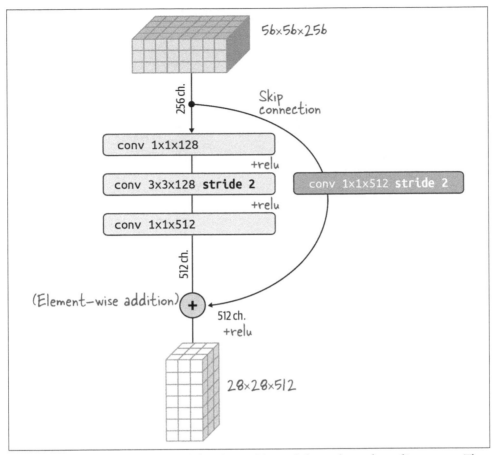

Figure 3-28. A residual block with height, width, and channel number adjustments. The number of channels is changed in the skip connection by using a 1x1 convolution instead of an identity function. Data height and width are downsampled by using one convolutional layer with a stride of 2 in both the convolutional path and the skip connection.

The ResNet architecture can be instantiated with various depths by stacking more and more residual blocks. Popular sizes are ResNet50 and ResNet101 (Figure 3-29).

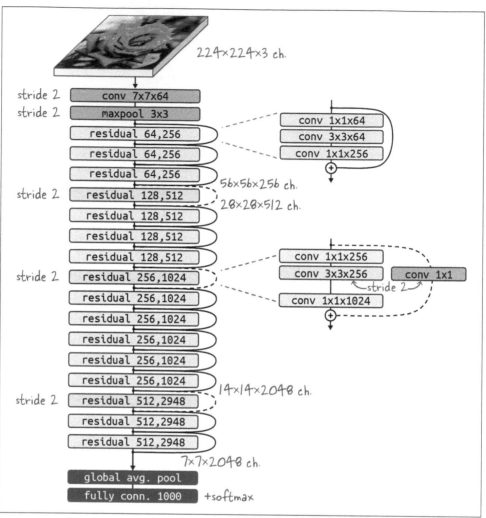

Figure 3-29. The ResNet50 architecture. Residual blocks with a stride of 2 have a skip connection implemented using a 1x1 convolution (dotted line). The ResNet 101 architecture is similar, with the "residual 256, 1,024" block repeated 23 times instead of 6.

In Figure 3-29, all the convolutional layers are ReLU-activated and use batch normalization. A network with this architecture can grow very deep—as the names indicate, 50, 100, or more layers are common for ResNets—but it is still able to figure out which layers need to have their weights adjusted for any given output error.

Skip connections seem to help gradients flow through the network during the optimization (backpropagation) phase. Several explanations have been suggested for this. Here are the three most popular ones.

The ResNet paper's authors theorize that the addition operation (see Figure 3-27) plays an important role. In a regular neural network, internal weights are adjusted to produce a desired output, such as a classification into one thousand classes. With skip connections, however, the goal of the neural network layers is to output the delta (or "residue") between the input and the desired final output. This, the authors argue, is an "easier" task for the network, but they don't elaborate on what makes it easier.

A second interesting explanation is that residual connections actually make the network shallower. During the gradient backpropagation phase, gradients flow both through convolutional layers, where they might decrease in magnitude, and through the skip connections, which leave them unchanged. In the paper "Residual Networks Behave Like Ensembles of Relatively Shallow Networks," (*https://arxiv.org/abs/1605.06431*) Veit et al. measured the intensity of gradients in a ResNet architecture. The result (Figure 3-30) shows how, in a 50-layer ResNet neural network, the signal can flow through various combinations of convolutional layers and skip connections.

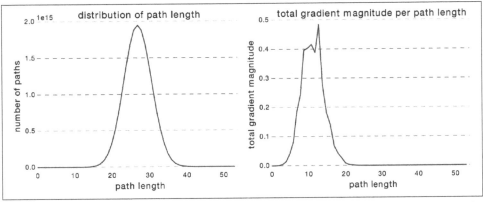

Figure 3-30. Theoretical distribution of path length in a ResNet50 model versus the path actually taken by meaningful gradients during backpropagation. Image from Veit et al., 2016 (https://arxiv.org/abs/1605.06431).

The most likely path lengths, measured in the number of convolutional layers traversed, are midway between 0 and 50 (left graph). However, Veit et al. measured that paths providing actually useful nonzero gradients in a trained ResNet were even shorter than that, traversing around 12 layers.

According to this theory, a deep 50- or 100-layer ResNet acts as an ensemble—i.e., a collection of shallower networks that optimally solve different parts of a classification problem. Taken together, they pool their classification strengths, but they still converge efficiently because they are not actually very deep. The benefit of the ResNet architecture compared to an actual ensemble of models is that it trains as a single model and learns to select the best path for each input by itself.

A third explanation looks at the topological landscape of the loss function optimized during training. In "Visualizing the Loss Landscape of Neural Nets" (*https://arxiv.org/abs/1712.09913*), Li et al. managed to picture the loss landscape in 3D rather than its original million or so dimensions and showed that good minima were much more accessible when skip connections were used (Figure 3-31).

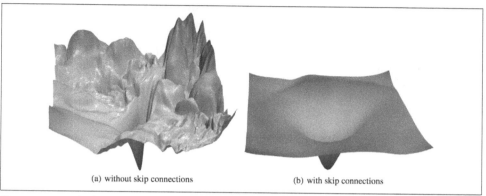

Figure 3-31. The loss landscape of a 56-layer ResNet as visualized through the "filter normalization scheme" of Li et al. Adding skip connections makes the global minimum much easier to reach. Image from Li et al., 2017 (https://arxiv.org/abs/1712.09913).

In practice, the ResNet architecture works very well and has become one of the most popular convolutional architectures in the field, as well as the benchmark against which all other advances are measured.

ResNet at a Glance

Architecture
    Convolutional modules with skip connections

Publication
    Kaiming He et al., "Deep Residual Learning for Image Recognition," 2015, *https://arxiv.org/abs/1512.03385*.

Code samples
    03g_finetune_RESNET50_flowers104.ipynb and *03g_fromzero_RESNET50_flowers104.ipynb*

Table 3-6. ResNet at a glance

Model	Parameters (excl. classif. head[a])	ImageNet accuracy	104 flowers F1 score[b] (fine-tuning)	104 flowers F1 score (trained from scratch)
ResNet50	23M	75%	94% prec.: 95%, recall: 94%	73% prec.: 76%, recall: 72%
Previous best for comparison:				
InceptionV3	22M	78%	95% prec.: 95%, recall: 94%	
SqueezeNet, 24 layers	2.7M			76% prec.: 77%, recall: 75%

[a] Excluding classification head from parameter counts for easier comparisons between architectures. Without the classification head, the number of parameters in the network is resolution-independent. Also, in fine-tuning examples, a different classification head might be used.

[b] For accuracy, precision, recall, and F1 score values, higher is better.

The classification performance is a bit below that achieved by InceptionV3, but the main goal of ResNet was to allow very deep architectures to still train and converge. Beyond ResNet50, ResNet101 and ResNet152 variants are also available with 101 and 152 layers.

DenseNet

The DenseNet architecture revisits the concept of skip connections with a radical new idea. In their paper (*https://arxiv.org/abs/1608.06993*) on DenseNet, Gao Huang et al. suggest feeding a convolutional layer with all the outputs of the previous layers, by creating as many skip connections as necessary. This time, data is combined by concatenation along the depth axis (channels) instead of being added, as in ResNet. Apparently, the intuition that led to the ResNet architecture—that data from skip connections should be added in because "residual" signals were easier to learn—was not fundamental. Concatenation works too.

Dense blocks are the basic building blocks of DenseNet. In a dense block, convolutions are grouped in pairs, with each pair of convolutions receiving as its input the output of all previous convolution pairs. In the dense block depicted in Figure 3-32, data is combined by concatenating it channel-wise. All convolutions are ReLU-activated and use batch normalization. Channel-wise concatenation only works if the height and width dimensions of the data are the same, so convolutions in a dense block are all of stride 1 and do not change these dimensions. Pooling layers will have to be inserted between dense blocks.

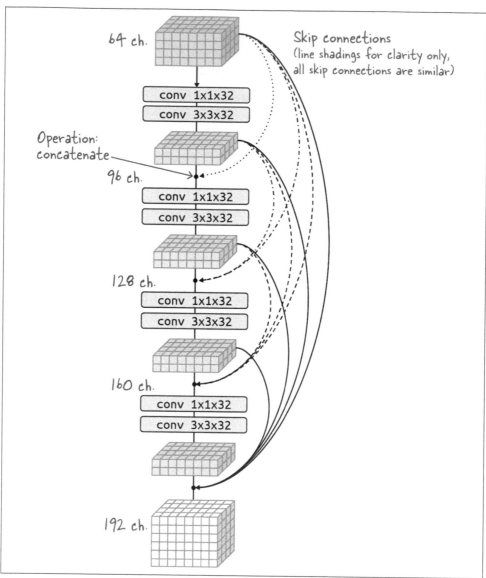

Figure 3-32. A "dense block," the basic building block of the DenseNet architecture. Convolutions are grouped in pairs. Each pair of convolutions receives as input the output of all previous convolution pairs. Notice that the number of channels grows linearly with the number of layers.

Intuitively, one would think that concatenating all previously seen outputs would lead to an explosive growth of the number of channels and parameters, but that is not in fact the case. DenseNet is surprisingly economical in terms of learnable parameters. The reason is that every concatenated block, which might have a relatively large number of channels, is always fed first through a 1x1 convolution that reduces it to a small number of channels, K. 1x1 convolutions are cheap in their number of parameters. A 3x3 convolution with the same number of channels (K) follows. The K resulting channels are then concatenated to the collection of all previously generated outputs. Each step, which uses a pair of 1x1 and 3x3 convolutions, adds exactly K channels to the data. Therefore, the number of channels grows only linearly with the number of convolutional steps in the dense block. The growth rate K is a constant throughout the network, and DenseNet has been shown to perform well with fairly low values of K (between $K=12$ and $K=40$ in the original paper).

Dense blocks and pooling layers are interleaved to create a full DenseNet network. Figure 3-33 shows a DenseNet121 with 121 layers, but the architecture is configurable and can easily scale beyond 200 layers.

The use of shallow convolutional layers ($K=32$, for example) is a characteristic feature of DenseNet. In previous architectures, convolutions with over one thousand filters were not rare. DenseNet can afford to use shallow convolutions because each convolutional layer sees all previously computed features. In other architectures, the data is transformed at each layer and the network must do active work to preserve a channel of data as-is, if that is the right thing to do. It must use some of its filter parameters to create an identity function, which is wasteful. DenseNet, the authors argue, is built to allow feature reuse and therefore requires far fewer filters per convolutional layer.

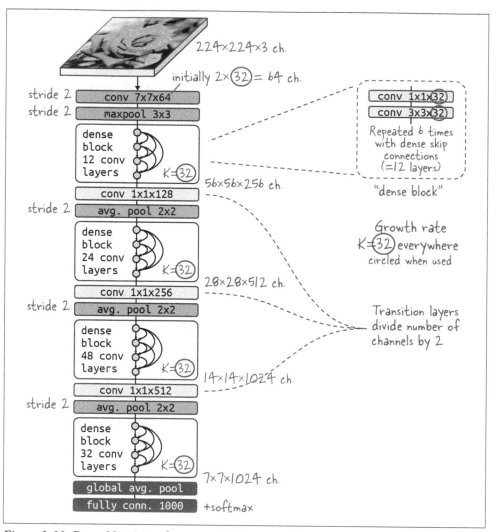

Figure 3-33. DenseNet121 architecture. With a growth rate K=32, all convolutional layers produce 32 channels of output, apart from the 1x1 convolutions used as transitions between dense blocks, which are designed to halve the number of channels. See previous figure for details about dense blocks. All convolutions are ReLU-activated and use batch normalization.

DenseNet at a Glance

Architecture
    Convolutional modules with a dense network of skip connections

Publication
    Gao Huang et al., "Densely Connected Convolutional Networks," 2016, *https://arxiv.org/abs/1608.06993.*

Code samples
    03h_finetune_DENSENET201_flowers104.ipynb   and   *03h_fromzero_DENSE-NET121_flowers104.ipynb*

Table 3-7. DenseNet at a glance

Model	Parameters (excl. classif. head[a])	ImageNet accuracy	104 flowers F1 score[b] (fine-tuning)	104 flowers F1 score (trained from scratch)
DenseNet201	18M	77%	95% prec.: 96%, recall: 95%	
DenseNet121	7M	75%		76% prec.: 80%, recall: 74%
Previous best for comparison:				
InceptionV3	22M	78%	95% prec.: 95%, recall: 94%	
SqueezeNet, 24 layers	2.7M			76% prec.: 77%, recall: 75%

[a] Excluding classification head from parameter counts for easier comparisons between architectures. Without the classification head, the number of parameters in the network is resolution-independent. Also, in fine-tuning examples, a different classification head might be used.
[b] For accuracy, precision, recall, and F1 score values, higher is better.

Depth-Separable Convolutions

Traditional convolutions filter all the channels of the input at once. They then use many filters to give the network the opportunity to do many different things with the same input channels. Let's take the example of a 3x3 convolutional layer applied to 8 input channels with 16 output channels. It has 16 convolutional filters of shape 3x3x8 (Figure 3-34).

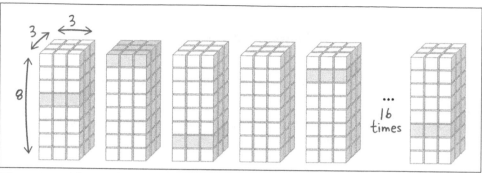

Figure 3-34. The weights of a 3x3 convolutional layer with 8 inputs and 16 outputs (16 filters). Many of the individual 3x3 filters are likely to be similar after training (shaded); for example, a horizontal line detector filter.

In each 3x3x8 filter, there are really two operations happening simultaneously: a 3x3 filter is applied to every input channel across the height and width of the image (spatial dimensions), and filtered outputs are recombined in various ways across channels. In short, the two operations are spatial filtering, combined with a linear recombination of the filtered outputs. If these two operations turned out to be independent (or separable), without affecting the performance of the network, they could be performed with fewer learnable weights. Let's see why.

If we look at the 16 filters of a trained layer, it is probable that the network had to reinvent the same 3x3 spatial filters in many of them, just because it wanted to combine them in different ways. In fact, this can be visualized experimentally (Figure 3-35).

Figure 3-35. Visualization of some of the 12x12 filters from the first convolutional layer of a trained neural network. Very similar filters have been reinvented multiple times. Image from Sifre, 2014 (https://oreil.ly/7Y4LL).

It looks like traditional convolutional layers use parameters inefficiently. That is why Laurent Sifre suggested, in section 6.2 of his 2014 thesis "Rigid-Motion Scattering for Image Classification," (*https://oreil.ly/7Y4LL*) to use a different kind of convolution called a *depth-separable convolution*, or just a *separable convolution*. The main idea is to filter the input, channel by channel, using a set of independent filters, and then combine the outputs separately using 1x1 convolutions, as depicted in Figure 3-36. The hypothesis is that there is little "shape" information to be extracted across channels, and therefore a weighted sum is all that is needed to combine them (a 1x1 convolution is a weighted sum of channels). On the other hand, there is a lot of "shape" information in the spatial dimensions of the image, and 3x3 filters or bigger are needed to catch it.

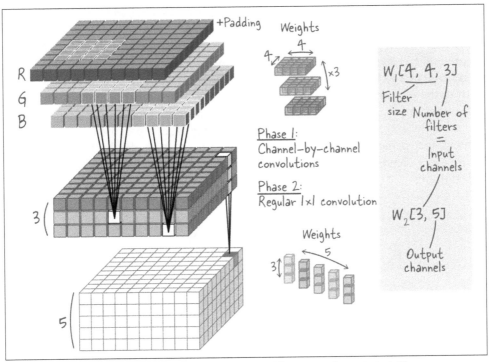

Figure 3-36. A 4x4 depth-separable convolutional layer. In phase 1, 4x4 filters are applied independently to each channel, producing an equal number of output channels. In phase 2, the output channels are then recombined using a 1x1 convolution (multiple weighted sums of the channels).

In Figure 3-36, the phase 1 filtering operation can be repeated with new filter weights to produce double or triple the number of channels. This is called a *depth multiplier*, but its usual value is 1, which is why this parameter was not represented in the calculation of the number of weights on the right.

The number of weights used by the example convolutional layer in Figure 3-36 can easily be computed:

- Using a separable 3x3x8x16 convolutional layer: 3 * 3 * 8 + 8 * 16 = 200 weights
- Using a traditional convolutional layer: 3 * 3 * 8 * 16 = 1,152 weights (for comparison)

Since separable convolutional layers do not need to reinvent each spatial filter multiple times, they are significantly cheaper in terms of learnable weights. The question is whether they are as efficient.

François Chollet argues in his paper "Xception: Deep Learning with Depthwise Separable Convolutions" (*https://arxiv.org/abs/1610.02357*) that separable convolutions are in fact a concept very similar to the Inception modules seen in a previous section. Figure 3-37(A) shows a simplified Inception module with three convolutional paths, each made of a 1x1 convolution followed by a 3x3 convolution. This is exactly equivalent to the representation in Figure 3-37(B), where a single 1x1 convolution outputs three times more channels than previously. Each of those blocks of channels is then picked up by a 3x3 convolution. From there, it only takes a parameter adjustment—namely, increasing the number of 3x3 convolutions—to arrive at Figure 3-37(C), where every channel coming out of the 1x1 convolutions is picked up by its own 3x3 convolution.

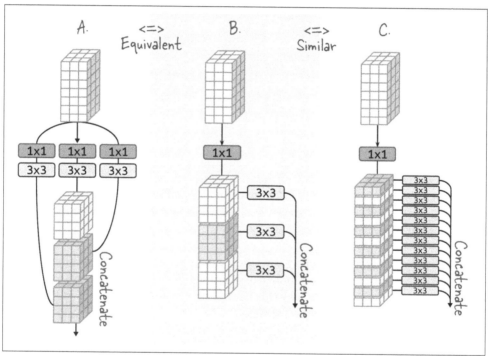

Figure 3-37. Architectural similarity between Inception modules and depth-separable convolutions: (A) a simplified Inception module with three parallel convolutional paths; (B) an exactly equivalent setup where there is a single 1x1 convolution but it outputs three times more channels; (C) a very similar setup with more 3x3 convolutions. This is exactly a separable convolution with the order of the 1x1 and 3x3 operations swapped.

Figure 3-37(C) actually represents a depth-separable convolution with the 1x1 (depthwise) and 3x3 (spatial) operations swapped around. In a convolutional architecture where these layers are stacked, this change in ordering does not matter much. In conclusion, a simplified Inception module is very similar in its functionality to a depth-separable convolution. This new building block is going to make convolutional architectures both simpler and more economical in terms of learnable weights.

Separable convolutional layers are available in Keras:

```
tf.keras.layers.SeparableConv2D(filters,
                                kernel_size,
                                strides=(1, 1),
                                padding='valid',
                                depth_multiplier=1)
```

The new parameter, compared to a traditional convolutional layer, is the depth_multiplier parameter. The following is a simplified description of the parameters (see the Keras documentation (*https://oreil.ly/0ymie*) for full details):

filters
> The number of output channels to produce in the final 1x1 convolution.

kernel_size
> The size of each spatial filter. This can be a single number, like 3 for a 3x3 filter, or a pair like (4, 2) for a rectangular 4x2 filter.

strides
> The step of the convolution for the spatial filtering.

padding
> 'valid' for no padding, or 'same' for zero-padding.

depth_multiplier
> The number of times the spatial filtering operation is repeated. Defaults to 1.

Xception

The Xception (*https://arxiv.org/abs/1610.02357*) architecture (Figure 3-38) combines separable convolutions with ResNet-style skip connections. Since separable convolutions are somewhat equivalent to Inception-style branching modules, Xception offers a combination of both ResNet and Inception architectural features in a simpler design. Xception's simplicity makes it a good choice when you want to implement your own convolutional backbone. The source code for the Keras implementation of Xception (*https://oreil.ly/rcCq6*) is easily accessible from the documentation.

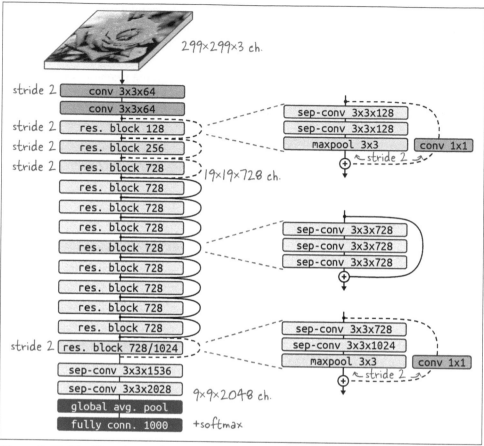

Figure 3-38. The Xception architecture with 36 convolutional layers. The architecture is inspired by ResNet but uses separable convolutions instead of traditional ones, except in the first two layers.

In Figure 3-38, all convolutional layers are ReLU-activated and use batch normalization. All separable convolutions use a depth multiplier of 1 (no channel expansion).

The residual blocks in Xception are different from their ResNet counterparts: they use 3x3 separable convolutions instead of the mix of 3x3 and 1x1 traditional convolutions in ResNet. This makes sense since 3x3 separable convolutions are already a combination of 3x3 and 1x1 convolutions (see Figure 3-36). This further simplifies the design.

It is also to be noted that although depth-separable convolutions have a depth multiplier parameter that allows the initial 3x3 convolutions to be applied multiple times to each input channel with independent weights, the Xception architecture obtains good results with a depth multiplier of 1. This is actually the most common practice. All other architectures described in this chapter that are based on depth-separable convolutions use them without the depth multiplier (leaving it at 1). It seems that adding parameters in the 1x1 part of the separable convolution is enough to allow the model to capture the relevant information in input images.

Xception at a Glance

Architecture
Residual blocks based on depth-separable convolutional layers

Publication
François Chollet, "Xception: Deep Learning with Depthwise Separable Convolutions," 2016, *https://arxiv.org/abs/1610.02357*.

Code samples
03i_finetune_XCEPTION_flowers104.ipynb and *03i_fromzero_XCEPTION_flowers104.ipynb*

Table 3-8. Xception at a glance

Model	Parameters (excl. classif. head[a])	ImageNet accuracy	104 flowers F1 score[b] (fine-tuning)	104 flowers F1 score (trained from scratch)
Xception	21M	79%	95% prec.: 95%, recall: 95%	83% prec.: 84%, recall: 82%
Previous best for comparison:				
DenseNet201	18M	77%	95% prec.: 96%, recall: 95%	
DenseNet121	7M	75%		76% prec.: 80%, recall: 74%
InceptionV3	22M	78%	95% prec.: 95%, recall: 94%	
SqueezeNet, 24 layers	2.7M			76% prec.: 77%, recall: 75%

[a] Excluding classification head from parameter counts for easier comparisons between architectures. Without the classification head, the number of parameters in the network is resolution-independent. Also, in fine-tuning examples, a different classification head might be used.
[b] For accuracy, precision, recall, and F1 score values, higher is better.

Neural Architecture Search Designs

The convolutional architectures described in the previous pages are all made of similar elements arranged in different ways: 3x3 and 1x1 convolutions, 3x3 separable convolutions, additions, concatenations... Couldn't the search for the ideal combination be automated? Let's look at architectures that can do this.

NASNet

Automating the search for the optimal combination of operations is precisely what the authors of the NASNet paper (*https://arxiv.org/abs/1707.07012*) did. However, a brute-force search through the entire set of possible operations would have been too large a task. There are too many ways to choose and assemble layers into a full neural network. Furthermore, each piece has many hyperparameters, like the number of its output channels or the size of its filters.

Instead, they simplified the problem in a clever way. Looking back at the Inception, ResNet, or Xception architectures (Figures 3-24, 3-29, and 3-38, respectively), it is easy to see that they are constructed from two types of repeated modules: one kind that leaves the width and height of the features intact ("normal cells") and another that divides them in half ("reduction cells"). The NASNet authors used an automated algorithm to design the structure of these basic cells (see Figure 3-39) and then assembled a convolutional architecture by hand, by stacking the cells with reasonable parameters (channel depth, for example). They then trained the resulting networks to see which module design worked the best.

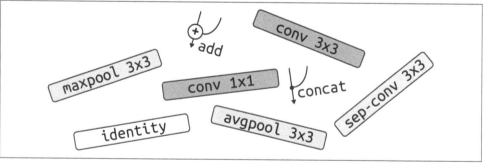

Figure 3-39. Some of the individual operations used as NASNet building blocks.

The search algorithm can either be a random search, which actually did not perform so badly in the study, or a more sophisticated one also based on neural networks called *reinforcement learning*. To learn more about reinforcement learning, see Andrej Karpathy's "Pong from Pixels" (*https://oreil.ly/Qjy9V*) post or Martin Görner's and Yu-Han Liu's "Reinforcement Learning Without a PhD" (*https://oreil.ly/BMIeQ*) Google I/O 2018 video.

Figure 3-40 shows the structure of the best normal and reduction cells found by the algorithm. Note that the search space allowed connections from not only the previous stage but also the one before, to mimic more densely connected architectures like DenseNet.

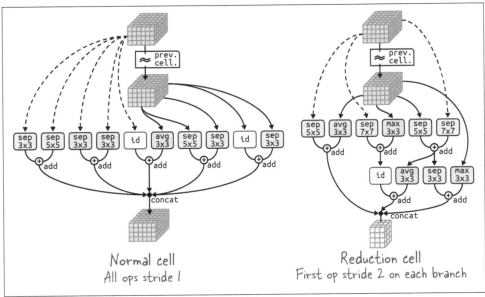

Figure 3-40. The best-performing convolutional cells found through neural architecture search in the NASNet paper. They are made of separable convolutions well as average and max-pooling layers.

The paper notes that separable convolutions are always used doubled ("sep 3x3" in Figure 3-40 actually indicates two consecutive 3x3 separable convolutions), which has been empirically found to increase performance.

Figure 3-41 shows how the cells are stacked to form a complete neural network.

Different NASNet scales can be obtained by adjusting the N and M parameters—for example, $N=7$ and $M=1,920$ for the most widely used variant, which has 22.6M parameters. All convolutional layers in the figure are ReLU-activated and use batch normalization.

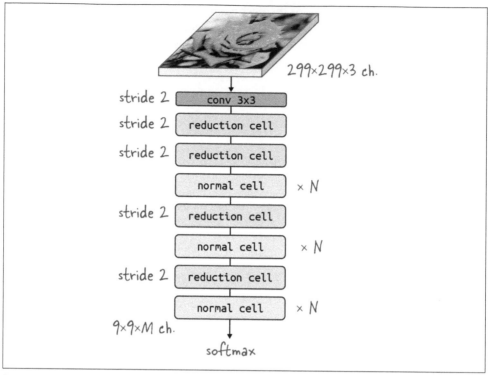

Figure 3-41. Stacking of the normal and reduction cells to create a complete neural network. Normal cells are repeated N times. The number of channels is multiplied by 2 in every reduction cell to obtain M output channels at the end.

There are a few interesting details to note about what the algorithm does:

- It only uses separable convolutions, although regular convolutions were part of the search space. This seems to confirm the benefits of separable convolutions.

- When merging branches, the algorithm chooses to add results rather than concatenate them. This is similar to ResNet but unlike Inception or DenseNet, which use concatenations. (Note that the last concatenation in each cell is forced by the architecture and was not chosen by the algorithm.)

- In the normal cell, the algorithm chooses multiple parallel branches, rather than fewer branches, and more layers of transformations. This is more like Inception, and less like ResNet.

- The algorithm uses separable convolutions with large 5x5 or 7x7 filters rather than implementing everything with 3x3 convolutions. This runs contrary to the "filter factorization" hypothesis outlined earlier in this chapter, and indicates that the hypothesis might not hold after all.

Some choices seem dubious, though, and are probably an artifact of the search space design. For example, in the normal cell, 3x3 average-pooling layers with a stride of 1 are basically blur operations. Maybe a blur is useful, but blurring the same input twice then adding the results is certainly not optimal.

NASNet at a Glance

Architecture
Complex, machine-generated

Publication
Barret Zoph et al., "Learning Transferable Architectures for Scalable Image Recognition," 2017, *https://arxiv.org/abs/1707.07012*.

Code sample
03j_finetune_NASNETLARGE_flowers104.ipynb

Table 3-9. NASNet at a glance

Model	Parameters (excl. classification head[a])	ImageNet accuracy	104 flowers F1 score[b] (fine-tuning)
NASNetLarge	85M	82%	89% precision: 92%, recall: 89%
Previous best for comparison:			
DenseNet201	18M	77%	95% precision: 96%, recall: 95%
Xception	21M	79%	95% precision: 95%, recall: 95%

[a] Excluding classification head from parameter counts for easier comparisons between architectures. Without the classification head, the number of parameters in the network is resolution-independent. Also, in fine-tuning examples, a different classification head might be used.
[b] For accuracy, precision, recall, and F1 score values, higher is better.

Despite its hefty weight count, NASNetLarge is not the best model for the 104 flowers dataset (achieving an F1 score of 89% versus 95% for the other models). This is probably because a large set of trainable parameters requires more training data.

The MobileNet Family

In the next couple of sections, we will describe the MobileNetV2/MnasNet/Efficient-Net family of architectures. MobileNetV2 (*https://arxiv.org/abs/1801.04381*) fits in this "neural architecture search" section because it introduces new building blocks that help design a more efficient search space. Although the initial MobileNetV2 was designed by hand, follow-up versions MnasNet (*https://arxiv.org/abs/1807.11626*) and EfficientNet (*https://arxiv.org/abs/1905.11946*) use the same building blocks for automated neural architecture search and end up with optimized but very similar architectures. Before we discuss this set of architectures, however, first we need to introduce two new building blocks: depthwise convolutions and inverted residual bottlenecks.

Depthwise convolutions

The first building block we need to explain in order to understand the MobileNetV2 architecture is depthwise convolutions. The MobileNetV2 (*https://arxiv.org/abs/1801.04381*) architecture revisits depth-separable convolutions and their interactions with skip connections. To make this fine-grained analysis possible, we must first split the depth-separable convolutions described previously (Figure 3-36) into their basic components:

- The spatial filtering part, called a depthwise convolution (Figure 3-42)
- A 1x1 convolution

In Figure 3-42, the filtering operation can be repeated with new filter weights to produce double or triple the number of channels. This is called a "depth multiplier" but its usual value is 1, which is why it is not represented in the picture.

Depthwise convolutional layers are available in Keras:

```
tf.keras.layers.DepthwiseConv2D(kernel_size,
                                strides=(1, 1),
                                padding='valid',
                                depth_multiplier=1)
```

Note that a depth-separable convolution, such as:

```
tf.keras.layers.SeparableConv2D(filters=128, kernel_size=(3,3))
```

can also be represented in Keras as a sequence of two layers:

```
tf.keras.layers.DepthwiseConv2D(kernel_size=(3,3))
tf.keras.layers.Conv2D(filters=128, kernel_size=(1,1))
```

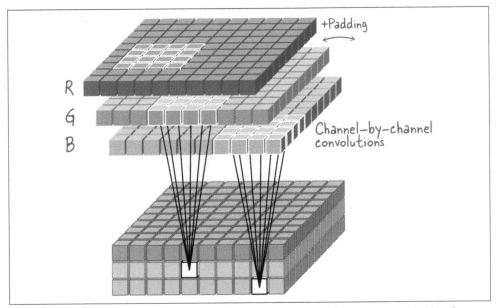

Figure 3-42. A depthwise convolutional layer. Convolutional filters are applied independently to each input channel, producing an equal number of output channels.

Inverted residual bottlenecks

The second and most important building block in the MobileNet family is the inverted residual bottleneck. Residual blocks used in ResNet or Xception architectures tend to keep the number of channels flowing through skip connections high (see Figure 3-43 below). In the MobileNetV2 paper (*https://arxiv.org/abs/1801.04381*), the authors make the hypothesis that the information that skip connections help preserve is inherently low-dimensional. This makes sense intuitively. If a convolutional block specializes in detecting, for example "cat whiskers," the information in its output ("whiskers detected at position (3, 16)") can be represented along three dimensions: class, *x*, *y*. Compared with the pixel representation of whiskers, it is low-dimensional.

The MobileNetV2 architecture introduces a new residual block design that places skip connections where the number of channels is low and expands the number of channels inside residual blocks. Figure 3-43 compares the new design to the typical residual blocks used in ResNet and Xception. The number of channels in ResNet blocks follows the sequence "many – few – many," with skip connections between the "many channels" stages. Xception does "many – many – many." The new MobileNetV2 design follows the sequence "few – many – few." The paper calls this technique *inverted residual bottlenecks*—"inverted" because it is the exact opposite of the ResNet approach, "bottleneck" because the number of channels is squeezed in between residual blocks, like the neck of a bottle.

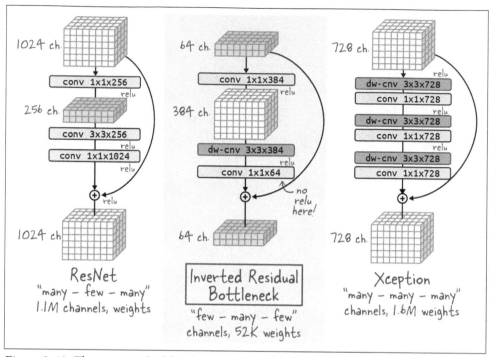

Figure 3-43. The new residual block design in MobileNetV2 (called an "inverted residual bottleneck"), compared with ResNet and Xception residual blocks. "dw-cnv" stands for depthwise convolution. Separable convolutions used by Xception are represented by their components: "dw-cnv" followed by "conv 1x1."

The goal of this new residual block is to offer the same expressivity as prior designs with a dramatically reduced weight count and, even more importantly, a reduced latency at inference time. MobileNetV2 was indeed designed to be used on mobile phones, where compute resources are scarce. The weight counts of the typical residual blocks represented in Figure 3-43 are 1.1M, 52K, and 1.6M respectively for the ResNet, MobileNetV2, and Xception blocks.

The authors of the MobileNetV2 paper argue that their design can achieve good results with fewer parameters because the information that flows between residual blocks is low-dimensional in nature and can therefore be represented in a limited number of channels. However, one construction detail is important: the last 1x1 convolution in the inverted residual block, the one that squeezes the feature map back to "few" channels, is not followed by a nonlinear activation. The MobileNetV2 paper covers this topic at some length, but the short version is that in a low-dimensional space, a ReLU activation would destroy too much information.

We are now ready to build a full MobileNetV2 model and then use neural architecture search to refine it into the optimized, but otherwise very similar, MnasNet and EfficientNet architectures.

MobileNetV2

We can now put together the MobileNetV2 convolutional stack. MobileNetV2 is built out of multiple inverted residual blocks, as shown in Figure 3-44.

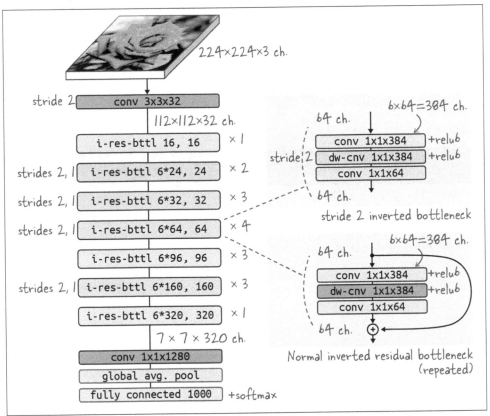

Figure 3-44. The MobileNetV2 architecture, based on repeated inverted residual bottle-necks. Repeat counts are in the center column. "conv" indicates regular convolutional layers, while "dw-cnv" denotes depthwise convolutions.

In Figure 3-44, inverted residual bottleneck blocks are marked "i-res-bttl N, M" and parameterized by their internal (N) and external channel depth (M). Every sequence marked "strides 2, 1" starts with an inverted bottleneck block with a stride of 2 and no skip connection. The sequence continues with regular inverted residual bottleneck blocks. All convolutional layers use batch normalization. Please note that the last convolutional layer in inverted bottleneck blocks does not use an activation function.

The activation function in MobileNetV2 is ReLU6, instead of the usual ReLU. Later evolutions of MobileNetV2 went back to using standard ReLU activation functions. The use of ReLU6 in MobileNetV2 is not a fundamental implementation detail.

MobileNetV2 at a Glance

Architecture
Sequence of inverted residual bottlenecks

Publication
Mark Sandler et al., "MobileNetV2: Inverted Residuals and Linear Bottlenecks," 2018, *https://arxiv.org/abs/1801.04381*.

Code sample
03k_finetune_MOBILENETV2_flowers104.ipynb

Table 3-10. MobileNetV2 at a glance

Model	Parameters (excl. classification head[a])	ImageNet accuracy	104 flowers F1 score[b] (fine-tuning)
MobileNetV2	2.3M	71%	92% precision: 92%, recall: 92%
Previous best for comparison:			
NASNetLarge	85M	82%	89% precision: 92%, recall: 89%
DenseNet201	18M	77%	95% precision: 96%, recall: 95%
Xception	21M	79%	95% precision: 95%, recall: 95%

[a] Excluding classification head from parameter counts for easier comparisons between architectures. Without the classification head, the number of parameters in the network is resolution-independent. Also, in fine-tuning examples, a different classification head might be used.
[b] For accuracy, precision, recall, and F1 score values, higher is better.

MobileNetV2 is optimized for a low weight count and sacrifices a bit of accuracy for it. Also, in the 104 flowers fine-tuning example, it converged significantly slower than other models. It can still be a good choice when mobile inference performance is important.

The MobileNetV2 simple structure of repeated inverted residual bottleneck blocks lends itself well to automated neural architecture search methods. That is how the MnasNet and EfficientNet architectures were created.

EfficientNet: Putting it all together

The team that created MobileNetV2 later refined the architecture through automated neural architecture search, using inverted residual bottlenecks as the building blocks of their search space. The MnasNet paper (*https://arxiv.org/abs/1807.11626*) summarizes their initial findings. The most interesting result of that research is that, once again, the automated algorithm reintroduced 5x5 convolutions into the mix. This was already the case in NASNet, as we saw earlier. This is interesting because all manually constructed architectures had standardized on 3x3 convolutions, justifying the choice with the filter factorization hypothesis. Apparently, larger filters like 5x5 are useful after all.

We'll skip a formal description of the MnasNet architecture in favor of its next iteration: EfficientNet (*https://arxiv.org/abs/1905.11946*). This architecture was developed using the exact same search space and network architecture search algorithm as MnasNet, but the optimization goal was tweaked toward prediction accuracy rather than mobile inference latency. Inverted residual bottlenecks from MobileNetV2 are again the basic building blocks.

EfficientNet is actually a family of neural networks of different sizes, where a lot of attention was paid to the scaling of the networks in the family. Convolutional architectures have three main ways of scaling:

- Use more layers.
- Use more channels in each layer.
- Use higher-resolution input images.

The EfficientNet paper points out that these three scaling axes are not independent: "If the input image is bigger, then the network needs more layers to increase the receptive field and more channels to capture more fine-grained patterns on the bigger image."

The novelty in the EfficientNetB0 through EfficientNetB7 family of neural networks is that they are scaled along all three scaling axes rather than just one, as was the case in earlier architecture families such as ResNet50/ResNet101/ResNet152. The EfficientNet family is today the workhorse of many applied machine learning teams because it offers optimal performance levels for every weight count. Research evolves fast though, and by the time this book is printed, it is probable that an even better architecture will have been discovered.

Figure 3-45 describes the baseline EfficientNetB0 architecture. Notice the similarity with MobileNetV2.

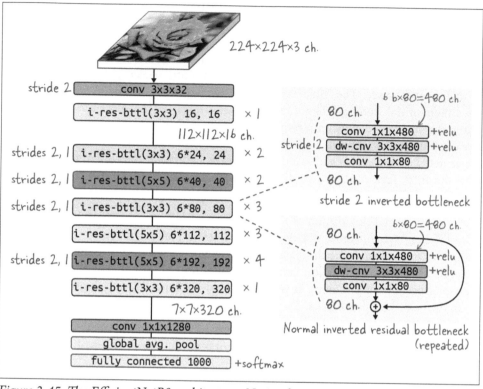

Figure 3-45. The EfficientNetB0 architecture. Notice the strong similarity with Mobile-NetV2 (Figure 3-44).

In Figure 3-45, sequences of inverted residual bottlenecks are noted [i-res-bttl(*KxK*) *P*Ch, Ch*] X *N*, where:

- *Ch* is the external number of channels output by each block.
- The internal number of channels is typically a multiple *P* of the external channels: *P*Ch*.
- *KxK* is the convolutional filter size, typically 3x3 or 5x5.
- *N* is the number of such consecutive layer blocks.

Every sequence marked "strides 2, 1" starts with an inverted bottleneck block with a stride of 2 and no skip connection. The sequence continues with regular inverted residual bottleneck blocks. As previously mentioned, "conv" indicates regular convolutional layers, while "dw-cnv" denotes depthwise convolutions.

EfficientNetB1 through B7 have the exact same general structure, with seven sequences of inverted residual bottlenecks; only the parameters differ. Figure 3-46 provides the scaling parameters for the entire family.

EfficientNetB0	EfficientNetB1	EfficientNetB2
ideal image res.: 224x224 px	ideal image res.: 240x240 px	ideal image res.: 260x260 px
weight count: 5.3M	weight count: 7.9M	weight count: 9.2M
[i-res-bttl(3x3) 16, 16] x 1	[i-res-bttl(3x3) 16, 16] x 2	[i-res-bttl(3x3) 16, 16] x 2
[i-res-bttl(3x3) 144, 24] x 2	[i-res-bttl(3x3) 144, 24] x 3	[i-res-bttl(3x3) 144, 24] x 3
[i-res-bttl(5x5) 240, 40] x 2	[i-res-bttl(5x5) 240, 40] x 3	[i-res-bttl(5x5) 288, 48] x 3
[i-res-bttl(3x3) 480, 80] x 3	[i-res-bttl(3x3) 480, 80] x 4	[i-res-bttl(3x3) 528, 88] x 4
[i-res-bttl(5x5) 672, 112] x 3	[i-res-bttl(5x5) 672, 112] x 4	[i-res-bttl(5x5) 720, 120] x 4
[i-res-bttl(5x5) 1152, 192] x 4	[i-res-bttl(5x5) 1152, 192] x 5	[i-res-bttl(5x5) 1248, 208] x 5
[i-res-bttl(3x3) 1920, 320] x 1	[i-res-bttl(3x3) 1920, 320] x 2	[i-res-bttl(3x3) 2112, 352] x 2

EfficientNetB3	EfficientNetB4	EfficientNetB5
ideal image res.: 300x300 px	ideal image res.: 380x380 px	ideal image res.: 456x456 px
weight count: 12.3M	weight count: 19.5M	weight count: 30.6M
[i-res-bttl(3x3) 24, 24] x 2	[i-res-bttl(3x3) 24, 24] x 2	[i-res-bttl(3x3) 24, 24] x 3
[i-res-bttl(3x3) 192, 32] x 3	[i-res-bttl(3x3) 192, 32] x 4	[i-res-bttl(3x3) 240, 40] x 5
[i-res-bttl(5x5) 288, 48] x 3	[i-res-bttl(5x5) 336, 56] x 4	[i-res-bttl(5x5) 384, 64] x 5
[i-res-bttl(3x3) 576, 96] x 5	[i-res-bttl(3x3) 672, 112] x 6	[i-res-bttl(3x3) 768, 128] x 7
[i-res-bttl(5x5) 816, 136] x 5	[i-res-bttl(5x5) 960, 160] x 6	[i-res-bttl(5x5) 1056, 176] x 7
[i-res-bttl(5x5) 1392, 232] x 6	[i-res-bttl(5x5) 1632, 272] x 8	[i-res-bttl(5x5) 1824, 304] x 9
[i-res-bttl(3x3) 2304, 384] x 2	[i-res-bttl(3x3) 2688, 448] x 2	[i-res-bttl(3x3) 3072, 512] x 3

EfficientNetB6	EfficientNetB7	EfficientNetB8
ideal image res.: 528x528 px	ideal image res.: 600x600 px	ideal image res.: 672x672 px
weight count: 43.3M	weight count: 66.7M	
[i-res-bttl(3x3) 32, 32] x 3	[i-res-bttl(3x3) 32, 32] x 4	[i-res-bttl(3x3) 32, 32] x 4
[i-res-bttl(3x3) 240, 40] x 6	[i-res-bttl(3x3) 288, 48] x 7	[i-res-bttl(3x3) 336, 56] x 8
[i-res-bttl(5x5) 432, 72] x 6	[i-res-bttl(5x5) 480, 80] x 7	[i-res-bttl(5x5) 528, 88] x 8
[i-res-bttl(3x3) 864, 144] x 8	[i-res-bttl(3x3) 960, 160] x 10	[i-res-bttl(3x3) 1056, 176] x 11
[i-res-bttl(5x5) 1200, 200] x 8	[i-res-bttl(5x5) 1344, 224] x 10	[i-res-bttl(5x5) 1488, 248] x 11
[i-res-bttl(5x5) 2064, 344] x 11	[i-res-bttl(5x5) 2304, 384] x 13	[i-res-bttl(5x5) 2544, 424] x 15
[i-res-bttl(3x3) 3456, 576] x 3	[i-res-bttl(3x3) 3840, 640] x 4	[i-res-bttl(3x3) 4224, 704] x 4

Figure 3-46. The EfficientNetB0 through EfficientNetB7 family, showing the parameters of the seven sequences of inverted residual bottlenecks that make up the EfficientNet architecture.

As shown in Figure 3-46, each neural network in the family has an ideal input image size. It has been trained on images of this size, though it can also be used with other image sizes. The number of layers and number of channels in each layer are scaled along with the input image size. The multiplier between the external and internal number of channels in inverted residual bottlenecks is always 6, apart from in the first row where it is 1.

So are these scaling parameters actually effective? The EfficientNet paper shows they are. The compound scaling outlined above is more efficient than scaling the network by layers, channels, or image resolution alone (Figure 3-47).

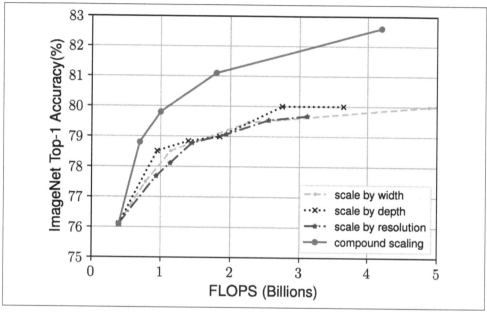

Figure 3-47. Accuracy of EfficientNet classifiers scaled using the compound scaling method from the EfficientNet paper versus scaling by a single factor: width (the number of channels in convolutional blocks), depth (the number of convolutional layers), or image resolution. Image from Tan & Le, 2019 (https://arxiv.org/abs/1905.11946).

The authors of the EfficientNet paper also used the class activation map technique from Zhou et al., 2016 (*https://arxiv.org/abs/1512.04150*) to visualize what the trained networks "see." Again, compound scaling achieves better results by helping the network focus on the important parts of the image (Figure 3-48).

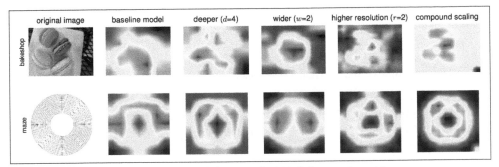

Figure 3-48. Class activation maps (Zhou et al., 2016) for two input images as seen through several EfficientNet variants. The model obtained through compound scaling (last column) focuses on more relevant regions with more object detail. Image from Tan & Le, 2019 (https://arxiv.org/abs/1905.11946).

EfficientNet also incorporates some additional optimizations. Briefly:

- Every inverted bottleneck block is further optimized through the "squeeze-excite" channel optimization, as per Jie et al., 2017 (*https://arxiv.org/abs/1709.01507*). This technique is a channel-wise attention mechanism that "renormalizes" output channels (i.e., boosts some and attenuates others) before the final 1x1 convolution of each block. Like any "attention" technique, it involves a small additional neural network that learns to produce the ideal renormalization weights. This additional network is not represented in Figure 3-45. Its contribution to the total count of learnable weights is small. This technique can be applied to any convolutional block, not just inverted residual bottlenecks, and boosts network accuracy by about one percentage point.

- Dropout is used in all members of the EfficientNet family to help with overfitting. Larger networks in the family use slightly larger dropout rates (0.2, 0.2, 0.3, 0.3, 0.4, 0.4, 0.5, and 0.5, respectively, for EfficientNetB0 through B7).

- The activation function used in EfficientNet is SiLU (also called Swish-1) as described in Ramachandran et al., 2017 (*https://arxiv.org/abs/1710.05941*). The function is $f(x) = x \cdot \text{sigmoid}(x)$.

- The training dataset was automatically expanded using the AutoAugment technique, as described in Cubuk et al., 2018 (*https://arxiv.org/abs/1805.09501*).

- The "stochastic depth" technique is used during training, as described in Huang et al., 2016 (*https://arxiv.org/abs/1603.09382*). We are not sure how effective this part was since the stochastic depth paper itself reports that the technique does not work with a ResNet152 trained on ImageNet. It might do something on deeper networks.

EfficientNet at a Glance

Architecture

Sequence of inverted residual bottlenecks

Code samples

03l_finetune_EFFICIENTNETB6_flowers104.ipynb, 03l_finetune_EFFICIENTNET B7_TFHUB_flowers104.ipynb, and *03l_fromzero_EFFICIENTNETB4_ flowers 104.ipynb*

Publication

Mingxing Tan and Quoc V. Le, "EfficientNet: Rethinking Model Scaling for Convolutional Neural Networks," 2019, *arXiv:1905.11946.*

EfficientNetB6 and B7 currently top the ImageNet classification charts with an accuracy of 84%. Fine-tuned on our 104 flowers dataset, however, they perform only marginally better than Xception, DenseNet201, or InceptionV3. All of these models tend to achieve precision and recall values of 95% on this dataset and saturate there. The dataset is probably too small to go further.

You will find a table summarizing all the results in the next section.

Beyond Convolution: The Transformer Architecture

The architectures for computer vision that are discussed in this chapter all rely on convolutional filters. Compared to the naive dense neural networks discussed in Chapter 2, convolutional filters reduce the number of weights necessary to learn how to extract information from images. However, as dataset sizes keep increasing, there comes a point where this weight reduction is no longer necessary.

Ashish Vaswani et al. proposed the Transformer architecture for natural language processing in a 2017 paper (*https://arxiv.org/abs/1706.03762*) with the catchy title "Attention Is All You Need." As the title indicates, the key innovation in the Transformer architecture is the concept of *attention*—having the model focus on some part of the input text sequence when predicting each word. For example, consider a model that needs to translate the French phrase "ma chemise rouge" into English ("my red shirt"). The model would learn to focus on the word *rouge* when predicting the second word of the English translation, *red*. The Transformer model achieves this by using *positional encodings*. Instead of simply representing the input phrase by its words, it adds the position of each word as an input: (ma, 1), (chemise, 2), (rouge, 3). The model then learns from the training dataset which word of the input it needs to focus on when predicting a specific word of the output.

The Vision Transformer (ViT) (*https://arxiv.org/abs/2010.11929*) model adapts the Transformer idea to work on images. The equivalent of words in images are square patches, so the first step is to take the input image and break it into patches, as shown in Figure 3-49 (the full code is available in *03m_transformer_flowers104.ipynb* on GitHub):

```
patches = tf.image.extract_patches(
    images=images,
    sizes=[1, self.patch_size, self.patch_size, 1],
    strides=[1, self.patch_size, self.patch_size, 1],
    rates=[1, 1, 1, 1],
    padding="VALID",
)
```

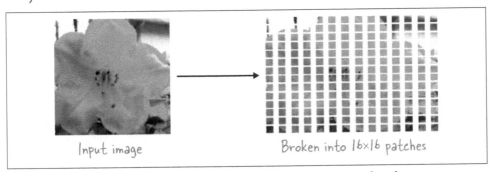

Figure 3-49. The input image is broken into patches that are treated as the sequence input to the Transformer.

The patches are represented by concatenating the patch pixel values and the patch position within the image:

```
encoded = (tf.keras.layers.Dense(...)(patch) +
          tf.keras.layers.Embedding(...)(position))
```

Note that the patch position is the ordinal number (5th, 6th, etc.) of the patch and is treated as a categorical variable. A learnable embedding is employed to capture closeness relationships between patches that have related content.

The patch representation is passed through multiple transformer blocks, each of which consists of an attention head (to learn which parts of the input to focus on):

```
x1 = tf.keras.layers.LayerNormalization()(encoded)
attention_output = tf.keras.layers.MultiHeadAttention(
    num_heads=num_heads, key_dim=projection_dim, dropout=0.1
)(x1, x1)
```

The attention output is used to add emphasis to the patch representation:

```
# Skip connection 1.
x2 = tf.keras.layers.Add()([attention_output, encoded])
# Layer normalization 2.
x3 = tf.keras.layers.LayerNormalization()(x2)
```

and passed through a set of dense layers:

```
# multilayer perceptron (mlp), a set of dense layers.
x3 = mlp(x3, hidden_units=transformer_units,
        dropout_rate=0.1)
# Skip connection 2 forms input to next block
encoded = tf.keras.layers.Add()([x3, x2])
```

The training loop is similar to that of any of the convolutional network architectures discussed in this chapter. Note that the ViT architecture requires a lot more data than convolutional network models—the authors suggest pretraining the ViT model on large amounts of data and then fine-tuning on smaller datasets. Indeed, training from scratch on the 104 flowers dataset yields only a 34% accuracy.

Even though not particularly promising at present for our relatively small dataset, the idea of applying the Transformer architecture to images is interesting, and a potential source of new innovations in computer vision.

Choosing a Model

This section will provide some tips on choosing a model architecture for your task. First of all, create a benchmark using code-free services to train ML models so that you have a good idea of what kind of accuracy is achievable on your problem. If you are training on Google Cloud, consider Google Cloud AutoML (*https://oreil.ly/bw0fE*), which utilizes neural architecture search (NAS). If you are using Microsoft Azure, consider Custom Vision AI (*https://www.customvision.ai*). DataRobot (*https://oreil.ly/I6GHs*) and H2O.ai (*https://oreil.ly/dubZl*) employ transfer learning for code-free image classification. It is unlikely that you will get an accuracy that is significantly higher than what these services provide out of the box, so you can use them as a way to quickly do a proof of concept before you invest too much time on an infeasible problem.

Performance Comparison

Let's summarize the performance numbers seen so far, first for fine-tuning (Table 3-11). Notice the new entrant at the bottom, called "ensemble." We will cover this in the next section.

Table 3-11. Eight model architectures fine-tuned on the 104 flowers dataset

Model	Parameters (excl. classification head[a])	ImageNet accuracy	104 flowers F1 score[b] (fine-tuning)
EfficientNetB6	40M	84%	95.5%
EfficientNetB7	64M	84%	95.5%
DenseNet201	18M	77%	95.4%
Xception	21M	79%	94.6%
InceptionV3	22M	78%	94.6%

Model	Parameters (excl. classification head[a])	ImageNet accuracy	104 flowers F1 score[b] (fine-tuning)
ResNet50	23M	75%	94.1%
MobileNetV2	2.3M	71%	92%
NASNetLarge	85M	82%	89%
VGG19	20M	71%	88%
Ensemble	79M (DenseNet210 + Xception + EfficientNetB6)	-	96.2%

[a] Excluding classification head from parameter counts for easier comparisons between architectures. Without the classification head, the number of parameters in the network is resolution-independent. Also, in fine-tuning examples, a different classification head might be used.

[b] For accuracy, precision, recall, and F1 score values, higher is better.

And now for training from scratch (Table 3-12). Since fine-tuning worked much better on the 104 flowers dataset, not all the models have been trained from scratch.

Table 3-12. Six model architectures trained from scratch on the 104 flowers dataset

Model	Parameters (excl. classification head[a])	ImageNet accuracy	104 flowers F1 score[b] (trained from scratch)
Xception	21M	79%	82.6%
SqueezeNet, 24 layers	2.7M	-	76.2%
DenseNet121	7M	75%	76.1%
ResNet50	23M	75%	73%
EfficientNetB4	18M	83%	69%
AlexNet	3.7M	60%	39%

[a] Excluding classification head from parameter counts for easier comparisons between architectures. Without the classification head, the number of parameters in the network is resolution-independent. Also, in fine-tuning examples, a different classification head might be used.

[b] For accuracy, precision, recall, and F1 score values, higher is better.

Xception takes the first spot here, which is a bit surprising since it is not the most recent architecture. Xception's author also noticed in his paper that his model seemed to work better than others when applied to real-world datasets other than ImageNet and other standard datasets used in academia. The fact that the second spot is taken by a SqueezeNet-like model quickly thrown together by the author of the book is significant. When you want to try your own architecture, SqueezeNet is both very simple to code and quite efficient. This model is also the smallest one in the selection. Its size is probably well adapted to the relatively small size of the 104 flowers dataset (approximately 20K pictures). The DenseNet architecture shares the second place with SqueezeNet. It is by far the most unconventional architecture in this selection, but it seems to have a lot of potential on unconventional datasets.

It might be worth looking at the other variations and versions of these models to pick the most suitable and most up-to-date one. As mentioned, EfficientNet was the state-of-the-art model at the time we wrote this book (January 2021). There might be something newer by the time you are reading it. You can check TensorFlow Hub (*https://www.tensorflow.org/hub*) for new models.

A last option is to use multiple models at the same time, a technique called *ensembling*. We'll look at this next.

Ensembling

When looking for the maximum accuracy, and when model size and inference times are not an issue, multiple models can be used at the same time and their predictions combined. Such *ensemble models* can often give better predictions than any of the models composing them. Their predictions are also more robust on real-life images. The key consideration when selecting models to ensemble is to choose models that are as different as possible from each other. Models with very different architectures are more likely to have different weaknesses. When combined in an ensemble, the strengths and weaknesses of different models will compensate for each other, as long as they are not in the same classes.

A notebook, *03z_ensemble_finetune_flowers104.ipynb*, is provided in the GitHub repository showcasing an ensemble of three models fine-tuned on the 104 flowers dataset: DenseNet210, Xception, and EfficientNetB6. As seen in Table 3-13, the ensemble wins by a respectable margin.

Table 3-13. Comparison of model ensembling versus individual models

Model	Parameters (excl. classification head[a])	ImageNet accuracy	104 flowers F1 score[b] (fine-tuning)
EfficientNetB6	40M	84%	95.5%
DenseNet201	18M	77%	95.4%
Xception	21M	79%	94.6%
Ensemble	79M		96.2%

[a] Excluding classification head from parameter counts for easier comparisons between architectures. Without the classification head, the number of parameters in the network is resolution-independent. Also, in fine-tuning examples, a different classification head might be used.
[b] For accuracy, precision, recall, and F1 score values, higher is better.

The easiest way to ensemble the three models is to average the class probabilities they predict. Another possibility, theoretically better, is to average their logits (the outputs of the last layer before softmax activation) and apply softmax on the averages to compute class probabilities. The sample notebook shows both options. On the 104 flowers dataset, they perform equally.

One point of caution when averaging logits is that logits, contrary to probabilities, are not normalized. They can have very different values in different models. Computing a weighted average instead of a simple average might help in that case. The training dataset should be used to compute the best weights.

Recommended Strategy

Here is our recommended strategy to tackle computer vision problems.

First, choose your training method based on the size of your dataset:

- If you have a very small dataset (less than one thousand images per label), use transfer learning.
- If you have a moderate-sized dataset (one to five thousand images per label), use fine-tuning.
- If you have a large dataset (more than five thousand images per label), train from scratch.

These numbers are rules of thumb and vary depending on the difficulty of the use case, the complexity of your model, and the quality of the data. You may have to experiment with a couple of the options. For example, the 104 flowers dataset has between one hundred and three thousand images per class, depending on the class; fine-tuning was still very effective on it.

Whether you are doing transfer learning, fine-tuning, or training from scratch, you will need to select a model architecture. Which one should you pick?

- If you want to roll your own layers, start with SqueezeNet. It's the simplest model that will perform well.
- For edge devices, you typically want to optimize for models that can be downloaded fast, occupy very little space on the device, and don't incur high latencies during prediction. For a small model that runs fast on low-power devices, consider MobileNetV2.
- If you don't have size/speed restrictions (such as if inference will be done on autoscaling cloud systems) and want the best/fanciest model, consider Efficient-Net.
- If you belong to a conservative organization that wants to stick with something tried and true, choose ResNet50 or one of its larger variants.

If training cost and prediction latency are not of concern, or if small improvements in model accuracy bring outside rewards, consider an ensemble of three complementary models.

Summary

This chapter focused on image classification techniques. It first explained how to use pretrained models and adapt them to a new dataset. This is by far the most popular technique and will work if the pretraining dataset and the target dataset share at least some similarities. We explored two variants of this technique: transfer learning, where the pretrained model is frozen and used as a static image encoder; and fine-tuning, where the weights of the pretrained model are used as initial values in a new training run on the new dataset. We then examined the historical and current state-of-the-art image classification architectures, from AlexNet to EfficientNets. All the building blocks of these architectures were explained, starting of course with convolutional layers, to give you a complete understanding of how these models work.

In Chapter 4, we will look at using any of these image model architectures to solve common computer vision problems.

Object Detection and Image Segmentation

So far in this book, we have looked at a variety of machine learning architectures but used them to solve only one type of problem—that of classifying (or regressing) an entire image. In this chapter, we discuss three new vision problems: object detection, instance segmentation, and whole-scene semantic segmentation (Figure 4-1). Other more advanced vision problems like image generation, counting, pose estimation, and generative models are covered in Chapters 11 and 12.

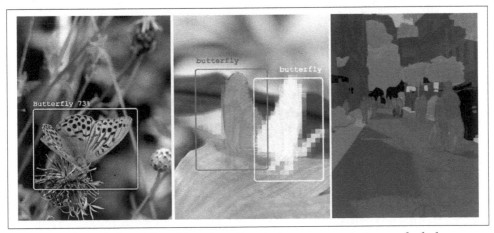

Figure 4-1. From left to right: object detection, instance segmentation, and whole-scene semantic segmentation. Images from Arthropods (https://oreil.ly/sRrvU) and Cityscapes (https://oreil.ly/rs9zf) datasets.

The code for this chapter is in the *04_detect_segment* folder of the book's GitHub repository (*https://github.com/GoogleCloudPlatform/ practical-ml-vision-book*). We will provide file names for code samples and notebooks where applicable.

Object Detection

Seeing is, for most of us, so effortless that, as we glimpse a butterfly from the corner of our eye and turn our head to enjoy its beauty, we don't even think about the millions of visual cells and neurons at play, capturing light, decoding the signals, and processing them into higher and higher levels of abstraction.

We saw in Chapter 3 how image recognition in ML works. However, the models presented in that chapter were built to classify an image as whole—they could not tell us where in the image a flower was. In this section, we will look at ways to build ML models that can provide this location information. This is a task known as *object detection* (Figure 4-2).

Figure 4-2. An object detection task. Image from Arthropods dataset (https://oreil.ly/ sRrvU).

In fact, convolutional layers do identify and locate the things they detect. The convolutional backbones from Chapter 3 already extract some location information. But in classification problems, the networks make no use of this information. They are trained on an objective where location does not matter. A picture of a butterfly is classified as such wherever the butterfly appears in the image. On the contrary, for object detection, we will add elements to the convolutional stack to extract and refine the location information and train the network to do so with maximum accuracy.

The simplest approach is to add something to the end of a convolutional backbone to predict bounding boxes around detected objects. That's the YOLO (You Only Look Once) approach, and we will start there. However, a lot of important information is also contained at intermediate levels in the convolutional backbone. To extract it, we will build more complex architectures called feature pyramid networks (FPNs) and illustrate their use with RetinaNet.

In this section, we will be using the Arthropod Taxonomy Orders Object Detection dataset (*https://oreil.ly/sRrvU*) (Arthropods for short), which is freely available on Kaggle.com (*http://kaggle.com*). The dataset contains seven categories—Coleoptera (beetles), Aranea (spiders), Hemiptera (true bugs), Diptera (flies), Lepidoptera (butterflies), Hymenoptera (bees, wasps, and ants), and Odonata (dragonflies)—as well as bounding boxes. Some examples are shown in Figure 4-3.

Figure 4-3. Some examples from the Arthropods dataset for object detection.

Besides YOLO, this chapter will also address the RetinaNet and Mask R-CNN architectures. Their implementations can be found in the TensorFlow Model Garden's official vision repository (*https://oreil.ly/FYKgH*). We will be using the new implementations located, at the time of writing, in the "beta" folder of the repository.

Example code showing how to apply these detection models on a custom dataset such as Arthropods can be found in *04_detect_segment* on GitHub, in the folder corresponding to Chapter 4.

In addition to the TensorFlow Model Garden, there is also an excellent step-by-step implementation of RetinaNet (*https://oreil.ly/LWG3c*) on the keras.io website.

YOLO

YOLO (you only look once) (*https://arxiv.org/abs/1506.02640*) is the simplest object detection architecture. It is not the most accurate, but it's one of the fastest when it comes to prediction times. For that reason, it is used in many real-time systems like security cameras. The architecture can be based on any convolutional backbone from Chapter 3. Images are processed through the convolutional stack as in the image classification case, but the classification head is replaced with an object detection and classification head.

More recent variations of the YOLO architecture exist (YOLOv2 (*https://arxiv.org/abs/1612.08242*), YOLOv3 (*https://arxiv.org/abs/1804.02767*), YOLOv4 (*https://arxiv.org/abs/2004.10934*)), but we will not be covering them here. We will use YOLOv1 as our first stepping-stone into object detection architectures, because it is the simplest one to understand.

YOLO grid

YOLOv1 (hereafter referred to as "YOLO" for simplicity) divides a picture into a grid of *NxM* cells—for example, 7x5 (Figure 4-4). For each cell, it tries to predict a bounding box for an object that would be centered in that cell. The predicted bounding box can be larger than the cell from which it originates; the only constraint is that the center of the box is somewhere inside the cell.

What does it mean to predict a bounding box? Let's take a look.

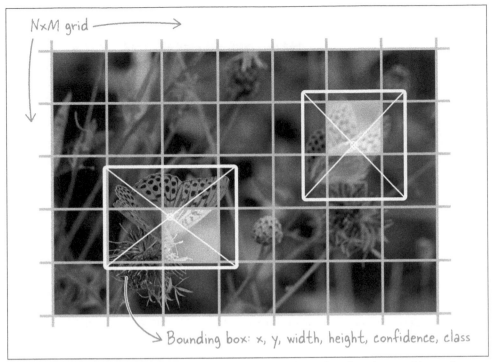

Figure 4-4. The YOLO grid. Each grid cell predicts a bounding box for an object whose center is somewhere in that cell. Image from Arthropods dataset (https://oreil.ly/sRrvU).

Object detection head

Predicting a bounding box amounts to predicting six numbers: the four coordinates of the bounding box (in this case, the x and y coordinates of the center, and the width and height), a confidence factor which tells us if an object has been detected or not, and finally, the class of the object (for example, "butterfly"). The YOLO architecture does this directly on the last feature map, as generated by the convolutional backbone it is using.

In Figure 4-5, the x- and y-coordinate calculations use a hyperbolic tangent (tanh) activation so that the coordinates fall in the [–1, 1] range. They will be the coordinates of the center of the detection box, relative to the center of the grid cell they belong to.

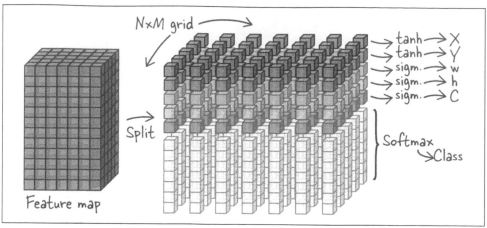

Figure 4-5. A YOLO detection head predicts, for every grid cell, a bounding box (x, y, w, h), the confidence C of there being an object in this location, and the class of the object.

Width and height (*w*, *h*) calculations use a sigmoid activation so as to fall in the [0, 1] range. They will represent the size of the detection box relative to the entire image. This allows detection boxes to be bigger than the grid cell they originate in. The confidence factor, *C*, is also in the [0, 1] range. Finally, a softmax activation is used to predict the class of the detected object. The tanh and sigmoid functions are depicted in Figure 4-6.

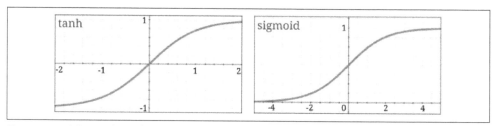

Figure 4-6. The tanh and sigmoid activation functions. Tanh outputs values in the [−1, 1] range, while the sigmoid function outputs them in the [0, 1] range.

An interesting practical question is how to obtain a feature map of exactly the right dimensions. In the example from Figure 4-4, it must contain exactly 7 * 5 * (5 + 7) values. The 7 * 5 is because we chose a 7x5 YOLO grid. Then, for each grid cell, five values are needed to predict a box (*x*, *y*, *w*, *h*, *C*), and seven additional values are needed because, in this example, we want to classify arthropods into seven categories (Coleoptera, Aranea, Hemiptera, Diptera, Lepidoptera, Hymenoptera, Odonata).

If you control the convolutional stack, you could try to tune it to get exactly 7 * 5 * 12 (420) outputs at the end. However, there is an easier way: flatten whatever feature map the convolutional backbone is returning and feed it through a fully connected layer with exactly that number of outputs. You can then reshape the 420 values into a 7x5x12 grid, and apply the appropriate activations as in Figure 4-5. The authors of the YOLO paper argue that the fully connected layer actually adds to the accuracy of the system.

Loss function

In object detection, as in any supervised learning setting, the correct answers are provided in the training data: ground truth boxes and their classes. During training the network predicts detection boxes, and it has to take into account errors in the boxes' locations and dimensions as well as misclassification errors, and also penalize detections of objects where there aren't any. The first step, though, is to correctly pair ground truth boxes with predicted boxes so that they can be compared. In the YOLO architecture, if each grid cell predicts a single box, this is straightforward. A ground truth box and a predicted box are paired if they are centered in the same grid cell (see Figure 4-4 for easier understanding).

However in the YOLO architecture, the number of detection boxes per grid cell is a parameter. It can be more than one. If you look back to Figure 4-5, you can see that it's easy enough for each grid cell to predict 10 or 15 (x, y, w, h, C) coordinates instead of 5 and generate 2 or 3 detection boxes instead of 1. But pairing these predictions with ground truth boxes requires more care. This is done by computing the *intersection over union* (IOU; see Figure 4-7) between all ground truth boxes and all predicted boxes within a grid cell, and selecting the pairings where the IOU is the highest.

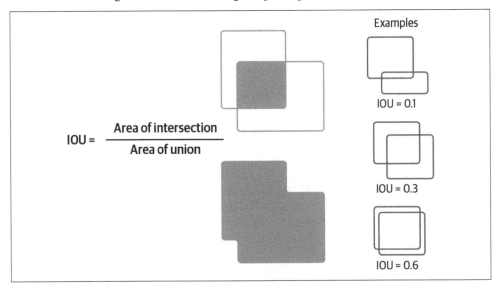

Figure 4-7. The IOU metric.

To summarize, ground truth boxes are assigned to grid cells by their centers and to the prediction boxes within these grid cells by IOU. With the pairings in place, we can now calculate the different parts of the loss:

Object presence loss
    Each grid cell that has a ground truth box computes:

$$L_{obj} = (1 - C)^2$$

Object absence loss
    Each grid cell that does not have a ground truth box computes:

$$L_{noobj} = (0 - C)^2 = C^2$$

Object classification loss
    Each grid cell that has a ground truth box computes:

$$L_{class} = cross\_entropy(p, \widehat{p})$$

where $\widehat{p}$ is the vector of predicted class probabilities and p is the one-hot-encoded target class.

Bounding box loss
    Each predicted box/ground truth box pairing contributes (predicted coordinate marked with a hat, the other coordinate is the ground truth):

$$L_{box} = (x - \widehat{x})^2 + (y - \widehat{y})^2 + (\sqrt{w} - \sqrt{\widehat{w}})^2 + (\sqrt{h} - \sqrt{\widehat{h}})^2$$

Notice here that the difference in box sizes is computed on the square roots of the dimensions. This is to mitigate the effect of large boxes, which tend to overwhelm the loss.

Finally, all the loss contributions from the grid cells are added together, with weighting factors. A common problem in object detection losses is that small losses from numerous cells with no object in them end up overpowering the loss from a lone cell that predicts a useful box. Weighting different parts of the loss can alleviate this problem. The authors of the paper used the following empirical weights:

$$\lambda_{obj} = 1 \quad \lambda_{noobj} = 0.5 \quad \lambda_{class} = 1 \quad \lambda_{box} = 5$$

YOLO limitations

The biggest limitation is that YOLO predicts a single class per grid cell and will not work well if multiple objects of different kinds are present in the same cell.

The second limitation is the grid itself: a fixed grid resolution imposes strong spatial constraints on what the model can do. YOLO models will typically not do well on collections of small objects, like a flock of birds, without careful tuning of the grid to the dataset.

Also, YOLO tends to localize objects with relatively low precision. The main reason for that is that it works on the last feature map from the convolutional stack, which is typically the one with the lowest spatial resolution and contains only coarse location signals.

Despite these limitations, the YOLO architecture is very simple to implement, especially with a single detection box per grid cell, which makes it a good choice when you want to experiment with your own code.

Note that it is not the case that every object is detected by looking at the information in a single grid cell. In a sufficiently deep convolutional neural network (CNN), every value in the last feature map, from which detection boxes are computed, depends on all the pixels of the original image.

If a higher accuracy is needed, you can step up to the next level: RetinaNet. It incorporates a number of ideas that improve upon the basic YOLO architecture, and is regarded, at the time of writing, as the state of the art of so-called *single-shot detectors*.

RetinaNet

RetinaNet (*https://arxiv.org/abs/1708.02002*), as compared to YOLOv1, has several innovations in its architecture and in the design of its losses. The neural network design includes feature pyramid networks which combine information extracted at multiple scales. The detection head predicts boxes starting from *anchor boxes* that change the bounding box representation to make training easier. Finally, the loss innovations include the focal loss, a loss specifically designed for detection problems, a smooth L1 loss for box regression, and non-max suppression. Let's look at each of these in turn.

Feature pyramid networks

When an image is processed by a CNN, the initial convolutional layers pick up low-level details like edges and textures. Further layers combine them into features with more and more semantic value. At the same time, pooling layers in the network reduce the spatial resolution of the feature maps (see Figure 4-8).

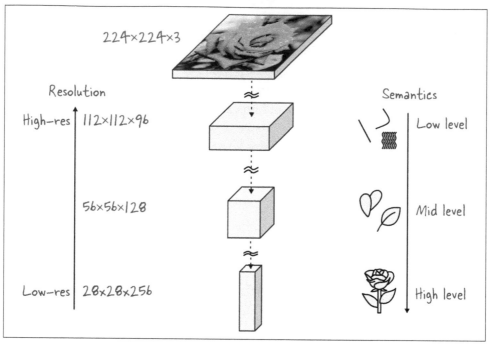

Figure 4-8. Feature maps at various stages of a CNN. As information progresses through the neural network, its spatial resolution decreases but its semantic content increases from low-level details to high-level objects.

The YOLO architecture only uses the last feature map for detection. It is able to correctly identify objects, but its localization accuracy is limited. Another idea would be to try and add a detection head at every stage. Unfortunately, in this approach, the heads working from the early feature maps would localize objects rather well but would have difficulty labeling them. At that early stage, the image has only gone through a couple of convolutional layers, which is not enough to classify it. Higher-level semantic information, like "this is a rose," needs tens of convolutional layers to emerge.

Still, one popular detection architecture, called the single-shot detector (SSD), is based on this idea. The authors of the SSD paper (*https://arxiv.org/abs/1512.02325*) made it work by connecting their multiple detection heads to multiple feature maps, all located toward the end of the convolutional stack.

What if we could combine all feature maps in a way that would surface both good spatial information and good semantic information at all scales? This can be done with a couple of additional layers forming a feature pyramid network (*https://arxiv.org/pdf/1612.03144.pdf*). Figure 4-9 offers a schematic view of an FPN compared to the YOLO and SSD approaches, while Figure 4-10 presents the detailed design.

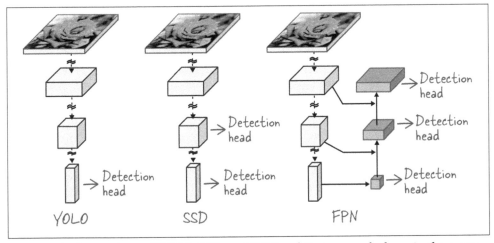

Figure 4-9. Comparison of YOLO, SSD, and FPN architectures and where, in the convolutional stack, they connect their detection head(s).

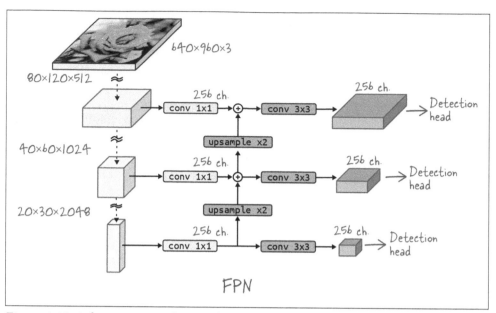

Figure 4-10. A feature pyramid network in detail. Feature maps are extracted from various stages of a convolutional backbone, and 1x1 convolutions squeeze every feature map to the same number of channels. Upsampling (nearest neighbor) then makes their spatial dimensions compatible so that they can be added up. The final 3x3 convolutions smooth out upsampling artifacts. Typically no activation functions are used in the FPN layers.

Here is what is happening in the FPN in Figure 4-10: in the downward path (convolutional backbone), convolutional layers gradually refine the semantic information in the feature maps, while pooling layers scale the feature maps down in their spatial dimensions (the *x* and *y* dimensions of the image). In the upward path, feature maps from the bottom layers containing good high-level semantic information get upsampled (using a simple nearest neighbor algorithm) so that they can be added, elementwise, to feature maps higher up in the stack. 1x1 convolutions are used in the lateral connections to bring all feature maps to the same channel depth and make the additions possible. The FPN paper (*https://arxiv.org/pdf/1612.03144.pdf*), for example, uses 256 channels everywhere. The resulting feature maps now contain semantic information at all scales, which was the initial goal. They are further processed through a 3x3 convolution, mostly to smooth out the effects of the upsampling.

There are typically no nonlinearities in the FPN layers. The authors of the FPN paper found them to have little impact.

A detection head can now take the feature maps at each resolution and produce box detections and classifications. The detection head can itself have multiple designs, which we will cover in the next two sections. It will, however, be shared across all the feature maps at different scales. This is why it was important to bring all the feature maps to the same channel depth.

The nice thing about the FPN design is that it is independent of the underlying convolutional backbone. Any convolutional stack from Chapter 3 will do, as long as you can extract intermediate feature maps from it—typically four to six, at various scales. You can even use a pretrained backbone. Typical choices are ResNet or EfficientNet, and pretrained versions of them can be found in TensorFlow Hub (*https://tfhub.dev/*).

There are multiple levels in a convolutional stack where features can be extracted and fed into the FPN. For each desired scale, many layers output feature maps of the same dimensions (see Figure 3-26 in the previous chapter). The best choice is the last feature map of a given block of layers outputting similarly sized features, just before a pooling layer halves the resolution again. This feature map is likely to contain the strongest semantic features.

It is also possible to extend an existing pretrained backbone with additional pooling and convolutional layers, for the sole purpose of feeding an FPN. These additional feature maps are typically small and therefore fast to process. They correspond to the lowest spatial resolution (see Figure 4-8) and can therefore improve the detection of large objects. The SSD paper (*https://arxiv.org/abs/1512.02325*) actually used this trick, and RetinaNet (*https://arxiv.org/abs/1708.02002*) does as well, as you will see in the architecture diagram later (Figure 4-15).

Anchor boxes

In the YOLO architecture, detection boxes are computed as deltas relative to a set of base boxes ($\Delta x = x - x_0$, $\Delta y = y - y_0$, $\Delta w = w - w_0$, $\Delta h = h - h_0$ are often referred to as "deltas" relative to some base box x_0, y_0, w_0, h_0 because of the Greek letter Δ, usually chosen to represent a "difference"). In that case, the base boxes were a simple grid overlaid on the image (see Figure 4-4).

More recent architectures have expanded on this idea by explicitly defining a set of so-called "anchor boxes" with various aspect ratios and scales (examples in Figure 4-11). Predictions are again small variations of the size and position of the anchors. The goal is to help the neural network predict small values around zero rather than large ones. Indeed, neural networks are able to solve complex nonlinear problems because they use nonlinear activation functions between their layers. However, most activation functions (sigmoid, ReLU) exhibit a nonlinear behavior around zero only. That's why neural networks are at their best when they predict small values around zero, and it's why predicting detections as small deltas relative to anchor boxes is helpful. Of course, this only works if there are enough anchor boxes of various sizes and aspect ratios that any object detection box can be paired (by max IOU) with an anchor box of closely matching position and dimensions.

Figure 4-11. Examples of anchor boxes of various sizes and aspect ratios used to predict detection boxes. Image from Arthropods dataset (https://oreil.ly/sRrvU).

We will describe in detail the approach taken in the RetinaNet architecture, as an example. RetinaNet uses nine different anchor types with:

- Three different aspect ratios: 2:1, 1:1, 1:2
- Three different sizes: 2^0, $2^{1/3}$, $2^{2/3}$ ($\simeq$ 1, 1.3, 1.6)

They are depicted in Figure 4-12.

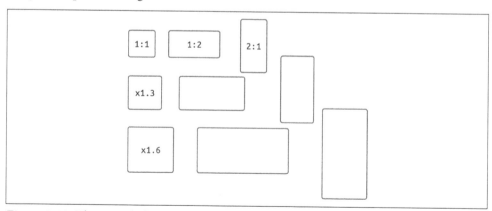

Figure 4-12. The nine different anchor types used in RetinaNet. Three aspect ratios and three different sizes.

Anchors, along with the feature maps computed by an FPN, are the inputs from which detections are computed in RetinaNet. The sequence of operations is as follows:

- The FPN reduces the input image into five feature maps (see Figure 4-10).

- Each feature map is used to predict bounding boxes relative to anchors at regularly spaced locations throughout the image. For example, a feature map of size 4x6 with 256 channels will use 24 (4 * 6) anchor locations in the image (see Figure 4-13).

- The detection head uses multiple convolutional layers to convert the 256-channel feature map into exactly 9 * 4 = 36 channels, yielding 9 detection boxes per location. The four numbers per detection box represent the deltas relative to the center (x, y), the width, and the height of the anchor. The precise sequence of the layers that compute detections from the feature maps is shown in Figure 4-15.

- Finally, each feature map from the FPN, since it corresponds to a different scale in the image, will use different scales of anchor boxes.

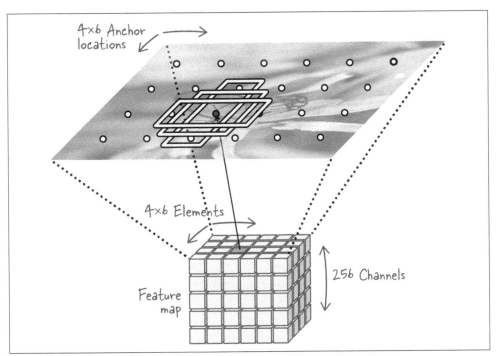

Figure 4-13. Conceptual view of the RetinaNet detection head. Each spatial location in a feature map corresponds to a series of anchors in the image, all centered at the same point. For clarity, only three such anchors are shown in the illustration, but RetinaNet would have nine at every location.

The anchors themselves are spaced regularly across the input image and sized appropriately for each level of the feature pyramid. For example in RetinaNet, the following parameters are used:

- The feature pyramid has five levels corresponding to scales P_3, P_4, P_5, P_6, and P_7 in the backbone. Scale P_n represents a feature map 2^n times smaller in width and height than the input image (see the complete RetinaNet view in Figure 4-15).
- Anchor base sizes are 32x32, 64x64, 128x128, 256x256, 512x512 pixels, at each feature pyramid level respectively ($= 4 * 2^n$, if n is the scale level).
- Anchor boxes are considered for every spatial location of every feature map in the feature pyramid, which means that the boxes are spaced every 8, 16, 32, 64, or 128 pixels across the input image at each feature pyramid level, respectively ($= 2^n$, if n is the scale level).

The smallest anchor box is therefore 32x32 pixels while the largest one is 812x1,624 pixels.

The anchor box settings must be tuned for every dataset so that they correspond to the detection box characteristics actually found in the training data. This is typically done by resizing input images rather than changing the anchor box generation parameters. However, on specific datasets with many small detections, or, on the contrary, mostly large objects, it can be necessary to tune the anchor box generation parameters directly.

The last step is to compute a detection loss. For that, predicted detection boxes must be paired with ground truth boxes so that detection errors can be evaluated.

The assignment of ground truth boxes to anchor boxes is based on the IOU metric computed between each set of boxes in one input image. All pairwise IOUs are computed and are arranged in a matrix with N rows and M columns, N being the number of ground truth boxes and M the number of anchor boxes. The matrix is then analyzed by columns (see Figure 4-14):

- An anchor is assigned to the ground truth box that has the largest IOU in its column, provided it is more than 0.5.
- An anchor box that has no IOU greater than 0.4 in its column is assigned to detect nothing (i.e., the background of the image).
- Any unassigned anchor at this point is marked to be ignored during training. Those are anchors with IOUs in the intermediate regions between 0.4 and 0.5.

Now that every ground truth box is paired with exactly one anchor box, it is possible to compute box predictions, classifications, and the corresponding losses.

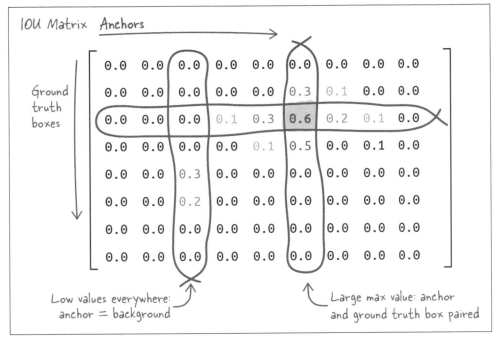

Figure 4-14. The pairwise IOU metric is computed between all ground truth boxes and all anchor boxes to determine their pairings. Anchors without a meaningful intersection with a ground truth box are deemed "background" and trained to detect nothing.

Architecture

The detection and classification heads transform the feature maps from the FPN into class predictions and bounding box deltas. Feature maps are three-dimensional. Two of their dimensions correspond to the x and y dimensions of the image and are called *spatial dimensions*; the third dimension is their number of channels.

In RetinaNet, for every spatial location in every feature map, the following parameters are predicted (with K = the number of classes and B = the number of anchor box types, so in our case $B=9$):

- The class prediction head predicts $B * K$ probabilities, one set of probabilities for every anchor type. This in effect predicts one class for every anchor.
- The detection head predicts $B * 4 = 36$ box deltas Δx, Δy, Δw, Δh. Bounding boxes are still parameterized by their center (x, y) as well as their width and height (w, h).

Both heads share a similar design, although with different weights, and the weights are shared across all scales in the feature pyramid.

Figure 4-15 represents a complete view of the RetinaNet architecture. It uses a ResNet50 (or other) backbone. The FPN extracts features from backbone levels P_3 though P_7, where P_n is the level where the feature map is reduced by a factor of 2^n in its width and height compared to the original image. The FPN part is described in detail in Figure 4-10. Every feature map from the FPN is fed through both a classification and a box regression head.

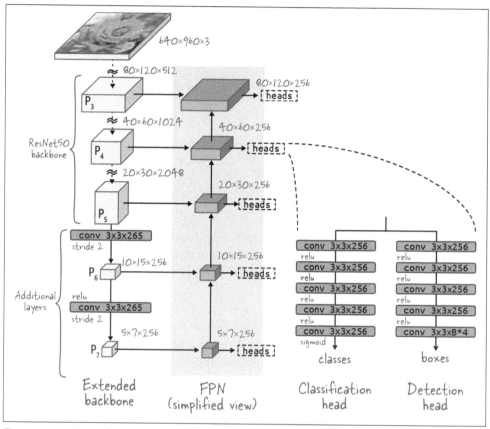

Figure 4-15. Complete view of the RetinaNet architecture. K is the number of target classes. B is the number of anchor boxes at each position, which is nine in RetinaNet.

The RetinaNet FPN taps into the three last scale levels available from the backbone. The backbone is extended with 2 additional layers using a stride of 2 to provide 2 additional scale levels to the FPN. This architectural choice allows RetinaNet to avoid processing very large feature maps, which would be time-consuming. The addition of the last two coarse scale levels also improves the detection of very large objects.

The classification and box regression heads themselves are made from a simple sequence of 3x3 convolutions. The classification head is designed to predict K binary classifications for every anchor, which is why it ends on a sigmoid activation. It looks like we are allowing multiple labels to be predicted for every anchor, but actually the goal is to allow the classification head to output all zeros, which will represent the "background class" corresponding to no detections. A more typical activation for classification would be softmax, but the softmax function cannot output all zeros.

The box regression ends with no activation function. It is computing the differences between the center coordinates (x, y), width, and height of the anchor box and detection box. Some care must be taken to allow the regressor to work in the $[-1, 1]$ range at all levels in the feature pyramid. The following formulas are used to achieve that:

- $X_{pixels} = X \times U \times W_A + X_A$
- $Y_{pixels} = Y \times U \times H_A + Y_A$
- $W_{pixels} = W_A \times e^{W \times V}$
- $H_{pixels} = H_A \times e^{H \times V}$

In these formulas, X_A, Y_A, W_A, and H_A are the coordinates of an anchor box (center coordinates, width, height), while X, Y, W, and H are the predicted coordinates relative to the anchor box (deltas). X_{pixels}, Y_{pixels}, W_{pixels}, and H_{pixels} are the actual coordinates, in pixels, of the predicted box (center and size). U and V are modulating factors that correspond to the expected variance of the deltas relative to the anchor box. Typical values are $U=0.1$ for coordinates, and $V=0.2$ for sizes. You can verify that values in the $[-1, 1]$ range for predictions result in predicted boxes that fall within ±10% of the position of the anchor and within ±20% of its size.

Focal loss (for classification)

How many anchor boxes are considered for one input image? Looking back at Figure 4-15, with an example input image of 640x960 pixels, the five different feature maps in the feature pyramid represent 80 * 120 + 40 * 60 + 20 * 30+ 10 * 15 + 5 * 7 = 12,785 locations in the input image. With 9 anchor boxes per location, that's slightly over 100K anchor boxes.

This means that 100K predicted boxes will be generated for every input image. In comparison, there are 0 to 20 ground truth boxes per image in a typical application. The problem this creates in detection models is that the loss corresponding to background boxes (boxes assigned to detect nothing) can overwhelm the loss corresponding to useful detections in the total loss. This happens even if background detections are already well trained and produce a small loss. This small value multiplied by 100K can still be orders of magnitude larger than the detection loss for actual detections. The end result is a model that cannot be trained.

The RetinaNet paper (*https://arxiv.org/abs/1708.02002*) suggested an elegant solution to this problem: the authors tweaked the loss function to produce much smaller values on empty backgrounds. They call this the *focal loss*. Here are the details.

We have already seen that RetinaNet uses a sigmoid activation to generate class probabilities. The output is a series of binary classifications, one for every class. A probability of 0 for every class means "background"; i.e., nothing to detect here. The classification loss used is the binary cross-entropy. For every class, it is computed from the actual binary class label y (0 or 1) and the predicted probability for the class p using the following formula:

$$CE(y, p) = -y \cdot \log(p) - (1 - y) \cdot \log(1 - p)$$

The focal loss is the same formula with a small modification:

$$FL(y, p) = -y \cdot (1 - p)^{\gamma} \cdot \log(p) - (1 - y) \cdot p^{\gamma} \cdot \log(1 - p)$$

For $y=0$ this is exactly the binary cross-entropy, but for higher values of γ the behavior is slightly different. To simplify, let's only consider the case of background boxes that do not belong to any class (i.e., where $y=0$ for all classes):

$$FL_{bkg}(p) = -p^{\gamma} \cdot \log(1 - p)$$

And let's plot the values of the focal loss for various values of p and γ (Figure 4-16).

As you can see in the figure, with $\gamma=2$, which was found to be an adequate value, the focal loss is much smaller than the regular cross-entropy loss, especially for small values of p. For background boxes, where there is nothing to detect, the network will quickly learn to produce small class probabilities p across all classes. With the cross-entropy loss, these boxes, even well classified as "background" with $p=0.1$ for example, would still be contributing a significant amount: $CE(0.1) = 0.05$. The focal loss is 100 times less: $FL(0.1) = 0.0005$.

With the focal loss, it becomes possible to add the losses from all anchor boxes—all 100K of them—and not worry about the total loss being overwhelmed by thousands of small losses from easy-to-classify background boxes.

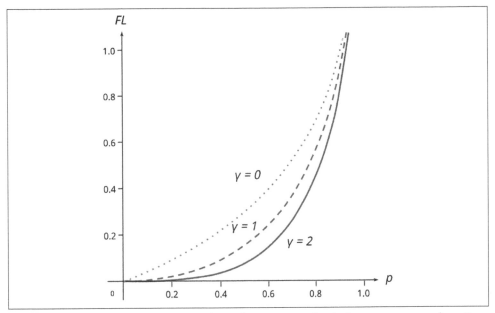

Figure 4-16. Focal loss for various values of γ. For γ=0, this is the cross-entropy loss. For higher values of γ, the focal loss greatly de-emphasizes easy-to-classify background regions where p is close to 0 for every class.

Smooth L1 loss (for box regression)

Detection boxes are computed by a regression. For regressions, the two most common losses are L1 and L2, also called *absolute loss* and *squared loss*. Their formulas are (computed between a target value a and the predicted value $\hat{a}$):

$$L1(a, \hat{a}) = |a - \hat{a}|$$
$$L2(a, \hat{a}) = (a - \hat{a})^2$$

The problem with the L1 loss is that its gradient is the same everywhere, which is not great for learning. The L2 loss is therefore preferred for regressions—but it suffers from a different problem. In the L2 loss, differences between the predicted and target values are squared, which means that the loss tends to get very large as the prediction and the target grow apart. This becomes problematic if you have some outliers, like a couple of bad points in the data (for example, a target box with the wrong size). The result will be that the network will try to fit the bad data point at the expense of everything else, which is not good either.

A good compromise between the two is the *Huber loss*, or *smooth L1 loss* (see Figure 4-17). It behaves like the L2 loss for small values and like the L1 loss for large values. Close to zero, it has the nice property that its gradient is larger when the differences are larger, and therefore it pushes the network to learn more where it is making the biggest mistakes. For large values, it becomes linear instead of quadratic and avoids being thrown off by a couple of bad target values. Its formula is:

$$L_\delta(a - \hat{a}) = \frac{1}{2}(a - \hat{a})^2 \ \text{for} |a - \hat{a}| \leq \delta$$

$$L_\delta = \delta\left(\left|a - \hat{a}\right| - \frac{1}{2}\delta\right) \quad \text{otherwise}$$

Where δ is an adjustable parameter. δ is the value around which the behavior switches from quadratic to linear. Another formula can be used to avoid the piecewise definition:

$$L_\delta(a - \hat{a}) = \delta^2\left(\sqrt{1 + \left(\frac{a - \hat{a}}{\delta}\right)^2} - 1\right)$$

This alternate form does not give the exact same values as the standard Huber loss, but it has the same behavior: quadratic for small values, linear for large ones. In practice, either form will work well in RetinaNet, with $\delta=1$.

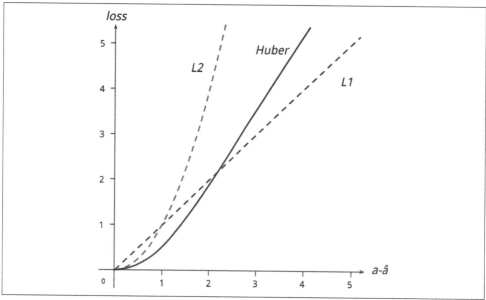

Figure 4-17. L1, L2, and Huber losses for regression. The desirable behaviors are quadratic for small values and linear for large ones. The Huber loss has both.

Non-maximum suppression

A detection network using numerous anchor boxes, such as RetinaNet, usually produces multiple candidate detections for every target box. We need an algorithm to select a single detection box for every detected object.

Non-maximum suppression (NMS) takes box overlap (IOU) and class confidence into account to select the most representative box for a given object (Figure 4-18).

Figure 4-18. On the left: multiple detections for the same object. On the right: a single box remaining after non-max suppression. Image from Arthropods dataset (https:// oreil.ly/sRrvU).

The algorithm uses a simple "greedy" approach: for every class, it considers the overlap (IOU) between all the predicted boxes. If two boxes overlap more than a given value A (IOU > A), it keeps the one with the highest class confidence. In Python-like pseudocode, for one given class:

```
def NMS(boxes, class_confidence):
    result_boxes = []
    for b1 in boxes:
        discard = False
        for b2 in boxes:
            if IOU(b1, b2) > A:
                if class_confidence[b2] > class_confidence[b1]:
                    discard = True
        if not discard:
            result_boxes.append(b1)
    return result_boxes
```

NMS works quite well in practice but it can have some unwanted side effects. Notice that the algorithm relies on a single threshold value (A). Changing this value changes the box filtering, especially for adjacent or overlapping objects in the original image. Take a look at the example in Figure 4-19. If the threshold is set at A=0.4, then the two boxes detected in the figure will be regarded as "overlapping" for the same class and the one with the lowest class confidence (the one on the left) will be discarded. That is obviously wrong. There are two butterflies to detect in this image and, before NMS, both were detected with a high confidence.

Figure 4-19. Objects close to each other create a problem for the non-max suppression algorithm. If the NMS threshold is 0.4, the box detected on the left will be discarded, which is wrong. Image from Arthropods dataset (https://oreil.ly/sRrvU).

Pushing the threshold value higher will help, but if it's too high the algorithm will fail to merge boxes that correspond to the same object. The usual value for this threshold is A=0.5, but it still causes objects that are close together to be detected as one.

A slight variation on the basic NMS algorithm is called *Soft-NMS* (*https://arxiv.org/abs/1704.04503*). Instead of removing non-maximum overlapping boxes altogether, it lowers their confidence score by the factor:

$$exp\left(-\frac{IOU^2}{\sigma}\right)$$

with σ being an adjustment factor that tunes the strength of the Soft-NMS algorithm. A typical value is σ=0.5. The algorithm is applied by considering the box with the highest confidence score for a given class (the *max box*), and decreasing the scores for all other boxes by this factor. The max box is then put aside and the operation is repeated on the remaining boxes until none remain.

For nonoverlapping boxes (IOU=0), this factor is 1. The confidence factors of boxes that do not overlap the max box are thus not affected. The factor gradually, but continuously, decreases as boxes overlap more with the max box. Highly overlapping boxes (IOU=0.9) get their confidence factor decreased by a lot (×0.2), which is the expected behavior because they are redundant with the max box and we want to get rid of them.

Since the Soft-NMS algorithm does not discard any boxes, a second threshold, based on the class confidence, is used to actually prune the list of detections.

The effect of Soft-NMS on the example from Figure 4-19 is shown in Figure 4-20.

Figure 4-20. Objects close to each other as handled by Soft-NMS. The detection box on the left is not deleted, but its confidence factor is reduced from 78% to 55%. Image from Arthropods dataset (https://oreil.ly/sRrvU).

 In TensorFlow, both styles of non-max suppression are available. Standard NMS is called `tf.image.non_max_suppression`, while Soft-NMS is called `tf.image.non_max_suppression_with_scores`.

Other considerations

In order to reduce the amount of data needed, it is customary to use a pretrained backbone.

Classification datasets are much easier to put together than object detection datasets. That's why readily available classification datasets are typically much larger than object detection datasets. Using a pretrained backbone from a classifier allows you to combine a generic large classification dataset with a task-specific object detection dataset and obtain a better object detector.

The pretraining is done on a classification task. Then the classification head is removed and the FPN and detection heads are added, initialized at random. The actual object detection training is performed with all weights trainable, which means that the backbone will be fine-tuned while the FPN and detection head train from scratch.

Since detection datasets tend to be smaller, data augmentation (which we will cover in more detail in Chapter 6) plays an important part in training. The basic data augmentation technique is to cut fixed-sized crops out of the training images at random, and at random zoom factors (see Figure 4-21). With target bounding boxes adjusted appropriately, this allows you to train the network with the same object at different locations in the image, at different scales and with different parts of the background visible.

Figure 4-21. Data augmentation for detection training. Fixed-size images are cut at random from each training image, potentially at different zoom factors. Target box coordinates are recomputed relative to the new boundaries. This provides more training images and more object locations from the same initial training data. Image from Arthropods dataset (https://oreil.ly/sRrvU).

A practical advantage of this technique is that it also provides fixed-sized training images to the neural network. You can train directly on a training dataset made up of images of different sizes and aspect ratios. The data augmentation takes care of getting all the images to the same size.

Finally, what drives training and hyperparameter tuning are metrics. Object detection problems have been the subject of multiple large-scale contests where detection metrics have been carefully standardized; this topic is covered in detail in "Metrics for Object Detection" on page 299 in Chapter 8.

Now that we have looked at object detection, let's turn our attention to another class of problems: image segmentation.

Segmentation

Object detection finds bounding boxes around objects and classifies them. *Instance segmentation* adds, for every detected object, a pixel mask that gives the shape of the object. *Semantic segmentation*, on the other hand, does not detect specific instances of objects but classifies every pixel of the image into a category like "road," "sky," or "people."

Mask R-CNN and Instance Segmentation

YOLO and RetinaNet, which we covered in the previous section, are examples of single-shot detectors. An image traverses them only once to produce detections. Another approach is to use a first neural network to suggest potential locations for objects to be detected, then use a second network to classify and fine-tune the locations of these proposals. These architectures are called *region proposal networks* (RPNs).

They tend to be more complex and therefore slower than single-shot detectors, but are also more accurate. There is a long list of RPN variants, all based on the original "regions with CNN features" idea: R-CNN (*https://arxiv.org/abs/1311.2524*), Fast R-CNN (*https://arxiv.org/abs/1504.08083*), Faster R-CNN (*https://arxiv.org/abs/1506.01497*), and more. The state of the art, at the time of writing, is Mask R-CNN (*https://arxiv.org/abs/1703.06870*), and that's the architecture we are going to dive into next.

The main reason why it is important to be aware of architectures like Mask R-CNN is not their marginally superior accuracy, but the fact that they can be extended to perform instance segmentation tasks. In addition to predicting a bounding box around detected objects, they can be trained to predict their outline—i.e., find every pixel belonging to each detected object (Figure 4-22). Of course, training them remains a supervised training task and the training data will have to contain ground truth segmentation masks for all objects. Unfortunately, masks are more time-consuming to generate by hand than bounding boxes and therefore instance segmentation datasets are harder to find than simple object detection datasets.

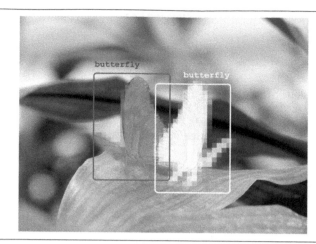

Figure 4-22. Instance segmentation involves detecting objects and finding all the pixels that belong to each object. The objects in the images are shaded with a pixel mask. Image from Arthropods dataset (https://oreil.ly/sRrvU).

Let's look at RPNs in detail, first analyzing how they perform classic object detection, then how to extend them for instance segmentation.

Region proposal networks

An RPN is a simplified single-shot detection network that only cares about two classes: objects and background. An "object" is anything labeled as such in the dataset (any class), and "background" is the designated class for a box that does not contain an object.

An RPN can use an architecture similar to the RetinaNet setup we looked at earlier: a convolutional backbone, a feature pyramid network, a set of anchor boxes, and two heads. One head is for predicting boxes and the other is for classifying them as object or background (we are not predicting segmentation masks yet).

The RPN has its own loss function, computed from a slightly modified training dataset: the class of any ground truth object is replaced with a single class "object." The loss function used for boxes is, as in RetinaNet, the Huber loss. For classes, since this is a binary classification, binary cross-entropy is the best choice.

Boxes predicted by the RPN then undergo non-max suppression. The top N boxes, sorted by their probability of being an "object," are regarded as box proposals or *regions of interest* (ROIs) for the next stage. N is usually around one thousand, but if fast inference is important, it can be as little as 50. ROIs can also be filtered by a minimal "object" score or a minimal size. In the TensorFlow Model Garden implementation, these thresholds are available even if they are set to zero by default. Bad ROIs can still be classified as "background" and rejected by the next stage, so letting them through at the RPN level is not a big problem.

One important practical consideration is that the RPN can be simple and fast if needed (see the example in Figure 4-23). It can use the output of the backbone directly, instead of using an FPN, and its classification and detection heads can use fewer convolutional layers. The goal is only to compute approximate ROIs around likely objects. They will be refined and classified in the next step.

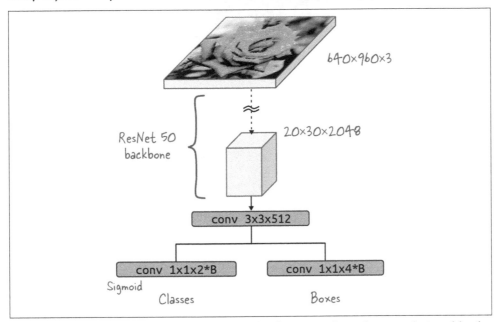

Figure 4-23. A simple region proposal network. The output from the convolutional backbone is fed through a two-class classification head (object or background) and a box regression head. B is the number of anchor boxes per location (typically three). An FPN can be used as well.

For example, the Mask R-CNN implementation in the TensorFlow Model Garden uses an FPN in its RPN but uses only three anchors per location, with aspect ratios of 0.5, 1.0, and 2.0, instead of the nine anchors per location used by RetinaNet.

R-CNN

We now have a set of proposed regions of interest. What next?

Conceptually, the R-CNN idea (Figure 4-24) is to crop the images along the ROIs and run the cropped images through the backbone again, this time with a full classification head attached to classify the objects (in our example, into "butterfly," "spider," etc.).

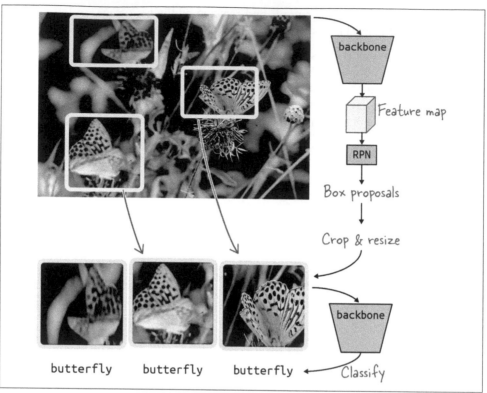

Figure 4-24. Conceptual view of an R-CNN. Images go through the backbone twice: the first time to generate regions of interest and the second time to classify the contents of these ROIs. Image from Arthropods dataset (https://oreil.ly/sRrvU).

In practice, however, this is too slow. The RPN can generate somewhere in the region of 50 to 2,000 proposed ROIs, and running them all through the backbone again would be a lot of work. Instead of cropping the image, the smarter thing to do is to crop the feature map directly, then run prediction heads on the result, as depicted in Figure 4-25.

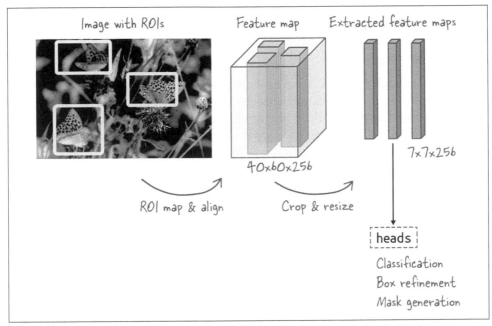

Image with ROIs   Feature map   Extracted feature maps

7×7×256

40×60×256

ROI map & align   Crop & resize

heads

Classification
Box refinement
Mask generation

Figure 4-25. A faster R-CNN or Mask R-CNN design. As previously, the backbone gener-
ates a feature map and the RPN predicts regions of interest from it (only the result is
shown). Then the ROIs are mapped back onto the feature map, and features are extrac-
ted and sent to the prediction heads for classification and more. Image from Arthropods
dataset (https://oreil.ly/sRrvU).

This is slightly more complex when an FPN is used. The feature extraction is still performed on a given feature map, but in a FPN there are several feature maps to choose
from. A ROI therefore must first be assigned to the most relevant FPN level. The
assignment is usually done using this formula:

$$n = floor\left(n_0 + log_2\left(\sqrt{wh}/224\right)\right)$$

where w and h are the width and height of the ROI, and n_0 is the FPN level where
typical anchor box sizes are closest to 224. Here, *floor* stands for rounding down to
the most negative number. For example, here are the typical Mask R-CNN settings:

- Five FPN levels, P_2, P_3, P_4, P_5, and P_6 (reminder: level P_n represents a feature map
  2^n times smaller in width and height than the input image)
- Anchor box sizes of 32x32, 64x64, 128x128, 256x256, and 512x512 on their
  respective levels (same as in RetinaNet)
- $n_0 = 4$

With these settings, we can verify that (for example) an ROI of 80x160 pixels would get assigned to level P_3 and an ROI of 200x300 to level P_4, which makes sense.

ROI resampling (ROI alignment)

Special care is needed when extracting the feature maps corresponding to the ROIs. The feature maps must be extracted and resampled correctly. The Mask R-CNN paper's authors discovered that any rounding error made during this process adversely affects detection performance. They called their precise resampling method *ROI alignment*.

For example, let's take an ROI of 200x300 pixels. It would be assigned to FPN level P_4, where its size relative to the P_4 feature map becomes (200 / 2^4, 300 / 2^4) = (12.5, 18.75). These coordinates should not be rounded. The same applies to its position.

The features contained in this 12.5x18.75 region of the P_4 feature map must then be sampled and aggregated (using either max pooling or average pooling) into a new feature map, typically of size 7x7. This is a well-known mathematical operation called *bilinear interpolation,* and we won't dwell on it here. The important point to remember is that cutting corners here degrades performance.

Class and bounding box predictions

The rest of the model is pretty standard. The extracted features go through multiple prediction heads in parallel—in this case:

- A classification head to assign a class to each object suggested by the RPN, or classify it as background
- A box refinement head that further adjusts the bounding box

To compute detection and classification losses, the same target box assignment algorithm is used as in RetinaNet, described in the previous section. The box loss is also the same (Huber loss). The classification head uses a softmax activation with a special class added for "background." In RetinaNet it was a series of binary classifications. Both work, and this implementation detail is not important. The total training loss is the sum of the final box and classification losses as well as the box and classification losses from the RPN.

The exact design of the class and detection heads is given later, in Figure 4-30. They are also very similar to what was used in RetinaNet: a straight sequence of layers, shared between all levels of the FPN.

Mask R-CNN adds a third prediction head for classifying individual pixels of objects. The result is a pixel mask depicting the silhouette of the object (see Figure 4-19). It can be used if the training dataset contains corresponding target masks. Before we explain how it works, however, we need to introduce a new kind of convolution, one

---

capable of creating pictures rather than filtering and distilling them: transposed convolutions.

Transposed convolutions

Transposed convolutions, sometimes also called *deconvolutions*, perform a learnable upsampling operation. Regular upsampling algorithms like nearest neighbor upsampling or bilinear interpolation are fixed operations. Transposed convolutions, on the other hand, involve learnable weights.

The name "transposed convolution" comes from the fact that in the matrix representation of a convolutional layer, which we are not covering in this book, the transposed convolution is performed using the same convolutional matrix as an ordinary convolution, but transposed.

The transposed convolution pictured in Figure 4-26 has a single input and a single output channel. The best way to understand what it does is to imagine that it is painting with a brush on an output canvas. The brush is a 3x3 filter. Every value of the input image is projected through the filter on the output. Mathematically, every element of the 3x3 filter is multiplied by the input value and the result is added to whatever is already on the output canvas. The operation is then repeated at the next position: in the input we move by 1, and in the output we move with a configurable stride (2 in this example). Any stride larger than 1 results in an upsampling operation. The most frequent settings are stride 2 with a 2x2 filter or stride 3 with a 3x3 filter.

If the input is a feature map with multiple channels, the same operation is applied to each channel independently, with a new filter each time; then all the outputs are added element by element, resulting in a single output channel.

It is of course possible to repeat this operation multiple times on the same feature map, with a new set of filters each time, which results in a feature map with multiple channels.

In the end, for a multichannel input and a multichannel output, the weights matrix of a transposed convolution will have the shape shown in Figure 4-27. This is, by the way, the same shape as a regular convolutional layer.

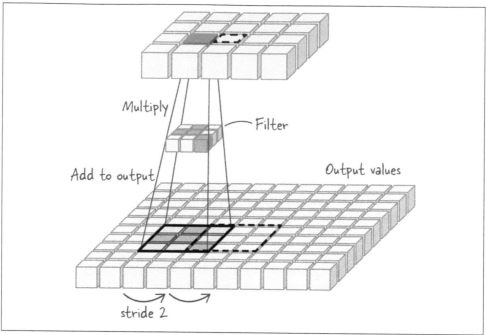

Figure 4-26. Transposed convolution. Each pixel of the original image (top) multiplies a 3x3 filter, and the result is added to the output. In a transposed convolution of stride 2, the output window moves by a step of 2 for every input pixel, creating a larger image (shifted output window pictured with a dashed outline).

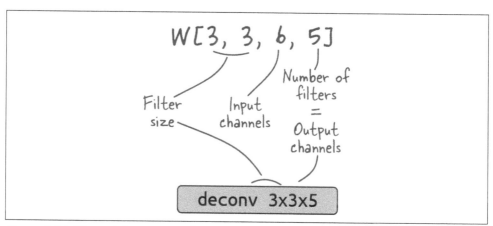

Figure 4-27. The weights matrix of a transposed convolutional layer, sometimes also called a "deconvolution." At the bottom is the schematic notation of deconvolutional layers that will be used for the models in this chapter.

Up-Convolution

Transposed convolutions are widely used in neural networks that generate images: autoencoders, generative adversarial networks (GANs), and so on. However, they have also been criticized for introducing "checkerboard" artifacts into the generated images (Odena et al., 2016 (*https://oreil.ly/39Dud*)), especially when their stride and filter size are not multiples of each other (Figure 4-28).

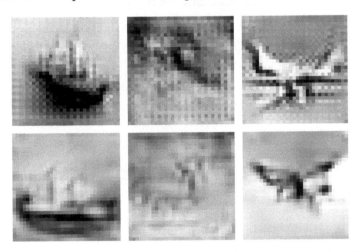

Figure 4-28. Transposed convolutions versus up-convolutions when used in a GAN. When transposed convolutions are used, an unwanted checkerboard pattern can appear (top row). This does not happen with up-convolutions. Image from Odena et al., 2016 (https://oreil.ly/39Dud).

Odena et al. suggest using a simple nearest neighbour resampling followed by a regular convolution, a combination called "up-convolution" (Figure 4-29), instead of transposed convolutions. Interestingly, as you may recall from "Feature pyramid networks" on page 139, this is exactly how upsampling was handled there.

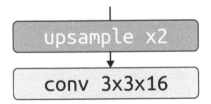

Figure 4-29. This is also a learnable upsampling operation. An "up-convolution" is a simple nearest neighbor upsampling operation followed by an ordinary convolutional layer.

Instance segmentation

Let's get back to Mask R-CNN, and its third prediction head that classifies individual pixels of objects. The output is a pixel mask outlining the silhouette of the object (see Figure 4-22).

Mask R-CNN and other RPNs work on a single ROI at a time, with a fairly high probability that this ROI is actually interesting, so they can do more work per ROI and with a higher precision. Instance segmentation is one such task.

The instance segmentation head uses transposed convolution layers to upsample the feature map into a black-and-white image that is trained to match the silhouette of the detected object.

Figure 4-30 shows the complete Mask R-CNN architecture.

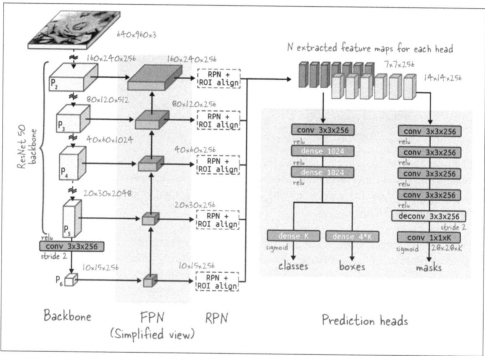

Figure 4-30. The Mask R-CNN architecture. N is the number of ROIs proposed by the RPN, and K is the number of classes; "deconv" denotes a transposed convolutional layer, which upsamples the feature maps to predict an object mask.

Notice that the mask head produces one mask per class. This seems to be redundant since there is a separate classification head. Why predict K masks for one object? In reality, this design choice increases the segmentation accuracy because it allows the segmentation head to learn class-specific hints about objects.

Another implementation detail is that the resampling and alignment of the feature maps to the ROIs is actually performed twice: once with a 7x7x256 output for the classification and detection head, and again with different settings (resampling to 14x14x256) specifically for the mask head to give it more detail to work with.

The segmentation loss is a simple pixel-by-pixel binary cross-entropy loss, applied once the predicted mask has been rescaled and upsampled to the same coordinates as the ground truth mask. Note that only the mask predicted for the predicted class is taken into account in the loss calculation. Other masks computed for the wrong classes are ignored.

We now have a complete picture of how Mask R-CNN works. One thing to notice is that with all the improvements added to the R-CNN family of detectors, Mask R-CNN is now a "two-pass" detector in name only. The input image effectively goes through the system only once. The architecture is still slower than RetinaNet but achieves a slightly higher detection accuracy and adds instance segmentation.

An extension of RetinaNet with an added mask head exists (RetinaMask (*https://arxiv.org/abs/1901.03353*)), but it does not outperform Mask R-CNN. Interestingly, the paper notes that adding the mask head and associated loss actually improves the accuracy of bounding box detections (the other head). A similar effect might explain some of the improved accuracy of Mask R-CNN too.

One limitation of the Mask R-CNN approach is that the predicted object masks are fairly low resolution: 28x28 pixels. The similar but not exactly equivalent problem of semantic segmentation has been solved with high-resolution approaches. We'll explore this in the next section.

U-Net and Semantic Segmentation

In semantic segmentation, the goal is to classify every pixel of the image into global classes like "road," "sky," "vegetation," or "people" (see Figure 4-31). Individual instances of objects, like individual people, are not separated. All "people" pixels across the entire image are part of the same "segment."

Figure 4-31. In semantic image segmentation, every pixel in the image is assigned a category (like "road," "sky," "vegetation," or "building"). Notice that "people," for example, is a single class across the whole image. Objects are not individualized. Image from Cityscapes (https://www.cityscapes-dataset.com).

For semantic image segmentation, a simple and quite often sufficient approach is called U-Net (*https://oreil.ly/yrwBW*). The U-Net is a convolutional network architecture that was designed for biomedical image segmentation (see Figure 4-32) and won a cell tracking competition in 2015.

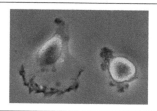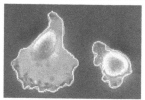

Figure 4-32. The U-Net architecture was designed to segment biomedical images such as these microscopy cell images. Images from Ronneberger et al., 2015 (https://oreil.ly/yrwBW).

The U-Net architecture is represented in Figure 4-33. A U-Net consists of an encoder which downsamples an image to an encoding (the lefthand side of architecture), and a mirrored decoder which upsamples the encoding back to the desired mask (the righthand side of the architecture). The decoder blocks have a number of skip connections (depicted by the horizontal arrows in the center) that directly connect from the encoder blocks. These skip connections copy features at a specific resolution and concatenate them channel-wise with specific feature maps in the decoder. This brings information at various levels of semantic granularity from the encoder directly into the decoder. (Note: cropping may be necessary on the skip connections because of slight size misalignments of the feature maps in corresponding levels of the encoder and decoder. Indeed, U-Net uses all convolutions without padding, which means that border pixels are lost at each layer. This design choice is not fundamental though, and padding can be used as well.)

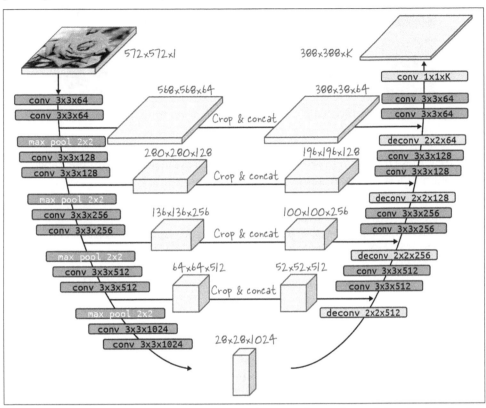

Figure 4-33. The U-Net architecture consists of mirrored encoder and decoder blocks that take on a U shape when depicted as shown here. Skip connections concatenate feature maps along the depth axis (channels). K is the target number of classes.

Images and labels

To illustrate U-Net image segmentation we'll use the Oxford Pets dataset (*https:// oreil.ly/GNyKx*), where each of the input images contains a label mask as shown in Figure 4-34. The label is an image in which pixels are assigned one of three integer values depending on whether they are background, the object outline, or the object interior.

Figure 4-34. Training images (top row) and labels (bottom row) from the Oxford Pets dataset.

We'll treat these three pixel values as the index of class labels and train the network to carry out multiclass classification:

```
model = ...
model.compile(optimizer='adam',
    loss=tf.keras.losses.SparseCategoricalCrossentropy(from_logits=True),
    metrics=['accuracy'])
model.fit(...)
```

The complete code is available in *04b_unet_segmentation.ipynb* on GitHub.

Architecture

Training a U-Net architecture from scratch requires a lot of trainable parameters. As discussed in "Other considerations" on page 155 it's difficult to label datasets for tasks such as object detection and segmentation. Therefore, to use the labeled data efficiently, it is better to use a pretrained backbone and employ transfer learning for the encoder block. As in Chapter 3, we can use a pretrained MobileNetV2 to create the encoding:

```
base_model = tf.keras.applications.MobileNetV2(
    input_shape=[128, 128, 3], include_top=False)
```

The decoder side will consist of upsampling layers to get back to the desired mask shape. The decoder also needs feature maps from specific layers of the encoder (skip connections). The layers of the MobileNetV2 model that we need can be obtained by name as follows:

```
layer_names = [
    'block_1_expand_relu',     # 64x64
    'block_3_expand_relu',     # 32x32
    'block_6_expand_relu',     # 16x16
    'block_13_expand_relu',    # 8x8
    'block_16_project',        # 4x4
]
base_model_outputs = [base_model.get_layer(name).output for name in layer_names]
```

The "down stack" or lefthand side of the U-Net architecture then consists of the image as input, and these layers as outputs. We are carrying out transfer learning, so the entire lefthand side does not need weight adjustments:

```
down_stack = tf.keras.Model(inputs=base_model.input,
                            outputs=base_model_outputs,
                            name='pretrained_mobilenet')
down_stack.trainable = False
```

Upsampling in Keras can be accomplished using a `Conv2DTranspose` layer. We also add batch normalization and nonlinearity to each step of the upsampling:

```
def upsample(filters, size, name):
  return tf.keras.Sequential([
     tf.keras.layers.Conv2DTranspose(filters, size,
                                     strides=2, padding='same'),
     tf.keras.layers.BatchNormalization(),
     tf.keras.layers.ReLU()
  ], name=name)

up_stack = [
    upsample(512, 3, 'upsample_4x4_to_8x8'),
    upsample(256, 3, 'upsample_8x8_to_16x16'),
    upsample(128, 3, 'upsample_16x16_to_32x32'),
    upsample(64, 3,  'upsample_32x32_to_64x64')
]
```

Each stage of the decoder up stack is concatenated with the corresponding layer of the encoder down stack:

```
for up, skip in zip(up_stack, skips):
    x = up(x)
    concat = tf.keras.layers.Concatenate()
    x = concat([x, skip])
```

Training

We can display the predictions on a few selected images using a Keras callback:

```
class DisplayCallback(tf.keras.callbacks.Callback):
  def on_epoch_end(self, epoch, logs=None):
     show_predictions(train_dataset, 1)

model.fit(train_dataset, ...,
          callbacks=[DisplayCallback()])
```

The result of doing so on the Oxford Pets dataset is shown in Figure 4-35. Note that the model starts out with garbage (top row), as one would expect, but then learns which pixels correspond to the animal and which pixels correspond to the background.

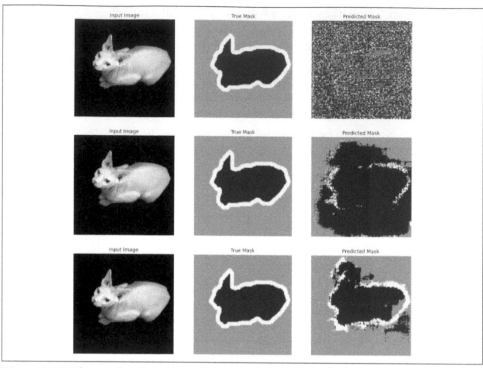

Figure 4-35. The predicted mask on the input image improves epoch by epoch as the model is trained.

However, because the model is trained to predict each pixel as background, outline, or interior independently of the other pixels, we see artifacts such as unclosed regions and disconnected pixels. The model doesn't realize that the region corresponding to the cat should be closed. That is why this approach is mostly used on images where the segments to be detected do not need to be contiguous, like the example in Figure 4-31, where the "road," "sky," and "vegetation" segments often have discontinuities.

An example of an application is in self-driving algorithms, to detect the road. Another is in satellite imagery, where a U-Net architecture was used to solve the hard problem of distinguishing clouds from snow; both are white, but snow coverage is useful ground-level information, whereas cloud obstruction means that the image needs to be retaken.

Summary

In this chapter, we looked at object detection and image segmentation methods. We started with YOLO, considering its limitations, and then discussed RetinaNet, which innovates over YOLO in terms of both the architecture and the losses used. We also discussed Mask R-CNN to carry out instance segmentation and U-Net to carry out semantic segmentation.

In the next chapters, we will delve more deeply into different parts of the computer vision pipeline using the simple transfer learning image classification architecture from Chapter 3 as our core model. The pipeline steps remain the same regardless of the backbone architecture or the problem being solved.

## CHAPTER 5

Creating Vision Datasets

To carry out machine learning on images, we need images. Of the use cases we looked at in Chapter 4, the vast majority were for supervised machine learning. For such models, we also need the correct answer, or *label*, to train the ML model. If you are going to train an unsupervised ML model or a self-supervised model like a GAN or autoencoder, you can leave out the labels. In this chapter, we will look at how to create a machine learning dataset consisting of images and labels.

 The code for this chapter is in the *05_create_dataset* folder of the book's GitHub repository (*https://github.com/GoogleCloudPlatform/ practical-ml-vision-book*). We will provide file names for code samples and notebooks where applicable.

Collecting Images

In most ML projects, the first stage is to collect the data. The data collection might be done in any number of ways: by mounting a camera at a traffic intersection, connecting to a digital catalog to obtain photographs of auto parts, purchasing an archive of satellite imagery, etc. It can be a logistical activity (mounting traffic cameras), a technical activity (building a software connector to the catalog database), or a commercial one (purchasing an image archive).

Photographs

Photographs are one of the most common sources of image data. These can include photographs taken from social media and other sources, and photographs taken under controlled conditions by permanently mounted cameras.

One of the first choices we need to make when collecting images is the placement of the camera and the size and resolution of the image. Obviously, the image has to frame whatever it is that we are interested in—for example, a camera mounted to photograph a traffic intersection would need to have an unobstructed view of the entire intersection.

Intuitively, it might seem that we will get the highest-accuracy models by training them on the highest-resolution images, and so we should endeavor to collect data at the highest resolution we can. However, high image resolutions come with several drawbacks:

- Larger images will require larger models—the number of weights in every layer of a convolutional model scales proportionally to the size of the input image. We'll need four times the number of parameters to train a model on 256x256 images than on 128x128 images, so training will take longer and will require more computational capacity and additional memory.

- The machines that we train ML models on have limited memory (RAM), so the larger the image size, the fewer images we can have in a batch. In general, larger batch sizes lead to smoother training curves. So, large images may be counterproductive in terms of accuracy.

- Higher-resolution images, especially those taken in outdoor and low-light environments, may have more noise. Smoothing the images down to a lower resolution might lead to faster training and higher accuracy.

- Collecting and saving a high-resolution image takes longer than collecting and saving a lower-resolution one. Therefore, to capture high-speed action, it might be necessary to use a lower resolution.

- Higher-resolution images take longer to transmit. So, if you are collecting images on the edge[1] and sending them to the cloud for inference, you can do faster inference by using smaller, lower-resolution images.

The recommendation, therefore, is to use the highest resolution that is warranted by the noise characteristics of your images and that your machine learning infrastructure budget can handle. Do not lower the resolution so much that the objects of interest cannot be resolved.

In general, it is worth using the highest-quality camera (in terms of lens, sensitivity, and so on) that your budget will allow—many computer vision problems are simplified if the images used during prediction will always be in focus, if the white balance will be consistent, and if the effect of noise on the images is minimal. Some of these problems can be rectified using image preprocessing (image preprocessing techniques will be covered in Chapter 6). Still, it is better to have images without these issues than to collect data and have to correct them after the fact.

Cameras can typically save photographs in a compressed (e.g., JPEG) or uncompressed (e.g., RAW) format. When saving JPEG photographs, we can often choose the quality. Lower-quality and lower-resolution JPEG files compress better, and so incur lower storage costs. As described previously, lower-resolution images will also reduce compute costs. Because storage is inexpensive relative to compute, our recommendation is to choose a high-quality threshold for the JPEGs (95%+) and store them at a lower resolution.

 The lowest resolution you can use depends on the problem. If you are trying to classify landscape photographs to determine whether they are of water or land, you might be able to get away with 12x16 images. If your aim is to identify the type of trees in those landscape photographs, you might need the pixels to be small enough to clearly pick up on the shapes of leaves, so you might need 768x1024 images.

---

1 This is common in Internet of Things (IoT) applications; see the Wikipedia entry on "Fog computing" (*https://oreil.ly/Txyj8*).

Use uncompressed images only if your images consist of human-generated content such as CAD drawings where the fuzzy edges of the JPEG compression might cause issues with recognition.

Imaging

Many instruments (X-rays, MRIs, spectroscopes, radars, lidars, and so on) create 2D or 3D images of a space. X-rays are projections of a 3D object and may be treated as grayscale images (see Figure 5-1). While typical photographs contain three (red, green, blue) channels, these images have only one channel.

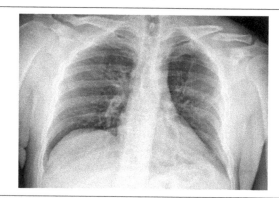

Figure 5-1. A chest X-ray can be treated as a grayscale image. Image courtesy of Google AI Blog (https://oreil.ly/RoyB0).

If the instrument measures multiple quantities, we can treat the reflectance at different wavelengths, Doppler velocity, and any other measured quantities as separate channels of the image. In tomography, the projections are of thin 3D slices, thus creating multiple cross-sectional images; these cross-sections may be treated as channels of a single image.

There are some special considerations associated with imagery data depending on the sensor geometry.

Polar grids

Radar and ultrasound are carried out in a polar coordinate system (see Figure 5-2). You can either treat the polar 2D data itself as the input image, or transform it into a Cartesian coordinate system before using it as an input to machine learning models. There are trade-offs in either approach: in the polar coordinate system there is no interpolation or repeated pixels but the size of a pixel varies throughout the image, whereas in the Cartesian coordinate system the pixel size is consistent but much of the data is missing, interpolated, or aggregated when remapped. For example, in Figure 5-2, many of the pixels at the bottom left will be missing and will have to be assigned some numerical value for ML purposes. Meanwhile, pixels at the bottom right will involve aggregation of many values from the pixel grid and pixels at the top will involve interpolation between the pixel values. The presence of all three situations in Cartesian images greatly complicates the learning task.

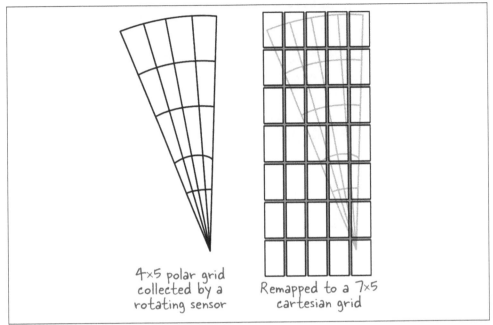

4×5 polar grid collected by a rotating sensor

Remapped to a 7×5 cartesian grid

Figure 5-2. Using a polar grid as-is versus remapping the data to a Cartesian grid.

We recommend using the polar grid as the input image to ML models, and including the distance of each pixel from the center (or the size of the pixel) as an additional input to the ML model. Because every pixel has a different size, the easiest way to incorporate this information is to treat the size of the pixel as an additional channel. This way we can take advantage of all of the image data without losing information through coordinate transformation.

Satellite channels

When working with satellite images, it might be worth working in the original satellite view or a parallax-corrected grid rather than remapping the images to Earth coordinates. If using projected map data, try to carry out the machine learning in the original projection of the data. Treat images collected of the same location at approximately the same time, but at different wavelengths, as channels (see Figure 5-3). Note that pretrained models are usually trained on three-channel images (RGB), so transfer learning and fine-tuning will not work, but the underlying architectures can work with any number of channels if you are training from scratch.

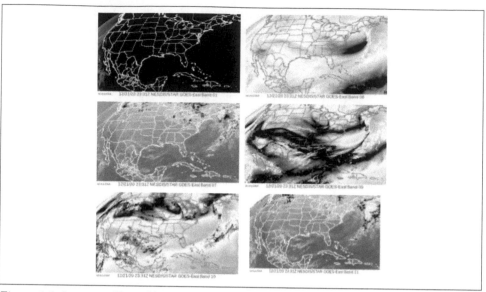

Figure 5-3. Images collected by instruments onboard the GOES-16 weather satellite at approximately the same time on December 21, 2020. Treat the original scalar values of these colorized images as six-channel images that are input to the model. Images courtesy of the US National Weather Service (https://oreil.ly/VTOBi).

Geospatial layers

If you have multiple map layers (e.g., land ownership, topography, population density; see Figure 5-4) collected in different projections, you will have to remap them into the same projection, line up the pixels, and treat these different layers as channels of an image. In such situations, it might be useful to include the latitude of the pixel as an additional input channel to the model so that changes in pixel size can be accounted for.

Categorical layers (such as land cover type) may have to be one-hot encoded so that the land cover type becomes five channels if there are five possible land cover types.

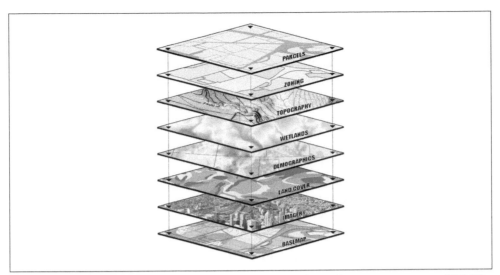

Figure 5-4. Geospatial layers can be treated as image channels. Image courtesy of USGS (https://oreil.ly/mmi41).

Proof of Concept

In many situations, you may not have the data on hand, and collecting it for a proof of concept would take too long. You may look into purchasing similar data to understand the feasibility of a project before investing in routine data collection. When purchasing images, keep in mind that you want to acquire images that are similar in quality, resolution, etc. to the images that you will ultimately be able to use in the actual project.

For example, many of the machine learning algorithms for the US GOES-16 satellite had to be developed before the satellite was launched. Naturally, there was no data available! In order to decide on the list of ML models that would be built on the GOES-16 data, similar-quality data already being collected by the European SEVIRI satellite was used to carry out proof-of-concept tests.

Another way to carry out a proof of concept is to simulate images. We will see an example of this in Chapter 11, where the ability to count tomatoes on a vine is illustrated through simulated images. When simulating images, it can be helpful to modify existing images rather than creating them from scratch. For example, the simulated tomato vine images might have been easier to generate if photographs of green vines, to which red tomatoes of different sizes could be added, had been readily available.

Do not train a model on perfect data and then try to apply it to imperfect images. For example, if you need a model to be able to identify flowers from photographs that hikers take on trails, you should not train the model on photographs taken by professional photographers that were subsequently retouched.

Data Types

So far, we have processed only photographs. As discussed in the previous section, there are other types of images, such as geospatial layers, MRI scans, or spectrograms of sound, to which machine learning can be applied. Mathematically, all that the ML techniques require is a 4D tensor (batch x height x width x channels) as input. As long as our data can be put into this form, computer vision methods may be applied.

Of course, you have to keep in mind the underlying concepts that make certain techniques work well. For example, you may not find success in applying convolutional filters to the problem of finding defective pixels (*https://oreil.ly/OIygm*) on computer monitors because convolutional filters work well only when there is spatial correlation between adjacent pixels.

Channels

A typical photograph is stored as a 24-bit RGB image with three channels (red, green, and blue), each of which is represented by an 8-bit number in the range 0–255. Some computer-generated images also have a fourth *alpha* channel, which captures the transparency of the pixel. The alpha channel is useful primarily to overlay or composite images together.

Scaling

Machine learning frameworks and pretrained models often expect that the pixel values are scaled from [0,255] to [0,1]. ML models typically ignore the alpha channel. In TensorFlow, this is done using:

```
# Read compressed data from file into a string.
img = tf.io.read_file(filename)
# Convert the compressed string to a 3D uint8 tensor.
img = tf.image.decode_jpeg(img, channels=3)
# Convert to floats in the [0,1] range.
img = tf.image.convert_image_dtype(img, tf.float32)
```

Channel order

The shape of a typical image input is [height, width, channels], where the number of channels is typically 3 for RGB images and 1 for grayscale. This is called a *channels-last* representation and is the default with TensorFlow. Earlier ML packages such as Theano and early versions of ML infrastructure such as Google's Tensor Processing Unit (TPU) v1.0 used a *channels-first* ordering. The channels-first order is more efficient in terms of computation because it reduces back-and-forth seeks within memory.[2] However, most image formats store the data pixel by pixel, so channels-last is the more natural data ingest and output format. The move from channels-first to channels-last is an example of ease of use being prioritized over efficiency as computational hardware becomes more powerful.

Because channel order can vary, Keras allows you to specify the order in the global *$HOME/.keras/keras.json* configuration file:

```
{
    "image_data_format": "channels_last",
    "backend": "tensorflow",
    "epsilon": 1e-07,
    "floatx": "float32"
}
```

The default is to use TensorFlow as the Keras backend, and therefore the image format defaults to `channels_last`. This is what we will do in this book. Because this is a global setting that will affect every model being run on the system, we strongly recommend that you don't fiddle with this file.

If you have an image that is channels-first and need to change it to channels-last, you can use `tf.einsum()`:

```
image = tf.einsum('chw->hwc', channels_first_image)
```

or simply do a transpose, providing the appropriate axes:

```
image = tf.transpose(channels_first_image, perm=(1, 2, 0))
```

---

2 See "Understanding Memory Formats" (*https://oreil.ly/HPmsI*) on the oneAPI Deep Neural Network Library.

Grayscale

If you have a grayscale image, or a simple 2D array of numbers, you may have to expand the dimensions to change the shape from [height, width] to [height, width, 1]:

```
image = tf.expand_dims(arr2d, axis=-1)
```

By specifying `axis=-1`, we ask for the channel dimension to be appended to the existing shape and the new channel dimension to be set to 1.

Geospatial Data

Geospatial data can either be generated from map layers or as a result of remote sensing from drones, satellites, radars, and the like.

Raster data

Geospatial data that results from maps often has *raster bands* (2D arrays of pixel values) that can be treated as channels. For example, you may have several raster bands covering a land area: population density, land cover type, flooding propensity, and so on. In order to apply computer vision techniques to such raster data, simply read the individual bands and stack them together to form an image:

```
image = tf.stack([read_into_2darray(b) for b in raster_bands], axis=-1)
```

In addition to raster data, you might also have vector data such as the locations of roads, rivers, states, or cities. In that case, you have to rasterize the data before using it in image-based ML models. For example, you might draw the roads or rivers as a set of one-pixel-wide line segments (see the top panel of Figure 5-5). If the vector data consists of polygons, such as state boundaries, you would rasterize the data by filling in the pixels that fall within the boundary. If there are 15 states, then you will end up with 15 raster images, with each image containing 1 in the pixels that are within the boundary of the corresponding state—this is the image equivalent of one-hot encoding categorical values (see the bottom panel of Figure 5-5). If the vector data consists of city boundaries, you'll have to decide whether to treat this as a Boolean value (the pixel value is 0 if rural, and 1 if it is a city) or a categorical variable (in which case, you'd generate *N* raster bands for the *N* cities in the dataset).

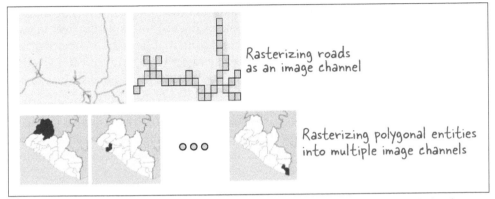

Figure 5-5. Rasterizing vector data. In the rasterized images, the 1s are highlighted. Map sources: OpenStreetMap (top) and Wikipedia (bottom).

The raster data will typically be in a geographic projection. Some projections (such as Lambert conformal) preserve areas, others (such as Mercator) preserve direction, and others (such as equidistant cylindrical) are chosen because they are simple to create. In our experience, any projection works fine for machine learning, but you should ensure that all the raster bands are in the same projection. It can also be helpful to add the latitude as an additional input channel if the size of a pixel will vary with latitude.

Remote sensing

Remotely sensed data is collected by an imaging instrument. If the instrument in question is a camera (as with a lot of drone images), the result will be an image with three channels. On the other hand, if there are multiple instruments on board the satellite capturing the images or if the instrument can operate at multiple frequencies, the result will be an image with a large number of channels.

Often, remote sensing images are colorized for visualization purposes. It is better to go back and get the raw numbers that are sensed by the instrument rather than using these colorized images.

Make sure that you read and normalize the images as we did for the photographs. For example, scale the values found in each image from 0 to 1. Sometimes the data will contain outliers. For example, bathymetric images may have outlier values due to ocean waves and tides. In such cases, it may be necessary to clip the data to a reasonable range before scaling it.

Remote sensing images will often contain missing data (such as the part of the image outside of the satellite horizon or areas of clutter in radar images). If it is possible to crop out the missing areas, do so. Impute missing values by interpolating over them if the missing areas are small. If the missing values consist of large areas, or occur in a significant fraction of the pixels, create a separate raster band that indicates whether the pixel is missing a true value or has been replaced by a sentinel value such as zero.

Both geospatial and remote sensing data require a significant amount of processing before they can be input into ML models. Because of this, it is worthwhile to have a scripted/automated data preparation step or pipeline that takes the raw images, processes them into raster bands, stacks them, and writes them out into an efficient format such as TensorFlow Records.

Audio and Video

Audio is a 1D signal whereas videos are 3D. It is better to use ML techniques that have been devised specifically for audio and video, but a simple first solution might involve applying image ML techniques to audio and video data. In this section, we'll discuss this approach. Audio and video ML frameworks are outside the scope of this book.

Spectrogram

To do machine learning on audio, it is necessary to split the audio into chunks and then apply ML to these time windows. The size of the time window depends on what's being detected—you need a few seconds to identify words, but a fraction of a second to identify instruments.

The result is a 1D signal, so it is possible to use Conv1D instead of Conv2D layers to process audio data. Technically speaking, this would be signal processing in the time space. However, the results tend to be better if audio signals are represented as spectrograms—a stacked view of the spectrum of frequencies in the audio signal as it varies over time. In a spectrogram, the x-axis of the image represents time and the y-axis represents the frequency. The pixel value represents the spectral density, which is the loudness of the audio signal at a specific frequency (see Figure 5-6). Typically, the spectral density is represented in decibels, so it is best to use the logarithm of the spectrogram as the image input.

To read and convert an audio signal into the log of the spectrogram, use the `scipy` package:

```
from scipy import signal
from scipy.io import wavfile
sample_rate, samples = wavfile.read(filename)
_, _, spectro = signal.spectrogram(samples, sample_rate)
img = np.log(spectro)
```

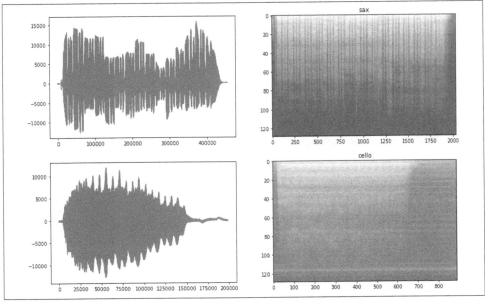

Figure 5-6. Audio signal (left) and spectrogram (right) of two musical instruments.

Natural Language Processing Using Computer Vision Techniques

In the spectrogram, we are computing the frequency characteristics of the signal at a point in time and then looking at the variation in this frequency to create a 2D image. This idea of grouping 1D objects into 2D in order to use computer vision techniques can also be applied to natural language processing problems!

For example, it is possible to take a document-understanding problem and treat it like a computer-vision problem. The idea is to use a pretrained embedding such as the Universal Sentence Encoder (USE) or BERT to convert sentences to embeddings (the full code is in *05_audio.ipynb* on GitHub):

```
paragraph = ...
embed = hub.load(
    https://tfhub.dev/google/universal-sentence-encoder/4")
embeddings = embed(paragraph.split('.'))
```

In this code snippet, we are splitting the paragraph into a list of sentences and applying the USE embedder to a set of sentences. Because embeddings is now a 2D tensor, it is possible to treat the paragraph/review/page/document (whatever your grouping unit is) as an image (see Figure 5-7). The image is 12x512 because there are 12 sentences in the paragraph and we used an embedding of size 512.

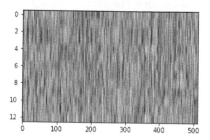

Figure 5-7. By stacking the text embeddings of sentences, we can treat a paragraph as an image. This is the representation of a paragraph from a Herman Hesse novel.

Frame by frame

Videos consist of *frames*, each of which is an image. The obvious approach to handling videos is to carry out image processing on the individual frames, and postprocess the results into an analysis of the entire video. We can use the OpenCV (cv2) package to read a video file in one of the standard formats and obtain a frame:

```
cap = cv2.VideoCapture(filename)
num_frames = int(cap.get(cv2.CAP_PROP_FRAME_COUNT))
for i in range(num_frames):
    readok, frame = cap.read()
    if readok:
        img = tf.convert_to_tensor(frame)
```

For example, we might classify the image frames, and treat the result of the video classification problem as the set of all the categories found in all the frames. The problem is that such an approach loses sight of the fact that adjacent frames in a video are highly correlated, just as adjacent pixels in an image are highly correlated.

Conv3D

Instead of processing videos one frame at a time, we can compute rolling averages of video frames and then apply computer vision algorithms. This approach is particularly useful when the videos are grainy. Unlike the frame-by-frame approach, the rolling average takes advantage of frame correlation to denoise the image.

A more sophisticated approach is to use 3D convolution. We read video clips into a 5D tensor with the shape [batch, time, height, width, channels], breaking the movie into short clips if necessary:

```
def read_video(filename):
    cap = cv2.VideoCapture(filename)
    num_frames = int(cap.get(cv2.CAP_PROP_FRAME_COUNT))
    frames = []
    for i in range(num_frames):
        readok, frame = cap.read()
        if readok:
            frames.append(frame)
    return tf.expand_dims(tf.convert_to_tensor(frames), -1)
```

Then, we apply `Conv3D` instead of `Conv2D` in our image processing pipeline. This is similar to a rolling average where the weights of each time step are learned from the data, followed by a nonlinear activation function.

Another approach is to use recurrent neural networks (RNNs) and other sequence methods that are more suitable for time-series data. However, because RNNs of video sequences are quite hard to train, the 3D convolutional approach tends to be more practical. An alternative is to extract features from the time signal using convolution and then pass the results of the convolution filter to a less complex RNN.

Manual Labeling

In many ML projects, the first step at which the data science team gets involved is in labeling the image data. Even if the labeling will be automated, the first few images in a proof of concept are almost always hand-labeled. The form and organization will differ based on the problem type (image classification or object detection) and whether an image can have multiple labels or only one.

To hand-label images, a *rater* views the image, determines the label(s), and records the label(s). There are two typical approaches to doing this recording: using a folder structure and a metadata table.

In a folder organization, raters simply move images to different folders depending on what their label is. All flowers that are daisies are stored in a folder named *daisy*, for example. Raters can do this quickly because most operating systems provide previews of images and handy ways to select groups of images and move them into folders (see Figure 5-8).

The problem with the folder approach is that it leads to duplication if an image can have multiple labels—for example, if an image contains both roses and daisies.

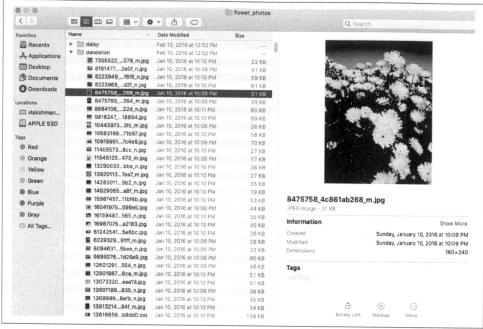

Figure 5-8. Preview images and quickly move them to the appropriate folder.

The alternative, and recommended, approach is to record the label(s) in a metadata table (such as in a spreadsheet or a CSV file) that has at least two columns—one column is the URL to the image file, and the other is the list of labels that are valid for the image:

```
$ gsutil cat gs://cloud-ml-data/img/flower_photos/all_data.csv | head -5
gs://cloud-ml-data/img/flower_photos/daisy/100080576_f52e8ee070_n.jpg,daisy
gs://cloud-ml-data/img/flower_photos/daisy/10140303196_b88d3d6cec.jpg,daisy
gs://cloud-ml-data/img/flower_photos/daisy/10172379554_b296050f82_n.jpg,daisy
gs://cloud-ml-data/img/flower_photos/daisy/10172567486_2748826a8b.jpg,daisy
gs://cloud-ml-data/img/flower_photos/daisy/10172636503_21bededa75_n.jpg,daisy
```

A good approach to marry the efficiency of the folder approach and the generalizability of the metadata table approach is to organize the images into folders and then use a script to crawl the images and create the metadata table.

Multilabel

If an image can be associated with multiple labels (for example, if an image can contain both daisies and sunflowers), one approach is to simply copy the image into both folders and have two separate lines:

```
gs://.../sunflower/100080576_f52e8ee070_n.jpg,sunflower
gs://.../daisy/100080576_f52e8ee070_n.jpg,daisy
```

However, having duplicates like this will make it more difficult to train a truly multi-label multiclass problem. A better approach is to make the labels column contain all the matching categories:

```
gs://.../multi/100080576_f52e8ee070_n.jpg,sunflower daisy
```

The ingest pipeline will have to parse the labels string to extract the list of matching categories using `tf.strings.split`.

Object Detection

For object detection, the metadata file needs to include the bounding box of the object in the image. This can be accomplished by having a third column that contains the bounding box vertices in a predefined order (such as counterclockwise starting from top-left). For segmentation problems, this column will contain a polygon rather than a bounding box (see Figure 5-9).

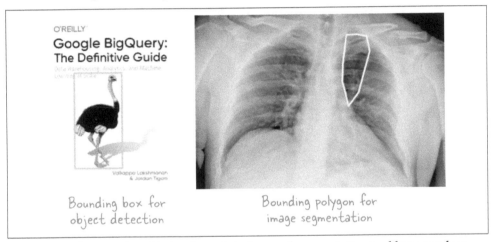

Figure 5-9. The metadata file in object detection and segmentation problems needs to include a bounding box or polygon, respectively.

Doughnut-shaped objects (with a center that is not part of the object) can be represented by a pair of polygons where the inner polygon has its vertices running in the opposite direction. To avoid this complexity, the segmentation boundaries are sometimes represented simply as a set of pixels instead of polygons.

Labeling at Scale

Manually labeling thousands of images is cumbersome and error-prone. How can we make it more efficient and accurate? One way is to use tools that make it possible to hand-label thousands of images efficiently. The other is to use methods to catch and correct labeling errors.

Labeling User Interface

A labeling tool should have a facility to display the image, and enable the rater to quickly select valid categories and save the rating to a database.

To support object identification and image segmentation use cases, the tool should have annotation capability and the ability to translate drawn bounding boxes or polygons into image pixel coordinates. The Computer Vision Annotation Tool (*https://oreil.ly/Mpmdq*) (see Figure 5-10) is a free, web-based video and image annotation tool that is available online (*https://cvat.org*) and can be installed locally. It supports a variety of annotation formats.

Figure 5-10. A tool for labeling images efficiently.

Multiple Tasks

Often, we will need to label images for multiple tasks. For example, we might need to classify the same images by flower type (daisy, tulip, …), color (yellow, red, …), location (indoors, outdoors, …), planting style (potted, in-ground, …), and so on. An efficient approach in such situations is to do the labeling using the interactive functionality of a Jupyter notebook (see Figure 5-11).

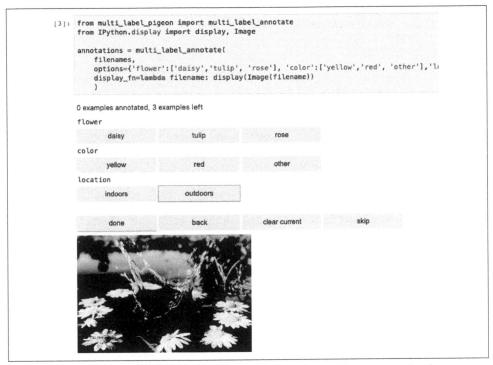

Figure 5-11. Efficiently labeling images for multiple tasks in a Jupyter notebook.

The functionality is provided by the Python package `multi-label-pigeon` (*https://oreil.ly/NLwqJ*):

```
annotations = multi_label_annotate(
    filenames,
    options={'flower':['daisy','tulip', 'rose'],
            'color':['yellow','red', 'other'],
            'location':['indoors','outdoors']},
    display_fn=lambda filename: display(Image(filename))
)
with open('label.json', 'w') as ofp:
    json.dump(annotations, ofp, indent=2)
```

The full code is in *05_label_images.ipynb* on GitHub for this book. The output is a JSON file with annotations for all the tasks for all the images:

```
{
    "flower_images/10172379554_b296050f82_n.jpg": {
        "flower": [
            "daisy"
        ],
        "color": [
            "red"
        ],
        "location": [
            "outdoors"
        ]
    },
```

Voting and Crowdsourcing

Manual labeling is subject to two challenges: human error and inherent uncertainty. Raters may get tired and wrongly identify an image. It may also be the case that the classification is ambiguous. Consider for example an X-ray image: radiologists may differ on whether something is a fracture or not.

In both these situations, it can be helpful to implement a voting system. For example, an image might be shown to two raters. If the raters agree, their label is assigned to the image. If the raters disagree, we can choose to do one of several things:

- Discard the image if we don't want to train using ambiguous data.
- Consider the image as belonging to a neutral class.
- Have the final label be determined by a third labeler, in effect making it a majority vote of three labelers. Of course, it is possible to increase the voting pool to any odd number.

Voting applies to multilabel problems as well. We just need to treat the incidence of each category as a binary classification problem, and then assign to an image all the labels on which a majority of raters agree.

Even object identification and segmentation boundaries can be determined via voting. An example of such a system is shown in Figure 5-12—the primary purpose of the CAPTCHA system is to identify whether a user is a robot or a human, but a secondary purpose is to crowdsource (*https://oreil.ly/9Ww3Y*) the labeling of images. It is clear that by decreasing the size of the tiles, it is possible to get a finer-grained labeling. By occasionally adding images or tiling, and collecting the results over many users, it is possible to get images successfully labeled.

Figure 5-12. Crowdsourcing object detection or segmentation polygons.

Labeling Services

Even with efficient labeling, it can take days or months to label all the images needed to train a state-of-the-art image model. This is not a productive use of a data scientist's time. Because of this, many *labeling services* have cropped up. These are businesses that distribute the work of labeling images among dozens of employees at low-cost locations. Typically, we have to provide a few sample images and a description of the technique that needs to be employed to label images.

Labeling services are a bit more sophisticated than crowdsourcing. These services work not only for well-known objects (stop signs, crosswalks, etc.), but also for tasks where a layperson can be taught to make the correct decision quickly (e.g., a fracture versus a scratch mark in X-ray images). That said, you would probably not use labeling services for tasks like identifying the molecular structure of a virus that would take significant domain expertise.

Examples of labeling services include AI Platform Data Labeling Service (*https://oreil.ly/V8vfu*), Clarifai (*https://oreil.ly/U4ylE*), and Lionbridge (*https://oreil.ly/NR5Z0*). You'd typically work with the procurement department of your organization to use such a service. You should also verify how these services handle sensitive or personally identifying data.

Automated Labeling

In many situations, it is possible to obtain labels in an automated way. These methods can be useful even if they are not 100% accurate because it is far more efficient for raters to correct automatically obtained labels than it is for them to assign labels to images one by one.

Labels from Related Data

As an example, you might be able to obtain the label for an image by looking at the section of the product catalog that the image appears in, or by doing entity extraction from the words that describe the image.

In some cases, ground truth is available by looking at only a few of the pixels of the image. For example, seismic images can be labeled at locations where wells were dug and core samples extracted. A radar image may be labeled using the readings of ground rain gauges at locations where those gauges are installed. These point labels may be used to label tiles of the original image. Alternatively, the point labels may be spatially interpolated, and the spatially interpolated data used as labels for tasks such as segmentation.

Noisy Student

It is possible to stretch the labeling of images using a Noisy Student (*https://arxiv.org/abs/1911.04252*) model. This approach works as follows:

- Manually label, say, 10,000 images.
- Use these images to train a small machine learning model. This is the *teacher model*.
- Use the trained machine learning model to predict the labels of, say, one million unlabeled images.
- Train a larger machine learning model, called the *student model*, on the combination of labeled and pseudo-labeled images. During the learning of the student model, employ dropout and random data augmentations (covered in Chapter 6) so that this model generalizes better than the teacher.
- Iterate by putting the student model back as the teacher.

It is possible to manually correct the pseudo-labels by choosing images where the machine learning models are not confident. This can be incorporated into the Noisy Student paradigm by doing the manual labeling before putting the student back as the new teacher model.

Self-Supervised Learning

In some cases, the machine learning approach can itself provide labels. For example, to create embeddings of images, we can train an autoencoder, as we will describe in Chapter 10. In an autoencoder, the image serves as its own label.

Another way that learning can be self-supervised is if the label will be known after some time. It may be possible to label a medical image based on the eventual outcome for the patient. If a patient subsequently develops emphysema, for example, that label can be applied to lung images taken of the patient a few months prior to the diagnosis. Such a labeling method works for many forecasts of future activity: a satellite weather image might be labeled based on the subsequent occurrence of cloud-to-ground lightning as detected by a ground-based network, and a dataset for predicting whether a user is going to abandon their shopping cart or cancel their subscription can be labeled based on the eventual action of the user. So, even if our images don't have a label immediately at capture time, it can be worth holding on to them until we eventually get a label for them.

Many data quality problems can be framed in a self-supervised way. For example, if the task is to fill in an image of the ground when clouds are obstructing the view, the model can be trained by artificially removing parts of a clear-sky image and using the actual pixel values as labels.

Bias

The ideal machine learning dataset is one that allows us to train a model that will be perfect when it is placed into production. If, on the other hand, certain examples are under- or overrepresented in the dataset in such a way as to produce lower accuracy in those scenarios when they are encountered in production, then we have a problem. The dataset is then said to be *biased*.

In this section, we will discuss sources of dataset bias, how to collect data for a training dataset in an unbiased way, and how to detect bias in your dataset.

Sources of Bias

Bias in a dataset is a characteristic of the dataset that will lead to unwanted behavior when the model is placed into production.

We find that many people confuse two related, but separate, concepts: bias and imbalance. Bias is different from imbalance—it is quite possible that less than 1% of the pictures taken by an automatic wildlife camera are of jaguars. A dataset of wildlife pictures that has a very small proportion of jaguars is to be expected: it's unbalanced, but this is not evidence of bias. We might downsample commonly occurring animals and upsample unusual ones to help the machine learning model learn to identify different types of wildlife better, but such upsampling does not make the dataset biased. Instead, dataset bias is any aspect of the dataset that causes the model to behave in unwanted ways.

There are three sources of bias. *Selection bias* happens when the model is trained on a skewed subset of the scenarios that it will encounter in production. *Measurement bias* occurs when the way an image is collected varies between training and production. *Confirmation bias* happens when the distribution of values in real life leads to the model reinforcing unwanted behaviors. Let's take a closer look at why each of these might occur; then we'll quickly show you how to detect bias in a dataset.

Selection Bias

Selection bias usually happens as a result of imperfect data collection—we mistakenly limit the source of our data, such that certain categories are excluded or poorly sampled. For example, suppose we're training a model to identify objects we sell. We might have trained the model on images in our product catalog, but this may have caused products from our partners to not be included. Therefore, the model will not recognize partner items that we sell but that were not in our product catalog. Similarly, an image model trained on photographs of houses found in county records may perform poorly on houses under construction if unfinished homes are not subject to county taxes, and are therefore not in the records.

A common reason for selection bias is that certain types of data are easier to collect than others. For example, it might be easier to collect images of French and Italian art than of Jamaican or Fijiian art. Datasets of artworks can therefore underrepresent certain countries or time periods. Likewise, previous years' product catalogs may be easy to find, but competitors' catalogs for this year might not be available yet, so our dataset might be up-to-date for our products but not for those of our competitors.

Sometimes selection bias happens simply because the training dataset is collected in a fixed time period, whereas the production time period is a lot more variable. For example, the training dataset might have been collected on a clear day, but the system is expected to work night and day, in clear weather and in rainy weather.

Selection bias can also happen as a result of outlier pruning and dataset cleanup. If we discard images of houseboats, barns, and mobile homes, the model will not be able to identify such buildings. If we are creating a dataset of seashells and discard any images of a shell with the animal still in it, then the model will perform poorly if shown a living crustacean.

To fix selection bias, it is necessary to work backward from the production system. What types of houses will need to be identified? Are there enough examples of such houses in the dataset? If not, the solution is to proactively collect such images.

Measurement Bias

Measurement bias occurs as a result of differences in the way an image is collected for training versus in production. These variations lead to systematic differences—perhaps we used a high-quality camera for the training images, but our production system employs an off-the-shelf camera that has a lower aperture, white balance, and/or resolution.

Measurement bias can also happen because of differences in who provides the data in training versus in production. For example, we may want to build a tool to help hikers identify wildflowers. If the training dataset consists of professional photographs, the photographs will include sophisticated effects like bokeh that will not be present in the photographs provided by a typical hiker for purposes of identification.

Measurement bias also happens when the labeling of images is done by a group of people. Different raters may have different standards, and inconsistencies in labeling can lead to poorer machine learning models.

Measurement bias can also be quite subtle. Perhaps all the photographs of foxes are taken against snow, whereas all the photographs of dogs are against grass. A machine learning model may learn to discriminate between snow and grass and achieve superior accuracy to a model that actually learns the features of foxes and dogs. So, we need to be mindful of what other things are within our images (and examine model explanations) to ensure our models learn the things we want them to learn.

Confirmation Bias

Remember when we said that many people confuse bias and imbalance? The difference and interrelationship between the two is particularly important when it comes to confirmation bias. A dataset may be biased even if it accurately represents an imbalanced real-world distribution—this is something that you should keep in mind as you read this section. Remember that bias in a dataset includes anything about the dataset that leads to unwanted behavior in ML models trained on that dataset.

Donald Rumsfeld, who was the US Secretary of Defense in 2002, famously listed three categories of knowledge (*https://oreil.ly/gmbxl*):

> There are known knowns; there are things we know we know. We also know there are known unknowns; that is to say we know there are some things we do not know. But there are also unknown unknowns—the ones we don't know we don't know. And if one looks throughout the history of our country and other free countries, it is the latter category that tends to be the difficult one.

Confirmation bias is bias that we don't know about when we collect the data but which can nevertheless play havoc with models trained on the dataset. Human reluctance to examine the reasons why certain imbalances exist can lead to ML models perpetuating existing biases.

Collecting data "in the wild" can lead to confirmation bias. For example, at the time of writing, firefighters tend to be predominantly men. If we were to collect a random sample of images of firefighters, chances are that all the images would be of male firefighters. A machine learning model trained on such a dataset, when shown an image of a woman firefighter, might generate the caption that this is a woman in costume at a Halloween party. That would be pretty offensive, wouldn't it? This is a made-up example, but it illustrates how an existing bias in society gets amplified when datasets reflect the real world. Do a search of recent news headlines about biased AI, and you will find any number of real-world disasters that have, at their core, a similar bias because they reflect real-world distributions.

A small-town newspaper will tend to cover events that occur in the town, and by virtue of this data being "in the wild," most of the photographs of concerts, fairs, and outdoor dining will contain images of the majority community. On the other hand, most of the photographs of minority-community teens that appear in the newspaper might be photographs of arrests. Arrest photographs of majority-community teens will also appear in the newspaper, but they will be greatly outnumbered by photographs of those teens in outdoor settings. Given such a dataset, a machine learning model will learn to associate minority-community members with jail and majority-community members with benign activities. Again, this is an example of a model confirming and perpetuating the bias of the newspaper editors because of what newspaper stories tend to cover.

Confirmation bias can also amplify existing biases in terms of labels. If a company trains a model to sort through job applications it has received and classify them based on who finally got hired, the model will learn any bias (whether it is in favor of elite colleges or against minority candidates) that the company's current interviewers have. If the company tends to hire very few Black candidates or highly favors Ivy League candidates, the model will learn and replicate that. The "unbiased" model has become extremely biased.

To address confirmation bias, we have to be aware of this blind spot that we have, and consciously move areas of unknown unknowns to one of the other two categories. We have to be aware of the existing biases in our company, in our industry, or in society and carefully validate that our dataset is not collected in such a way as to amplify that bias. The recommended approach involves both awareness (of potential bias) and active data collection (to mitigate this bias).

Detecting Bias

To detect bias, you can carry out *sliced evaluations*—essentially, compute the objective function of your model, but only on members of a group. Compare this with the value of the metric for non-members of the group. Then investigate any groups for which the sliced metrics are very different from that of the overall dataset. You can also apply a Bayesian approach and calculate measures such as "what are the chances that a retinal scan will be categorized as diseased if the sample is from a racial minority?"

The Aequitas Fairness Tree approach (*https://oreil.ly/eE64O*) suggests which metric to monitor depending on whether the ML model is used punitively or assistively.

Creating a Dataset

Once we have collected a set of images and labeled them, we are ready to train an ML model with those images. However, we will have to split the dataset into three parts: training, validation, and testing sets. We will also want to take the opportunity to store the image data in a more efficient format for ML. Let's look at both of these steps and how our training program would read files in this format.

Splitting Data

The dataset of images and labels will have to be split into three parts, for training, validation, and testing. The actual proportion is up to us, but something like 80:10:10 is common.

The training dataset is the set of examples that are presented to the model. The optimizer uses these examples to tune the weights of the model so as to reduce the error, or *loss*, on the training dataset. The loss on the training dataset at the end of training is not, however, a reliable measure of the performance of the model. To estimate that, we have to use a dataset of examples that have not been shown to the model during its training process. That is the purpose of the validation dataset.

If we were training only one model, and training it only once, we would need only the training and validation datasets (in this case, an 80:20 split is common). However, it is very likely that we will retry the training with a different set of hyperparameters —perhaps we will change the learning rate, or decrease the dropout, or add a couple more layers to the model. The more of these hyperparameters we optimize against the validation dataset, the more the skill of the model on the validation dataset gets incorporated into the structure of the model itself. The validation dataset is thus no longer a reliable estimate of how the model will perform when given net new data.

Our final evaluation (of the model fit on the training dataset, and using parameters optimized on the validation dataset) is carried out on the test dataset.

Splitting the dataset at the beginning of each training run is not a good idea. If we do this, every experiment will have different training and validation datasets, which defeats the purpose of retaining a truly independent test dataset. Instead, we should split once, and then continue using the same training and validation datasets for all our hyperparameter tuning experiments. Therefore, we should save the training, validation, and test CSV files and use these consistently throughout the model lifecycle.

Sometimes, we might want to do cross-validation on the dataset. To do this, we train the model multiple times using different splits of the first 90% into training and validation datasets (the test dataset remains the same 10%). In such a case, we'd write out multiple training and validation files. Cross-validation is common on small datasets, but much less common in machine learning on large datasets such as those used in image models.

TensorFlow Records

The CSV file format mentioned in the previous section is not recommended for large-scale machine learning because it relies on storing image data as individual JPEG files, which is not very efficient. A more efficient data format to use is Tensor-Flow Records (TFRecords). We can convert our JPEG image files into TFRecords using Apache Beam.

First, we define a method to create a TFRecord given the image filename and the label of the image:

```
def create_tfrecord(filename, label, label_int):
    img = read_and_decode(filename)
    dims = img.shape
    img = tf.reshape(img, [-1])  # flatten to 1D array
    return tf.train.Example(features=tf.train.Features(feature={
        'image': _float_feature(img),
        'shape': _int64_feature([dims[0], dims[1], dims[2]]),
        'label': _string_feature([label]),
        'label_int': _int64_feature([label_int])
    })).SerializeToString()
```

The TFRecord is a dictionary with two main keys: image and label. Because different images can have different sizes, we also take care to store the shape of the original image. To save time looking up the index of the label during training, we also store the label as an integer.

 Besides efficiency, TFRecords give us the ability to embed image metadata such as the label, bounding box, and even additional ML inputs such as the location and timestamp of the image as part of the data itself. This way, we don't need to rely on ad hoc mechanisms such as the file/directory name or external files to encode metadata.

The image itself is a flattened array of floating-point numbers—for efficiency, we are doing the JPEG decoding and scaling before writing to the TFRecords. This way, it is not necessary to redo these operations as we iterate over the training dataset:

```
def read_and_decode(filename):
    img = tf.io.read_file(filename)
    img = tf.image.decode_jpeg(img, channels=IMG_CHANNELS)
    img = tf.image.convert_image_dtype(img, tf.float32)
    return img
```

As well as being more efficient, decoding the images and scaling their values to [0, 1] before writing them out to TFRecords has two other advantages. First, this puts the data in the exact form required by the image models in TensorFlow Hub (see Chapter 3). Second, it allows the reading code to use the data without having to know whether the files were in JPEG or PNG or some other image format.

 An equally valid approach is to store the data in the TFRecord as JPEG bytes, rely on TensorFlow's decode_image() function to read the data, and scale the image values to [0, 1] in the preprocessing layer of the model. Because the JPEG bytes are compressed using an algorithm tailored for images, the resulting files can be smaller than gzipped TFRecord files consisting of raw pixel values. Use this approach if bandwidth is more important than decoding time. Another benefit of this approach is that the decoding operation is usually pipelined on the CPU while the model trains on a GPU, so it might be essentially free.

The Apache Beam pipeline consists of getting the training, validation, and test CSV files, creating TFRecords, and writing the three datasets with appropriate prefixes. For example, the training TFRecord files are created using:

```
with beam.Pipeline() as p:
    (p
    | 'input_df' >> beam.Create(train.values)
    | 'create_tfr' >> beam.Map(lambda x: create_tfrecord(
            x[0], x[1], LABELS.index(x[1])))
    | 'write' >> beam.io.tfrecordio.WriteToTFRecord(
            'output/train', file_name_suffix='.gz')
    )
```

While there are several advantages to decoding and scaling the pixel values before writing them out to TFRecords, the floating-point pixel data tends to take up more space than the original byte stream. This drawback is addressed in the preceding code by compressing the TFRecord files. The TFRecord writer will automatically compress the output files when we specify that the filename suffix should be .gz.

Running at scale

The previous code is fine for transforming a few images, but when you have thousands to millions of images, you'll want a more scalable, resilient solution. The solution needs to be fault-tolerant, able to be distributed to multiple machines, and capable of being monitored using standard DevOps tools. Typically, we'd also want to pipe the output to a cost-efficient blob storage as new images come streaming in. Ideally, we'd want this to be done in a serverless way so that we don't have to manage and scale up/down this infrastructure ourselves.

One solution that addresses these production needs of resilience, monitoring, streaming, and autoscaling is to run our Apache Beam code on Google Cloud Dataflow rather than in a Jupyter notebook:

```
with beam.Pipeline('DataflowRunner', options=opts) as p:
```

The options can be obtained from the command line using standard Python constructs (like `argparse`) and will typically include the Cloud project to be billed and the Cloud region in which to run the pipeline. Besides Cloud Dataflow, other runners for Apache Beam include Apache Spark and Apache Flink.

As long as we are creating a pipeline like this, it can be helpful to capture all the steps of our workflow within it, including the step of splitting the dataset. We can do this as follows (the full code is in *jpeg_to_tfrecord.py* on GitHub):

```
with beam.Pipeline(RUNNER, options=opts) as p:
    splits = (p
            | 'read_csv' >> beam.io.ReadFromText(arguments['all_data'])
            | 'parse_csv' >> beam.Map(lambda line: line.split(','))
            | 'create_tfr' >> beam.Map(lambda x: create_tfrecord(
                    x[0], x[1], LABELS.index(x[1])))
            | 'assign_ds' >> beam.Map(assign_record_to_split)
            )
```

where the `assign_record_to_split()` function assigns each record to one of the three splits:

```
def assign_record_to_split(rec):
    rnd = np.random.rand()
    if rnd < 0.8:
        return ('train', rec)
    if rnd < 0.9:
        return ('valid', rec)
    return ('test', rec)
```

At this point, splits consists of tuples like:

```
('valid', 'serialized-tfrecord...')
```

These can then be farmed out into three sets of sharded files with the appropriate prefixes:

```
for s in ['train', 'valid', 'test']:
    _ = (splits
            | 'only_{}'.format(s) >> beam.Filter(lambda x: x[0] == s)
            | '{}_records'.format(s) >> beam.Map(lambda x: x[1])
            | 'write_{}'.format(s) >> beam.io.tfrecordio.WriteToTFRecord(
                    os.path.join(OUTPUT_DIR, s), file_name_suffix='.gz')
            )
```

When this program is run, the job will be submitted to the Cloud Dataflow service, which will execute the entire pipeline (see Figure 5-13) and create TFRecord files corresponding to all three splits with names like *valid-00000-of-00005.gz*.

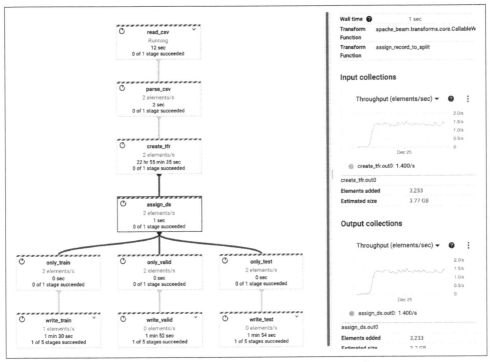

Figure 5-13. Running the dataset creation pipeline in Cloud Dataflow.

Balancing Flexibility and Maintainability

Because ML training is so computationally expensive, it can be worth the duplication in storage to create efficient, ready-to-train-on datasets for your ML projects. There are two drawbacks, however. First, each of your ML projects will typically involve different preprocessing steps (more on this in Chapter 6), and creating separate datasets for each project can lead to increased storage costs. That's why, in this chapter, we did something intermediate—while we decoded the JPEG images and scaled them to be in the range [0, 1], we left them in the original size. Resizing is one of the preprocessing steps that will be done in the training data pipeline because each ML project will tend to want to resize the images differently.

The second drawback is that such extracted datasets run the risk of running afoul of the data governance policies in place at your organization. There might be regulatory and compliance risks associated with extracting image data from the original data lake (where presumably all access is logged and monitored, and data is appropriately aged off) and storing intermediate files or sample metadata, which are potentially harder to track and might need to be saved in different and less-governed storage locations (like hard disks of a cluster for fast I/O during the ML process).

Changing the input from CSV files to Cloud pub/sub will convert this pipeline from a batch pipeline to a streaming one. All the intermediate steps remain the same, and the resulting sharded TFRecords (which are in a format conducive for machine learning) can function as our ML *data lake*.

TensorFlow Recorder

In the previous sections we looked at how to manually create TFRecord files, carrying out some extract, transform, load (ETL) operations along the way. If you already have data in Pandas or CSV files, it may be much more convenient to use the TFRecorder Python package (*https://oreil.ly/w7f80*), which adds a `tensorflow.to_tfr()` method to a Pandas dataframe:

```
import pandas as pd
import tfrecorder
csv_file = './all_data_split.csv'
df = pd.read_csv(csv_file, names=['split', 'image_uri', 'label'])
df.tensorflow.to_tfr(output_dir='gs://BUCKET/data/output/path')
```

The CSV files in this example are assumed to have lines that look like this:

```
valid,gs://BUCKET/img/abc123.jpg,daisy
train,gs://BUCKET/img/def123.jpg,tulip
```

TFRecorder will serialize the images into TensorFlow Records.

Running TFRecorder at scale in Cloud Dataflow involves adding a few parameters to the call:

```
df.tensorflow.to_tfr(
    output_dir='gs://my/bucket',
    runner='DataflowRunner',
    project='my-project',
    region='us-central1',
    tfrecorder_wheel='/path/to/my/tfrecorder.whl')
```

For details on how to create and load a wheel to be used, please check the TFRecorder documentation (*https://oreil.ly/1osx7*).

Reading TensorFlow Records

To read TensorFlow Records, use a `tf.data.TFRecordDataset`. To read all the training files into a TensorFlow dataset, we can pattern match and then pass the resulting files into `TFRecordDataset()`:

```
train_dataset = tf.data.TFRecordDataset(
    tf.data.Dataset.list_files(
        'gs://practical-ml-vision-book/flowers_tfr/train-*')
    )
```

The full code is in *06a_resizing.ipynb* on GitHub, but in a notebook in the folder for Chapter 6 because that's when we actually have to read these files.

The dataset at this point contains protobufs. We need to parse the protobufs based on the schema of the records that we wrote to the files. We specify that schema as follows:

```
feature_description = {
    'image': tf.io.VarLenFeature(tf.float32),
    'shape': tf.io.VarLenFeature(tf.int64),
    'label': tf.io.FixedLenFeature([], tf.string,
default_value=''),
        'label_int': tf.io.FixedLenFeature([], tf.int64, default_value=0),
}
```

Compare this with the code we used to create the TensorFlow Record:

```
return tf.train.Example(features=tf.train.Features(feature={
    'image': _float_feature(img),
    'shape': _int64_feature([dims[0], dims[1], dims[2]]),
    'label': _string_feature(label),
    'label_int': _int64_feature([label_int])
}))
```

The `label` and `label_int` have a fixed length (1), but the `image` and its `shape` are variable length (since they are arrays).

Given the proto and the feature description (or schema), we can read in the data using the function `parse_single_example()`:

```
rec = tf.io.parse_single_example(proto, feature_description)
```

For storage efficiency, variable-length arrays are stored as sparse tensors (see "What Is a Sparse Tensor?" on page 208). We can make them dense and reshape the flattened image array into a 3D tensor, giving us the full parsing function:

```
def parse_tfr(proto):
    feature_description = ...
    rec = tf.io.parse_single_example(proto, feature_description)
    shape = tf.sparse.to_dense(rec['shape'])
    img = tf.reshape(tf.sparse.to_dense(rec['image']), shape)
    return img, rec['label_int']
```

We can now apply the parsing function to every proto that is read using `map()`:

```
train_dataset = tf.data.TFRecordDataset(
    [filename for filename in tf.io.gfile.glob(
        'gs://practical-ml-vision-book/flowers_tfr/train-*')
    ]).map(parse_tfr)
```

At this point, the training dataset gives us the image and its label, which we can use just like the image and label we obtained from the CSV dataset in Chapter 2.

Summary

In this chapter, we looked at how to create vision datasets consisting of images and the labels associated with those images. The images can be photographs or can be produced by sensors that create 2D or 3D projections. It is possible to align several such images into a single image by treating the individual image's values as channels.

Image labeling often has to be done manually, at least in the beginning stages of a project. We looked at different types of labels for different problem types, how to organize the labels, how to efficiently label images, and how to use voting to reduce errors in the labels. Labels can sometimes be extracted automatically from the eventual outcome, or from ancillary datasets. It is also possible to set up an iterative Noisy Student process to create pseudo-labels.

We also discussed dataset bias, the causes of bias, and how to lower the chances of bias in our datasets. We will look at how to diagnose bias in Chapter 8.

Finally, we saw how to create training and validation, test splits of our data, and store these three image datasets efficiently in a data lake. In the next two chapters, you will learn how to train ML models on the datasets you created for that purpose. In Chapter 6, we will explore how to preprocess images for machine learning, and in Chapter 7 we will discuss how to train ML models on the preprocessed images.

Preprocessing

In Chapter 5, we looked at how to create training datasets for machine learning. This is the first step of the standard image processing pipeline (see Figure 6-1). The next stage is preprocessing the raw images in order to feed them into the model for training or inference. In this chapter, we will look at why images need to be preprocessed, how to set up preprocessing to ensure reproducibility in production, and ways to implement a variety of preprocessing operations in Keras/TensorFlow.

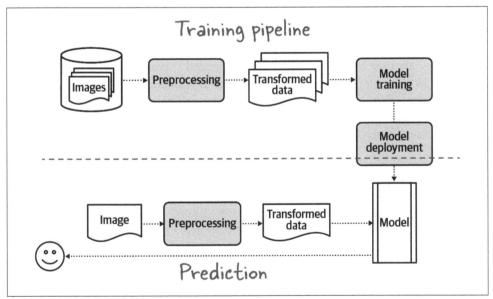

Figure 6-1. Raw images have to be preprocessed before they are fed into the model, both during training (top) and during prediction (bottom).

The code for this chapter is in the *06_preprocessing* folder of the book's GitHub repository (*https://github.com/GoogleCloudPlatform/practical-ml-vision-book*). We will provide file names for code samples and notebooks where applicable.

Reasons for Preprocessing

Before raw images can be fed into an image model, they usually have to be preprocessed. Such preprocessing has several overlapping goals: shape transformation, data quality, and model quality.

Shape Transformation

The input images typically have to be transformed into a consistent size. For example, consider a simple DNN model:

```
model = tf.keras.Sequential([
    tf.keras.layers.Flatten(input_shape=(512, 256, 3)),
    tf.keras.layers.Dense(128,
                          activation=tf.keras.activations.relu),
    tf.keras.layers.Dense(len(CLASS_NAMES), activation='softmax')
])
```

This model requires that the images fed into it are 4D tensors with an inferred batch size, 512 columns, 256 rows, and 3 channels. Every layer that we have considered so far in this book needs a shape to be specified at construction. Sometimes the specification can be inferred from previous layers, and does not have to be explicit: the first Dense layer takes the output of the Flatten layer and therefore is built to have 512 * 256 * 3 = 393,216 input nodes in the network architecture. If the raw image data is not of this size, then there is no way to map each input value to the nodes of the network. So, images that are not of the right size have to be transformed into tensors with this exact shape. Any such transformation will be carried out in the preprocessing stage.

Data Quality Transformation

Another reason to do preprocessing is to enforce data quality. For example, many satellite images have a terminator line (see Figure 6-2) because of solar lighting or the Earth's curvature.

Solar lighting can lead to different lighting levels in different parts of the image. Since the terminator line moves throughout the day and its location is known precisely from the timestamp, it can be helpful to normalize each pixel value taking into account the solar illumination that the corresponding point on the Earth receives. Or, due to the Earth's curvature and the point of view of the satellite, there might be parts of the images that were not sensed by the satellite. Such pixels might be masked or assigned a value of -inf. In the preprocessing step, it is necessary to handle this somehow because neural networks will expect to see a finite floating-point value; one option is to replace these pixels with the mean value in the image.

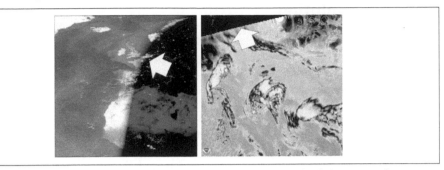

Figure 6-2. Impact of solar lighting (left) and Earth's curvature (right). Images from NASA © Living Earth and the NOAA GOES-16 satellite.

Even if your dataset doesn't consist of satellite imagery, it's important to be aware that data quality problems, like the ones described here for satellite data, pop up in many situations. For example, if some of your images are darker than others, you might want to transform the pixel values within the images to have a consistent white balance.

Improving Model Quality

A third goal of preprocessing is to carry out transformations that help improve the accuracy of models trained on the data. For example, machine learning optimizers work best when data values are small numbers. So, in the preprocessing stage, it can be helpful to scale the pixel values to lie in the range [0, 1] or [−1, 1].

Some transformations can help improve model quality by increasing the effective size of the dataset that the model was trained on. For example, if you are training a model to identify different types of animals, an easy way to double the size of your dataset is to *augment* it by adding flipped versions of the images. In addition, adding random perturbations to images results in more robust training as it limits the extent to which the model overfits.

Of course, we have to be careful when applying left-to-right transformations. If we are training a model with images that contain a lot of text (such as road signs), augmenting images by flipping them left to right would reduce the ability of the model to recognize the text. Also, sometimes flipping the images can destroy information that we require. For example, if we are trying to identify products in a clothing store, flipping images of buttoned shirts left to right may destroy information. Men's shirts have the button on the wearer's right and the button hole on the wearer's left, whereas women's shirts are the opposite. Flipping the images randomly would make it impossible for the model to use the position of the buttons to determine the gender the clothes were designed for.

Size and Resolution

As discussed in the previous section, one of the key reasons to preprocess images is to ensure that the image tensors have the shape expected by the input layer of the ML model. In order to do this, we usually have to change the size and/or resolution of the images being read in.

Consider the flower images that we wrote out into TensorFlow Records in Chapter 5. As explained in that chapter, we can read those images using:

```
train_dataset = tf.data.TFRecordDataset(
    [filename for filename in tf.io.gfile.glob(
        'gs://practical-ml-vision-book/flowers_tfr/train-*')
    ]).map(parse_tfr)
```

Let's display five of those images:

```
for idx, (img, label_int) in enumerate(train_dataset.take(5)):
    print(img.shape)
    ax[idx].imshow((img.numpy()));
```

As is clear from Figure 6-3, the images all have different sizes. The second image, for example (240x160), is in portrait mode, whereas the third image (281x500) is horizontally elongated.

Figure 6-3. Five of the images in the 5-flowers training dataset. Note that they all have different dimensions (marked on top of the image).

Using Keras Preprocessing Layers

When the input images are of different sizes, we need to preprocess them to the shape expected by the input layer of the ML model. We did this in Chapter 2 using a TensorFlow function when we read the images, specifying the desired height and width:

```
img = tf.image.resize(img, [IMG_HEIGHT, IMG_WIDTH])
```

Keras has a preprocessing layer called `Resizing` that offers the same functionality. Typically we will have multiple preprocessing operations, so we can create a Sequential model that contains all of those operations:

```
preproc_layers = tf.keras.Sequential([
    tf.keras.layers.experimental.preprocessing.Resizing(
        height=IMG_HEIGHT, width=IMG_WIDTH,
        input_shape=(None, None, 3))
    ])
```

To apply the preprocessing layer to our images, we could do:

```
train_dataset.map(lambda img: preproc_layers(img))
```

However, this won't work because the `train_dataset` provides a tuple (img, label) where the image is a 3D tensor (height, width, channels) while the Keras Sequential model expects a 4D tensor (batchsize, height, width, channels).

The simplest solution is to write a function that adds an extra dimension to the image at the first axis using `expand_dims()` and removes the batch dimension from the result using `squeeze()`:

```
def apply_preproc(img, label):
    # add to a batch, call preproc, remove from batch
    x = tf.expand_dims(img, 0)
    x = preproc_layers(x)
    x = tf.squeeze(x, 0)
    return x, label
```

With this function defined, we can apply the preprocessing layer to our tuple using:

```
train_dataset.map(apply_preproc)
```

 Normally, we don't have to call `expand_dims()` and `squeeze()` in a preprocessing function because we apply the preprocessing function after a `batch()` call. For example, we would normally do:

```
train_dataset.batch(32).map(apply_preproc)
```

Here, however, we can't do this because the images that come out of the `train_dataset` are all of different sizes. To solve this problem, we can add an extra dimension as shown or use ragged batches (*https://oreil.ly/LbavM*).

The result is shown in Figure 6-4. Notice that all the images are now the same size, and because we passed in 224 for the IMG_HEIGHT and IMG_WIDTH, the images are squares. Comparing this with Figure 6-3, we notice that the second image has been squashed vertically whereas the third image has been squashed in the horizontal dimension and stretched vertically.

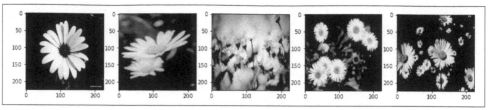

Figure 6-4. The effect of resizing the images to a shape of (224, 224, 3). Intuitively, stretching and squashing flowers will make them harder to recognize, so we would like to preserve the aspect ratio of the input images (the ratio of height to width). Later in this chapter, we will look at other preprocessing options that can do this.

The Keras `Resizing` layer (*https://oreil.ly/pUrsF*) offers several interpolation options when doing the squashing and stretching: `bilinear`, `nearest`, `bicubic`, `lanczos3`, `gaussian`, and so on. The default interpolation scheme (`bilinear`) retains local structures, whereas the `gaussian` interpolation scheme is more tolerant of noise. In practice, however, the differences between different interpolation methods are pretty minor.

The Keras preprocessing layers have an advantage that we will delve deeper into later in this chapter—because they are part of the model, they are automatically applied during prediction. Choosing between doing preprocessing in Keras or in TensorFlow thus often comes down to a trade-off between efficiency and flexibility; we will expand upon this later in the chapter.

Using the TensorFlow Image Module

In addition to the `resize()` function that we used in Chapter 2, TensorFlow offers a plethora of image processing functions in the `tf.image` module (*https://oreil.ly/K8r7W*). We used `decode_jpeg()` from this module in Chapter 5, but TensorFlow also has the ability to decode PNG, GIF, and BMP and to convert images between color and grayscale. There are methods to work with bounding boxes and to adjust contrast, brightness, and so on.

In the realm of resizing, TensorFlow allows us to retain the aspect ratio when resizing by cropping the image to the desired aspect ratio and stretching it:

```
img = tf.image.resize(img, [IMG_HEIGHT, IMG_WIDTH],
                      preserve_aspect_ratio=True)
```

or padding the edges with zeros:

```
img = tf.image.resize_with_pad(img, [IMG_HEIGHT, IMG_WIDTH])
```

We can apply this function directly to each (img, label) tuple in the dataset as follows:

```
def apply_preproc(img, label):
    return (tf.image.resize_with_pad(img, 2*IMG_HEIGHT, 2*IMG_WIDTH),
            label)
train_dataset.map(apply_preproc)
```

The result is shown in Figure 6-5. Note the effect of padding in the second and third panels in order to avoid stretching or squashing the input images while providing the desired output size.

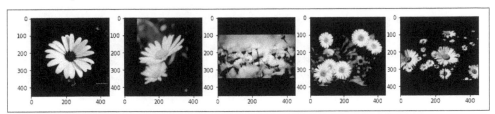

Figure 6-5. Resizing the images to (448, 448) with padding.

The eagle-eyed among you may have noticed that we resized the images to be larger than the desired height and width (twice as large, actually). The reason for this is that it sets us up for the next step.

While we've preserved the aspect ratio by specifying a padding, we now have padded images with black borders. This is not desirable either. What if we now do a "center crop"—i.e., crop these images (which are larger than what we want anyway) in the center?

Mixing Keras and TensorFlow

A center-cropping function is available in TensorFlow, but to keep things interesting, let's mix TensorFlow's `resize_with_pad()` and Keras's `CenterCrop` functionality.

In order to call an arbitrary set of TensorFlow functions as part of a Keras model, we wrap the function(s) inside a Keras `Lambda` layer:

```
tf.keras.layers.Lambda(lambda img:
                    tf.image.resize_with_pad(
                        img, 2*IMG_HEIGHT, 2*IMG_WIDTH))
```

Here, because we want to do the resize and follow it by a center crop, our preprocessing layers become:

```
preproc_layers = tf.keras.Sequential([
    tf.keras.layers.Lambda(lambda img:
                        tf.image.resize_with_pad(
                            img, 2*IMG_HEIGHT, 2*IMG_WIDTH),
                        input_shape=(None, None, 3)),
    tf.keras.layers.experimental.preprocessing.CenterCrop(
        height=IMG_HEIGHT, width=IMG_WIDTH)
    ])
```

Note that the first layer (`Lambda`) carries an `input_shape` parameter. Because the input images will be of different sizes, we specify the height and width as `None`, which leaves the values to be determined at runtime. However, we do specify that there will always be three channels.

The result of applying this preprocessing is shown in Figure 6-6. Note how the aspect ratio of the flowers is preserved and all the images are 224x224.

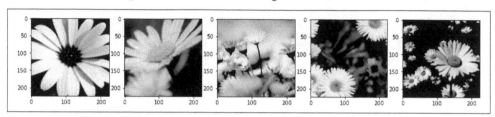

Figure 6-6. The effect of applying two processing operations: a resize with pad followed by a center crop.

At this point, you have seen three different places to carry out preprocessing: in Keras, as a preprocessing layer; in TensorFlow, as part of the `tf.data` pipeline; and in Keras, as part of the model itself. As mentioned earlier, choosing between these comes down to a trade-off between efficiency and flexibility; we'll explore this in more detail later in this chapter.

Model Training

Had the input images all been the same size, we could have incorporated the preprocessing layers into the model itself. However, because the input images vary in size, they cannot be easily batched. Therefore, we will apply the preprocessing in the ingest pipeline before doing the batching:

```
train_dataset = tf.data.TFRecordDataset(
    [filename for filename in tf.io.gfile.glob(
        'gs://practical-ml-vision-book/flowers_tfr/train-*')
    ]).map(parse_tfr).map(apply_preproc).batch(batch_size)
```

The model itself is the same MobileNet transfer learning model that we used in Chapter 3 (the full code is in *06a_resizing.ipynb* on GitHub):

```
layers = [
    hub.KerasLayer(
        "https://tfhub.dev/.../mobilenet_v2/...",
        input_shape=(IMG_HEIGHT, IMG_WIDTH, IMG_CHANNELS),
        trainable=False,
        name='mobilenet_embedding'),
    tf.keras.layers.Dense(num_hidden,
                          activation=tf.keras.activations.relu,
                          name='dense_hidden'),
```

```
        tf.keras.layers.Dense(len(CLASS_NAMES),
                          activation='softmax',
                          name='flower_prob')
]
model = tf.keras.Sequential(layers, name='flower_classification')
model.compile(optimizer=tf.keras.optimizers.Adam(learning_rate=lrate),
              loss=tf.keras.losses.SparseCategoricalCrossentropy(
                  from_logits=False),
              metrics=['accuracy'])
history = model.fit(train_dataset, validation_data=eval_dataset, epochs=10)
```

The model training converges and the validation accuracy plateaus at 0.85 (see Figure 6-7).

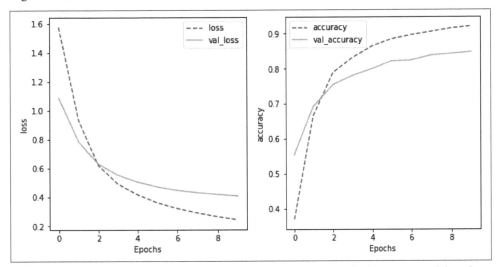

Figure 6-7. The loss and accuracy curves for a MobileNet transfer learning model with preprocessed layers as input.

Comparing Figure 6-7 against Figure 3-3, it seems that we have fared worse with padding and center cropping than with the naive resizing we did in Chapter 3. Even though the validation datasets are different in the two cases, and so the accuracy numbers are not directly comparable, the difference in accuracy (0.85 versus 0.9) is large enough that it is quite likely that the Chapter 6 model is worse than the Chapter 3 one. Machine learning is an experimental discipline, and we would not have known this unless we tried. It's quite possible that on a different dataset, fancier preprocessing operations will improve the end result; you have to try multiple options to figure out which method works best for your dataset.

Some prediction results are shown in Figure 6-8. Note that the input images all have a natural aspect ratio and are center cropped.

Figure 6-8. Images as input to the model, and predictions on those images.

Training-Serving Skew

During inference, we need to carry out the exact same set of operations on the image that we did during training (see Figure 6-1). Recall that we did preprocessing in three places:

1. When creating the file. When we wrote out the TensorFlow Records in Chapter 5, we decoded the JPEG files and scaled the input values to [0, 1].

2. When reading the file. We applied the function `parse_tfr()` to the training dataset. The only preprocessing this function did was to reshape the image tensor to [height, width, 3], where the height and width are the original size of the image.

3. In the Keras model. We then applied `preproc_layers()` to the images. In the last version of this method, we resized the images with padding to 448x448 and then center cropped them to 224x224.

In the inference pipeline, we have to perform all those operations (decoding, scaling, reshaping, resizing, center cropping) on the images provided by clients.[1] If we were to miss an operation or carry it out slightly differently between training and inference, it would cause potentially incorrect results. The condition where the training and inference pipelines diverge (therefore creating unexpected or incorrect behavior during inference not seen during training) is called *training-serving skew*. In order to prevent training-serving skew, it is ideal if we can reuse the exact same code both in training and for inference.

Broadly, there are three ways that we can set things up so that all the image preprocessing done during training is also done during inference:

---

1 Reality is more complex. There might be data preprocessing (e.g., data augmentation, covered in the next section) that you would only want to apply during training. Not all data preprocessing needs to be consistent between training and inference.

- Put the preprocessing in functions that are called from both the training and inference pipelines.
- Incorporate the preprocessing into the model itself.
- Use `tf.transform` to create and reuse artifacts.

Let's look at each of these methods. In each of these cases, we'll want to refactor the training pipeline so as to make it easier to reuse all the preprocessing code during inference. The easier it is to reuse code between training and inference, the more likely it is that subtle differences won't crop up and cause training-serving skew.

Reusing Functions

The training pipeline in our case reads TensorFlow Records consisting of already decoded and scaled JPEG files, whereas the prediction pipeline needs to key off the path to an *individual* image file. So, the preprocessing code will not be identical, but we can still collect all the preprocessing into functions that are reused and put them in a class that we'll call _Preprocessor.[2] The full code is available in *06b_reuse_functions.ipynb* on GitHub.

The methods of the preprocessor class will be called from two functions, one to create a dataset from TensorFlow Records and the other to create an individual image from a JPEG file. The function to create a preprocessed dataset is:

```
def create_preproc_dataset(pattern):
    preproc = _Preprocessor()
    trainds = tf.data.TFRecordDataset(
        [filename for filename in tf.io.gfile.glob(pattern)]
    ).map(preproc.read_from_tfr).map(
        lambda img, label: (preproc.preprocess(img), label))
    return trainds
```

There are three functions of the preprocessor that are being invoked: the constructor, a way to read TensorFlow Records into an image, and a way to preprocess the image. The function to create an individual preprocessed image is:

```
def create_preproc_image(filename):
    preproc = _Preprocessor()
    img = preproc.read_from_jpegfile(filename)
    return preproc.preprocess(img)
```

---

2 Ideally, all the functions in this class would be private and only the functions `create_preproc_dataset()` and `create_preproc_image()` would be public. Unfortunately, at the time of writing, `tf.data`'s map functionality doesn't handle the name wrangling that would be needed to use private methods as lambdas. The underscore in the name of the class reminds us that its methods are meant to be private.

Here too, we are using the constructor and preprocessing method, but we're using a different way to read the data. Therefore, the preprocessor will require four methods.

The constructor in Python consists of a method called __init__():

```
class _Preprocessor:
    def __init__(self):
        self.preproc_layers = tf.keras.Sequential([
            tf.keras.layers.experimental.preprocessing.CenterCrop(
                height=IMG_HEIGHT, width=IMG_WIDTH),
                input_shape=(2*IMG_HEIGHT, 2*IMG_WIDTH, 3)
        ])
```

In the __init__() method, we set up the preprocessing layers.

To read from a TFRecord we use the parse_tfr() function from Chapter 5, now a method of our class:

```
def read_from_tfr(self, proto):
    feature_description = ... # schema
    rec = tf.io.parse_single_example(
        proto, feature_description
    )
    shape = tf.sparse.to_dense(rec['shape'])
    img = tf.reshape(tf.sparse.to_dense(rec['image']), shape)
    label_int = rec['label_int']
    return img, label_int
```

Preprocessing consists of taking the image, sizing it consistently, putting into a batch, invoking the preprocessing layers, and unbatching the result:

```
def preprocess(self, img):
    x = tf.image.resize_with_pad(img, 2*IMG_HEIGHT, 2*IMG_WIDTH)
    # add to a batch, call preproc, remove from batch
    x = tf.expand_dims(x, 0)
    x = self.preproc_layers(x)
    x = tf.squeeze(x, 0)
    return x
```

When reading from a JPEG file, we take care to do all the steps that were carried out when the TFRecord files were written out:

```
def read_from_jpegfile(self, filename):
    # same code as in 05_create_dataset/jpeg_to_tfrecord.py
    img = tf.io.read_file(filename)
    img = tf.image.decode_jpeg(img, channels=IMG_CHANNELS)
    img = tf.image.convert_image_dtype(img, tf.float32)
    return img
```

Now, the training pipeline can create the training and validation datasets using the create_preproc_dataset() function that we have defined:

```
train_dataset = create_preproc_dataset(
    'gs://practical-ml-vision-book/flowers_tfr/train-*'
).batch(batch_size)
```

The prediction code (which will go into a serving function, covered in Chapter 9) will take advantage of the `create_preproc_image()` function to read individual JPEG files and then invoke `model.predict()`.

Preprocessing Within the Model

Note that we did not have to do anything special to reuse the model itself for prediction. For example, we did not have to write different variations of the layers: the Hub layer representing MobileNet and the dense layer were all transparently reusable between training and prediction.

Any preprocessing code that we put into the Keras model will be automatically applied during prediction. Therefore, let's take the center-cropping functionality out of the _Preprocessor class and move it into the model itself (see *06b_reuse_functions.ipynb* on GitHub for the code):

```
class _Preprocessor:
    def __init__(self):
        # nothing to initialize
        pass

    def read_from_tfr(self, proto):
        # same as before

    def read_from_jpegfile(self, filename):
        # same as before

    def preprocess(self, img):
        return tf.image.resize_with_pad(img, 2*IMG_HEIGHT, 2*IMG_WIDTH)
```

The CenterCrop layer moves into the Keras model, which now becomes:

```
layers = [
    tf.keras.layers.experimental.preprocessing.CenterCrop(
        height=IMG_HEIGHT, width=IMG_WIDTH,
        input_shape=(2*IMG_HEIGHT, 2*IMG_WIDTH, IMG_CHANNELS),
    ),
    hub.KerasLayer(...),
    tf.keras.layers.Dense(...),
    tf.keras.layers.Dense(...)
]
```

Recall that the first layer of a Sequential model is the one that carries the `input_shape` parameter. So, we have removed this parameter from the Hub layer and added it to the CenterCrop layer. The input to this layer is twice the desired size of the images, so that's what we specify.

The model now includes the `CenterCrop` layer and its output shape is 224x224, our desired output shape:

```
Model: "flower_classification"
```

Layer (type)	Output Shape	Param #
center_crop (CenterCrop)	(None, 224, 224, 3)	0
mobilenet_embedding (KerasLa	(None, 1280)	2257984
dense_hidden (Dense)	(None, 16)	20496
flower_prob (Dense)	(None, 5)	85

Of course, if both the training and prediction pipelines read the same data format, we could get rid of the preprocessor completely.

Where to Do Preprocessing

Could we not have also moved the `resize_with_pad()` functionality into the Keras model to get rid of the _Preprocessor class entirely? Not at the time this section was being written—Keras models require batched inputs, and it's much easier to write models where batches contain elements of the same shape. Because our input images have different shapes, we need to resize them to something consistent before feeding them to the Keras model. Ragged tensors (*https://oreil.ly/INIra*), which were experimental at the time of writing, will make this unnecessary.

How do you choose whether to have the center cropping done in TensorFlow as part of the `tf.data` pipeline or as a Keras layer and part of the model? Choosing whether to carry out a particular bit of preprocessing in the `tf.data` pipeline or in a Keras layer comes down to five factors:

Efficiency
> If we will always need to carry out center cropping, it is more efficient to have that be part of the preprocessing pipeline because we will be able to cache the results, either by writing out already cropped images into the TensorFlow Records or by adding `.cache()` to the pipeline. If it's done in the Keras model, this preprocessing will have to be carried out during each training iteration.

Experimentation
> Having the center cropping as a Keras layer is more flexible. As just one example, we can choose to experiment with cropping the images at 50% or 70% for different models. We can even treat the cropping ratio as a model hyperparameter.

Maintainability
> Any code in a Keras layer is automatically reused in training and inference, so using Keras layers is less error-prone.

Flexibility

We haven't discussed this yet, however, when you have operations that need to be carried out differently in training and inference (for example, the data augmentation methods that we will discuss shortly), it is much easier to have those operations be within a Keras layer.

Acceleration

Commonly, operations in the `tf.data` pipeline are carried out on the CPU and operations in the model function are carried out on the GPU (device placement can be changed, but this is the usual default). Given this default, having code in the model function is a way to take advantage of acceleration and distribution strategies.

Decide where to carry out preprocessing by balancing these considerations. Normally, you will lay out your preprocessing operations and draw a line of separation, doing some operations in `tf.data` and some in the model function.

Note that if you need to preprocess the labels in any way, it's easier to do this in `tf.data` because a Keras Sequential model does not pass the labels through its layers. If you do need to pass the labels through, you will have to switch to the Keras Functional API and pass in a dictionary of features, replacing the image component at each step. See the GAN example in Chapter 12 for an illustration of this approach.

Using tf.transform

What we did in the previous section—writing a `_Preprocessor` class and expecting to keep `read_from_tfr()` and `read_from_jpegfile()` consistent in terms of the preprocessing that is carried out—is hard to enforce. This will be a perennial source of bugs in your ML pipelines because ML engineering teams tend to keep fiddling around with preprocessing and data cleanup routines.

For example, suppose we write out already cropped images into TFRecords for efficiency. How can we ensure that this cropping happens during inference? To mitigate training-serving skew, it is best if we save all the preprocessing operations in an artifacts registry and automatically apply these operations as part of the serving pipeline.

The TensorFlow library that does this is TensorFlow Transform (*https://oreil.ly/ 25SxU*) (`tf.transform`). To use `tf.transform`, we need to:

- Write an Apache Beam pipeline to carry out analysis of the training data, precompute any statistics needed for the preprocessing (e.g., mean/variance to use for normalization), and apply the preprocessing.
- Change the training code to read the preprocessed files.
- Change the training code to save the transform function along with the model.

- Change the inference code to apply the saved transform function.

Let's look at each of these briefly (the full code is available in *06h_tftransform.ipynb* on GitHub).

Writing the Beam pipeline

The Beam pipeline to carry out the preprocessing is similar to the pipeline we used in Chapter 5 to convert the JPEG files into TensorFlow Records. The difference is that we use the built-in functionality of TensorFlow Extended (TFX) to create a CSV reader:

```
RAW_DATA_SCHEMA = schema_utils.schema_from_feature_spec({
    'filename': tf.io.FixedLenFeature([], tf.string),
    'label': tf.io.FixedLenFeature([], tf.string),
})
csv_tfxio = tfxio.CsvTFXIO(file_pattern='gs://.../all_data.csv'],
                           column_names=['filename', 'label'],
                           schema=RAW_DATA_SCHEMA)
And we use this class to read the CSV file:
img_records = (p
               | 'read_csv' >> csv_tfxio.BeamSource(batch_size=1)
               | 'img_record' >> beam.Map(
                   lambda x: create_input_record(x[0], x[1]))
              )
```

The input record at this point contains the JPEG data read, and a label index, so we specify this as the schema (see *jpeg_to_tfrecord_tft.py*) to create the dataset that will be transformed:

```
IMG_BYTES_METADATA = tft.tf_metadata.dataset_metadata.DatasetMetadata(
    schema_utils.schema_from_feature_spec({
        'img_bytes': tf.io.FixedLenFeature([], tf.string),
        'label': tf.io.FixedLenFeature([], tf.string),
        'label_int': tf.io.FixedLenFeature([], tf.int64)
    })
)
```

Transforming the data

To transform the data, we pass in the original data and metadata to a function that we call tft_preprocess():

```
raw_dataset = (img_records, IMG_BYTES_METADATA)
transformed_dataset, transform_fn = (
    raw_dataset | 'tft_img' >>
    tft_beam.AnalyzeAndTransformDataset(tft_preprocess)
)
```

The preprocessing function carries out the resizing operations using TensorFlow functions:

```
def tft_preprocess(img_record):
    img = tf.map_fn(decode_image, img_record['img_bytes'],
                    fn_output_signature=tf.uint8)
    img = tf.image.convert_image_dtype(img, tf.float32)
    img = tf.image.resize_with_pad(img, IMG_HEIGHT, IMG_WIDTH)
    return {
        'image': img,
        'label': img_record['label'],
        'label_int': img_record['label_int']
    }
```

Saving the transform

The resulting transformed data is written out as before. In addition, the transformation function is written out:

```
transform_fn | 'write_tft' >> tft_beam.WriteTransformFn(
    os.path.join(OUTPUT_DIR, 'tft'))
```

This creates a SavedModel that contains all the preprocessing operations that were carried out on the raw dataset.

Reading the preprocessed data

During training, the transformed records can be read as follows:

```
def create_dataset(pattern, batch_size):
    return tf.data.experimental.make_batched_features_dataset(
        pattern,
        batch_size=batch_size,
        features = {
            'image': tf.io.FixedLenFeature(
                [IMG_HEIGHT, IMG_WIDTH, IMG_CHANNELS], tf.float32),
            'label': tf.io.FixedLenFeature([], tf.string),
            'label_int': tf.io.FixedLenFeature([], tf.int64)
        }
    ).map(
        lambda x: (x['image'], x['label_int'])
    )
```

These images are already scaled and resized and so can be used directly in the training code.

Transformation during serving

We need to make the transformation function artifacts (that were saved using Write TransformFn()) available to the prediction system. We can do this by ensuring that the WriteTransformFn() writes the transform artifacts to a Cloud Storage location that is accessible to the serving system. Alternatively, the training pipeline can copy over the transform artifacts so that they are available alongside the exported model.

At prediction time, all the scaling and preprocessing operations are loaded and applied to the image bytes sent from the client:

```
preproc = tf.keras.models.load_model(
    '.../tft/transform_fn').signatures['transform_signature']
preprocessed = preproc(img_bytes=tf.convert_to_tensor(img_bytes)...)
```

We then call `model.predict()` on the preprocessed data:

```
pred_label_index = tf.math.argmax(model.predict(preprocessed))
```

In Chapter 7, we will look at how to write a serving function that does these operations on behalf of the client.

Benefits of tf.transform

Note that with `tf.transform` we have avoided having to make the trade-offs inherent in either putting preprocessing code in the `tf.data` pipeline or including it as part of the model. We now get the best of both approaches—efficient training and transparent reuse to prevent training-serving skew:

- The preprocessing (scaling and resizing of input images) happens only once.
- The training pipeline reads already preprocessed images, and is therefore fast.
- The preprocessing functions are stored into a model artifact.
- The serving function can load the model artifact and apply the preprocessing before invoking the model (details on how are covered shortly).

The serving function doesn't need to know the details of the transformations, only where the transform artifacts are stored. A common practice is to copy over these artifacts to the model output directory as part of the training program, so that they are available alongside the model itself. If we change the preprocessing code, we simply run the preprocessing pipeline again; the model artifact containing the preprocessing code gets updated, so the correct preprocessing gets applied automatically.

There are other advantages to using `tf.transform` beyond preventing training-serving skew. For example, because `tf.transform` iterates over the entire dataset once before training has even started, it is possible to use global statistics of the dataset (e.g., the mean) to scale the values.

Data Augmentation

Preprocessing is useful for more than simply reformatting images to the size and shape required by the model. Preprocessing can also be a way to improve model quality through *data augmentation*.

Data augmentation is a data-space solution to the problem of insufficient data (or insufficient data of the right kind)—it is a set of techniques that enhance the size and quality of training datasets with the goal of creating machine learning models that are more accurate and that generalize better.

Deep learning models have lots of weights, and the more weights there are, the more data is needed to train the model. If our dataset is too small relative to the size of the ML model, the model can employ its parameters to memorize the input data, which results in overfitting (a condition where the model performs well on training data, but produces poor results on unseen data at inference time).

As a thought experiment, consider an ML model with one million weights. If we have only 10,000 training images, the model can assign 100 weights to each image, and these weights can home in on some characteristic of each image that makes it unique in some way—for example, perhaps this is the only image where there is a bright patch centered around a specific pixel. The problem is that such an overfit model will not perform well after it is put into production. The images that the model will be required to predict will be different from the training images, and the noisy information it has learned won't be helpful. We need the ML model to *generalize* from the training dataset. For that to happen, we need a lot of data, and the larger the model we want, the more data we need.

Data augmentation techniques involve taking the images in the training dataset and transforming them to create new training examples. Existing data augmentation methods fall into three categories:

- Spatial transformation, such as random zooming, cropping, flipping, rotation, and so on
- Color distortion to change brightness, hue, etc.
- Information dropping, such as random masking or erasing of different parts of the image

Let's look at each of these in turn.

Spatial Transformations

In many cases, we can flip or rotate an image without changing its essence. For example, if we are trying to detect types of farm equipment, flipping the images horizontally (left to right, as shown in the top row of Figure 6-9) would simply simulate the equipment as seen from the other side. By augmenting the dataset using such image transformations, we are providing the model with more variety—meaning more examples of the desired image object or class in varying sizes, spatial locations, orientations, etc. This will help create a more robust model that can handle these kinds of variations in real data.

Figure 6-9. Some geometric transformations of an image of a tractor in a field. Photograph by author.

However, flipping the image vertically (top to bottom, as shown on the left side of Figure 6-9) is not a good idea, for a few reasons. First, the model is not expected to correctly classify an upside-down image in production, so there is no point in adding this image to the training dataset. Second, a vertically flipped tractor image makes it more difficult for the ML model to identify features like the cabin that are not vertically symmetric. Flipping the image vertically thus both adds an image type that the model is not required to classify correctly and makes the learning problem tougher.

> Make sure that augmenting data makes the training dataset larger, but does not make the problem more difficult. In general, this is the case only if the augmented image is typical of the images that the model is expected to predict on, and not if the augmentation creates a skewed, unnatural image. Information dropping methods, discussed shortly, are an exception to this rule.

Keras supports several data augmentation layers (*https://oreil.ly/8r8Z6*), including RandomTranslation, RandomRotation, RandomZoom, RandomCrop, RandomFlip, and so on. They all work similarly.

The RandomFlip layer will, during training, randomly either flip an image or keep it in its original orientation. During inference, the image is passed through unchanged. Keras does this automatically; all we have to do is add this as one of the layers in our model:

```
tf.keras.layers.experimental.preprocessing.RandomFlip(
    mode='horizontal',
    name='random_lr_flip/none'
)
```

The `mode` parameter controls the types of flips that are allowed, with a `horizontal` flip being the one that flips the image left to right. Other modes are `vertical` and `horizontal_and_vertical`.

In the previous section, we center cropped the images. When we do a center crop, we lose a considerable part of the image. To improve our training performance, we could consider augmenting the data by taking random crops of the desired size from the input images. The `RandomCrop` layer in Keras will do random crops during training (so that the model sees different parts of each image during each epoch, although some of them will now include the padded edges and may not even include the parts of the image that are of interest) and behave like a `CenterCrop` during inference.

The full code for this example is in *06d_augmentation.ipynb* on GitHub. Combining these two operations, our model layers now become:

```
layers = [
    tf.keras.layers.experimental.preprocessing.RandomCrop(
        height=IMG_HEIGHT//2, width=IMG_WIDTH//2,
        input_shape=(IMG_HEIGHT, IMG_WIDTH, IMG_CHANNELS),
        name='random/center_crop'
    ),
    tf.keras.layers.experimental.preprocessing.RandomFlip(
        mode='horizontal',
        name='random_lr_flip/none'
    ),
    hub.KerasLayer(
        "https://tfhub.dev/.../mobilenet_v2/...",
        trainable=False,
        name='mobilenet_embedding'),
    tf.keras.layers.Dense(
        num_hidden,
        kernel_regularizer=regularizer,
        activation=tf.keras.activations.relu,
        name='dense_hidden'),
    tf.keras.layers.Dense(
        len(CLASS_NAMES),
        kernel_regularizer=regularizer,
        activation='softmax',
        name='flower_prob')
]
```

And the model itself becomes:

```
Model: "flower_classification"

Layer (type)                    Output Shape              Param #
=================================================================
random/center_crop (RandomCr    (None, 224, 224, 3)       0

random_lr_flip/none (RandomF    (None, 224, 224, 3)       0

mobilenet_embedding (KerasLa    (None, 1280)              2257984

dense_hidden (Dense)            (None, 16)                20496

flower_prob (Dense)             (None, 5)                 85
```

Training this model is similar to training without augmentation. However, we will need to train the model longer whenever we augment data—intuitively, we need to train for twice as many epochs in order for the model to see both flips of the image. The result is shown in Figure 6-10.

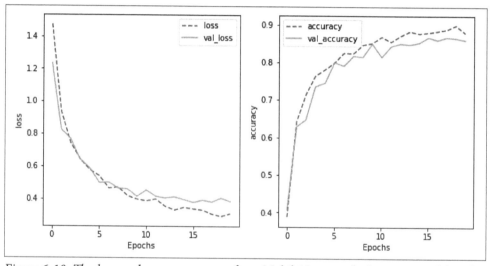

Figure 6-10. The loss and accuracy curves for a MobileNet transfer learning model with data augmentation. Compare to Figure 6-7.

Comparing Figure 6-10 with Figure 6-7, we notice how much more resilient the model training has become with the addition of data augmentation. Note that the training and validation loss are pretty much in sync, as are the training and validation accuracies. The accuracy, at 0.86, is only slightly better than before (0.85); the important thing is that we can be more confident about this accuracy because of the much better behaved training curves.

By adding data augmentation, we have dramatically lowered the extent of overfitting.

Color Distortion

It's important to not limit yourself to the set of augmentation layers that are readily available. Think instead about what kinds of variations of the images the model is likely to encounter in production. For example, it is likely that photographs provided to an ML model (especially if these are photographs by amateur photographers) will vary quite considerably in terms of lighting. We can therefore increase the effective size of the training dataset and make the ML model more resilient if we augment the data by randomly changing the brightness, contrast, saturation, etc. of the training images. While Keras has several built-in data augmentation layers (like RandomFlip (*https://oreil.ly/818dT*)), it doesn't currently support changing the contrast[3] and brightness. So, let's implement this ourselves.

We'll create a data augmentation layer from scratch that will randomly change the contrast and brightness of an image. The class will inherit from the Keras Layer class and take two arguments, the ranges within which to adjust the contrast and the brightness (the full code is in *06e_colordistortion.ipynb* on GitHub):

```
class RandomColorDistortion(tf.keras.layers.Layer):
    def __init__(self, contrast_range=[0.5, 1.5],
                 brightness_delta=[-0.2, 0.2], **kwargs):
        super(RandomColorDistortion, self).__init__(**kwargs)
        self.contrast_range = contrast_range
        self.brightness_delta = brightness_delta
```

When invoked, this layer will need to behave differently depending on whether it is in training mode or not. If not in training mode, the layer will simply return the original images. If it is in training mode, it will generate two random numbers, one to adjust the contrast within the image and the other to adjust the brightness. The actual adjustment is carried out using methods available in the tf.image module:

```
def call(self, images, training=False):
    if not training:
        return images

    contrast = np.random.uniform(
        self.contrast_range[0], self.contrast_range[1])
    brightness = np.random.uniform(
        self.brightness_delta[0], self.brightness_delta[1])

    images = tf.image.adjust_contrast(images, contrast)
    images = tf.image.adjust_brightness(images, brightness)
    images = tf.clip_by_value(images, 0, 1)
    return images
```

---

3 RandomContrast (*https://oreil.ly/ZX7QN*) was added between the time this section was written and when the book went to press.

It's important that the implementation of the custom augmentation layer consists of TensorFlow functions so that these functions can be implemented efficiently on a GPU. See Chapter 7 for recommendations on writing efficient data pipelines.

The effect of this layer on a few training images is shown in Figure 6-11. Note that the images have different contrast and brightness levels. By invoking this layer many times on each input image (once per epoch), we ensure that the model gets to see many color variations of the original training images.

Figure 6-11. Random contrast and brightness adjustment on three of the training images. The original images are shown in the first panel of each row, and four generated images are shown in the other panels. If you're looking at grayscale images, please refer to 06e_colordistortion.ipynb on GitHub to see the effect of the color distortion.

The layer itself can be inserted into the model after the RandomFlip layer:

```
layers = [
    ...
    tf.keras.layers.experimental.preprocessing.RandomFlip(
        mode='horizontal',
        name='random_lr_flip/none'
    ),
    RandomColorDistortion(name='random_contrast_brightness/none'),
    hub.KerasLayer ...
]
```

The full model will then have this structure:

```
Model: "flower_classification"

_____
Layer (type)                    Output Shape            Param #
==============================================================
random/center_crop (RandomCr    (None, 224, 224, 3)        0
_____
random_lr_flip/none (RandomF    (None, 224, 224, 3)        0
_____
random_contrast_brightness/n    (None, 224, 224, 3)        0
_____
mobilenet_embedding (KerasLa    (None, 1280)            2257984
_____
dense_hidden (Dense)            (None, 16)                20496
_____
flower_prob (Dense)             (None, 5)                  85
==============================================================
Total params: 2,278,565
Trainable params: 20,581
Non-trainable params: 2,257,984
```

Training of the model remains identical. The result is shown in Figure 6-12. We get better accuracy than with just geometric augmentation (0.88 instead of 0.86) and the training and validation curves remain totally in sync, indicating that overfitting is under control.

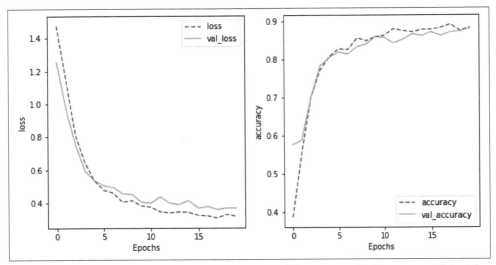

Figure 6-12. The loss and accuracy curves for a MobileNet transfer learning model with geometric and color augmentation. Compare to Figure 6-7 and 6-10.

Information Dropping

Recent research highlights some new ideas in data augmentation that involve making more dramatic changes to the images. These techniques *drop* information from the images in order to make the training process more resilient and to help the model attend to the important features of the images. They include:

Cutout (https://arxiv.org/abs/1708.04552)
> Randomly mask out square regions of input during training. This helps the model learn to disregard uninformative parts of the image (such as the sky) and attend to the discriminative parts (such as the petals).

Mixup (https://arxiv.org/abs/1710.09412)
> Linearly interpolate a pair of training images and assign as their label the corresponding interpolated label value.

CutMix (https://arxiv.org/abs/1905.04899)
> A combination of cutout and mixup. Cut patches from different training images and mix the ground truth labels proportionally to the area of the patches.

GridMask (https://arxiv.org/pdf/2001.04086.pdf)
> Delete uniformly distributed square regions while controlling the density and size of the deleted regions. The underlying assumption is that images are intentionally collected—uniformly distributed square regions tend to be the background.

Cutout and GridMask involve preprocessing operations on a single image and can be implemented similar to how we implemented the color distortion. Open source code for cutout (*https://oreil.ly/fGHK6*) and GridMask (*https://oreil.ly/3tzFk*) is available on GitHub.

Mixup and CutMix, however, use information from multiple training images to create synthetic images that may bear no resemblance to reality. In this section we'll look at how to implement mixup, since it is simpler. The full code is in *06f_mixup.ipynb* on GitHub.

The idea behind mixup is to linearly interpolate a pair of training images and their labels. We can't do this in a Keras custom layer because the layer only receives images; it doesn't get the labels. Therefore, let's implement a function that receives a batch of images and labels and does the mixup:

```
def augment_mixup(img, label):
    # parameters
    fracn = np.rint(MIXUP_FRAC * len(img)).astype(np.int32)
    wt = np.random.uniform(0.5, 0.8)
```

In this code, we have defined two parameters: `fracn` and `wt`. Instead of mixing up all the images in the batch, we will mix up a fraction of them (by default, 0.4) and keep the remaining images (and labels) as they are. The parameter `fracn` is the number of images in the batch that we have to mix up. In the function we will also choose a weighting factor, `wt`, of between 0.1 and 0.4 to interpolate the pair of images.

To interpolate, we need pairs of images. The first set of images will be the first `fracn` images in the batch:

```
img1, label1 = img[:fracn], label[:fracn]
```

How about the second image in each pair? We'll do something quite simple: we'll pick the next image, so that the first image gets interpolated with the second, the second with the third, and so on. Now that we have the pairs of images/labels, interpolating can be done as follows:

```
def _interpolate(b1, b2, wt):
    return wt*b1 + (1-wt)*b2
interp_img = _interpolate(img1, img2, wt)
interp_label = _interpolate(label1, label2, wt)
```

The results are shown in Figure 6-13. The top row is the original batch of five images. The bottom row is the result of mixup: 40% of 5 is 2, so the first two images are the ones that are mixed up, and the last three images are left as-is. The first mixed-up image is obtained by interpolating the first and second original images, with a weight of 0.63 to the first and 0.37 to the second. The second mixed-up image is obtained by mixing up the second and third images from the top row. Note that the labels (the array above each image) show the impact of the mixup as well.

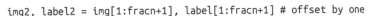

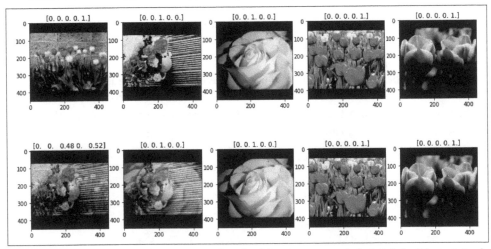

Figure 6-13. The results of mixup on a batch of five images and their labels. The original images are in the top row, and the first two images (40% of the batch) in the bottom row are the ones that are mixed up.

At this point, we have `fracn` interpolated images built from the first `fracn+1` images (we need `fracn+1` images to get `fracn` pairs, since the `fracnth` image is interpolated with the `fracn+1th` one). We then stack the interpolated images and the remaining unaltered images to get back a `batch_size` of images:

```
img = tf.concat([interp_img, img[fracn:]], axis=0)
label = tf.concat([interp_label, label[fracn:]], axis=0)
```

The `augment_mixup()` method can be passed into the `tf.data` pipeline that is used to create the training dataset:

```
train_dataset = create_preproc_dataset(...) \
    .shuffle(8 * batch_size) \
    .batch(batch_size, drop_remainder=True) \
    .map(augment_mixup)
```

There are a couple of things to notice in this code. First, we have added a `shuffle()` step to ensure that the batches are different in each epoch (otherwise, we won't get any variety in our mixup). We ask `tf.data` to drop any leftover items in the last batch, because computation of the parameter n could run into problems on very small batches. Because of the shuffle, we'll be dropping different items each time, so we're not too bothered about this.

 `shuffle()` works by reading records into a buffer, shuffling the records in the buffer, and then providing the records to the next step of the data pipeline. Because we want the records in a batch to be different during each epoch, we will need the size of the shuffle buffer to be much larger than the batch size—shuffling the records within a batch won't suffice. Hence, we use:

```
.shuffle(8 * batch_size)
```

Interpolating labels is not possible if we keep the labels as sparse integers (e.g., 4 for tulips). Instead, we have to one-hot encode the labels (see Figure 6-13). Therefore, we make two changes to our training program. First, our `read_from_tfr()` method does the one-hot encoding instead of simply returning `label_int`:

```
def read_from_tfr(self, proto):
    ...
    rec = tf.io.parse_single_example(
        proto, feature_description
    )
    shape = tf.sparse.to_dense(rec['shape'])
    img = tf.reshape(tf.sparse.to_dense(rec['image']), shape)
    label_int = rec['label_int']
    return img, tf.one_hot(label_int, len(CLASS_NAMES))
```

Second, we change the loss function from `SparseCategoricalCrossentropy()` to `CategoricalCrossentropy()` since the labels are now one-hot encoded:

```
model.compile(optimizer=tf.keras.optimizers.Adam(learning_rate=lrate),
              loss=tf.keras.losses.CategoricalCrossentropy(
                  from_logits=False),
              metrics=['accuracy'])
```

On the 5-flowers dataset, mixup doesn't improve the performance of the model—we got the same accuracy (0.88, see Figure 6-14) with mixup as without it. However, it might help in other situations. Recall that information dropping helps the model learn to disregard uninformative parts of the image and mixup works by linearly interpolating pairs of training images. So, information dropping via mixup would work well in situations where only a small section of the image is informative, and where the pixel intensity is informative—think, for example, of remotely sensed imagery where we are trying to identify deforested patches of land.

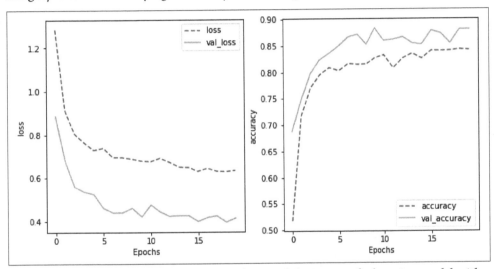

Figure 6-14. The loss and accuracy curves for a MobileNet transfer learning model with mixup. Compare to Figure 6-12.

Interestingly, the validation accuracy and loss are now better than the training accuracy. This is logical when we recognize that the training dataset is "harder" than the validation dataset—there are no mixed-up images in the validation set.

Forming Input Images

The preprocessing operations we have looked at so far are one-to-one, in that they simply modify the input image and provide a single image to the model for every image that is input. This is not necessary, however. Sometimes, it can be helpful to use the preprocessing pipeline to break down each input into multiple images that are then fed to the model for training and inference (see Figure 6-15).

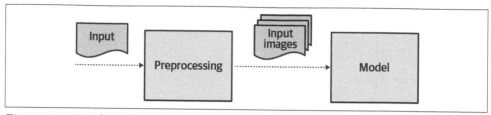

Figure 6-15. Breaking down a single input into component images that are used to train the model. The operation used to break an input into its component images during training also has to be repeated during inference.

One method of forming the images that are input to a model is *tiling*. Tiling is useful in any field where we have extremely large images and where predictions can be carried out on parts of the large image and then assembled. This tends to be the case for geospatial imagery (identifying deforested areas), medical images (identifying cancerous tissue), and surveillance (identifying liquid spills on a factory floor).

Imagine that we have a remotely sensed image of the Earth and would like to identify forest fires (see Figure 6-16). To do this, a machine learning model would have to predict whether an individual pixel contains a forest fire or not. The input to such a model would be a *tile*, the part of the original image immediately surrounding the pixel to be predicted. We can preprocess geospatial images to yield equal-sized tiles that are used to train ML models and obtain predictions from them.

Figure 6-16. Remotely sensed image of wildfires in California. Image courtesy of NOAA.

For each of the tiles, we'll need a label that signifies whether or not there is fire within the tile. To create these labels, we can take fire locations called in by fire lookout towers and map them to an image the size of the remotely sensed image (the full code is in *06g_tiling.ipynb* on GitHub):

```
fire_label = np.zeros((338, 600))
for loc in fire_locations:
    fire_label[loc[0]][loc[1]] = 1.0
```

To generate the tiles, we will extract patches of the desired tile size and stride forward by half the tile height and width (so that the tiles overlap):

```
tiles = tf.image.extract_patches(
    images=images,
    sizes=[1, TILE_HT, TILE_WD, 1],
    strides=[1, TILE_HT//2, TILE_WD//2, 1],
    rates=[1, 1, 1, 1],
    padding='VALID')
```

The result, after a few reshaping operations, is shown in Figure 6-17. In this figure, we are also annotating each tile by its label. The label for an image tile is obtained by looking for the maximum value within the corresponding label tile (this will be 1.0 if the tile contains a `fire_location` point):

```
labels = tile_image(labels)
labels = tf.reduce_max(labels, axis=[1, 2, 3])
```

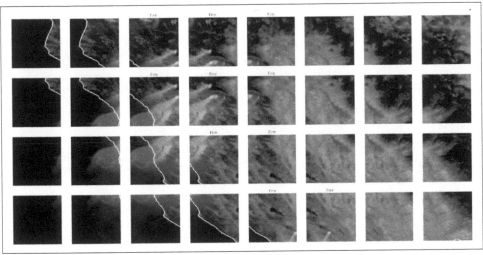

Figure 6-17. Tiles generated from a remotely sensed image of wildfires in California. Tiles with fire are labeled "Fire." Image courtesy of NOAA.

These tiles and their labels can now be used to train an image classification model. By reducing the stride by which we generate tiles, we can augment the training dataset.

Summary

In this chapter, we looked at various reasons why the preprocessing of images is needed. It could be to reformat and reshape the input data into the data type and shape required by the model, or to improve the data quality by carrying out operations such as scaling and clipping. Another reason to do preprocessing is to perform data augmentation, which is a set of techniques to increase the accuracy and resilience of a model by generating new training examples from the existing training dataset. We also looked at how to implement each of these types of preprocessing, both as Keras layers and by wrapping TensorFlow operations into Keras layers.

In the next chapter, we will delve into the training loop itself.

## CHAPTER 7

Training Pipeline

The stage after preprocessing is model training, during which the machine learning model will read in the training data and use that data to adjust its weights (see Figure 7-1). After training, the model is saved or exported so that it can be deployed.

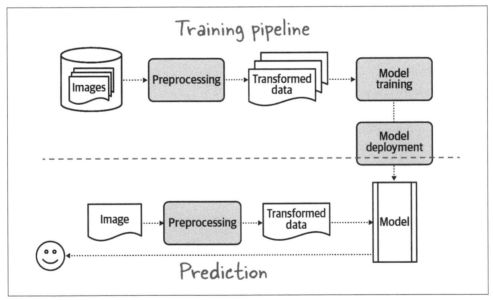

Figure 7-1. In the model training process, the ML model is trained on preprocessed data and then exported for deployment. The exported model is used to make predictions.

In this chapter, we will look at ways to make the ingestion of training (and validation) data into the model more efficient. We will take advantage of time slicing between the different computational devices (CPUs and GPUs) available to us, and examine how to make the whole process more resilient and reproducible.

The code for this chapter is in the *07_training* folder of the book's GitHub repository (*https://github.com/GoogleCloudPlatform/ practical-ml-vision-book*). We will provide file names for code samples and notebooks where applicable.

Efficient Ingestion

A significant part of the time it takes to train machine learning models is spent on ingesting data—reading it and transforming it into a form that is usable by the model. The more we can do to streamline and speed up this stage of the training pipeline, the more efficient we can be. We can do this by:

Storing data efficiently
> We should preprocess the input images as much as possible, and store the preprocessed values in a way that is efficient to read.

Parallelizing the reading of data
> When ingesting data, the speed of storage devices tends to be a bottleneck. Different files may be stored on different disks, or can be read via different network connections, so it is often possible to parallelize the reading of data.

Preparing images in parallel with training
> If we can preprocess the images on the CPU in parallel with training on the GPU, we should do so.

Maximizing GPU utilization
> As much as possible, we should try to carry out matrix and mathematical operations on the GPU, since it is many orders of magnitude faster than a CPU. If any of our preprocessing operations involve these operations, we should push them to the GPU.

Let's look at each of these ideas in more detail.

Storing Data Efficiently

Storing images as individual JPEG files is not very efficient from a machine learning perspective. In Chapter 5, we discussed how to convert JPEG images into TensorFlow Records. In this section, we will explain why TFRecords are an efficient storage mechanism, and consider trade-offs between flexibility and efficiency in terms of the amount of preprocessing that is carried out before the data is written out.

TensorFlow Records

Why store images as TensorFlow Records? Let's consider what we're looking for in a file format.

We know that we are going to be reading these images in batches, so it will be best if we can read an entire batch of images using a single network connection rather than open up one connection per file. Reading a batch all at once will also provide greater throughput to our machine learning pipeline and minimize the amount of time the GPU is waiting for the next batch of images.

Ideally, we would like the files to be around 10–100 MB in size. This allows us to balance the ability to read the images from multiple workers (one for every GPU) and the need to have each file open long enough to amortize the latency of reading the first byte over many batches.

Also, we would like the file format to be such that bytes read from the file can be mapped immediately to an in-memory structure without the need to parse the file or handle storage layout differences (such as endianness) between different types of machines.

The file format that meets all these criteria is TensorFlow Records. We can store the image data for training, validation, and testing into separate TFRecord files, and shard the files at around 100 MB each. Apache Beam has a handy TFRecord writer that we used in Chapter 5.

Storing preprocessed data

We can improve the performance of our training pipeline if we don't have to do the preprocessing in the training loop. We might be able to carry out the desired preprocessing on the JPEG images and then write out the preprocessed data rather than the raw data.

In practice, we will have to split the preprocessing operations between the ETL pipeline that creates the TensorFlow Records and the model code itself. Why not do it all in the ETL pipeline or all in the model code? The reason is that preprocessing operations applied in the ETL pipeline are done only once instead of in each epoch of the model training. However, there will always be preprocessing operations that are specific to the model that we are training or that need to be different during each epoch. These cannot be done in the ETL pipeline—they must be done in the training code.

In Chapter 5, we decoded our JPEG files, scaled them to lie between [0, 1], flattened out the array, and wrote the flattened array out to TensorFlow Records:

```
def create_tfrecord(filename, label, label_int):
    img = tf.io.read_file(filename)
    img = tf.image.decode_jpeg(img, channels=IMG_CHANNELS)
    img = tf.image.convert_image_dtype(img, tf.float32)
    img = tf.reshape(img, [-1]) # flatten to 1D array
    return tf.train.Example(features=tf.train.Features(feature={
        'image': _float_feature(img),
        ...
    })).SerializeToString()
```

The operations that we did before writing the TensorFlow Records were chosen explicitly.

We could have done less if we'd wanted—we could have simply read the JPEG files and written out the contents of each file as a string into the TensorFlow Records:

```
def create_tfrecord(filename, label, label_int):
    img = tf.io.read_file(filename)
    return tf.train.Example(features=tf.train.Features(feature={
        'image': _bytes_feature(img),
        ...
    })).SerializeToString()
```

Had we been concerned about potentially different file formats (JPEG, PNG, etc.) or image formats not understood by TensorFlow, we could have decoded each image, converted the pixel values into a common format, and written out the compressed JPEG as a string.

We could also have done much more. For example, we could have created an embedding of the images and written out not the image data, but only the embeddings:

```
embedding_encoder = tf.keras.Sequential([
    hub.KerasLayer(
        "https://tfhub.dev/.../mobilenet_v2/...",
        trainable=False,
        input_shape=(256, 256, IMG_CHANNELS),
        name='mobilenet_embedding'),
])

def create_tfrecord(filename, label, label_int):
    img = tf.io.read_file(filename)
    img = tf.image.decode_jpeg(img, channels=IMG_CHANNELS)
    img = tf.image.convert_image_dtype(img, tf.float32)
    img = tf.resize(img, [256, 256, 3])
    embed = embedding_encoder(filename)
    embed = tf.reshape(embed, [-1]) # flatten to 1D array
    return tf.train.Example(features=tf.train.Features(feature={
        'image_embedding': _float_feature(embed),
        ...
    })).SerializeToString()
```

The choice of what operations to perform comes down to a trade-off between efficiency and reusability. It's also affected by what types of reusability we envision. Remember that ML model training is a highly iterative, experimental process. Each training experiment will iterate over the training dataset multiple times (specified by the number of epochs). Therefore, each TFRecord in the training dataset will have to be processed multiple times. The more of the processing we can carry out before writing the TFRecords, the less processing has to be carried out in the training pipeline itself. This will result in faster and more efficient training and higher data throughput. This advantage is multiplied manyfold because we normally do not just train a model once; we run multiple experiments with multiple hyperparameters. On the other hand, we have to make sure that the preprocessing that we are carrying out is desirable for all the ML models that we want to train using this dataset—the more preprocessing we do, the less reusable our dataset might become. We should also not enter the realm of micro-optimizations that improve speed minimally but make the code much less clear or reusable.

If we write out the image embeddings (rather than the pixel values) to TensorFlow Records, the training pipeline will be hugely efficient since the embedding computation typically involves passing the image through one hundred or more neural network layers. The efficiency gains can be considerable. However, this presupposes that we will be doing transfer learning. We cannot train an image model from scratch using this dataset. Of course, storage being much less expensive than compute, we might also find that it is advantageous to create two datasets, one of the embeddings and the other of the pixel values.

Because TensorFlow Records can vary in terms of how much preprocessing has been carried out, it is a good practice to document this in the form of metadata. Explain what data is present in the records, and how that data was generated. General-purpose tools like Google Cloud Data Catalog (*https://oreil.ly/T2W2N*), Collibra (*https://oreil.ly/MZNaZ*), and Informatica (*https://oreil.ly/MsFaX*) can help here, as can custom ML frameworks like the Feast feature store (*https://oreil.ly/t3Rh2*).

Reading Data in Parallel

Another way to improve the efficiency of ingesting data into the training pipeline is to read the records in parallel. In Chapter 6, we read the written-out TFRecords and preprocessed them using:

```
preproc = _Preprocessor()
trainds = tf.data.TFRecordDataset(pattern)
            .map(preproc.read_from_tfr)
            .map(_preproc_img_label)
```

In this code, we are doing three things:

1. Creating a `TFRecordDataset` from a pattern
2. Passing each record in the files to `read_from_tfr()`, which returns an (img, label) tuple
3. Preprocessing the tuples using `_preproc_img_label()`

Parallelizing

There are a couple of improvements that we can make to our code, assuming that we are running on a machine with more than one virtual CPU (most modern machines have at least two vCPUs, often more). First, we can ask TensorFlow to automatically interleave reading when we create the dataset:

```
tf.data.TFRecordDataset(pattern, num_parallel_reads=AUTO)
```

Second, the two `map()` operations can be parallelized using:

```
.map(preproc.read_from_tfr, num_parallel_calls=AUTOTUNE)
```

Measuring performance

In order to measure the performance impact of these changes, we need to go through the dataset and carry out some mathematical operations. Let's compute the mean of all the images. To prevent TensorFlow from optimizing away any calculations (see the following sidebar), we'll compute the mean only of pixels that are above some random threshold that is different in each iteration of the loop:

```
def loop_through_dataset(ds, nepochs):
    lowest_mean = tf.constant(1.)
    for epoch in range(nepochs):
        thresh = np.random.uniform(0.3, 0.7)  # random threshold
        ...
        for (img, label) in ds:
            ...
            mean = tf.reduce_mean(tf.where(img > thresh, img, 0))
            ...
```

Measuring Performance Impacts

When carrying out measurements of performance, we have to make sure that the optimizer doesn't realize that our code is unnecessary to compute. For example, in the following code, the optimizer would realize that we are not using the mean at all and simply optimize away the calculations:

```
for iter in range(100):
    mean = tf.reduce_mean(img)
```

One way to prevent this is to use the mean somehow. For example, we can find the lowest mean found in the loop and make sure to print or return it:

```
    lowest_mean = tf.constant(1.)
for iter in range(100):
    mean = tf.reduce_mean(img)
    lowest_mean = mean if mean < lowest_mean
return(lowest_mean)
```

However, the optimizer is capable of recognizing that `img` doesn't change and that `reduce_mean()` will return the same value, so it will get moved out of the loop. That's why we are adding a random threshold to our code.

Table 7-1 shows the result of measuring the performance of the preceding loop when ingesting the first 10 TFRecord files using different mechanisms. It is clear that while the additional parallelization increases the overall CPU time, the actual wall-clock time reduces with each bout of parallelization. We get a 35% reduction in the time spent by making the maps parallel and by interleaving two datasets.

Table 7-1. Time taken to loop through a small dataset when the ingestion is done in different ways

Method	CPU time	Wall time
Plain	7.53 s	7.99 s
Parallel map	8.30 s	5.94 s
Interleave	8.60 s	5.47 s
Interleave + parallel map	8.44 s	5.23 s

Will this performance gain carry over to machine learning models? To test this, we can try training a simple linear classification model instead of using the `loop_through_dataset()` function:

```
def train_simple_model(ds, nepochs):
    model = tf.keras.Sequential([
        tf.keras.layers.Flatten(
            input_shape=(IMG_HEIGHT, IMG_WIDTH, IMG_CHANNELS)),
        tf.keras.layers.Dense(len(CLASS_NAMES), activation='softmax')
    ])
    model.compile(optimizer=tf.keras.optimizers.Adam(),
                  loss=tf.keras.losses.SparseCategoricalCrossentropy(
                      from_logits=False),
                  metrics=['accuracy'])
    model.fit(ds, epochs=nepochs)
```

The result, shown in Table 7-2, illustrates that the performance gains do hold up—we get a 25% speedup between the first and last rows. As the complexity of the model increases, the I/O plays a smaller and smaller role in the overall timing, so it makes sense that the improvement is less.

Table 7-2. Time taken to train a linear ML model on a small dataset when the ingestion is done in different ways

Method	CPU time	Wall time
Plain	9.91 s	9.39 s
Parallel map	10.7 s	8.17 s
Interleave	10.5 s	7.54 s
Interleave + parallel map	10.3 s	7.17 s

Looping through a dataset is faster than training an actual ML model on the full training dataset. Use it as a lightweight way to exercise your ingestion code for the purposes of tuning the performance of the I/O part.

Maximizing GPU Utilization

Because GPUs are more efficient at doing machine learning model operations, our goal should be to maximize their utilization. If we rent GPUs by the hour (as we do in a public cloud), maximizing GPU utilization will allow us to take advantage of their increased efficiency to get an overall lower cost per training run than we would get if we were to train on CPUs.

There are three factors that will affect our model's performance:

1. Every time we move data between the CPU and the GPU, that transfer takes time.

2. GPUs are efficient at matrix math. The more operations we do on single items, the less we are taking advantage of the performance speedup offered by a GPU.

3. GPUs have limited memory.

These factors play a role in the optimizations that we can do to improve the performance of our training loop. In this section, we will look at three core ideas in maximizing GPU utilization: efficient data handling, vectorization, and staying in the graph.

Efficient data handling

When we are training our model on a GPU, the CPU will be idle while the GPU is calculating gradients and doing weight updates.

It can be helpful to give the CPU something to do—we can ask it to *prefetch* the data, so that the next batch of data is ready to pass to the GPU:

```
ds = create_preproc_dataset(
    'gs://practical-ml-vision-book/flowers_tfr/train' + PATTERN_SUFFIX
).prefetch(AUTOTUNE)
```

If we have a small dataset, especially one where the images or TensorFlow Records have to be read across a network, it can also be helpful to cache them locally:

```
ds = create_preproc_dataset(
    'gs://practical-ml-vision-book/flowers_tfr/train' + PATTERN_SUFFIX
).cache()
```

Table 7-3 shows the impact of prefetching and caching on how long it takes to train a model.

Table 7-3. Time taken to train a linear ML model on a small dataset when the input records are prefetched and/or cached

Method	CPU time	Wall time
Interleave + parallel	9.68 s	6.37 s
Cache	6.16 s	4.36 s
Prefetch + cache	5.76 s	4.04 s

In our experience, caching tends to work only for small (toy) datasets. For large datasets, you are likely to run out of local storage.

Vectorization

Because GPUs are good at matrix manipulation, we should attempt to give the GPU the maximum amount of data it can handle at one time. Instead of passing images one at a time, we should send in a batch of images—this is called *vectorization*.

To batch records, we can do:

```
ds = create_preproc_dataset(
    'gs://practical-ml-vision-book/flowers_tfr/train' + PATTERN_SUFFIX
).prefetch(AUTOTUNE).batch(32)
```

It's important to realize the entire Keras model operates on batches. Therefore, the `RandomFlip` and `RandomColorDistortion` preprocessing layers that we added do not process one image at a time; they process batches of images.

The larger the batch size is, the faster the training loop will be able to get through an epoch. There are diminishing returns, however, to increasing the batch size. Also, there is a limit imposed by the memory limit of the GPU. It's worth doing a cost–benefit analysis of using larger, more expensive machines with more GPU memory and training for a shorter period of time versus using smaller, less expensive machines and training for longer.

When training on Google's Vertex AI, GPU memory usage and utilization are automatically reported for every job. Azure allows you to configure containers (*https://oreil.ly/J2dhk*) for GPU monitoring. Amazon CloudWatch provides GPU monitoring on AWS. If you are managing your own infrastructure, use GPU tools like `nvidia-smi` (*https://oreil.ly/bSEhN*) or AMD System Monitor (*https://oreil.ly/PIaLQ*). You can use these to diagnose how effectively your GPUs are being used, and whether there is headroom in GPU memory to increase your batch size.

In Table 7-4, we show the impact of changing the batch size on a linear model. Larger batches are faster, but there are diminishing returns and we'll run out of on-board GPU memory beyond a certain point. The faster performance with increasing batch size is one of the reasons why TPUs, with their large on-board memory and interconnected cores that share the memory, are so cost-effective.

Table 7-4. Time taken to train a linear ML model at different batch sizes

Method	CPU time	Wall time
Batch size 1	11.4 s	8.09 s
Batch size 8	9.56 s	6.90 s
Batch size 16	9.90 s	6.70 s
Batch size 32	9.68 s	6.37 s

A key reason that we implemented the random flip, color distortion, and other pre-processing and data augmentation steps as Keras layers in Chapter 6 has to do with batching. We could have done the color distortion using a `map()` as follows:

```
trainds = tf.data.TFRecordDataset(
        [filename for filename in tf.io.gfile.glob(pattern)]
    ).map(preproc.read_from_tfr).map(_preproc_img_label
    ).map(color_distort).batch(32)
```

where `color_distort()` is:

```
def color_distort(image, label):
    contrast = np.random.uniform(0.5, 1.5)
    brightness = np.random.uniform(-0.2, 0.2)
    image = tf.image.adjust_contrast(image, contrast)
    image = tf.image.adjust_brightness(image, brightness)
    image = tf.clip_by_value(image, 0, 1)
    return image, label
```

But this would have been inefficient since the training pipeline would have to do color distortion one image at a time. It is much more efficient if we carry out preprocessing operations in Keras layers. This way, the preprocessing is done on the whole batch in one step. An alternative would be to vectorize the color distortion operation by writing the code as:

```
    ).batch(32).map(color_distort)
```

This would also cause the color distortion to happen on a batch of data. Best practice, however, is to write preprocessing code that follows the `batch()` operation in a Keras layer. There are two reasons for this. First, the separation between ingestion code and model code is cleaner and more maintainable if we consistently make the call to `batch()` a hard boundary. Second, keeping preprocessing in a Keras layer (see Chapter 6) makes it easier to reproduce the preprocessing functionality in the inference pipeline since all the model layers are automatically exported.

Staying in the graph

Because executing mathematical functions is much more efficient on a GPU than on a CPU, TensorFlow reads the data using the CPU, transfers the data to the GPU, then runs all our code that belongs to the tf.data pipeline (the code in the map() calls, for example) on the GPU. It also runs all the code in the Keras model layers on the GPU. Since we are sending the data directly from the tf.data pipeline to the Keras input layer, there is no need to transfer the data—the data stays within the TensorFlow graph. The data and model weights all remain in the GPU memory.

This means that we have to be extremely careful to make sure that we don't do anything that would involve moving the data out of the TensorFlow graph once the CPU has delivered the data to the GPU. Data transfers carry extra overhead, and any code executed on the CPU will tend to be slower.

Iteration. As an example, suppose we are reading a satellite image of California wildfires and wish to apply a specific formula based on photometry to the RGB pixel values to transform them into a single "grayscale" image (see Figure 7-2 and the full code in *07b_gpumax.ipynb* on GitHub):

```
def to_grayscale(img):
    rows, cols, _ = img.shape
    result = np.zeros([rows, cols], dtype=np.float32)
    for row in range(rows):
        for col in range(cols):
            red = img[row][col][0]
            green = img[row][col][1]
            blue = img[row][col][2]
            c_linear = 0.2126 * red + 0.7152 * green + 0.0722 * blue
            if c_linear > 0.0031308:
                result[row][col] = 1.055 * pow(c_linear, 1/2.4) - 0.055
            else:
                result[row][col] = 12.92 * c_linear
    return result
```

There are three problems with this function:

- It needs to iterate through the image pixels:

    ```
    rows, cols, _ = img.shape
        for row in range(rows):
            for col in range(cols):
    ```

- It needs to read individual pixel values:

    ```
    green = img[row][col][1]
    ```

- It needs to change output pixel values:

    ```
    result[row][col] = 12.92 * c_linear
    ```

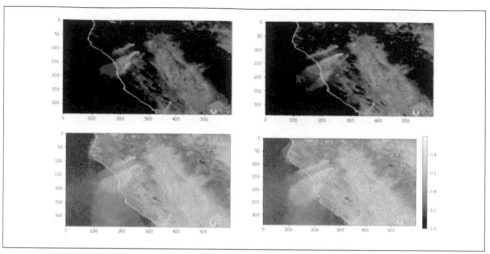

Figure 7-2. Top: original images with three channels. Bottom: transformed images with only one channel. Image of wildfires in California courtesy of NOAA.

These operations cannot be done in the TensorFlow graph. Therefore, to call the function, we need to bring it out of the graph using `.numpy()`, do the transformation, and then push the result back into the graph as a tensor (`gray` is converted into a tensor for the `reduce_mean()` operation).

Using tf.py_function() to Call Pure Python Code

There are times when we will have to invoke pure Python functionality from our TensorFlow programs. Maybe we have to do some time zone conversions and we need access to the `pytz` library, or maybe we get some data in JSON format and we need to invoke `json.loads()`.

In order to drop out of the TensorFlow graph, run a Python function, and get its result back into the TensorFlow graph, use `tf.py_function()`:

```
def to_grayscale(img):
    return tf.py_function(to_grayscale_numpy, [img],
                          tf.float32)
```

Now, `to_grayscale()` can be used as if it were implemented using TensorFlow operations:

```
ds = tf.data.TextLineDataset(...).map(to_grayscale)
```

There are three parameters to `py_function()`: the name of the function to wrap, the input tensor(s), and the output type. In our case, the wrapped function will be:

```
def to_grayscale_numpy(img):
    # The conversion from a tensor happens here.
    img = img.numpy()
    rows, cols, _ = img.shape
    result = np.zeros([rows, cols], dtype=np.float32)
    ...
    # The conversion back happens here.
    return tf.convert_to_tensor(result)
```

Note that we are still calling numpy() to bring the img tensor out of the graph, so that we can iterate through it, and we are taking the result (a numpy array) and converting it to a tensor so that it can be used in the remainder of the TensorFlow code.

Using py_function() is merely a way to call out to Python functions from Tensor-Flow. It does not do any optimizations or acceleration.

Slicing and conditionals.   We can avoid the explicit iteration and pixel-wise read/write by using TensorFlow's slicing functionality:

```
def to_grayscale(img):
    # TensorFlow slicing functionality
    red = img[:, :, 0]
    green = img[:, :, 1]
    blue = img[:, :, 2]
    c_linear = 0.2126 * red + 0.7152 * green + 0.0722 * blue
```

Note that the last line of this code snippet is actually operating on tensors (red is a tensor, not a scalar) and uses operator overloading (the + is actually tf.add()) to invoke TensorFlow functions.

But how do we do the if statement in the original?

```
if c_linear > 0.0031308:
    result[row][col] = 1.055 * pow(c_linear, 1 / 2.4) - 0.055
else:
    result[row][col] = 12.92 * c_linear
```

The if statement assumes that c_linear is a single floating-point value, whereas now c_linear is a 2D tensor.

To push a conditional statement into the graph and avoid setting pixel values individually, we can use tf.cond() and/or tf.where():

```
gray = tf.where(c_linear > 0.0031308,
                1.055 * tf.pow(c_linear, 1 / 2.4) - 0.055,
                12.92 * c_linear)
```

One key thing to realize is that all the three parameters to tf.where() in this example are actually 2D tensors. Note also the use of tf.pow() rather than pow(). Given the choice between tf.cond() and tf.where(), use tf.where() as it is faster.

This results in a more than 10x speedup.

Matrix math. The computation of c_linear can be optimized further. This is what we had:

```
red = img[:, :, 0]
green = img[:, :, 1]
blue = img[:, :, 2]
c_linear = 0.2126 * red + 0.7152 * green + 0.0722 * blue
```

If we look carefully at this calculation, we'll see that we don't need the slicing. Instead, we can write the computation as a matrix multiplication if we take the constants and put them into a 3x1 tensor:

```
def to_grayscale(img):
    wt = tf.constant([[0.2126], [0.7152], [0.0722]]) # 3x1 matrix
    c_linear = tf.matmul(img, wt)  # (ht,wd,3) x (3x1) -> (ht, wd)
    gray = tf.where(c_linear > 0.0031308,
                    1.055 * tf.pow(c_linear, 1 / 2.4) - 0.055,
                    12.92 * c_linear)
    return gray
```

With this optimization, we get an additional 4x speedup.

Batching. Once we have written the calculation of c_linear using matrix math, we also realize that we don't need to process the data one image at a time. We can process a batch of images all at once. We can do the calculations on a batch of images using either a custom Keras layer or a Lambda layer.

Let's wrap the grayscale calculation into the call() statement of a custom Keras layer:

```
class Grayscale(tf.keras.layers.Layer):
    def __init__(self, **kwargs):
        super(Grayscale, self).__init__(kwargs)

    def call(self, img):
        wt = tf.constant([[0.2126], [0.7152], [0.0722]]) # 3x1 matrix
        c_linear = tf.matmul(img, wt)  #(N, ht,wd,3)x(3x1)->(N, ht, wd)
        gray = tf.where(c_linear > 0.0031308,
                        1.055 * tf.pow(c_linear, 1 / 2.4) - 0.055,
                        12.92 * c_linear)
        return gray # (N, ht, wd)
```

An important thing to note is that the input matrix is now a 4D tensor, with the first dimension being the batch size. The result is therefore a 3D tensor.

Clients calling this code can compute the mean of each image to get back a 1D tensor of means:

```
tf.keras.layers.Lambda(lambda gray: tf.reduce_mean(gray, axis=[1, 2]))
```

We can combine these two layers into a Keras model, or prepend them to an existing model:

```
preproc_model = tf.keras.Sequential([
    Grayscale(input_shape=(336, 600, 3)),
    tf.keras.layers.Lambda(lambda gray: tf.reduce_mean(
                            gray, axis=[1, 2]))  # note axis change
])
```

The timings of all the methods we discussed in this section are shown in Table 7-5.

Table 7-5. Time taken when the grayscale computation is carried out in different ways

Method	CPU time	Wall time
Iterate	39.6 s	41.1 s
Pyfunc	39.7 s	41.1 s
Slicing	4.44 s	3.07 s
Matmul	1.22 s	2.29 s
Batch	1.11 s	2.13 s

Saving Model State

So far in this book, we have been training a model and then using the trained model to immediately make a few predictions. This is highly unrealistic—we will want to train our model, and then keep the trained model around to continue making predictions with it. We will need to save the model's state so that we can quickly read in the trained model (its structure and its final weights) whenever we want.

We will want to save the model not just to predict from it, but also to resume training. Imagine that we have trained a model on one million images and are carrying out predictions with that model. If a month later we receive one thousand new images, it would be good to continue the training of the original model for a few steps with the new images instead of training from scratch. This is called fine-tuning (and was discussed in Chapter 3).

So, there are two reasons to save model state:

- To make inferences from the model
- To resume training

What these two use cases require are quite different. It's easiest to understand the difference between the two use cases if we consider the RandomColorDistortion data augmentation layer that is part of our model. For the purposes of inference, this layer can be removed completely. However, in order to resume training, we may need to know the full state of the layer (consider, for example, that we lower the amount of distortion the longer we train).

Saving the model for inference is called *exporting* the model. Saving the model in order to resume training is called *checkpointing*. Checkpoints are much larger in size than exports because they include a lot more internal state.

Exporting the Model

To export a trained Keras model, use the `save()` method:

```
os.mkdir('export')
model.save('export/flowers_model')
```

The output directory will contain a protobuf file called *saved_model.pb* (which is why this format is often referred to as the TensorFlow SavedModel format), the variable weights, and any assets such as vocabulary files that the model needs for prediction.

 An alternative to SavedModel is Open Neural Network Exchange (ONNX), an open source, framework-agnostic ML model format that was introduced by Microsoft and Facebook. You can use the `tf2onnx` tool (*https://oreil.ly/ZXkFo*) to convert a TensorFlow model to ONNX.

Invoking the model

We can interrogate the contents of a SavedModel using the command-line tool `saved_model_cli` that comes with TensorFlow:

```
saved_model_cli show --tag_set all --dir export/flowers_model
```

This shows us that the prediction signature (see the following sidebar) is:

```
inputs['random/center_crop_input'] tensor_info:
    dtype: DT_FLOAT
    shape: (-1, 448, 448, 3)
    name: serving_default_random/center_crop_input:0
```

The given SavedModel `SignatureDef` contains the following output(s):

```
outputs['flower_prob'] tensor_info:
    dtype: DT_FLOAT
    shape: (-1, 5)
    name: StatefulPartitionedCall:0
Method name is: tensorflow/serving/predict
```

Signature of a TensorFlow Function

The signature of a function is the name of the function, the parameters it takes, and what it returns. The typical Python function is written to be *polymorphic* (i.e., applicable to values of different types). For example, this will work when a and b are floats as well as when they are both strings:

```
def myfunc(a, b):
    return (a + b)
```

This is because Python is an interpreted (as opposed to a compiled) language—the code gets executed when it's called, and at runtime, the interpreter knows whether you are passing it floats or strings. Indeed, when we inspect the signature of this function using Python's reflection capability:

```
from inspect import signature
print(signature(myfunc).parameters)
print(signature(myfunc).return_annotation)
```

we get back simply:

```
OrderedDict([('a', <Parameter "a">), ('b', <Parameter "b">)])
<class 'inspect._empty'>
```

meaning the parameters can be of any type and the return type is unknown.

It is possible to provide type hints to Python3 by explicitly specifying the input and output types:

```
def myfunc(a: int, b: float) -> float:
    return (a + b)
```

Note that these type hints are not checked by the runtime—it is still possible to pass strings to this function. The type hints are meant for use by code editors and linting tools. However, Python's reflection capability does read the type hints and tell us more details about the signature:

```
OrderedDict([('a', <Parameter "a: int">), ('b', <Parameter "b: float">)])
<class 'float'>
```

While this is nice, type hints are not sufficient for TensorFlow programs. We also need to specify the shapes of tensors. We do that by adding an annotation to our function:

```
@tf.function(input_signature=[
    tf.TensorSpec([3,5], name='a'),
    tf.TensorSpec([5,8], name='b')
])
def myfunc(a, b):
    return (tf.matmul(a,b))
```

The @tf.function annotation *auto-graphs* the function by walking through it and figures out the shape and type of the output tensor. We can examine the information that TensorFlow now has about the signature by calling get_concrete_function() and passing in an eager tensor (a tensor that is immediately evaluated):

```
print(myfunc.get_concrete_function(tf.ones((3,5)), tf.ones((5,8))))
```

This results in:

```
ConcreteFunction myfunc(a, b)
    Args:
```

```
        a: float32 Tensor, shape=(3, 5)
        b: float32 Tensor, shape=(5, 8)
    Returns:
        float32 Tensor, shape=(3, 8)
```

Note that the full signature includes the name of the function (myfunc), the parameters (a, b), the parameter types (float32), the parameter shapes ((3, 5) and (5, 8)), and the output tensor's type and shape.

Therefore, to invoke this model we can load it and call the predict() method, passing in a 4D tensor with the shape [num_examples, 448, 448, 3], where num_examples is the number of examples we want to predict on at once:

```
serving_model = tf.keras.models.load_model('export/flowers_model')
img = create_preproc_image('../dandelion/9818247_e2eac18894.jpg')
batch_image = tf.reshape(img, [1, IMG_HEIGHT, IMG_WIDTH, IMG_CHANNELS])
batch_pred = serving_model.predict(batch_image)
```

The result is a 2D tensor with the shape [num_examples, 5] which represents the probability for each type of flower. We can look for the maximum of these probabilities to obtain the prediction:

```
pred = batch_pred[0]
pred_label_index = tf.math.argmax(pred).numpy()
pred_label = CLASS_NAMES[pred_label_index]
prob = pred[pred_label_index]
```

All this is still highly unrealistic, however. Do we really expect that a client who needs the prediction for an image will know enough to do the reshape(), argmax(), and so on? We need to provide a much simpler signature for our model to be usable.

Usable signature

A more usable signature for our model is one that doesn't expose all the internal details of the training (such as the size of the images the model was trained on).

What kind of signature would be easiest for a client to use? Instead of asking them to send us a tensor with the image contents, we can simply ask them for a JPEG file. And instead of returning a tensor of logits, we can send back easy-to-understand information extracted from the logits (the full code is in *07c_export.ipynb* on GitHub):

```
@tf.function(input_signature=[tf.TensorSpec([None,], dtype=tf.string)])
def predict_flower_type(filenames):
    ...
    return {
        'probability': top_prob,
        'flower_type_int': pred_label_index,
        'flower_type_str': pred_label
    }
```

Note that while we are at it, we might as well make the function more efficient—we can take a batch of filenames and do the predictions for all the images at once. Vectorizing brings efficiency gains at prediction time as well, not just during training!

Given a list of filenames, we can get the input images using:

```
input_images = [create_preproc_image(f) for f in filenames]
```

However, this involves iterating through the list of filenames and moving data back and forth from accelerated TensorFlow code to unaccelerated Python code. If we have a tensor of filenames, we can achieve the effect of iteration while keeping all the data in the TensorFlow graph by using `tf.map_fn()`. With that, our prediction function becomes:

```
input_images = tf.map_fn(
    create_preproc_image,
    filenames,
    fn_output_signature=tf.float32
)
```

Next, we invoke the model to get the full probability matrix:

```
batch_pred = model(input_images)
```

We then find the maximum probability and the index of the maximum probability:

```
top_prob = tf.math.reduce_max(batch_pred, axis=1)
pred_label_index = tf.math.argmax(batch_pred, axis=1)
```

Note that we are being careful to specify the `axis` as 1 (`axis=0` is the batch dimension) when finding the maximum probability and the argmax. Finally, where in Python we could simply do:

```
pred_label = CLASS_NAMES[pred_label_index]
```

the TensorFlow in-graph version is to use `tf.gather()`:

```
pred_label = tf.gather(params=tf.convert_to_tensor(CLASS_NAMES),
                       indices=pred_label_index)
```

This code converts the `CLASS_NAMES` array into a tensor and then indexes into it using the `pred_label_index` tensor. The resulting values are stored in the `pred_label` tensor.

 You can often replace Python iterations by `tf.map_fn()` and deference arrays (read the *n*th element of an array) by using `tf.gather()`, as we have done here. Slicing using the [:, :, 0] syntax is very useful as well. The difference between `tf.gather()` and slicing is that `tf.gather()` can take a tensor as the index, whereas slices are constants. In really complex situations, `tf.dynamic_stitch()` can come in handy.

Using the signature

With the signature defined, we can specify our new signature as the serving default:

```
model.save('export/flowers_model',
          signatures={
              'serving_default': predict_flower_type
          })
```

Note that the API allows us to have multiple signatures in the model—this is useful if we want to add versioning to our signature, or support different signatures for different clients. We will explore this further in Chapter 9.

With the model exported, the client code to do a prediction now becomes simplicity itself:

```
serving_fn = tf.keras.models.load_model('export/flowers_model'
                                        ).signatures['serving_default']
filenames = [
    'gs://.../9818247_e2eac18894.jpg',
    ...
    'gs://.../8713397358_0505cc0176_n.jpg'
]
pred = serving_fn(tf.convert_to_tensor(filenames))
```

The result is a dictionary and can be used as follows:

```
print(pred['flower_type_str'].numpy().decode('utf-8'))
```

A few input images and their predictions are shown in Figure 7-3. The point to note is that the images are all different sizes. The client doesn't need to know any of the internal details of the model in order to invoke it. It's also worth noting that the "string" type in TensorFlow is only an array of bytes. We have to pass these bytes into a UTF-8 decoder to get proper strings.

Figure 7-3. Model predictions on a few images.

Checkpointing

So far, we have focused on how to export the model for inference. Now, let's look at how to save the model in order to resume training. Checkpointing is typically done not only at the end of training, but also in the middle of training. There are two reasons for this:

- It might be helpful to go back and select the model at the point where the validation accuracy is highest. Recall that the training loss keeps decreasing the longer we train, but at some epoch, the validation loss starts to rise because of overfitting. When we observe that, we have to pick the checkpoint of the previous epoch because it had the lowest validation error.
- Machine learning on production datasets can take several hours to several days. The chances that a machine will crash during such a long time period are uncomfortably high. Therefore, it's a good idea to have periodic backups so that we can resume training from an intermediate point rather than starting from scratch.

Checkpointing is implemented in Keras by means of *callbacks*—functionality that is invoked during the training loop by virtue of being passed in as a parameter to the `model.fit()` function:

```
model_checkpoint_cb = tf.keras.callbacks.ModelCheckpoint(
    filepath='./chkpts',
    monitor='val_accuracy', mode='max',
    save_best_only=True)
history = model.fit(train_dataset,
                    validation_data=eval_dataset,
                    epochs=NUM_EPOCHS,
                    callbacks=[model_checkpoint_cb])
```

Here, we are setting up the callback to overwrite a previous checkpoint if the current validation accuracy is higher.

While we are doing this, we might as well set up early stopping—even if we initially start out thinking that we need to train for 20 epochs, we can stop the training once the validation error hasn't improved for 2 consecutive epochs (specified by the `patience` parameter):

```
early_stopping_cb = tf.keras.callbacks.EarlyStopping(
    monitor='val_accuracy', mode='max',
    patience=2)
```

The callbacks list now becomes:

```
callbacks=[model_checkpoint_cb, early_stopping_cb]
```

When we train using these callbacks, training stops after eight epochs, as shown in Figure 7-4.

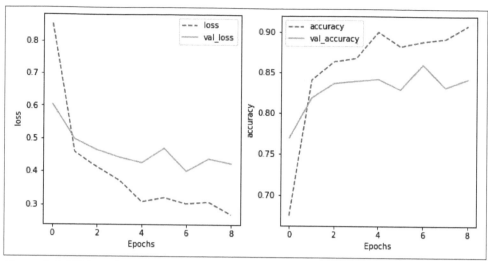

Figure 7-4. With early stopping, model training stops once the validation accuracy no longer increases.

To start from the last checkpoint in the output directory, call:

```
model.load_weights(checkpoint_path)
```

Full fault resilience is provided by the `BackupAndRestore` (*https://oreil.ly/JD3a1*) callback which, at the time of writing, was experimental.

Distribution Strategy

To distribute processing among multiple threads, accelerators, or machines, we need to parallelize it. We have looked at how to parallelize the ingestion. However, our Keras model is not parallelized; it runs on only one processor. How do we run our model code on multiple processors?

To distribute the model training, we need to set up a *distribution strategy*. There are several available, but they're all used in a similar way—you first create a strategy using its constructor, then create the Keras model within the scope of that strategy (here, we're using `MirroredStrategy`):

```
strategy = tf.distribute.MirroredStrategy()
with strategy.scope():
    layers = [
        ...
    ]
    model = tf.keras.Sequential(layers)
model.compile(...)
history = model.fit(...)
```

What is `MirroredStrategy`? What other strategies are available, and how do we choose between them? We will answer each of these questions in the next sections.

 What device does the code run on? All TensorFlow instructions that create trainable variables (such as Keras models or layers) must be created within the `strategy.scope()`, with the exception of `model.compile()`. You can call the `compile()` method wherever you want. Even though this method technically creates variables such as optimizer slots, it has been implemented to use the same strategy as the model. Also, you can create your ingestion (`tf.data`) pipeline wherever you want. It will always run on the CPU and it will always distribute data to workers appropriately.

Choosing a Strategy

Image ML models tend to be deep, and the input data is dense. For such models, there are three contending distribution strategies:

`MirroredStrategy`
: Makes mirrors of the model structure on each of the available GPUs. Each weight in the model is mirrored across all the replicas and kept in sync through identical updates that happen at the end of each batch. Use `MirroredStrategy` whenever you have a single machine, whether that machine has one GPU or multiple GPUs. This way, your code will require no changes when you attach a second GPU.

`MultiWorkerMirroredStrategy`
: Extends the `MirroredStrategy` idea to GPUs spread across multiple machines. In order to get the multiple workers communicating, you need to set up the `TF_CONFIG` (*https://oreil.ly/m2U4N*) variable correctly—we recommend using a public cloud service (such as Vertex Training) where this is automatically done for you.

`TPUStrategy`
: Runs the training job on TPUs, which are specialized application-specific integrated chips (ASICs) that are custom-designed for machine learning workloads. TPUs get their speedup through a custom matrix multiplication unit, high-speed on-board networking to connect up to thousands of TPU cores, and a large shared memory. They are available commercially only on Google Cloud Platform. Colab offers free TPUs with some limitations, and Google Research provides academic researchers access to TPUs through the TensorFlow Research Cloud program (*https://oreil.ly/qdEOw*).

All three of these strategies are forms of *data parallelism*, where each batch is split among the workers, and then an all-reduce operation (*https://oreil.ly/0Zhcg*) is carried out. Other available distribution strategies, like `CentralStorage` and `Parameter Server`, are designed for sparse/massive examples and are not a good fit for image models where an individual image is dense and small.

 We recommend maximizing the number of GPUs on a single machine with `MirroredStrategy` before moving on to multiple workers with `MultiWorkerMirroredStrategy` (more on this in the following section). TPUs are usually more cost-effective than GPUs, especially when you move to larger batch sizes. The current trend in GPUs (such as with the 16xA100) is to provide multiple powerful GPUs on a single machine so as to make this strategy work for more and more models.

Creating the Strategy

In this section, we will cover the specifics of the three strategies commonly used to distribute the training of image models.

MirroredStrategy

To create a `MirroredStrategy` instance, we can simply call its constructor (the full code is in *07d_distribute.ipynb* on GitHub):

```
def create_strategy():
    return tf.distribute.MirroredStrategy()
```

To verify whether we are running on a machine with GPUs set up, we can use:

```
if (tf.test.is_built_with_cuda() and
    len(tf.config.experimental.list_physical_devices("GPU")) > 1)
```

This is not a requirement; `MirroredStrategy` will work on a machine with only CPUs.

Starting a Jupyter notebook on a machine with two GPUs and using `MirroredStrat egy`, we see an immediate speedup. Where an epoch took about 100 s to process on a CPU, and 55 s on a single GPU, it takes only 29 s when we have two GPUs.

When training in a distributed manner, you must make sure to increase the batch size. This is because a batch is split between the GPUs, so if a single GPU has the resources to process a batch size of 32, two GPUs will be able to easily handle 64. Here, 64 is the global batch size, and each of the two GPUs will have a local batch size of 32. Larger batch sizes are typically associated with better behaved training curves. We will experiment with different batch sizes in "Hyperparameter tuning" on page 42.

Sometimes, it is helpful for consistency and for debugging purposes to have a strategy even if you are not distributing the training code or using GPUs. In such cases, use OneDeviceStrategy:

```
tf.distribute.OneDeviceStrategy('/cpu:0')
```

MultiWorkerMirroredStrategy

To create a `MultiWorkerMirroredStrategy` instance, we can again simply call its constructor:

```
def create_strategy():
    return tf.distribute.MultiWorkerMirroredStrategy()
```

To verify that the `TF_CONFIG` environment variable is set up correctly, we can use:

```
tf_config = json.loads(os.environ["TF_CONFIG"])
```

and check the resulting config.

If we use a managed ML training system like Google's Vertex AI or Amazon Sage-Maker, these infrastructure details will be taken care of for us.

When using multiple workers, there are two details that we need to take care of: shuffling and virtual epochs.

Shuffling. When all the devices (CPUs, GPUs) are on the same machine, each batch of training examples is split among the different device workers and the resulting gradient updates are made *synchronously*—each device worker returns its gradient, the gradients are averaged across the device workers, and the computed weight update is sent back to the device workers for the next step.

When the devices are spread among multiple machines, having the central loop wait for all the workers on every machine to finish with a batch will lead to significant wastage of compute resources, as all the workers will have to wait for the slowest one. Instead, the idea is to have workers process data in parallel and for gradient updates to be averaged if they are available—a late-arriving gradient update is simply dropped from the calculation. Each worker receives the weight update that is current as of this time.

When we apply gradient updates *asynchronously* like this, we cannot split a batch across the different workers because then our batches would be incomplete, and our model will want equal-sized batches. So, we will have to have each worker reading full batches of data, computing the gradient, and sending in a gradient update for each full batch. If we do that, there is no use having all the workers reading the same data—we want every worker's batches to contain different examples. By shuffling the dataset, we can ensure that the workers are all working on different training examples at any point in time.

Even if we are not doing distributed training, it's a good idea to randomize the order in which the data is read by the tf.data pipeline. This will help reduce the chances that, say, one batch contains all daisies and the next batch contains all tulips. Such bad batches can play havoc with the gradient descent optimizer.

We can randomize the data that is read in two places:

- When we obtain the files that match the pattern, we shuffle these files:

```
files = [filename for filename
    # shuffle so that workers see different orders
    in tf.random.shuffle(tf.io.gfile.glob(pattern))
]
```

- After we preprocess the data, and just before we batch, we shuffle the records within a buffer that is larger than the batch size:

```
trainds = (trainds
    .shuffle(8 * batch_size)  # Shuffle for distribution ...
    .map(preproc.read_from_tfr, num_parallel_calls=AUTOTUNE)
    .map(_preproc_img_label, num_parallel_calls=AUTOTUNE)
    .prefetch(AUTOTUNE)
)
```

- The more ordered your dataset is, the larger your shuffle buffer needs to be. If your dataset is initially sorted by label, only a buffer size covering the entire dataset will work. In that case, it's better to shuffle the data ahead of time, when preparing the training dataset.

Virtual epochs. We often wish to train for a fixed number of training examples, not a fixed number of epochs. Since the number of training steps in an epoch depends on the batch size, it is easier to key off the total number of training examples in the dataset and compute what the number of steps per epoch ought to be:

```
num_steps_per_epoch = None
if (num_training_examples > 0):
    num_steps_per_epoch = (num_training_examples // batch_size)
```

We call a training cycle consisting of this number of steps a *virtual epoch* and train for the same number of epochs as before.

We specify the number of steps per virtual epoch as a parameter to model.fit():

```
history = model.fit(train_dataset,
                    validation_data=eval_dataset,
                    epochs=num_epochs,
                    steps_per_epoch=num_steps_per_epoch)        )
```

What if we get the number of training examples in the dataset wrong? Suppose we specify the number as 4,000, but there are actually 3,500 examples? We will have a problem, because the dataset will finish before 4,000 examples are encountered. We can prevent that from happening by making the training dataset repeat upon itself indefinitely:

```
if (num_training_examples > 0):
    train_dataset = train_dataset.repeat()
```

This also works when we underestimate the number of training examples in the dataset—the next set of examples simply carry over to the next epoch. Keras knows that when a dataset is infinite, it should use the number of steps per epoch to decide when the next epoch starts.

TPUStrategy

While MirroredStrategy is meant for one or more GPUs on a single machine, and MultiWorkerMirroredStrategy is meant for GPUs on multiple machines, TPUStrategy allows us to distribute to a custom ASIC chip called the TPU, shown in Figure 7-5.

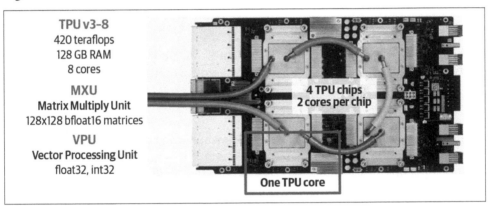

Figure 7-5. A tensor processing unit.

To create a TPUStrategy instance, we can call its constructor, but we have to pass a parameter to this constructor:

```
tpu = tf.distribute.cluster_resolver.TPUClusterResolver().connect()
return tf.distribute.TPUStrategy(tpu)
```

Because TPUs are multiuser machines, the initialization will wipe out the existing memory on the TPU, so we have to make sure to initialize the TPU system before we do any work in our program.

In addition, we add an extra parameter to model.compile():

```
model.compile(steps_per_execution=32)
```

This parameter instructs Keras to send multiple batches to the TPU at once. In addition to lowering communication overhead, this gives the compiler the opportunity to optimize TPU hardware utilization across multiple batches. With this option, it is no longer necessary to push batch sizes to very high values to optimize TPU performance.

It is worth noting what the user does not need to worry about—in TensorFlow/Keras, the complicated code to distribute the data is taken care of for you automatically in `strategy.distribute_dataset()`. At the time of writing, this is code you have to write by hand in PyTorch.

It's not enough to simply write the software, though; we also need to set up the hardware. For example, to use `MultiWorkerMirroredStrategy`, we will also need to launch a cluster of machines that coordinate the task of training an ML model.

To use `TPUStrategy`, we will need to launch a machine with a TPU attached to it. We can accomplish this using:

```
gcloud compute tpus execution-groups create \
    --accelerator-type v3-32 --no-forward-ports --tf-version 2.4.1 \
    --name somevmname --zone europe-west4-a \
    --metadata proxy-mode=project_editors
```

Distribution strategies are easier to implement if we use a service that manages the hardware infrastructure for us. We'll defer the hardware setup to the next section.

Serverless ML

While Jupyter notebooks are good for experimentation and training, it's a lot easier for ML engineers to maintain code in production if it's organized into Python packages. It is possible to use a tool like Papermill (*https://oreil.ly/AL4I9*) to directly execute a notebook. We recommend, however, that you treat notebooks as expendable, and keep your production-ready code in standalone Python files with associated unit tests.

By organizing code into Python packages, we also make it easy to submit the code to a fully managed ML service such as Google's Vertex AI, Azure ML, or Amazon Sage-Maker. Here, we'll demonstrate Vertex AI, but the others are similar in concept.

Creating a Python Package

To create a Python package, we have to organize files in a folder structure where each level is marked by an *__init__.py* file. The *__init__.py* file, which runs any initialization code the package needs, is required, but it can be empty. The simplest structure that would be sufficient is to have:

```
trainer/
        __init__.py
        07b_distribute.py
```

Reusable modules

How do we get code in a notebook into the file *07b_distribute.py*? An easy way to reuse code between Jupyter notebooks and the Python package is to export the Jupyter notebook to a *.py* file and then remove code whose only purpose is to display graphs and other output in the notebook. Another possibility is to base all the code development in the standalone files and simply `import` the necessary modules from the notebook cells as needed.

The reason that we create a Python package is that packages make it much easier to make our code reusable. However, it is unlikely that this model is the only one that we will train. For maintainability reasons, we suggest that you have an organizational structure like this (the full code is in *serverlessml* on GitHub):

```
flowers/                     Top-level package
    __init__.py              Initialize the flowers package
    classifier/              Subpackage for the classification model
        __init__.py
        model.py             Most of the code in the Jupyter notebook
        train.py             argparse and then launches model training
        ...
    ingest/                  Subpackage for reading data
        __init__.py
        tfrecords.py         Code to read from TensorFlow Records
        ...
    utils/                   Subpackage for code reusable across models
        __init__.py
        augment.py           Custom layers for data augmentation
        plots.py             Various plotting functions
        ...
```

Use Jupyter notebooks for experimentation, but at some point, move the code into a Python package and maintain that package going forward. From then on, if you need to experiment, call the Python package from the Jupyter notebook.

Invoking Python modules

Given files in the structure outlined in the previous section, we can invoke the training program using:

```
python3 -m flowers.classifier.train --job-dir /tmp/flowers
```

This is also a good time at which to make all the hyperparameters to the module settable as command-line parameters. For example, we will want to experiment with different batch sizes, so we make the batch size a command-line parameter:

```
python3 -m flowers.classifier.train --job-dir /tmp/flowers \
        --batch_size 32 --num_hidden 16 --lrate 0.0001 ...
```

Within the entrypoint Python file, we'll use Python's `argparse` library to pass the command-line parameters to the `create_model()` function.

It's best to try to make every aspect of your model configurable. Besides the L1 and L2 regularizations, it's a good idea to make data augmentation layers optional as well.

Because the code has been split across multiple files, you will find yourself needing to call functions that are now in a different file. So, you will have to add import statements of this form to the caller:

```
from flowers.utils.augment import *
from flowers.utils.util import *
from flowers.ingest.tfrecords import *
```

Installing dependencies

While the package structure we've shown is sufficient to create and run a module, it is quite likely that you will need the training service to `pip install` Python packages that you need. The way to specify that is to create a *setup.py* file in the same directory as the package, so that the overall structure becomes:

```
serverlessml/          Top-level directory
    setup.py           File to specify dependencies
    flowers/           Top-level package
        __init__.py
```

The *setup.py* file looks like this:

```
from setuptools import setup, find_packages
setup(
    name='flowers',
    version='1.0',
    packages=find_packages(),
    author='Practical ML Vision Book',
    author_email='abc@nosuchdomain.com',
    install_requires=['python-package-example']
)
```

 Verify that you got the packaging and imports correct by doing two things from within the top-level directory (the directory that contains *setup.py*):

```
python3 ./setup.py dist
python3 -m flowers.classifier.train \
        --job-dir /tmp/flowers \
        --pattern '-00000-*' --num_epochs 1
```

Also look at the generated *MANIFEST.txt* file to ensure that all the desired files are there. If you need ancillary files (text files, scripts, and so on), you can specify them in *setup.py*.

Submitting a Training Job

Once we have a locally callable module, we can put the module source in Cloud Storage (e.g., `gs://${BUCKET}/flowers-1.0.tar.gz`) and then submit jobs to Vertex Training to have it run the code for us on the cloud hardware of our choice.

For example, to run on a machine with a single CPU, we'd create a configuration file (let's call it *cpu.yaml*) specifying the CustomJobSpec:

```
workerPoolSpecs:
  machineSpec:
    machineType: n1-standard-4
  replicaCount: 1
  pythonPackageSpec:
    executorImageUri: us-docker.pkg.dev/vertex-ai/training/tf-cpu.2-4:latest
    packageUris: gs://{BUCKET}/flowers-1.0.tar.gz
    pythonModule: flowers.classifier.train
    args:
    - --pattern="-*"
    - --num_epochs=20
    - --distribute="cpu"
```

We'd then provide that configuration file when starting the training program:

```
gcloud ai custom-jobs create \
  --region=${REGION} \
  --project=${PROJECT} \
  --python-package-uris=gs://${BUCKET}/flowers-1.0.tar.gz \
  --config=cpu.yaml \
  --display-name=${JOB_NAME}
```

A key consideration is that if we have developed the code using Python 3.7 and TensorFlow 2.4, we need to ensure that Vertex Training uses the same versions of Python and TensorFlow to run our training job. We do this using the `executorIma geUri` setting. Not all combinations (*https://oreil.ly/PyqU2*) of runtimes and Python versions are supported, since some versions of TensorFlow may have had issues that were subsequently fixed. If you are developing on Vertex Notebooks, there will be a corresponding runtime on Vertex Training and Vertex Prediction (or an upgrade path to get to a consistent state). If you are developing in a heterogeneous environment, it's worth verifying that your development, training, and deployment environments support the same environment in order to prevent nasty surprises down the line.

Container or Python Package?

The purpose of putting our training code into a Python package is to make it easier to install on ephemeral infrastructure. Because we won't have the ability to log in to such machines and install software packages interactively, we want to make the installation of our training software completely automated. Python packages provide us that ability. Another way to capture dependencies, that works beyond just Python, is to containerize your training code. A container is a lightweight bundle of software that includes everything needed to run an application—besides our Python code, it will also include the Python installation itself, any system tools and system libraries that we require (such as video decoders), and all our settings (such as configuration files, authentication keys, and environment variables).

Because Vertex Training accepts both Python modules and container images, we can capture the Python and TensorFlow dependencies by building a container image that contains our training code as well as the versions of Python and TensorFlow that we need. In the container, we'd also install any extra packages our code requires. To make container creation easier, TensorFlow provides a base container image (*https://oreil.ly/7qmS1*). If you are developing using Vertex Notebooks, every Notebook instance has a corresponding container image (*https://oreil.ly/fj748*) that you can use as your base (we will do this in the next section). Therefore, creating a container to run your training code is quite straightforward.

Given that both Python packages and containers are relatively easy to create, which one should you use?

Using Python packages for training can help you organize your code better and fosters reuse and maintainability. Furthermore, if you provide a Python package to Vertex Training, it will install the package on a *machine-* and *framework-optimized* container, something that you would be hard pressed to do if you were building your own containers.

On the other hand, using a container for training is much more flexible. For example, a container is a good option in a project where you need to use old or unsupported versions of a runtime or need to install proprietary software components such as database connectors to internal systems.

So, the choice comes down to what you value more: efficiency (in which case you'd choose a Python package) or flexibility (in which case you'd choose a container).

In the training code, a `OneDeviceStrategy` should be created:

```
strategy = tf.distribute.OneDeviceStrategy('/cpu:0')
```

Using the `gcloud` command to launch a training job makes it easy to incorporate model training in scripts, invoke the training job from Cloud Functions, or schedule the training job using Cloud Scheduler.

Next, let's walk through the hardware setups corresponding to the different distribution scenarios that we have covered so far. Each scenario here corresponds to a different distribution strategy.

Running on multiple GPUs

To run on a single machine with one, two, four, or more GPUs, we can add a snippet like this to the YAML configuration file:

```
workerPoolSpecs:
  machineSpec:
    machineType: n1-standard-4
    acceleratorType: NVIDIA_TESLA_T4
    acceleratorCount: 2
  replicaCount: 1
```

and launch the `gcloud` command as before, making sure to specify this configuration file in `--config`.

In the training code, a `MirroredStrategy` instance should be created.

Distribution to multiple GPUs

To run on multiple workers, each of which has several GPUs, the configuration YAML file should include lines similar to the following:

```
workerPoolSpecs:
  - machineSpec:
      machineType: n1-standard-4
      acceleratorType: NVIDIA_TESLA_T4
      acceleratorCount: 1
  - machineSpec:
      machineType: n1-standard-4
      acceleratorType: NVIDIA_TESLA_T4
      acceleratorCount: 1
    replicaCount: 1
```

Remember that if you are using multiple worker machines, you should use virtual epochs by declaring the number of training examples that you will term as an epoch. Shuffling is also required. The code example in *serverlessml* on GitHub does both these things.

In the training code, a `MultiWorkerMirroredStrategy` instance should be created.

Distribution to TPU

To run on a Cloud TPU, the configuration file YAML looks like this (choose the version of TPU (*https://oreil.ly/vHMhx*) that is most appropriate (*https://oreil.ly/mVeTS*) at the time you are reading this):

```
workerPoolSpecs:
    - machineSpec:
            machineType: n1-standard-4
            acceleratorType:TPU_V2
            acceleratorCount: 8
```

In the training code, a TPUStrategy instance should be created.

You can use Python's error handling mechanism to create a boilerplate method for creating the distribution strategy appropriate for the hardware configuration:

```
def create_strategy():
    try:
        # detect TPUs
        tpu = tf.distribute.cluster_resolver.TPUClusterResolver().connect()
        return tf.distribute.experimental.TPUStrategy(tpu)
    except ValueError:
        # detect GPUs
        return tf.distribute.MirroredStrategy()
```

Now that we have looked at how to train a single model, let's consider how to train a family of models and pick the best one.

Hyperparameter Tuning

In the process of creating our ML model, we have made many arbitrary choices: the number of hidden nodes, the batch size, the learning rate, the L1/L2 regularization amounts, and so on. The overall number of possible combinations is massive, so it's preferable to take an optimization approach where we specify a budget (e.g., "try 30 combinations") and instead ask a hyperparameter optimization technique to choose the best settings.

In Chapter 2, we looked at the in-built Keras Tuner. However, that only works if your model and dataset are small enough that the entire training process can be carried out wrapped within the tuner. For more realistic ML datasets, it's better to use a fully managed service.

Fully managed hyperparameter training services provide a combination of parameter values to the training program, which then trains the model and reports on performance metrics (accuracy, loss, etc.). So, the hyperparameter tuning service requires that we:

- Specify the set of parameters to tune, the search space (the range of values each parameter can take, for example that the learning rate has to be between 0.0001 and 0.1), and the search budget.

- Incorporate a given combination of parameters into the training program.

- Report how well the model performed when using that combination of parameters.

In this section, we'll discuss hyperparameter tuning on Vertex AI as an example of how this works.

Specifying the search space

We specify the search space in the YAML configuration provided to Vertex AI. For example, we might have:

```
displayName: "FlowersHpTuningJob"
maxTrialCount: 50
parallelTrialCount: 2
studySpec:
  metrics:
  - metricId: accuracy
    goal: MAXIMIZE
  parameters:
  - parameterId: l2
    scaleType: UNIT_LINEAR_SCALE
    doubleValueSpec:
      minValue: 0
      maxValue: 0.2
  - parameterId: batch_size
    scaleType: SCALE_TYPE_UNSPECIFIED
    discreteValueSpec:
      values:
      - 16
      - 32
      - 64
  algorithm: ALGORITHM_UNSPECIFIED
```

In this YAML listing, we are specifying (see if you can find the corresponding lines):

- The goal, which is to maximize the accuracy that is reported by the trainer
- The budget, which is a total of 50 trials carried out 2 at a time
- That we want to stop a trial early if it looks unlikely to do better than we have already seen
- Two parameters, l2 and batch_size:
  — The possible L2 regularization strengths (between 0 and 0.2)
  — The batch size, which can be one of 16, 32, or 64

- The algorithm type, which if unspecified uses Bayesian Optimization

Using parameter values

Vertex AI will invoke our trainer, passing specific values for l2 and batch_size as command-line parameters. So, we make sure to list them in the argparse:

```
parser.add_argument(
    '--l2',
    help='L2 regularization', default=0., type=float)
parser.add_argument(
    '--batch_size',
    help='Number of records in a batch', default=32, type=int)
```

We have to incorporate these values into the training program. For example, we'll use the batch size as:

```
train_dataset = create_preproc_dataset(
    'gs://...' + opts['pattern'],
    IMG_HEIGHT, IMG_WIDTH, IMG_CHANNELS
).batch(opts['batch_size'])
```

It's helpful at this point to step back and think carefully about all the implicit choices that we have made in the model. For example, our CenterCrop augmentation layer was:

```
tf.keras.layers.experimental.preprocessing.RandomCrop(
    height=IMG_HEIGHT // 2, width=IMG_WIDTH // 2,
    input_shape=(IMG_HEIGHT, IMG_WIDTH, IMG_CHANNELS),
    name='random/center_crop'
)
```

The number 2 is baked in, yet the truly fixed thing is the size of the image (224x224x3) that the MobileNet model requires. It's worth experimenting with whether we should center crop the images to 50% the original size, or use some other ratio. So, we make crop_ratio one of the hyperparameters:

```
- parameterName: crop_ratio
  type: DOUBLE
  minValue: 0.5
  maxValue: 0.8
  scaleType: UNIT_LINEAR_SCALE
```

and use it as follows:

```
IMG_HEIGHT = IMG_WIDTH = round(MODEL_IMG_SIZE / opts['crop_ratio'])
tf.keras.layers.experimental.preprocessing.RandomCrop(
    height=MODEL_IMG_SIZE, width=MODEL_IMG_SIZE,
    input_shape=(IMG_HEIGHT, IMG_WIDTH, IMG_CHANNELS),
    name='random/center_crop'
)
```

Reporting accuracy

After we train the model using the hyperparameters that were supplied to the trainer on the command line, we need to report back to the hyperparameter tuning service. What we report back is whatever we specified as the `hyperparameterMetricTag` in the YAML file:

```
hpt = hypertune.HyperTune()
accuracy = ...
hpt.report_hyperparameter_tuning_metric(
    hyperparameter_metric_tag='accuracy',
    metric_value=accuracy,
    global_step=nepochs)
```

Result

On submitting the job, hyperparameter tuning is launched and 50 trials are carried out, 2 at a time. The hyperparameters for these trials are chosen using a Bayesian optimization approach, and because we specified two parallel trials, the optimizer starts with two random initial starting points. Whenever a trial finishes, the optimizer determines which part of the input space needs further exploration and a new trial is launched.

The cost of the job is determined by the infrastructure resources used to train the model 50 times. Running the 50 trials 2 at a time causes the job to finish twice as fast as if we'd run them only one at a time. If we were to run the 50 trials 10 at a time, the job would finish 10 times faster but cost the same—however, the first 10 trials wouldn't get much of a chance to incorporate information from the previously finished trials, and future trials, on average, are unable to take advantage of the information from 9 already-started trials. We recommend using as many total trials as your budget allows and as few prallel trials as your patience allows! You can also resume an already completed hyperparameter job (specify `resumePreviousJobId` in the YAML) so you can continue the search if you find more budget or more patience.

The results are shown in the web console (see Figure 7-6).

HyperTune trials

	Trial ID	accuracy ↓	Training step	Elapsed time	l2	batch_size	num_hidden	with_color_distort	
○ ✓	33	0.88601	1,000	3 min 31 sec	0	64	24	0	⋮
○ ✓	37	0.88083	1,000	5 min 2 sec	0	64	24	0	⋮
○ ✓	48	0.88083	1,000	6 min 34 sec	0	64	24	0	⋮
○ ✓	23	0.87824	1,000	4 min 33 sec	0	64	24	1	⋮
○ ✓	50	0.87824	1,000	5 min 4 sec	0	16	8	0	⋮
○ ✓	6	0.87565	1,000	3 min 32 sec	0.0684	64	24	0	⋮
○ ✓	11	0.87565	1,000	5 min 2 sec	0.02894	64	24	0	⋮
○ ✓	12	0.87306	1,000	6 min 4 sec	0	64	24	0	⋮
○ ✓	14	0.87306	1,000	4 min 1 sec	0	64	24	0	⋮
○ ✓	35	0.87306	1,000	5 min 32 sec	0	64	24	0	⋮

Rows per page: 10 ▼   1 – 10 of 50   ‹ ›

Figure 7-6. The results of hyperparameter tuning.

Based on the tuning, the highest accuracy (0.89) is obtained with the following settings: `l2=0`, `batch_size=64`, `num_hidden=24`, `with_color_distort=0`, `crop_ratio=0.70706`.

Continuing tuning

Looking at these results, it is striking that the optimal values for `num_hidden` and `batch_size` are the highest values we tried. Given this, it might be a good idea to continue the hyperparameter tuning process and explore even higher values. At the same time, we can reduce the search space for the `crop_ratio` by making it a set of discrete values (0.70706 should probably be just 0.7).

This time, we don't need Bayesian optimization. We just want the hyperparameter service to carry out a grid search of 45 possible combinations (this is also the budget):

```
- parameterId: batch_size
  scaleType: SCALE_TYPE_UNSPECIFIED
  discreteValueSpec:
    values:
    - 48
    - 64
    - 96
- parameterId: num_hidden
  scaleType: SCALE_TYPE_UNSPECIFIED
  discreteValueSpec:
    values:
    - 16
    - 24
    - 32
- parameterId: crop_ratio
  scaleType: SCALE_TYPE_UNSPECIFIED
  discreteValueSpec:
    values:
    - 0.65
```

```
- 0.70
- 0.75
- 0.80
- 0.85
```

After this new training run, we get a report as before, and we can select the best set of parameters. When we did this, it turned out that `batch_size=64`, `num_hidden=24` was indeed the best—better than choosing 96 for the batch size or 32 for the number of hidden nodes—but with `crop_ratio=0.8`.

Deploying the Model

Now that we have a trained model, let's deploy it for online predictions. The TensorFlow SavedModel format is supported by a serving system called TensorFlow Serving. A Docker container (*https://oreil.ly/nS7ZA*) for TensorFlow Serving is available for you to deploy this in a container orchestration system like Google Kubernetes Engine, Google Cloud Run, Amazon Elastic Kubernetes Service, AWS Lambda, Azure Kubernetes Service, or on premises using Kubernetes. Managed versions of TensorFlow Serving are available in all the major clouds. Here, we'll show you how to deploy the SavedModel into Google's Vertex AI.

Vertex AI also provides model management and versioning capabilities. In order to use these functionalities, we'll create an endpoint called *flowers* to which we will deploy multiple model versions:

```
gcloud ai endpoints create --region=us-central1 --display-name=flowers
```

Suppose, for example, that hyperparameter tuning trial #33 was the best and contains the model we want to deploy. This command will create a model called `txf` (for transfer learning) and deploy it into the flowers endpoint:

```
MODEL_LOCATION="gs://...}/33/flowers_model"
gcloud ai models upload ---display-name=txf \
         --container-image-uri=".../tf2-cpu.2-1:latest" -artifact-uri=$MODEL_LOCATION
gcloud ai endpoints deploy-model $ENDPOINT_ID  --model=$MODEL_ID \
         ... --region=us-central1  --traffic-split=
```

Once the model is deployed, we can do an HTTP POST of a JSON request to the model to obtain predictions. For example, posting:

```
{"instances": [
    {"filenames": "gs://cloud-ml-data/.../9853885425_4a82356f1d_m.jpg"},
    {"filenames": "gs://cloud-ml-data/../8713397358_0505cc0176_n.jpg"}
]}
```

returns:

```
{
    "predictions": [
        {
            "probability": 0.9999885559082031,
```

```
          "flower_type_int": 1,
          "flower_type_str": "dandelion"
      },
      {

          "probability": 0.9505964517593384,
          "flower_type_int": 4,
          "flower_type_str": "tulips"
      }
    ]
}
```

Of course, we could post this request from any program capable of sending an HTTP POST request (see Figure 7-7).

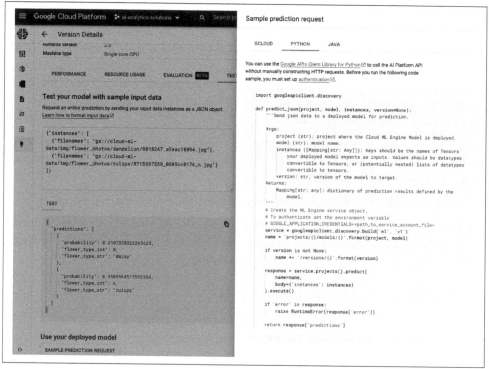

Figure 7-7. Left: trying out the deployed model from the Google Cloud Platform console. Right: example code for replicating in Python.

How would someone use this model? They would have to upload an image file to the cloud, and send the path to the file to the model for predictions. This process is a bit onerous. Can the model not directly accept the contents of an image file? We'll look at how to improve the serving experience in Chapter 9.

Summary

In this chapter, we covered various aspects of building a training pipeline. We started by considering efficient storage in TFRecords files, and how to read that data efficiently using a `tf.data` pipeline. This included parallel execution of map functions, interleaved reading of datasets, and vectorization. The optimization ideas carried over into the model itself, where we looked at how to parallelize model execution across multiple GPUs, multiple workers, and on TPUs.

We then moved on to operationalization considerations. Rather than managing infrastructure, we looked at how to carry out training in a serverless way by submitting a training job to Vertex AI, and how to use this paradigm to carry out distributed training. We also looked at how to use Vertex AI's hyperparameter tuning service to achieve better model performance. For predictions, we need autoscaling infrastructure, so we looked at how to deploy a SavedModel into Vertex AI. Along the way, you learned about signatures, how to customize them, and how to get predictions out of a deployed model.

In the next chapter, we will look at how to monitor the deployed model.

## CHAPTER 8

Model Quality and Continuous Evaluation

So far in this book, we have covered the design and implementation of vision models. In this chapter, we will dive into the important topic of monitoring and evaluation. In addition to beginning with a high-quality model, we also want to maintain that quality. In order to ensure optimal operation, it is important to obtain insights through monitoring, calculate metrics, understand the quality of the model, and continuously evaluate its performance.

Monitoring

So, we've trained our model on perhaps millions of images, and we are very happy with its quality. We've deployed it to the cloud, and now we can sit back and relax while it makes great predictions forever into the future... Right? Wrong! Just as we wouldn't leave a small child alone to manage him or herself, we also don't want to leave our models alone out in the wild. It's important that we constantly monitor their quality (using metrics like accuracy) and computational performance (queries per second, latency, etc.). This is especially true when we're constantly retraining models on new data that may contain distribution changes, errors, and other issues that we'll want to be aware of.

TensorBoard

Often ML practitioners train their models without fully considering all the details. They submit a training job and check it every now and then until the job is finished. Then they make predictions using the trained model to see how it's performing. This may not seem like a big deal if the training jobs take a few minutes. However, many computer vision projects, especially with datasets that contain millions of images, have training jobs that take days or weeks. It would be terrible if something went wrong with the training early on and we didn't notice until training was complete, or until we tried to use the model to make some predictions.

There is a great monitoring tool called TensorBoard that is distributed with Tensor-Flow that we can use to avoid just this scenario. TensorBoard is an interactive dashboard (see Figure 8-1) that displays summaries saved during model training and evaluation. You can use it as a historical record of experiments run, for comparing different versions of your model or code, and for analyzing training jobs.

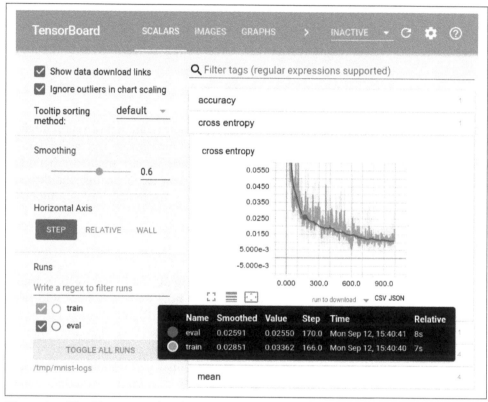

Figure 8-1. The TensorBoard scalar summary UI.

TensorBoard allows us to monitor loss curves to make sure that the model training is still progressing, and it hasn't stopped improving. We can also display and interact with any other evaluation metrics we have in our model, such as accuracy, precision, or AUC—for example, we can perform filtering across multiple series, smoothing, and outlier removal, and we're able to zoom in and out.

Weight Histograms

We can also explore histograms in TensorBoard, as shown in Figure 8-2. We can use these to monitor weights, gradients, and other scalar quantities that have too many values to inspect individually.

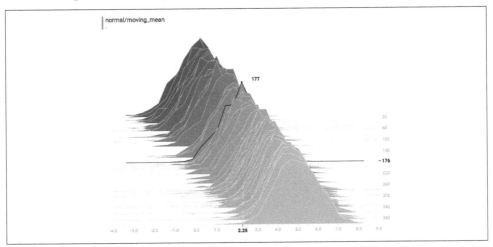

Figure 8-2. The TensorBoard histogram UI. Model weights are on the horizontal axis and the training step number is on the vertical axis.

What Should the Weight Distributions Look Like?

Each layer of a neural network can have thousands or millions of weights. As with any large collection of values, they form a distribution. The distribution of weights at the beginning of training and at the end can be very different. Usually the initial distribution is based on our weight initialization strategy, whether that be samples from a random normal distribution or a random uniform distribution, with or without normalization factors, and so on.

As the model gets trained and converges, however, the central limit theorem (CLT) tells us that the weight distribution should ideally start to look more Gaussian. It states that if we have a population with mean μ and standard deviation σ, then given a large enough number of random samples, the distribution of the sample means should be approximately Gaussian. But if we have a systematic problem in our model, then the weights will reflect that problem and may be skewed toward zero values (an indication of the presence of "dead layers," which happen if input values are poorly scaled) or very large ones (which happens as a result of overfitting). Thus, by looking at the weight distribution, we can diagnose whether there is a problem.

If our weight distribution is not looking Gaussian, there are a few things we can do. We can scale our input values from [0, 1] to [−1, 1] if the distribution is skewed toward zero values. If the problem is in intermediate layers, try adding batch normalization. If the distribution tends toward large values, we can try adding regularization or increasing the dataset size. Other issues can be resolved through trial and error. Perhaps we chose our initialization strategy poorly, and it made it hard for the weights to move to the standard regime of small, normally distributed weights. In that case, we can try changing the initialization method.

We may also be having gradient issues that could be moving the weights away from a Gaussian distribution. We can fix this by adding gradient clipping, constraints, or penalties (for example, adding a loss term that grows the farther gradients stray from a set value). Additionally, the order and distribution of examples in our mini-batches can affect the evolution of our weight distribution, so experimenting with those parameters might help make the weight distribution more Gaussian.

Device Placement

We can output the TensorFlow model graph to TensorBoard for visualization and exploration, as shown in Figure 8-3. .

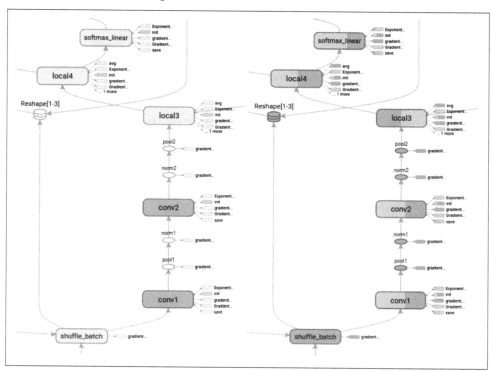

Figure 8-3. TensorBoard model graph visualizations: structure view (left) and device view (right).

The default structure view shows which nodes share the same structure, and the device view shows which nodes are on which device(s), with a color per device. We can also see TPU compatibility and more. This can allow us to ensure that our model code is being accelerated properly.

Data Visualization

TensorBoard can display examples of specific types of data, such as images (on the Images tab, shown on the left in Figure 8-4) or audio (on the Audio tab). This way, we can get feedback as training is progressing; for example, with image generation, we can see live how our generated images are looking. For classification problems, TensorBoard also has the ability to display confusion matrices, as seen on the right in Figure 8-4, so we can monitor metrics per class throughout a training job (more on this in "Metrics for Classification" on page 289).

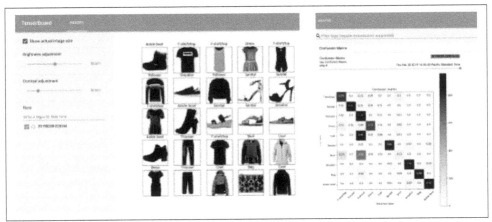

Figure 8-4. The TensorBoard Images tab allows you to visualize training images (left) and view a confusion matrix (right) to see where the classifier is making most of its mistakes.

Training Events

We can add a TensorBoard callback to our model using code like the following:

```
tensorboard_callback = tf.keras.callbacks.TensorBoard(
    log_dir='logs', histogram_freq=0, write_graph=True,
    write_images=False, update_freq='epoch', profile_batch=2,
    embeddings_freq=0, embeddings_metadata=None, **kwargs
)
```

We specify the directory path where the TensorBoard event logs will get written to disk using the `log_dir` argument. `histogram_freq` and `embeddings_freq` control how often (in epochs) those two types of summaries are written; if you specify a value of zero they are not computed or displayed. Note that validation data, or at least a split, needs to be specified when fitting the model for histograms to show. Furthermore, for embeddings, we can pass a dictionary to the argument `embeddings_meta data` that maps layer names to a filename where the embedding metadata will be saved.

If we want to see the graph in TensorBoard, we can set the `write_graph` argument to `True`; however, the event log files can get quite sizable if our model is large. The update frequency is specified through the `update_freq` argument. Here it is set to update every epoch or batch, but we can set it to an integer value to have it update after that number of batches. We can visualize model weights as images in Tensor-Board using the Boolean argument `write_images`. Lastly, if we want to profile the performance of our compute characteristics, such as the contributions to the step time, we can set `profile_batch` to an integer or tuple of integers and it will profile that batch or range of batches. Setting the value to zero disables profiling.

Once defined, we can add the TensorBoard callback to `model.fit()`'s callbacks list as shown here:

```
history = model.fit(
    train_dataset,
    epochs=10,
    batch_size=1,
    validation_data=validation_dataset,
    callbacks=[tensorboard_callback]
)
```

The simplest way to run TensorBoard is to open a terminal and run the following bash command:

```
tensorboard --logdir=<path_to_your_logs>
```

You can provide other arguments, for example to change the default port Tensor-Board uses, but to quickly get it up and running you simply need to specify the `log dir`.

The summaries typically include loss and evaluation metric curves. However, we can use callbacks to emit other potentially useful summaries, like images and weight histograms, depending on our use case. We can also print out and/or log the loss and eval metrics while training is taking place, as well as have periodic evaluations of generated images or other model outputs that we can then inspect for diminishing returns in improvement. Lastly, if training locally with `model.fit()`, we can inspect the history output and look at the loss and eval metrics and how they change over time.

Model Quality Metrics

Even if you are using a validation set, looking at the validation loss doesn't really give a clear picture of how well the model is performing. Enter the evaluation metrics! These are metrics that are calculated based on the model's predictions on unseen data that allow us to evaluate how the model is doing in terms that are related to the use case.

Metrics for Classification

As you learned in previous chapters, image classification involves assigning labels to images that indicate which class they belong to. Labels can be mutually exclusive, with only a single label applying to any given image, or it may be possible for multiple labels to describe an image. In both the single-label and multilabel cases, we typically predict a probability across each of the classes for an image. Since our predictions are probabilities and our labels are usually binary (0 if the image is not that class and 1 if it is), we need some way to convert predictions into a binary representation so we can compare them with the actual labels. To do that, we typically set a threshold: any predicted probabilities below the threshold become a 0, and any predicted probabilities above it become a 1. In binary classification the default threshold is normally 0.5, giving an equal chance for both choices.

Binary classification

There are many metrics for single-label classification that are used in practice, but the best choice depends on our use case. In particular, different evaluation metrics are appropriate for binary and multiclass classification. Let's begin with binary classification.

The most common evaluation metric is accuracy. This is a measure of how many predictions our model got right. To figure that out, it's also useful to calculate four other metrics: true positives, true negatives, false positives, and false negatives. True positives are when the label is 1, indicating that the example belongs to a certain class, and the prediction is also 1. Similarly, true negatives are when the label is 0, indicating that the example does not belong to that class, and the prediction is also 0. Conversely, a false positive is when the label is 0 but the prediction is 1, and a false negative is when the label is 1 but the prediction is 0. Taken together, these create something called a *confusion matrix* for the set of predictions, which is a 2x2 grid that counts the number of each of these four metrics, as can be seen in Figure 8-5.

		Actual class	
		Yes	**No**
Predicted class	**Yes**	TP	FP
	No	FN	TN

Figure 8-5. A binary classification confusion matrix.

We can add these four metrics to our Keras model as follows:

```
model.compile(
    optimizer="sgd",
    loss="mse",
    metrics=[
        tf.keras.metrics.TruePositives(),
        tf.keras.metrics.TrueNegatives(),
        tf.keras.metrics.FalsePositives(),
        tf.keras.metrics.FalseNegatives(),
    ]
)
```

Classification accuracy is the percentage of correct predictions, so it's calculated by dividing the number of predictions the model got right by the total number of predictions it made. Using the four confusion matrix metrics, this can be expressed as:

$$accuracy = \frac{TP + TN}{TP + TN + FP + FN}$$

In TensorFlow, we can add an accuracy metric to our Keras model like this:

```
model.compile(optimizer="sgd", loss="mse",
    metrics=[tf.keras.metrics.Accuracy()]
)
```

This counts the number of predictions that matched the labels and then divides by the total number of predictions.

If our predictions and labels are all either 0 or 1, as in the case of binary classification, then we could instead add the following TensorFlow code:

```
model.compile(optimizer="sgd", loss="mse",
    metrics=[tf.keras.metrics.BinaryAccuracy()]
)
```

In this case the predictions are most likely probabilities that are thresholded to 0 or 1 and then compared with the actual labels to see what percentage of them match.

If our labels are categorical, one-hot encoded, then we could instead add the following TensorFlow code:

```
model.compile(optimizer="sgd", loss="mse",
    metrics=[tf.keras.metrics.CategoricalAccuracy()]
)
```

This is more common for the multiclass case and usually involves comparing a vector of predicted probabilities for each class to a one-hot-encoded vector of labels for each example.

A problem with accuracy, however, is that it works well only when the classes are balanced. For example, suppose our use case is to predict whether a retinal image depicts eye disease. Let's say we have screened one thousand patients, and only two of them actually have eye disease. A biased model that predicts that every image shows a healthy eye would be correct 998 times and wrong only twice, thus achieving 99.8% accuracy. While that might sound impressive, this model is actually useless to us because it will completely fail to detect the cases we're actually looking for. For this specific problem, accuracy is not a useful evaluation metric. Thankfully, there are other combinations of the confusion matrix values that can be more meaningful for imbalanced datasets (and also for balanced ones).

If, instead, we were interested in the percentage of positive predictions that our model got right, then we would be measuring the *prediction precision*. In other words, how many patients really have eye disease out of all the ones the model predicted to have eye disease? Precision is calculated as follows:

$$precision = \frac{TP}{TP + FP}$$

Similarly, if we wanted to know the percentage of positive examples that our model was able to correctly identify, then we would be measuring the *prediction recall*. In other words, of the patients who really had the eye disease, how many did the model find? Recall is calculated as:

$$recall = \frac{TP}{TP + FN}$$

In TensorFlow, we can add these two metrics to our Keras model using:

```
model.compile(optimizer="sgd", loss="mse",
    metrics=[tf.keras.metrics.Precision(), tf.keras.metrics.Recall()]
)
```

We could also add a thresholds argument either as a float in the range [0, 1] or a list or tuple of float values if we want the metrics calculated at thresholds other than 0.5.

As you can see, with precision and recall the numerators are identical and the denominators only differ in whether they include false positives or false negatives.

Therefore, typically when one goes up, the other goes down. So how do we find a good balance point between the two? We can add another metric, the F1 score:

$$F_1 = 2 * \frac{precision * recall}{precision + recall}$$

The F1 score is simply the harmonic mean between precision and recall. Like accuracy, precision, and recall, it has a range between 0 and 1. An F1 score of 1 indicates a model with perfect precision and recall and thus perfect accuracy. An F1 score of 0 means either the precision or the recall is 0, which means that there are no true positives. This indicates either that we have a terrible model or that our evaluation dataset contains no positive examples at all, denying our model the chance to learn how to predict positive examples well.

A more general metric known as the F_β score adds a real-valued constant between 0 and 1, β, which allows us to scale the importance of precision or recall in the F-score equation:

$$F_\beta = \left(1 + \beta^2\right) * \frac{precision * recall}{\beta^2 * precision + recall}$$

This is useful if we want to use a more aggregate measure than precision or recall alone, but the costs associated with false positives and false negatives are different; it allows us to optimize for the one we care about the most.

All the evaluation metrics we've looked at so far require us to choose a classification threshold which determines whether the probabilities are high enough to become positive class predictions or not. But how do we know where to set the threshold? Of course, we could try many possible threshold values and then choose the one that optimizes the metric we care most about.

However, if we're using multiple thresholds, there is another way to compare models across all thresholds at once. This first involves building curves out of metrics across a grid of thresholds. The two most popular curves are the *receiver operating characteristic* (ROC) and *precision-recall* curves. ROC curves have the true positive rate, also known as the sensitivity or recall, on the y-axis; and the false positive rate, also known as 1-specificity (the true negative rate) or fallout, along the x-axis. The false positive rate is defined as:

$$FPR = \frac{FP}{FP + TN}$$

Precision-recall curves have precision on the y-axis and recall on the x-axis.

Suppose we've chosen a grid of two hundred equally spaced thresholds, and calculated the thresholded evaluation metrics for both the horizontal and vertical axes for either type of curve. Of course, plotting these points will create a line that extends across all two hundred thresholds.

Generating curves like these can help us with threshold selection. We want to choose a threshold that optimizes the metric of interest. It could be one of these statistical metrics, or, better yet, a metric relevant to the business or use case at hand, such as the economic cost of missing a patient who has eye disease versus carrying out additional unnecessary screening of a patient who doesn't have eye disease.

We can summarize this information into a single number by calculating the *area under the curve* (AUC). As we can see on the left side of Figure 8-6, a perfect classifier would have an AUC of 1 because there would be a 100% true positive rate and a 0% false positive rate. A random classifier would have an AUC of 0.5 because the ROC curve would fall along the $y = x$-axis, which shows that the numbers of true positives and false positives grow at equal rates. If we calculate an AUC less than 0.5, then that means our model is performing *worse* than a random classifier; an AUC of 0 means the model was perfectly wrong about every prediction. All else being equal, a higher AUC is usually better, with the possible range being between 0 and 1.

The precision-recall (PR) curve is similar, as we can see on the right of Figure 8-6; however, not every point in PR space may be obtained, and thus the range is less than [0, 1]. The actual range depends on how skewed the data's class distributions are.

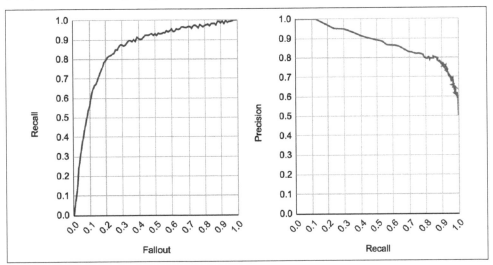

Figure 8-6. Left: ROC curve. Right: precision-recall curve.

So, which curve should we use when comparing classification models? If the classes are well sampled and balanced, then calculating the AUC-ROC is recommended.

Otherwise, if the classes are imbalanced or skewed, then AUC-PR is the recommended choice. Here is the TensorFlow code to add the AUC evaluation metric:

```
tf.keras.metrics.AUC(
    num_thresholds=200, curve="ROC",
    summation_method="interpolation",
    thresholds=None, multi_label=False
)
```

We can set the number of thresholds to calculate the four confusion metrics via the `num_thresholds` argument, which will create that number of equally spaced thresholds between 0 and 1. Alternatively, we can provide a list of float thresholds within the range [0, 1] that `tf.keras.metrics.AUC()` will use instead to calculate the AUC.

We can also set the type of curve via the `curve` argument to either `"ROC"` or `"PR"` to use an ROC or precision-recall curve, respectively.

Lastly, since we are performing binary classification, we set `multi_label` to `False`. Otherwise, it would calculate the AUC for each class and then average.

Multiclass, single-label classification

If we instead have a multiclass classification problem, let's say with three classes (dog, cat, and bird), then the confusion matrix will look like Figure 8-7. Notice that instead of a 2x2 matrix we now have a 3x3 matrix; thus, in general, it will be an $n \times n$ matrix where n is the number of classes. A key difference between the binary classification problem and the multiclass classification problem is that we don't have true negatives anymore, because those are now the "true positives" of the other classes.

		Actual classes		
		Dog	Cat	Bird
Predicted classes	Dog			
	Cat			
	Bird			

Figure 8-7. A multiclass confusion matrix with three classes.

Remember, for multiclass, single-label classification, even though we have multiple classes, each instance still belongs to one and only one class. The labels are mutually exclusive. It is either a picture of a dog, a cat, or a bird, not more than one of these things.

How can we fit our binary classification confusion matrix metrics into our multiclass version? Let's walk through an example. If we have an image that is labeled a dog and we predict correctly that it is a dog, then the count in the dog-dog cell of the matrix gets incremented by one. This is what we called a true positive in the binary classification version. But what if instead our model predicted "cat"? It's obviously a false something, but it doesn't really fit into the false positive or false negative camps. It's just…false, wrong.

Thankfully, we don't have to leap too far to get our multiclass confusion matrix to work for us. Let's look at the confusion matrix again, with values filled in this time (Figure 8-8).

			Actual classes		
			Dog	Cat	Bird
Predicted classes	Dog		150	50	50
	Cat		30	125	60
	Bird		20	25	90

Figure 8-8. A dog, cat, bird multiclass classification confusion matrix example.

We can see that this is a balanced dataset, because each class has two hundred examples. However, it is not a perfect model since it is not a purely diagonal matrix; it has gotten many examples wrong, as evidenced by the off-diagonal counts. If we want to be able to calculate the precision, recall, and other metrics, then we must look at each class individually.

Looking only at the dog class, our confusion matrix contracts to what we see in Figure 8-9. We can see in this figure that our true positives are where the image was actually a dog and we predicted a dog, which was the case for 150 examples. The false positives are where we predicted the image was a dog but it was not (i.e., it was a cat or a bird). Therefore, to get this count we add together the 50 examples from the dog-cat cell and the 50 examples from the dog-bird cell. To find the count of false negatives, we do the opposite: these are cases where we should have predicted a dog but didn't, so to get their total we add together the 30 examples from the cat-dog cell and the 20 examples from the bird-dog cell. Lastly, the true negative count is the sum of the rest of the cells, where we correctly said that those images were not pictures of dogs. Remember, even though the model might have gotten cats and birds mixed up with each other in some cases, because for now we are only looking at the dog class those values all get lumped together in the true negative count.

		Actual dog	
		Yes	No
Predicted dog	Yes	TP = 150	FP = 50 + 50
	No	FN = 30 + 20	TN = 125 + 25 + 60 + 90

Figure 8-9. The dog classification confusion matrix.

Once we've done this for every class, we can calculate the composite metrics (precision, recall, F1 score, etc.) for each class. We can then take the unweighted average of each of these to get the macro versions of these metrics—for example, averaging the precisions across all classes would give the macro-precision. There is also a micro version, where instead we add up all of the true positives from each of the individual class confusion matrices into a global true positive count and do the same for the other three confusion metrics. However, since this was done globally, the micro-precision, micro-recall, and micro-F1 score will all be the same. Lastly, instead of using an unweighted average as we did in the macro versions, we could weight each class's individual metric by the total number of samples of that class. This would then give us the weighted precision, weighted recall, and so on. This can be useful if we have imbalanced classes.

Since these all still used thresholds to convert the predicted class probabilities into a 1 or 0 for the winning class, we can use these combined metrics for various thresholds to make ROC or precision-recall curves to find the AUC for comparing threshold-agnostic model performance.

Multiclass, multilabel classification

In binary (single-class, single-label) classification, the probabilities are mutually exclusive and each example either is the positive class or is not. In multiclass single-label classification the probabilities are again mutually exclusive, so each example can belong to one and only one class, but there are no positive and negative classes. The third type of classification problem is multiclass multilabel classification, where the probabilities are no longer mutually exclusive. An image doesn't necessarily have to be of just a dog or just a cat. If both are in the image, then the labels for both dog and cat can be 1, and therefore a good model should predict a value close to 1 for each of those classes, and a value close to 0 for any other classes.

What evaluation metrics can we use for the multilabel case? We have several options, but first let's define some notation. We'll define Y to be the set of actual labels, Z to be the set of predicted labels, and the function I to be the indicator function.

A harsh and challenging metric to maximize is the *exact match ratio* (EMR), also known as the *subset accuracy*:

$$EMR = \frac{1}{n} \sum_{i=1}^{n} I(Y_i = Z_i)$$

This measures the percentage of examples where we got *all* of the labels exactly right. Note that this does not give partial credit. If we were supposed to predict that one hundred classes are in an image but we only predict 99 of them, then that example isn't counted as an exact match. The better the model, the higher the EMR should be.

A less strict metric we could use is the *Hamming score*, which is effectively the multi-label accuracy:

$$HS = \frac{1}{n} \sum_{i=1}^{n} \frac{|Y_i \cap Z_i|}{|Y_i \cup Z_i|}$$

Here we are measuring the ratio of predicted correct labels to the total number of labels, predicted and actual, for each example, averaged across all examples. We want to maximize this quantity. This is similar to the Jaccard index or intersection over union (IOU), which we looked at in Chapter 4.

There is also a *Hamming loss* that can be used, which has a range of $[0, 1]$:

$$HL = \frac{1}{kn} \sum_{i=1}^{n} \sum_{l=1}^{k} \left[I(l \in Z_i \wedge l \notin Y_i) + I(l \notin Z_i \wedge l \in Y_i) \right]$$

Different from the Hamming score, the Hamming loss measures the relevance of an example to a class label that is incorrectly predicted and then averages that measure. Therefore, we are able to capture two kinds of errors: in the first term of the sum we are measuring the prediction error where we predicted an incorrect label, and for the second term we are measuring the missing error where a relevant label was not predicted. This is similar to an exclusive or (XOR) operation. We sum over the number of examples n and the number of classes k and normalize the double sum by those two numbers. If we only had one class, this would simplify to essentially 1 – accuracy for binary classification. Since this is a loss, the smaller the value, the better.

We also have multilabel forms of precision, recall, and F1 score. For precision, we average the ratio of predicted correct labels to the total number of actual labels.

$$precision = \frac{1}{n} \sum_{i=1}^{n} \frac{|Y_i \cap Z_i|}{|Z_i|}$$

Similarly for recall, where instead we average the ratio of predicted correct labels to the total number of predicted labels:

$$recall = \frac{1}{n} \sum_{i=1}^{n} \frac{|Y_i \cap Z_i|}{|Z_i|}$$

For F1 score, it is similar to before as the harmonic mean of precision and recall:

$$F_1 = \frac{1}{n} \sum_{i=1}^{n} \frac{2|Y_i \cap Z_i|}{|Y_i| + |Z_i|}$$

Of course we can also calculate the AUC of a ROC curve or precision-recall curve using the macro version, where we calculate the AUCs per class and then average them.

Metrics for Regression

For image regression problems, there are also evaluation metrics that we can use to see how well our model is performing on data outside of training. For all of the following regression metrics, our goal is to minimize them as much as possible.

The most well-known and standard metric is *mean squared error* (MSE):

$$MSE = \frac{1}{n} \sum_{i=1}^{n} \left(Y_i - \widehat{Y}_i\right)^2$$

MSE, as its name suggests, is the mean of the squared error between the predicted and actual continuous labels. This is a mean-unbiased estimator which has great sensitivity due to the quadratic term, but this sensitivity means a few outliers can unduly influence it.

The *root mean squared error* (RMSE), which is just the square root of the mean squared error, is also used:

$$RMSE = \sqrt{\frac{1}{n} \sum_{i=1}^{n} \left(Y_i - \widehat{Y}_i\right)^2}$$

A slightly simpler and more interpretable metric is the *mean absolute error* (MAE):

$$MAE = \frac{1}{n} \sum_{i=1}^{n} \left|Y_i - \widehat{Y}_i\right|$$

The MAE is just the absolute difference between continuous predictions and labels. Compared to the MSE/RMSE with their squared exponents, the MAE is not as prone to being skewed by a few outliers. Also, unlike MSE, which is a mean-unbiased estimator, where the estimator's sample mean is the same as the distributional mean, MAE is instead a median-unbiased estimator, where the estimator overestimates as frequently as it underestimates.

In an effort to make regression more robust, we can also try the Huber loss metric. This is also less sensitive to outliers than having a squared error loss:

$$HL_\delta\left(Y, \widehat{Y}\right) = \frac{1}{n} \sum_{i=1}^{n} \begin{cases} \frac{1}{2}\left(Y_i - \widehat{Y}_i\right)^2 & for \left|Y_i - \widehat{Y}_i\right| \leq \delta \\ \delta\left|Y_i - \widehat{Y}_i\right| - \frac{1}{2}\delta^2 & otherwise \end{cases}$$

As you can see, we get the best of both worlds with this metric. We declare a constant threshold, δ; if the absolute residual is less than this value we use the squared term, and otherwise we use the linear term. This way we can benefit from the sensitivity of the squared mean–unbiased estimator of the quadratic term for values close to zero and the robustness of the median-unbiased estimator of the linear term for values further from zero.

Metrics for Object Detection

Essentially, most of the usual object detection evaluation metrics are the same as the classification metrics. However, instead of comparing predicted and actual labels for an entire image, we are comparing the objects detected versus the objects that are actually there using bounding boxes, as we saw in Chapter 4.

One of the most common object detection metrics is the intersection over union:

$$IOU = \frac{area\left(\widehat{B} \cap B\right)}{area\left(\widehat{B} \cup B\right)}$$

The numerator is the area of the intersection of our predicted bounding box and the actual bounding box. The denominator is the union of our predicted bounding box and the actual bounding box. We can see this graphically in Figure 8-10.

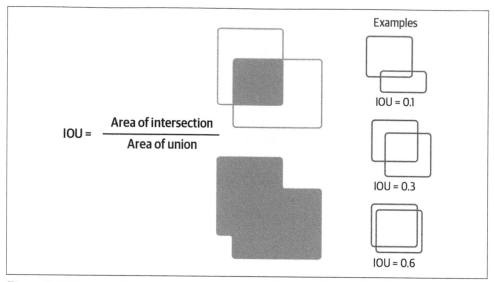

$$IOU = \frac{\text{Area of intersection}}{\text{Area of union}}$$

Figure 8-10. Intersection over union is the area of overlap divided by the area of union.

With perfect overlap, the two areas will be equal and thus the IOU will be 1. With no overlap, there will be 0 in the numerator and therefore the IOU will be 0. Thus, the bounds of IOU are [0, 1].

We can also use a form of the classification confusion metrics, such as true positives. As with classification, calculating these requires a threshold, but instead of thresholding a predicted probability, we threshold the IOU. In other words, if a bounding box's IOU is over a certain value, then we declare that that object has been detected. Threshold values are typically 50, 75, or 95%.

A true positive in this case would be considered a correct detection. This occurs when the predicted and actual bounding boxes have an IOU greater than or equal to the threshold. A false positive, on the other hand, would be considered a wrong detection. This occurs when the predicted and actual bounding boxes have an IOU less than the threshold. A false negative would be considered a missed detection, where an actual bounding box was not detected at all.

Lastly, true negatives don't apply for object detection. A true negative is a correct missed detection. If we remember our per-class multiclass confusion matrices, the true negative was the sum of all of the other cells not used in the other three confusion metrics. Here, the true negatives would be all of the bounding boxes that we could have placed on the image and not triggered one of the other three confusion metrics. Even for small images the number of permutations of these kinds of not-placed bounding boxes would be enormous, so it doesn't make sense to use this confusion metric.

Precision in this case equals the number of true positives divided by the number of all detections. This measures the model's ability to identify only the relevant objects within the image:

$$precision = \frac{TP}{alldetections}$$

In object detection, recall measures the model's ability to find all of the relevant objects within the image. Therefore, it equals the number of true positives divided by the number of all actual bounding boxes:

$$recall = \frac{TP}{allactualboundingboxes}$$

Just like with classification, these composite metrics can be used to create curves using different threshold values. Some of the most common are precision-recall curves (like the ones we've seen before) and recall-IOU curves, which typically plot IOU in the range [0.5, 1.0].

We can also calculate the average precision and average recall using the precision-recall and recall-IOU curves. In order to smooth out any perturbations in the curve, we typically interpolate the precision at multiple recall levels before performing the actual average precision calculation, as shown in Figure 8-11.

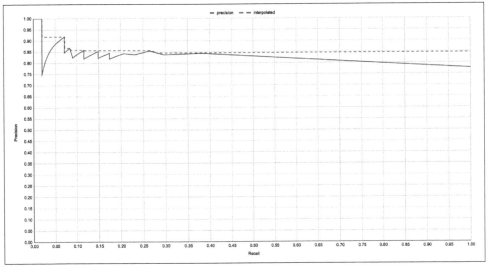

Figure 8-11. An interpolated precision-recall curve.

We do something similar for average recall. In the formula, the interpolated precision at a chosen recall level r is the maximum of the precision p found for any recall level r' that is greater than or equal to r:

$$pinterpolated = max_{r' \geq r}[p(r')]$$

The traditional interpolation method is to choose 11 equally spaced recall levels; however, more recently practitioners have been experimenting with choosing all unique recall levels for interpolation. The average precision is thus the area under the interpolated precision-recall curve:

$$AP = \frac{1}{n}\sum_{i=1}^{n-1}(r_{i+1} - r_i)pinterpolated(r_{i+1})$$

This is the end of the story for precision if we only have one class, but often in object detection we have many classes, all of which have different detection performances. Therefore, it can be useful to calculate the *mean average precision* (mAP), which is just the mean of each class's average precision:

$$mAP = \frac{1}{k}\sum_{l=1}^{k}AP_l$$

To calculate average recall, as mentioned previously, we use the recall-IOU curve instead of the precision-recall curve used for average precision. It is essentially the recall averaged over all IOUs (specifically, IOUs that are at least 50%) and thus becomes two times the area under the recall-IOU curve:

$$AR = 2\int_{0.5}^{1}recall(u)du$$

As we did for the multiclass objection detection case for average precision, we can find the *mean average recall* (mAR) by averaging the average recalls across all classes:

$$mAR = \frac{1}{k}\sum_{l=1}^{k}AR_l$$

For instance segmentation tasks, the metrics are exactly the same as for detection. IOU can equally well be defined for boxes or masks.

Now that we have explored the available evaluation metrics for models, let's look at how we use them for understanding model bias and for continuous evaluation.

Quality Evaluation

The evaluation metrics computed on the validation dataset during training are computed in aggregate. Such aggregate metrics miss a number of subtleties that are needed to truly gauge a model's quality. Let's take a look at sliced evaluations, a technique to catch these subtleties, and how to use sliced evaluations to identify bias in a model.

Sliced Evaluations

Evaluation metrics are usually calculated based on a holdout dataset that is similar to the training dataset in distribution. This typically gives us a good overall view of model health and quality. However, the model may perform much worse on some slices of the data than others, and these deficiencies can be lost in the ocean of calculating on the entire dataset.

Therefore, it can often be a good idea to analyze model quality on a more granular level. We can do this by taking slices of the data based on classes or other separating characteristics and calculating the usual evaluation metrics on each one of those subsets. Of course, we should still calculate the evaluation metrics using all of the data so that we can see how individual subsets vary from the superset. You can see an example of these sliced evaluation metrics in Figure 8-12.

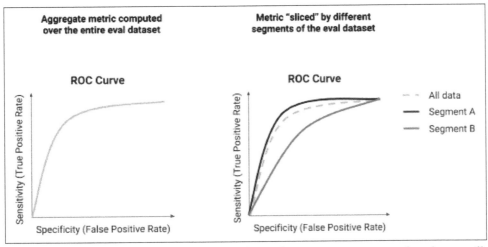

Figure 8-12. A sliced ROC curve for two different data segments compared to the overall ROC curve.

Some use cases place special importance on certain segments of the data, so these are prime targets to apply sliced evaluation metrics to in order to keep a close eye on them.

This doesn't just have to be a passive monitoring exercise, though! Once we know the sliced evaluation metrics, we can then make adjustments to our data or model to bring each of the sliced metrics in line with our expectations. This could be as simple as augmenting the data more for a particular class or adding some more complexity to the model to be able to understand those problematic slices better.

Next, we'll look at a specific example of a segment that we may need to do sliced evaluations on.

Fairness Monitoring

Image ML models have been shown to perform poorly on some segments of the population. For example, a 2018 study (*https://oreil.ly/CnSW8*) showed that commercially available facial analysis programs had dramatically higher error rates at identifying the gender of darker-skinned women as compared to lighter-skinned men. In 2020, many Twitter users reported (*https://oreil.ly/oVOZR*) that Twitter's photo preview feature appears to favor white faces over Black faces. Meanwhile, Zoom's facial recognition appeared to remove Black faces (*https://oreil.ly/9v8op*) when using a virtual background. And in 2015, Google Photos mistakenly labeled (*https://oreil.ly/Mw5LC*) a selfie of a Black couple as being an image of gorillas.

Considering these high-profile and distressing mistakes by highly capable engineering teams, it is clear that if our computer vision problems involve human subjects, we should attempt to safeguard against such errors by carrying out sliced evaluations where the segments consist of individuals belonging to different races and genders. This will allow us to diagnose whether there is a problem.

Poor model performance on subjects of different genders and races cannot be addressed simply by ensuring that all races and genders are present in the training and evaluation datasets. There may be deeper problems. Photographic filters and processing techniques were historically optimized (*https://oreil.ly/JFpNx*) to best represent lighter skin tones, and this causes problems with lighting effects on darker-toned individuals. Therefore, preprocessing and data augmentation methods may have to be incorporated into our model-training pipelines in order to correct for this effect. Also, ML model training focuses initially on common cases, and only later on rarer examples. This means that techniques such as early stopping, pruning, and quantization might amplify biases (*https://arxiv.org/abs/1911.05248*) against minorities. It is not, in other words, "just" a data problem. Addressing fairness issues requires examination of the entire machine learning pipeline.

Sliced evaluations are an invaluable tool to diagnose whether such biases exist in the models that have been trained. This means that we should perform these evaluations for any segment of the population that we are concerned might be treated unfairly.

Continuous Evaluation

How often should we carry out sliced evaluations? It's important to constantly be evaluating our models even after we deploy them. This can help us catch things that could be going wrong early. For instance, we might have prediction drift because the inference input distribution is slowly shifting over time. There also could be a sudden event that causes a major change in the data, which in turn causes the model's behavior to change.

Continuous evaluation typically consists of seven steps:

1. Randomly sample and save the data being sent for model predictions. For example, we might choose to save 1% of all the images sent to the deployed model.

2. Carry out predictions with the model as usual and send them back to the client—but make sure to also save the model's prediction for each of the sampled images.

3. Send the samples for labeling. We can use the same labeling approach as was used for the training data—for example, we can use a labeling service, or label the data a few days later based on the eventual outcome.

4. Compute evaluation metrics over the sampled data, including sliced evaluation metrics.

5. Plot moving averages of the evaluation metrics. For example, we might plot the average Hubert loss over the past seven days.

6. Look for changes in the averaged evaluation metrics over time, or specific thresholds that are exceeded. We might choose to send out an alert, for example, if the accuracy for any monitored segment drops below 95% or if the accuracy this week is more than 1% lower than the accuracy the previous week.

7. We might also choose to periodically retrain or fine-tune the model after adding the sampled and subsequently labeled data to the training dataset.

When to retrain is a decision that we need to make. Some common choices include retraining whenever the evaluation metric falls below a certain threshold, retraining every X days, or retraining once we have X new labeled examples.

Whether to train from scratch or just fine tune is another decision that we need to make. The typical choice is to fine tune the model if the new samples are a small fraction of the original training data and to train from scratch once the sampled data starts to approach about 10% of the number of examples in the original dataset.

Summary

In this chapter, we discussed the importance of monitoring our models during training. We can use the amazing graphical UI of TensorBoard to watch our loss and other metrics throughout training, and to verify that the model is converging and getting better over time. Additionally, since we don't want to overtrain our models, by creating checkpoints and enabling early stopping we can halt training at the best moment.

We also discussed many quality metrics that we can use to evaluate our models on unseen data to get a better measure of how well they're doing. There are different metrics for image classification, image regression, and object detection, although some of them resurface in slightly different forms among the various problem types. In fact, image classification has three different subfamilies of classification metrics, depending on both the number of classes and the number of labels per image.

Finally, we looked at performing sliced evaluations on subsets of our data to not only be aware of our model's gaps but also to help us brainstorm fixes to close those gaps. This practice can help us monitor for bias, to make sure that we are being as fair as possible and understand the inherent risks of using our model.

## CHAPTER 9

Model Predictions

The primary purpose of training machine learning models is to be able to use them to make predictions. In this chapter, we will take a deep dive into several considerations and design choices involved in deploying trained ML models and using them to make predictions.

 The code for this chapter is in the *09_deploying* folder of the book's GitHub repository (*https://github.com/GoogleCloudPlatform/ practical-ml-vision-book*). We will provide file names for code samples and notebooks where applicable.

Making Predictions

To *invoke* a trained model—i.e., to use it to make predictions—we have to load the model from the directory into which it was exported and call the serving signature. In this section, we will look at how to do this. We will also look at how to improve the maintainability and performance of invoked models.

Exporting the Model

To obtain a serving signature to invoke, we must export our trained model. Let's quickly recap these two topics—exporting and model signatures—which were covered in much greater detail in "Saving Model State" on page 255 in Chapter 7. Recall that a Keras model can be exported (see the notebook *07c_export.ipynb* on GitHub) using code like this:

```
model.save('gs://practical-ml-vision-book/flowers_5_trained')
```

This saves the model in TensorFlow SavedModel format. We discussed examining the signature of the prediction function using the command-line tool `saved_model_cli`.

By default the signature matches the input layer of the Keras model that was saved, but it is possible to export the model with a different function by explicitly specifying it (see Figure 9-1):

```
model.save('export/flowers_model',
           signatures={
               'serving_default': predict_flower_type
           })
```

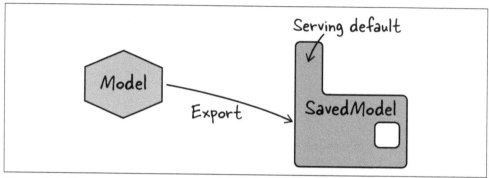

Figure 9-1. Exporting a model creates a SavedModel that has a default signature for serving predictions. In this case, the model on the left is the Python object in memory, and the SavedModel is what is persisted to disk.

The `predict_flower_type()` function carries a `@tf.function` annotation, as explained in "Signature of a TensorFlow Function" on page 256 in Chapter 7:

```
@tf.function(input_signature=[tf.TensorSpec([None,], dtype=tf.string)])
def predict_flower_type(filenames):
    ...
```

Suppose, for the examples in the first part of this chapter, that we have exported the model with the `predict_flower_type()` function as its default serving function.

Using In-Memory Models

Imagine we are programming a client that needs to call this model and obtain predictions from it for some input. The client could be a Python program from which we wish to invoke the model. We would then load the model into our program and obtain the default serving function as follows (full code in *09a_inmemory.ipynb* on GitHub):

```
serving_fn = tf.keras.models.load_model(MODEL_LOCATION
                                        ).signatures['serving_default']
```

If we pass in a set of filenames to the serving function, we obtain the corresponding predictions:

```
filenames = [
    'gs://.../9818247_e2eac18894.jpg',
    ...
    'gs://.../8713397358_0505cc0176_n.jpg'
]
pred = serving_fn(tf.convert_to_tensor(filenames))
```

The result is a dictionary. The maximum likelihood prediction can be obtained from the tensor by looking in the dictionary for the specific key and calling .numpy():

```
pred['flower_type_str'].numpy()
```

In this prediction situation, the model was loaded and invoked directly within the client program (see Figure 9-2). The input to the model had to be a tensor, and so the client program had to create a tensor out of the filename strings. Because the output of the model was also a tensor, the client program had to obtain a normal Python object using .numpy().

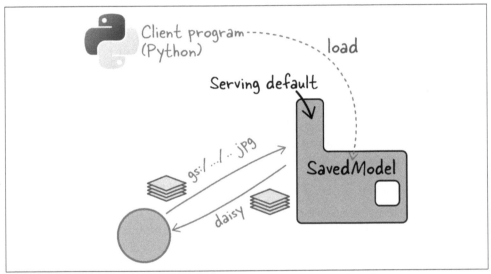

Figure 9-2. A client program written in Python loads the SavedModel into its memory, sends a tensor containing filenames to the in-memory model, and receives a tensor containing the predicted labels.

A few input images and their predictions are shown in Figure 9-3. Note that because of the care we took in Chapters 5 and 7 to replicate the preprocessing operations in the serving function, clients can send us images of any size—the server will resize the images to what the model requires.

Figure 9-3. A selection of images and their corresponding predictions.

There are, nevertheless, two key problems with this in-memory approach: abstraction and performance. Let's look at what these problems are and how to address them.

Improving Abstraction

It is usually the case that the machine learning engineers and data scientists who develop an ML model have different tools and skills at their disposal than the application developers who are integrating the ML predictions into user-facing applications. You want the ML prediction API to be such that it can be used by someone without any knowledge of TensorFlow or programming in React, Swift, or Kotlin. This is why abstraction is necessary.

We have abstracted away the model's details to some extent—the client doesn't need to know the required size of the images (indeed, note in Figure 9-3 that the images are all of different sizes) or the architecture of the ML model being used for classification. However, the abstraction is not complete. We do have some requirements for the client programmer:

- The client machine will need to have the TensorFlow libraries installed.

- At the time of writing, TensorFlow APIs are callable only from Python, C (*https://oreil.ly/H4zVq*), Java (*https://oreil.ly/WOP0O*), Go (*https://oreil.ly/bRhdh*), and JavaScript (*https://oreil.ly/vvODq*). Therefore, the client will have to be written in one of those languages.

- Because the client programmer has to call functions like `tf.convert_to_ten sor()` and `.numpy()`, they must understand concepts like tensor shapes and eager execution.

To improve the abstraction, it would be better if we could invoke the model using a protocol such as HTTPS that can be used from many languages and environments. Also, it would be better if we could supply the inputs in a generic format such as JSON, and obtain the results in the same format.

Improving Efficiency

In the in-memory approach, the model is loaded and invoked directly within the client program. So, the client will need:

- Considerable on-board memory, since image models tend to be quite large
- Accelerators such as GPUs or TPUs, as otherwise the computation will be quite slow

As long as we make sure to run the client code on machines with enough memory and with accelerators attached, are we OK? Not quite.

Performance problems tend to manifest themselves in four scenarios:

Online prediction
> We may have many concurrent clients that need the predictions in near real time. This is the case if we are building interactive tools, such as one that offers the ability to load product photographs onto an ecommerce website. Since there may be many thousands of simultaneous users, we need to ensure that the predictions are carried out at a low latency for all these concurrent users.

Batch prediction
> We might need to carry out inference on a large dataset of images. If each image takes 300 ms to process, the inference on 10,000 images will take nearly an hour. We might need the results faster.

Stream prediction
> We might need to carry out inference on images as they stream into our system. If we receive around 10 images a second, and it takes 100 ms to process each image, we will barely be able to keep up with the incoming stream, so any traffic spikes will cause the system to start falling behind.

Edge prediction
> Low-connectivity clients might need the predictions in near real time. For example, we might need to identify defects in the parts on a factory conveyor belt even as it is moving. For this to happen, we need the image of the belt to get processed as quickly as possible. We may not have the network bandwidth to send that image to a powerful machine in the cloud and get the results back within the time budget imposed by the moving conveyor belt. This is also the situation in cases where an app on a mobile phone needs to make a decision based on what the phone camera is being pointed at. Because the factory or mobile phone sits on the edge of the network, where network bandwidth isn't as high as it would be between two machines in a cloud data center, this is called *edge prediction*.

In the following sections, we'll dive into each of these scenarios and look at techniques for dealing with them.

Online Prediction

For online prediction, we require a microservices architecture—model inference will need to be carried out on powerful servers with accelerators attached. Clients will request model inference by sending HTTP requests and receiving HTTP responses. Using accelerators and autoscaling infrastructure addresses the performance problem, while using HTTP requests and responses addresses the abstraction problem.

TensorFlow Serving

The recommended approach for online prediction is to deploy the model using TensorFlow Serving as a web microservice that responds to POST requests. The request and response will not be tensors, but abstracted into a web-native message format such as JSON.

Deploying the model

TensorFlow Serving is just software, so we also need some infrastructure. User requests will have to be dynamically routed to different servers, which will need to autoscale to deal with traffic peaks. You can run TensorFlow Serving on managed services like Google Cloud's Vertex AI, Amazon SageMaker, or Azure ML (see Figure 9-4). Acceleration on these platforms is available both via GPUs and through custom-built accelerators like AWS Inferentia and Azure FPGA. Although you can install the TensorFlow Serving module or Docker container into your favorite web application framework, we don't recommend this approach since you won't get the benefits of the optimized ML serving systems and infrastructure management that the cloud providers' ML platforms offer.

To deploy the SavedModel as a web service on Google Cloud, we'd point gcloud at the Google Cloud Storage location to which the model was exported and deploy the resulting model to a Vertex AI endpoint. Please see the code in GitHub for details.

When deploying the model, we can also specify the machine type, type of accelerators, and minimum and maximum replica counts.

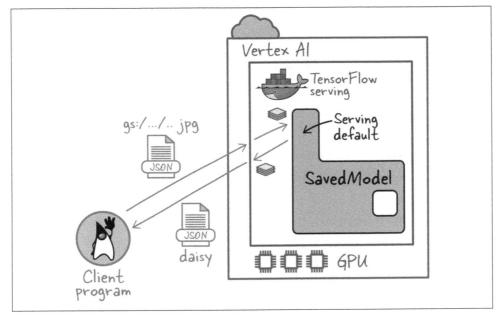

Figure 9-4. Online model predictions served through a REST API.

Making predictions

Predictions can be obtained from any machine that is capable of making an HTTPS call to the server on which the model is deployed (see Figure 9-4). The data is sent back and forth as JSON messages, and TensorFlow Serving converts the JSON into tensors to send to the SavedModel.

We can try out the deployed model by creating a JSON request:

```
{
    "instances": [
        {
            "filenames": "gs://.../9818247_e2eac18894.jpg"
        },
        {
            "filenames": "gs://.../9853885425_4a82356f1d_m.jpg"
        },
    ]
}
```

and sending it to the server using gcloud:

```
gcloud ai endpoints predict ${ENDPOINT_ID} \
    --region=${REGION} \
    --json-request=request.json
```

One key thing to note is that the JSON request consists of a set of instances, each of which is a dictionary. The items in the dictionary correspond to the inputs specified in the model signature. We can view the model signature by running the command-line tool `saved_model_cli` on the SavedModel:

```
saved_model_cli show --tag_set serve \
    --signature_def serving_default --dir ${MODEL_LOCATION}
```

In the case of the flowers model, this returns:

```
inputs['filenames'] tensor_info:
    dtype: DT_STRING
    shape: (-1)
    name: serving_default_filenames:0
```

That's how we knew that each instance in the JSON needed a string element called `filenames`.

Because this is just a REST API, it can be invoked from any programming language that is capable of sending an HTTPS POST request. Here's how to do it in Python:

```
api = ('https://{}-aiplatform.googleapis.com/v1/projects/' +
       '{}/locations/{}/endpoints/{}:predict'.format(
       REGION, PROJECT, REGION, ENDPOINT_ID))
```

The header contains the client's authentication token. This can be retrieved programmatically using:

```
token = (GoogleCredentials.get_application_default()
             .get_access_token().access_token)
```

We have seen how to deploy the model and obtain predictions from it, but the API is whatever signature the model was exported with. Next, let's look at how to change this.

Modifying the Serving Function

Currently, the flowers model has been exported so that it takes a filename as input and returns a dictionary consisting of the most likely class (e.g., daisy), the index of this class (e.g., 2), and the probability associated with this class (e.g., 0.3). Suppose we wish to change the signature so that we also return the filename that the prediction is associated with.

This sort of scenario is quite common because it is impossible to anticipate the exact signature that we will need in production when a model is exported. In this case, we want to pass input parameters from the client through to the response. A need for such *pass-through parameters* is quite common, and different clients will want to pass through different things.

While it is possible to go back, change the trainer program, retrain the model, and re-export the model with the desired signature, it is more convenient to simply change the signature of the exported model.

Changing the default signature

To change the signature, first we load the exported model:

```
model = tf.keras.models.load_model(MODEL_LOCATION)
```

Then we define a function with the desired new signature, making sure to invoke the old signature on the model from within the new function:

```
@tf.function(input_signature=[tf.TensorSpec([None,], dtype=tf.string)])
def pass_through_input(filenames):
    old_fn = model.signatures['serving_default']
    result = old_fn(filenames) # has flower_type_int etc.
    result['filename'] = filenames # pass through
    return result
```

If the client instead wanted to supply a sequence number and asked us to pass this through in the response, we could do that as follows:

```
@tf.function(input_signature=[tf.TensorSpec([None,], dtype=tf.string),
                              tf.TensorSpec([], dtype=tf.int64)])
def pass_through_input(filenames, sequenceNumber):
    old_fn = model.signatures['serving_default']
    result = old_fn(filenames) # has flower_type_int etc.
    result['filename'] = filenames # pass through
    result['sequenceNumber'] = sequenceNumber # pass through
    return result
```

Finally, we export the model with our new function as the serving default:

```
model.save(NEW_MODEL_LOCATION,
          signatures={
              'serving_default': pass_through_input
          })
```

We can verify the resulting signature using saved_model_cli and ensure that the file-name is included in the output:

```
outputs['filename'] tensor_info:
    dtype: DT_STRING
    shape: (-1)
    name: StatefulPartitionedCall:0
```

Multiple signatures

What if you have multiple clients, and each of them wants a different signature? TensorFlow Serving allows you to have multiple signatures in a model (although only one of them will be the serving default).

For example, suppose we want to support both the original signature and the pass-through version. In this case, we can export the model with two signatures (see Figure 9-5):

```
model.save('export/flowers_model2',
          signatures={
              'serving_default': old_fn,
              'input_pass_through': pass_through_input
          })
```

where `old_fn` is the original serving signature that is obtained via:

```
model = tf.keras.models.load_model(MODEL_LOCATION)
old_fn = model.signatures['serving_default']
```

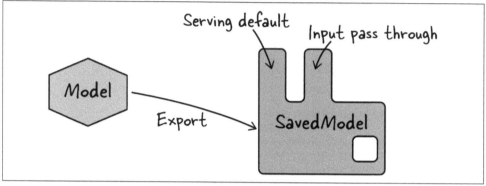

Figure 9-5. Exporting a model with multiple signatures.

Clients who wish to invoke the nondefault serving signature will have to specifically include a signature name in their requests:

```
{
    "signature_name": "input_pass_through",
    "instances": [
        {
            "filenames": "gs://.../9818247_e2eac18894.jpg"
        },
        ...
    ]
}
```

Others will get the response corresponding to the default serving function.

Handling Image Bytes

We have, so far, been sending a filename to the service and asking for the classification result. This works well for images that have been uploaded to the cloud already, but can introduce friction if that's not the case. If the image is not already in the cloud, it would be ideal for the client code to send us the JPEG bytes corresponding to the file contents. That way, we can avoid an intermediate step of uploading the image data to the cloud before invoking the prediction model.

Loading the model

To change the model in this situation, we could load the exported model and change the input signature to be:

```
@tf.function(input_signature=[tf.TensorSpec([None,], dtype=tf.string)])
def predict_bytes(img_bytes):
```

But what would this implementation do? In order to invoke the existing model signature, we will need the user's file to be available to the server. So, we'd have to take the incoming image bytes, write them to a temporary Cloud Storage location, and then send it to the model. The model would then read this temporary file back into memory. This is pretty wasteful—how can we get the model to directly use the bytes we are sending it?

To do this, we need to decode the JPEG bytes, preprocess them the same way that we did during model training, and then invoke `model.predict()`. For that, we need to load the last (or best) checkpoint saved during model training:

```
CHECK_POINT_DIR='gs://.../chkpts'
model = tf.keras.models.load_model(CHECK_POINT_DIR)
```

We can also load the exported model using the same API:

```
EXPORT_DIR='gs://.../export'
model = tf.keras.models.load_model(EXPORT_DIR)
```

Adding a prediction signature

Having loaded the model, we use this model to implement the prediction function:

```
@tf.function(input_signature=[tf.TensorSpec([None,], dtype=tf.string)])
def predict_bytes(img_bytes):
    input_images = tf.map_fn(
        preprocess, # preprocessing function used in training
        img_bytes,
        fn_output_signature=tf.float32
    )
    batch_pred = model(input_images) # same as model.predict()
    top_prob = tf.math.reduce_max(batch_pred, axis=[1])
    pred_label_index = tf.math.argmax(batch_pred, axis=1)
    pred_label = tf.gather(tf.convert_to_tensor(CLASS_NAMES),
                            pred_label_index)
    return {
        'probability': top_prob,
        'flower_type_int': pred_label_index,
        'flower_type_str': pred_label
    }
```

In that code snippet, note that we need to get access to the preprocessing functions used in training, perhaps by importing a Python module. The preprocessing function has to be the same as what was used in training:

```
def preprocess(img_bytes):
    img = tf.image.decode_jpeg(img_bytes, channels=IMG_CHANNELS)
    img = tf.image.convert_image_dtype(img, tf.float32)
    return tf.image.resize_with_pad(img, IMG_HEIGHT, IMG_WIDTH)
```

We might as well also implement another method to predict from the filename:

```
@tf.function(input_signature=[tf.TensorSpec([None,], dtype=tf.string)])
def predict_filename(filenames):
    img_bytes = tf.map_fn(
        tf.io.read_file,
        filenames
    )
    result = predict_bytes(img_bytes)
    result['filename'] = filenames
    return result
```

This function simply reads in the file (using `tf.io.read_file()`) and then invokes the other prediction method.

Exporting signatures

Both of these functions can be exported, so that clients have the choice of supplying either the filename or the byte contents:

```
model.save('export/flowers_model3',
           signatures={
               'serving_default': predict_filename,
               'from_bytes': predict_bytes
           })
```

Base64 encoding

In order to provide the contents of a local image file to the web service, we read the file contents into memory and send them over the wire. Because it is very possible that the JPEG files will contain special characters that will confuse the JSON parser on the server side, it is necessary to base64-encode the file contents before sending them (the full code is available in *09d_bytes.ipynb* on GitHub):

```
def b64encode(filename):
    with open(filename, 'rb') as ifp:
        img_bytes = ifp.read()
        return base64.b64encode(img_bytes)
```

The base64-encoded data can then be incorporated into the JSON message that is sent as follows:

```
data = {
    "signature_name": "from_bytes",
    "instances": [
        {
            "img_bytes": {"b64": b64encode('/tmp/test1.jpg')}
        },
```

```
        {
            "img_bytes": {"b64": b64encode('/tmp/test2.jpg')}
        },
    ]
}
```

Note the use of the special b64 element to denote base64 encoding. TensorFlow Serving understands this and decodes the data on the other end.

Batch and Stream Prediction

Doing batch prediction one image at a time is unacceptably slow. A better solution is to carry out the predictions in parallel. Batch prediction is an embarrassingly parallel problem—predictions on two images can be performed entirely in parallel because there is no data to transfer between the two prediction routines. However, attempts to parallelize the batch prediction code on a single machine with many GPUs often run into memory issues because each of the threads will need to have its own copy of the model. Using Apache Beam, Apache Spark, or any other big data processing technology that allows us to distribute data processing across many machines is a good way to improve batch prediction performance.

We also need multiple machines for streaming prediction (such as in response to a clickstream of events through Apache Kafka, Amazon Kinesis, or Google Cloud Pub/Sub), for the same reasons that we require them for batch prediction—to carry out inference on the images as they arrive in parallel without causing out-of-memory problems. However, because streaming workloads tend to be spiky, we also require this infrastructure to autoscale—we should provision more machines at traffic peaks and scale down to a minimal number of machines at traffic lows. Apache Beam on Cloud Dataflow provides this capability. Therefore, we suggest using Beam for improving the performance of streaming prediction. Happily, the same code that is used for batch prediction in Beam will also work unchanged for streaming prediction.

The Apache Beam Pipeline

The solution to both batch and streaming prediction involves Apache Beam. We can write a Beam transform to carry out inference as part of the pipeline:

```
| 'pred' >> beam.Map(ModelPredict(MODEL_LOCATION))
```

We can reuse the model prediction code that we used in in-memory prediction by loading the serving function from the exported model:

```
class ModelPredict:
    def __init__(self, model_location):
        self._model_location = model_location
```

```
def __call__(self, filename):
    serving_fn = (tf.keras.models.load_model(self._model_location)
                    .signatures['serving_default'])
    result = serving_fn(tf.convert_to_tensor([filename]))
    return {
        'filenames': filename,
        'probability': result['probability'].numpy()[0],
        'pred_label': result['flower_type_str'].numpy()[0]
    }
```

However, there are two issues with this code. First, we are processing the files one at a time. TensorFlow graph operations are faster if we can carry them out in batches, so we'll want to batch up the filenames. Second, we are loading the model for each element. Ideally, we'd load the model once and reuse it. Because Beam is a distributed system, however, we actually have to load the model once *on each worker* (see Figure 9-6). To do that, we must use a shared *handle* (essentially a shared connection to the service) that is acquired by each worker. This handle has to be acquired through a weak reference so that if a worker is decommissioned (due to low traffic) and then reactivated (due to a traffic peak), Beam does the right thing and reloads the model in that worker.

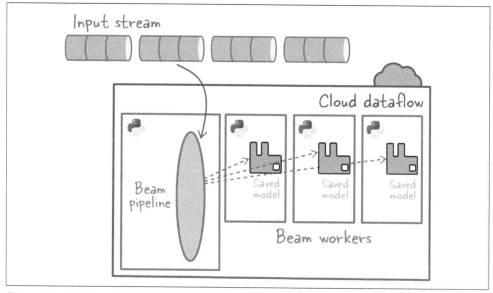

Figure 9-6. Batch prediction uses distributed workers to process the input data in parallel. This architecture also works for stream prediction.

To use the shared handle, we modify the model prediction code as follows:

```
class ModelPredict:
    def __init__(self, shared_handle, model_location):
        self._shared_handle = shared_handle
```

```
            self._model_location = model_location

    def __call__(self, filenames):
        def initialize_model():
            logging.info('Loading Keras model from ' +
                         self._model_location)
            return (tf.keras.models.load_model(self._model_location)
                    .signatures['serving_default'])

        serving_fn = self._shared_handle.acquire(initialize_model)
        result = serving_fn(tf.convert_to_tensor(filenames))
        return {
            'filenames': filenames,
            'probability': result['probability'].numpy(),
            'pred_label': result['flower_type_str'].numpy()
        }
```

The shared handle, whose capability is provided by Apache Beam, ensures that connections are reused within a worker and reacquired after passivation. In the pipeline,
we create the shared handle and make sure to batch the elements before calling model
prediction (you can see the full code in *09a_inmemory.ipynb* on GitHub):

```
with beam.Pipeline() as p:

    shared_handle = Shared()

    (p
     | ...
     | 'batch' >> beam.BatchElements(
                    min_batch_size=1, max_batch_size=32)
     | 'addpred' >> beam.Map(
                    ModelPredict(shared_handle, MODEL_LOCATION) )
    )
```

The same code works for both batch and streaming predictions.

> If you are grouping the images, then the groups are already a batch
> of images and so there is no need to explicitly batch them:
> ```
> | 'groupbykey' >> beam.GroupByKey()  # (usr, [files])
> | 'addpred' >> beam.Map(lambda x:
>                  ModelPredict(shared_handle,
>                          MODEL_LOCATION)(x[1]))
> ```

We can run the Apache Beam code at scale using Cloud Dataflow.

Managed Service for Batch Prediction

If we have deployed the model as a web service to support online prediction, then an
alternative to using the Beam on Dataflow batch pipeline is to also use Vertex AI to
carry out batch prediction:

```
gcloud ai custom-jobs create \
    --display_name=flowers_batchpred_$(date -u +%y%m%d_%H%M%S) \
    --region ${REGION} \
    --project=${PROJECT} \

--worker-pool-spec=machine-type='n1-highmem-2',container-image-uri=${IMAGE}
```

Performance-wise, the best approach depends on the accelerators that are available in your online prediction infrastructure versus what is available in your big data infrastructure. Since online prediction infrastructure can use custom ML chips, this approach tends to be better. Also, Vertex AI batch prediction is easier to use because we don't have to write code to handle batched requests.

Invoking Online Prediction

Writing our own batch prediction pipeline in Apache Beam is more flexible because we can do additional transformations in our pipeline. Wouldn't it be great if we could combine the Beam and REST API approaches?

We can do this by invoking the deployed REST endpoint from the Beam pipeline instead of invoking the model that is in memory (the full code is in *09b_rest.ipynb* on GitHub):

```
class ModelPredict:
    def __init__(self, project, model_name, model_version):
        self._api = ('https://ml.googleapis.com/...:predict'
            .format(project, model_name, model_version))

    def __call__(self, filenames):
        token = (GoogleCredentials.get_application_default()
                .get_access_token().access_token)
        data = {
            "instances": []
        }
        for f in filenames:
            data['instances'].append({
                "filenames" : f
            })
        headers = {'Authorization': 'Bearer ' + token }
        response = requests.post(self._api, json=data, headers=headers)
        response = json.loads(response.content.decode('utf-8'))
        for (a,b) in zip(filenames, response['predictions']):
            result = b
            result['filename'] = a
            yield result
```

If we combine the Beam approach with the REST API approach as shown here, we will be able to support streaming predictions (something the managed service doesn't do). We also gain a couple of performance advantages:

- A deployed online model can be scaled according to the computational needs of the model. Meanwhile, the Beam pipeline can be scaled on the data rate. This ability to independently scale the two parts can lead to cost savings.

- A deployed online model can make more effective use of GPUs because the entire model code is on the TensorFlow graph. Although you can run the Dataflow pipeline on GPUs, GPU use is less effective because the Dataflow pipeline does many other things (like reading data, grouping keys, etc.) that do not benefit from GPU acceleration.

These two performance benefits have to be balanced against the increased networking overhead, however—using an online model adds a network call from the Beam pipeline to the deployed model. Measure the performance to determine whether the in-memory model is better for your needs than the REST model. In practice, we have observed that the larger the model is, and the more instances there are in the batch, the greater are the performance advantages of invoking the online model from Beam rather than hosting the model in memory.

Edge ML

Edge ML is becoming increasingly important because the number of devices with computational capabilities has been growing dramatically in recent years. These include smartphones, connected appliances in homes and factories, and instruments placed outdoors. If these edge devices have a camera, then they are candidates for machine learning use cases on images.

Constraints and Optimizations

Edge devices tend to have a few constraints:

- They may have no connectivity to the internet, and even if they do have connectivity, the connection might be spotty and have low bandwidth. It is, therefore, necessary to carry out ML model inference on the device itself so that we do not wait for the duration of a round trip to the cloud.

- There may be privacy constraints, and it may be desired that image data never leaves the device.

- Edge devices tend to have limited memory, storage, and computing power (at least compared to typical desktop or cloud machines). Therefore, the model inference has to be done in an efficient way.

- The use case often requires that the device have low cost, be small, use very little power, and not get too hot.

For edge prediction, therefore, we need a low-cost, efficient, on-device ML accelerator. In some cases, the accelerator will already be built in. For example, modern mobile phones tend to have an on-board GPU. In other cases, we will have to incorporate an accelerator into the design of the instrument. We can buy edge accelerators to attach or incorporate into instruments (such as cameras and X-ray scanners) when they are being built.

In conjunction with selecting fast hardware, we also need to ensure that we do not overtax the device. We can do that by taking advantage of approaches that reduce the computational requirements of image models so that they operate efficiently on the edge.

TensorFlow Lite

TensorFlow Lite is a software framework for carrying out TensorFlow model inference on edge devices. Note that TensorFlow Lite is not a version of TensorFlow—we cannot train models using TensorFlow Lite. Instead, we train a model using regular TensorFlow, and then convert the SavedModel into an efficient form for use on edge devices (see Figure 9-7).

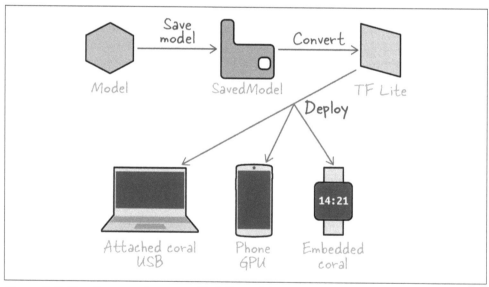

Figure 9-7. Creating an edge-runnable ML model.

To convert a SavedModel file into a TensorFlow Lite file, we need to use the `tf.lite` converter tool. We can do so from Python as follows:

```
converter = tf.lite.TFLiteConverter.from_saved_model(MODEL_LOCATION)
tflite_model = converter.convert()
with open('export/model.tflite', 'wb') as ofp:
    ofp.write(tflite_model)
```

In order to get efficient edge predictions, we need to do two things. First, we should make sure to use an edge-optimized (*https://oreil.ly/0GYY0*) model such as Mobile-Net. MobileNet tends to be about 40x faster than models like Inception thanks to optimizations such as pruning connections during training and using a piecewise linear approximation of the activation function (see Chapter 3).

Second, we should carefully select how to quantize the model weights. The appropriate choice for quantization depends on the device to which we are deploying the model. For example, the Coral Edge TPU works best if we quantize the model weights to integers. We can do quantization to integers by specifying some options on the converter:

```python
converter = tf.lite.TFLiteConverter.from_saved_model(saved_model_dir)
converter.optimizations = [tf.lite.Optimize.DEFAULT]
converter.representative_dataset = training_dataset.take(100)
converter.target_spec.supported_ops = [tf.lite.OpsSet.TFLITE_BUILTINS_INT8]
converter.inference_input_type = tf.int8  # or tf.uint8
converter.inference_output_type = tf.int8  # or tf.uint8
tflite_model = converter.convert()
```

In this code, we ask the optimizer to look at one hundred representative images (or whatever the model input is) from our training dataset to determine how best to quantize the weights without losing the model's predictive power. We also ask the conversion process to use only int8 arithmetic, and specify that the input and output types for the model will be int8.

Quantizing the model weights from float32 to int8 allows the Edge TPU to use one-fourth the memory and to accelerate the arithmetic by carrying it out on integers, which is an order of magnitude faster than using floats. Quantization tends to incur about a 0.2 to 0.5% loss in accuracy, although this depends on the model and dataset.

Once we have a TensorFlow Lite model file, we download the file to the edge device or package the model file with the application that is installed onto the device.

Running TensorFlow Lite

To obtain predictions from the model, the edge devices need to run a TensorFlow Lite interpreter. Android comes with an interpreter written in Java. To do inference from within an Android program, we can do:

```java
try (Interpreter tflite = new Interpreter(tf_lite_file)) {
    tflite.run(inputImageBuffer.getBuffer(), output);
}
```

Similar interpreters for iOS are available in Swift and Objective-C.

The ML Kit framework (*https://oreil.ly/9c3xb*) supports many common edge uses, like text recognition, barcode scanning, face detection, and object detection. ML Kit is well integrated with Firebase, a popular software development kit (SDK) for mobile applications. Before you roll your own ML solution, check that it is not already available in ML Kit.

For non-phone devices, use the Coral Edge TPU. At the time of writing, the Coral Edge TPU is available in three forms:

- A dongle that can be attached via USB3 to an edge device such as a Raspberry Pi
- A baseboard with Linux and Bluetooth
- A standalone chip that is small enough to be soldered onto an existing board

The Edge TPU tends to provide a 30–50x speedup over a CPU.

Using the TensorFlow Lite interpreter on Coral involves setting and retrieving the interpreter state:

```
interpreter = make_interpreter(path_to_tflite_model)
interpreter.allocate_tensors()
common.set_input(interpreter, imageBuffer)
interpreter.invoke()
result = classify.get_classes(interpreter)
```

 To run models on microcontrollers like Arduino, use TinyML,[1] not TensorFlow Lite. A microcontroller is a small computer on a single circuit board and does not require any operating system. TinyML provides a customized TensorFlow library (*https://oreil.ly/lppxk*) designed to run on embedded devices without an operating system and only tens of kilobytes of memory. TensorFlow Lite, on the other hand, is a set of tools that optimize ML models to run on edge devices that do have an operating system.

Processing the Image Buffer

On the edge device we will have to process the image in the camera buffer directly, so we will be processing only one image at a time. Let's change the serving signature appropriately (full code in *09e_tflite.ipynb* on GitHub):

---

1 Pete Warden and Daniel Situnayake, *TinyML* (O'Reilly, 2019).

```
@tf.function(input_signature=[
        tf.TensorSpec([None, None, 3], dtype=tf.float32)])
def predict_flower_type(img):
    img = tf.image.resize_with_pad(img, IMG_HEIGHT, IMG_WIDTH)
    ...
    return {
        'probability': tf.squeeze(top_prob, axis=0),
        'flower_type': tf.squeeze(pred_label, axis=0)
    }
```

We then export it:

```
model.save(MODEL_LOCATION,
        signatures={
            'serving_default': predict_flower_type
        })
```

and convert this model to TensorFlow Lite.

Federated Learning

With TensorFlow Lite, we trained the model on the cloud and converted the cloud-trained model to a file format that was copied over to the edge device. Once the model is on the edge device, it is no longer retrained. However, data drift and model drift will occur on edge ML models just as they do on cloud models. Therefore, we will have to plan on saving at least a sample of the images to a disk on the device, and periodically retrieving the images to a centralized location.

Recall, though, that one of the reasons to carry out inference on the edge is to support privacy-sensitive use cases. What if we don't want the image data to ever leave the device?

One solution to this privacy concern is *federated learning*. In federated learning, devices collaboratively learn a shared prediction model while each of the devices keeps its training data on-device. Essentially, each device computes a gradient update and shares only the gradient (not the original image) with its neighbors, or *federation*. The gradient updates across multiple devices are averaged by one or more members of the federation, and only the aggregate is sent to the cloud. It is also possible for a device to further fine-tune the shared prediction model based on interactions that happen on the device (see Figure 9-8). This allows for privacy-sensitive personalization to happen on each device.

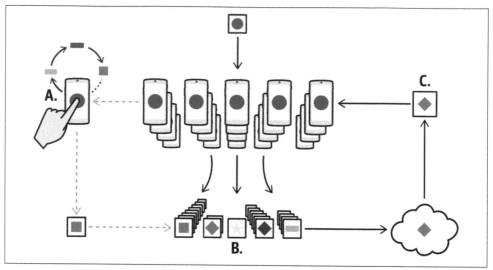

Figure 9-8. In federated learning, the model on the device (A) is improved based on both its own interactions and data from many other devices, but data never leaves the device. Many users' updates are aggregated (B) to form a consensus change (C) to the shared model, after which the procedure is repeated. Image courtesy of the Google AI Blog (https://oreil.ly/tBoB0).

Even with this approach, model attacks could still extract some sensitive information out of the trained model. To further boost privacy protection, federated learning can be combined with *differential privacy* (*https://arxiv.org/abs/1412.7584*). An open source framework to implement federated learning is available in the TensorFlow repository (*https://oreil.ly/D5UQC*).

Summary

In this chapter, we looked at how to invoke a trained model. We improved the abstraction provided by the prediction API and discussed how to improve the inference performance. For batch predictions, we suggested using a big data tool like Apache Beam and distributing the predictions over many machines.

For scaled concurrent, real-time predictions, we suggested deploying the model as a microservice using TensorFlow Serving. We also discussed how to change the signature of the model to support multiple requirements, and to accept image byte data sent directly over the wire. We also demonstrated making the model more efficient for deploying to the edge using TensorFlow Lite.

At this point, we have covered all the steps of the typical machine learning pipeline, from dataset creation to deployment for predictions. In the next chapter, we will look at a way to tie them all together into a pipeline.

## CHAPTER 10

Trends in Production ML

So far in this book, we have looked at computer vision as a problem to be solved by data scientists. Because machine learning is used to solve real-world business problems, however, there are other roles that interface with data scientists to carry out machine learning—for example:

ML engineers

ML models built by data scientists are put into production by ML engineers, who tie together all the steps of a typical machine learning workflow, from dataset creation to deployment for predictions, into a machine learning pipeline. You will often hear this being described as *MLOps*.

End users

People who make decisions based on ML models tend to not trust black-box AI approaches. This is especially true in domains such as medicine, where end users are highly trained specialists. They will often require that your AI models are *explainable*—explainability is widely considered a prerequisite for carrying out AI responsibly.

Domain experts

Domain experts can develop ML models using code-free frameworks. As such, they often help with data collection, validation, and problem viability assessment. You may hear this being described as ML being "democratized" through *no-code* or *low-code* tools.

In this chapter, we'll look at how the needs and skills of people in these adjacent roles increasingly affect the ML workflow in production settings.

The code for this chapter is in the *10_mlops* folder of the book's GitHub repository (*https://github.com/GoogleCloudPlatform/practical-ml-vision-book*). We will provide file names for code samples and notebooks where applicable.

Machine Learning Pipelines

Figure 10-1 shows a high-level view of the machine learning pipeline. In order to create a web service that takes an image file and identifies the flower in it, as we have depicted throughout this book, we need to perform the following steps:

- Create our dataset by converting our JPEG images into TensorFlow Records, with the data split into training, validation, and test datasets.
- Train an ML model to classify flowers (we carried out hyperparameter tuning to select the best model, but let's assume that we can predetermine the parameters).
- Deploy the model for serving.

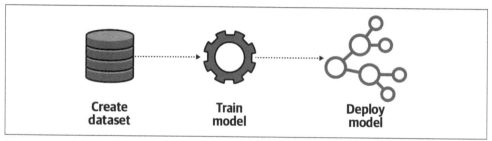

Figure 10-1. The end-to-end ML pipeline.

As you'll see in this section, in order to complete these steps in an ML pipeline we have to:

- Set up a cluster on which to execute the pipeline.
- Containerize our codebase, since the pipeline executes containers.
- Write pipeline components corresponding to each step of the pipeline.
- Connect the pipeline components so as to run the pipeline in one go.
- Automate the pipeline to run in response to events such as the arrival of new data.

First, though, let's discuss why we need an ML pipeline in the first place.

The Need for Pipelines

After we have trained our model on the original dataset, what happens if we get a few hundred more files to train on? We need to carry out the same set of operations to process those files, add them to our datasets, and retrain our model. In a model that depends heavily on having fresh data (say, one used for product identification rather than flower classification), we might need to perform these steps on a daily basis.

As new data arrives for a model to make predictions on, it is quite common for the model's performance to start to degrade because of *data drift*—that is, the newer data might be different from the data it was trained on. Perhaps the new images are of a higher resolution, or from a season or place we don't have in our training dataset. We can also anticipate that a month from now, we'll have a few more ideas that we will want to try. Perhaps one of our colleagues will have devised a better augmentation filter that we want to incorporate, or a new version of MobileNet (the architecture we are doing transfer learning from) might have been released. Experimentation to change our model's code will be quite common and will have to be planned for.

Ideally, we'd like a framework that will help us schedule and operationalize our ML pipelines and allow for constant experimentation. Kubeflow Pipelines provides a software framework that can represent any ML pipeline we choose in its domain-specific language (DSL). It runs on Kubeflow, a Kubernetes framework optimized for running TensorFlow models (see Figure 10-2). The managed Kubeflow Pipelines executor on Google Cloud is called Vertex Pipelines. The pipeline itself can execute the steps on the Kubernetes cluster (for on-premises work) or call out to Vertex Training, Vertex Prediction, and Cloud Dataflow on Google Cloud. Metadata about experiments and steps can be stored in the cluster itself, or in Cloud Storage and Cloud SQL.

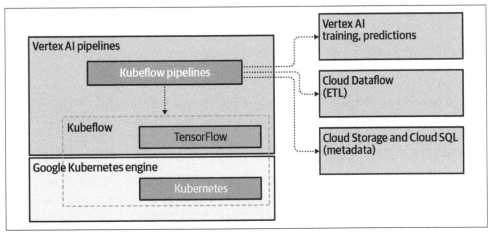

Figure 10-2. The Kubeflow Pipelines API runs on TensorFlow and Kubernetes.

Most ML pipelines follow a pretty standard set of steps: data validation, data transformation, model training, model evaluation, model deployment, and model monitoring. If your pipeline follows these steps, you can take advantage of the higher-level abstractions TensorFlow Extended (TFX) provides in the form of Python APIs. This way, you don't need to work at the level of the DSL and containerized steps. TFX (*https://oreil.ly/1AOvG*) is beyond the scope of this book.

Kubeflow Pipelines Cluster

To execute Kubeflow pipelines, we need a cluster. We can set one up on Google Cloud by navigating to the AI Platform Pipelines console (*https://oreil.ly/SYUlx*) and creating a new instance. Once started, we will get a link to open up the Pipelines dashboard and a Settings icon that provides the host URL (see Figure 10-3).

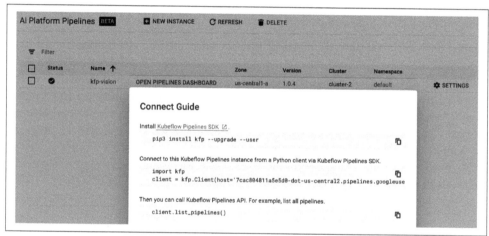

Figure 10-3. AI Platform Pipelines provides a managed execution environment for Kubeflow Pipelines.

We can develop pipelines in a Jupyter notebook, then deploy them to the cluster. Follow along with the full code in *07e_mlpipeline.ipynb* on GitHub.

Containerizing the Codebase

Once we have our cluster, the first step of our pipeline needs to transform the JPEG files into TensorFlow Records. Recall that we wrote an Apache Beam program called *jpeg_to_tfrecord.py* in Chapter 5 to handle this task. In order to make this repeatable, we need to make it a container where all the dependencies are captured.

We developed it in a Jupyter notebook, and fortunately the Notebooks service on Vertex AI releases a container image corresponding to each Notebook instance type.

Therefore, to build a container that is capable of executing that program, we need to do the following:

- Get the container image corresponding to the Notebook instance.

- Install any additional software dependencies. Looking through all our notebooks, we see that we need to install two additional Python packages: `apache-beam[gcp]` and `cloudml-hypertune`.

- Copy over the script. Because we will probably need other code from the repository as well for other tasks, it's probably better to copy over the entire repository.

This Dockerfile (the full code is in *Dockerfile* on GitHub) performs those three steps:

```
FROM gcr.io/deeplearning-platform-release/tf2-gpu
RUN python3 -m pip install --upgrade apache-beam[gcp] cloudml-hypertune
RUN mkdir -p /src/practical-ml-vision-book
COPY . /src/practical-ml-vision-book/
```

 Those of you familiar with Dockerfiles will recognize that there is no `ENTRYPOINT` in this file. That's because we will set up the entry point in the Kubeflow component—all the components for our pipeline will use this same Docker image.

We can push the Docker image to a container registry using standard Docker functionality:

```
full_image_name=gcr.io/${PROJECT_ID}/practical-ml-vision-book:latest
docker build -t "${full_image_name}" .
docker push "$full_image_name"
```

Writing a Component

For every component that we need, we'll first load its definition from a YAML file and then use it to create the actual component.

The first component we need to create is the dataset (see Figure 10-1). From Chapter 5, we know that the step involves running *jpeg_to_tfrecord.py*. We define the component in a file named *create_dataset.yaml*. It specifies these input parameters:

```
inputs:
- {name: runner, type: str, default: 'DirectRunner', description: 'DirectRunner...'}
- {name: project_id, type: str, description: 'Project to bill Dataflow job to'}
- {name: region, type: str, description: 'Region to run Dataflow job in'}
- {name: input_csv, type: GCSPath, description: 'Path to CSV file'}
- {name: output_dir, type: GCSPath, description: 'Top-level directory...'}
- {name: labels_dict, type: GCSPath, description: 'Dictionary file...'}
```

It also specifies the implementation, which is to call a script called *create_dataset.sh* that you'll find in *create_dataset.sh* on GitHub. The arguments to the script are constructed from the inputs to the component:

```
implementation:
    container:
        image: gcr.io/[PROJECT-ID]/practical-ml-vision-book:latest
        command: [
            "bash",
            "/src/practical-ml-vision-book/.../create_dataset.sh"
        ]
        args: [
            {inputValue: output_dir},
            {outputPath: tfrecords_topdir},
            "--all_data", {inputValue: input_csv},
            "--labels_file", {inputValue: labels_dict},
            "--project_id", {inputValue: project_id},
            "--output_dir", {inputValue: output_dir},
            "--runner", {inputValue: runner},
            "--region", {inputValue: region},
        ]
```

The *create_dataset.sh* script simply forwards everything to the Python program:

```
cd /src/practical-ml-vision-book/05_create_dataset
python3 -m jpeg_to_tfrecord $@
```

Why do we need the extra level of indirection here? Why not simply specify python3 as the command (instead of the bash call to the shell script)? That's because, besides just calling the converter program, we also need to perform additional functionality like creating folders, passing messages to subsequent steps of our Kubeflow pipelines, cleaning up intermediate files, and so on. Rather than update the Python code to add unrelated Kubeflow Pipelines functionality to it, we'll wrap the Python code within a bash script that will do the setup, message passing, and teardown. More on this shortly.

We will call the component from the pipeline as follows:

```
create_dataset_op = kfp.components.load_component_from_file(
    'components/create_dataset.yaml'
)
create_dataset = create_dataset_op(
    runner='DataflowRunner',
    project_id=project_id,
    region=region,
    input_csv='gs://cloud-ml-data/img/flower_photos/all_data.csv',
    output_dir='gs://{}/data/flower_tfrecords'.format(bucket),
    labels_dict='gs://cloud-ml-data/img/flower_photos/dict.txt'
)
```

If we pass in `DirectRunner` instead of `DataflowRunner`, the Apache Beam pipeline executes on the Kubeflow cluster itself (albeit slowly and on a single machine). This is useful for executing on premises.

Given the `create_dataset_op` component that we have just created, we can create a pipeline that runs this component as follows:

```
create_dataset_op = kfp.components.load_component_from_file(
    'components/create_dataset.yaml'
)

@dsl.pipeline(
    name='Flowers Transfer Learning Pipeline',
    description='End-to-end pipeline'
)
def flowerstxf_pipeline(
    project_id=PROJECT,
    bucket=BUCKET,
    region=REGION
):
    # Step 1: Create dataset
    create_dataset = create_dataset_op(
        runner='DataflowRunner',
        project_id=project_id,
        region=region,
        input_csv='gs://cloud-ml-data/img/flower_photos/all_data.csv',
        output_dir='gs://{}/data/flower_tfrecords'.format(bucket),
        labels_dict='gs://cloud-ml-data/img/flower_photos/dict.txt'
    )
```

We then compile this pipeline into a *.zip* file:

```
pipeline_func = flowerstxf_pipeline
pipeline_filename = pipeline_func.__name__ + '.zip'
import kfp.compiler as compiler
compiler.Compiler().compile(pipeline_func, pipeline_filename)
```

and submit that file as an experiment:

```
import kfp
client = kfp.Client(host=KFPHOST)
experiment = client.create_experiment('from_notebook')
run_name = pipeline_func.__name__ + ' run'
run_result = client.run_pipeline(
    experiment.id,
    run_name,
    pipeline_filename,
    {
        'project_id': PROJECT,
        'bucket': BUCKET,
        'region': REGION
```

```
        }
    )
```

We can also upload the *.zip* file, submit the pipeline, and carry out experiments and runs using the Pipelines dashboard.

Connecting Components

We now have the first step of our pipeline. The next step (see Figure 10-1) is to train an ML model on the TensorFlow Records created in the first step.

The dependency between the create_dataset step and the train_model step is expressed as follows:

```
create_dataset = create_dataset_op(...)
train_model = train_model_op(
    input_topdir=create_dataset.outputs['tfrecords_topdir'],
    region=region,
    job_dir='gs://{}/trained_model'.format(bucket)
)
```

In this code, notice that one of the inputs to train_model_op() depends on the output of create_dataset. Connecting the two components in this manner makes Kubeflow Pipelines wait for the create_dataset step to complete before starting the train_model step.

The underlying implementation involves the create_dataset step writing out the value for the tfrecords_topdir into a local temporary file whose name will be automatically generated by Kubeflow Pipelines. So, our create_dataset step will have to take this additional input and populate the file. Here's how we write the output directory name to the file in *create_dataset.sh* (the parameters for Kubeflow to provide to this script are specified in the YAML file):

```
#!/bin/bash -x
OUTPUT_DIR=$1
shift
COMPONENT_OUT=$1
shift

# run the Dataflow pipeline
cd /src/practical-ml-vision-book/05_create_dataset
python3 -m jpeg_to_tfrecord $@

# for subsequent components
mkdir -p $(dirname $COMPONENT_OUT)
echo "$OUTPUT_DIR" > $COMPONENT_OUT
```

The script writes the name of the output directory to the component output file, removes the two parameters from the command-line arguments (that's what the

---

shift does in bash), and passes along the rest of the command-line parameters to `jpeg_to_tfrecord`.

The `train_model` step is similar to the `create_dataset` step in that it uses the code-base container and invokes a script to train the model:

```
name: train_model_caip
...
implementation:
    container:
        image: gcr.io/[PROJECT-ID]/practical-ml-vision-book:latest
        command: [
            "bash",
            "/src/practical-ml-vision-book/.../train_model_caip.sh",
        ]
        args: [
            {inputValue: input_topdir},
            {inputValue: region},
            {inputValue: job_dir},
            {outputPath: trained_model},
        ]
```

We can turn this into a local training run on the cluster by replacing the call to Vertex AI Training by a call to `gcloud ai-platform local`. See *train_model_kfp.sh* in the book's GitHub repository for details.

The script writes out the directory in which the trained model is stored:

```
echo "${JOB_DIR}/flowers_model" > $COMPONENT_OUT
```

The deploy step does not require any custom code. To deploy the model, we can use the deploy operator that comes with Kubeflow Pipelines:

```
deploy_op = kfp.components.load_component_from_url(
    'https://.../kubeflow/pipelines/.../deploy/component.yaml')
deploy_model = deploy_op(
    model_uri=train_model.outputs['trained_model'],
    model_id='flowers',
    version_id='txf',
    ...)
```

As the pipeline is run, the logs, steps, and artifacts passed between steps show up in the console (see Figure 10-4).

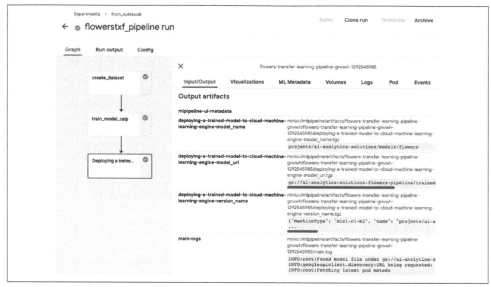

Figure 10-4. Information about a pipeline that has been run is displayed in the Vertex Pipelines console.

Automating a Run

Because we have a Python API to submit new runs of an experiment, it is quite straightforward to incorporate this Python code into a Cloud Function or a Cloud Run container. The function will then get invoked in response to a Cloud Scheduler trigger, or whenever new files are added to a storage bucket.

Caching in Kubeflow

The results of previous runs are cached and simply returned back if a component is run again with the same set of inputs and output strings. Unfortunately, Kubeflow Pipelines doesn't check the contents of Google Cloud Storage directories, so it doesn't know that the contents of a bucket may have changed even if the input parameter (the bucket) remains the same. Therefore, the caching tends to be of limited use. Because of that, you might want to explicitly set *staleness* criteria for the cache:

```
create_dataset.execution_options.caching_strategy.max_cache_staleness = "P7D"
```

The time duration for which data should be cached is represented in ISO 8601 format (*https://oreil.ly/yHek7*). P7D, for example, indicates that the output should be cached for 7 days. To effectively use caching, you have to incorporate timestamps into the names of your input and output directories.

The experiment-launching code can also be invoked in response to continuous integration (CI) triggers (such as GitHub/GitLab Actions) to carry out retraining any time new code is committed. The necessary continuous integration, continuous deployment (CD), permission management, infrastructure authorization, and authentication together form the realm of *MLOps*. MLOps is beyond the scope of this book, but the ML Engineering on Google Cloud Platform (*https://oreil.ly/Vy94n*), MLOps on Azure (*https://oreil.ly/lf6ea*), and Amazon SageMaker MLOps Workshop (*https://oreil.ly/9Cym0*) GitHub repositories contain instructions to help get you started on the respective platforms.

We have seen how pipelines address the need of ML engineers to tie together all the steps of a typical machine learning workflow into an ML pipeline. Next, let's look at how explainability meets the needs of decision makers.

Explainability

When we present an image to our model, we get a prediction. But why do we get that prediction? What is the model using to decide that a flower is a daisy or a tulip? Explanations of how AI models work are useful for several reasons:

Trust
> Human users may not trust a model that doesn't explain what it is doing. If an image classification model says that an X-ray depicts a fracture but does not point out the exact pixels it used to make its determination, few doctors will trust the model.

Troubleshooting
> Knowing what parts of an image are important to make a determination can be useful to diagnose why the model is making an error. For example, if a dog is identified as a fox, and the most relevant pixels happen to be of snow, it is likely that the model has wrongly learned to associate the background (snow) with foxes. To correct this error we will have to collect examples of foxes in other seasons or dogs in snow, or augment the dataset by pasting foxes and dogs into each others' scenes.

Bias busting
> If we are using image metadata as input to our model, examining the importance of features associated with sensitive data can be very important to determining sources of bias. For example, if a model to identify traffic violations treats potholes in the road as an important feature, this might be because the model is learning the biases in the training dataset (perhaps more tickets were handed out in poorer/less well maintained areas than in wealthy ones).

There are two types of explanations: global and instance-level. The term *global* here highlights that these explanations are a property of the whole model after training, as opposed to each individual prediction at inference time. These methods rank the inputs to the model by the extent to which they *explain* the variance (*https://oreil.ly/kZi7q*) of the predictions. For example, we may say that `feature1` explains 36% of the variance, `feature2` 23%, and so on. Because global feature importance is based on the extent to which different features contribute to the variance, these methods are calculated on a dataset consisting of many examples, such as the training or the validation dataset. However, global feature importance methods are not that useful in computer vision because there are no explicit, human-readable features when images are directly used as inputs to models. We will therefore not consider global explanations any further.

The second type of explanation is a measure of *instance-level* feature importance. These explanations attempt to explain each individual prediction and are invaluable in fostering user trust and for troubleshooting errors. These methods are more common in image models, and will be covered next.

Techniques

There are four methods that are commonly employed to interpret or explain the predictions of image models. In increasing order of sophistication, they are:

- Local Interpretable Model-agnostic Explanations (LIME) (*https://arxiv.org/abs/1602.04938*)
- Kernel Shapley Additive Explanations (KernelSHAP) (*https://arxiv.org/abs/1705.07874*)
- Integrated Gradients (IG) (*https://arxiv.org/abs/1703.01365*)
- Explainable Representations through AI (xRAI) (*https://arxiv.org/abs/2012.06006*)

Let's look at each of these in turn.

LIME

LIME perturbs the input image by first identifying patches of the image that consist of contiguous similar pixels (see Figure 10-5), then replacing some of the patches with a uniform value, essentially removing them. It then asks the model to make a prediction on the perturbed image. For each perturbed image, we get a classification probability. These probabilities are spatially weighted based on how similar the perturbed image is to the original. Finally, LIME presents the patches with the highest positive weights as the explanation.

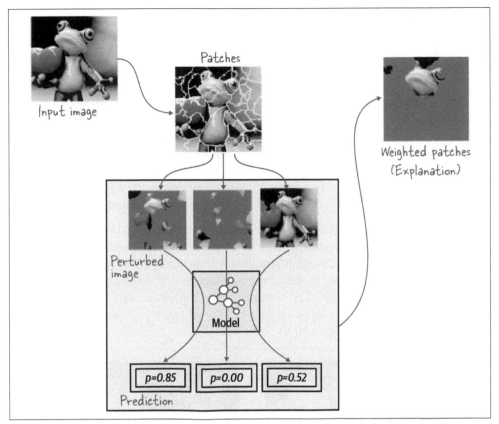

Figure 10-5. How LIME works, adapted from Ruberio et al., 2016 (https://oreil.ly/ xMFO7). In the bottom panel, p represents the predicted probability of the image being that of a frog.

KernelSHAP

KernelSHAP is similar to LIME, but it weights the perturbed instances differently. LIME weights instances that are similar to the original image very low, on the theory that they possess very little extra information. KernelSHAP, on the other hand, weights the instances based on a distribution derived from game theory. The more patches are included in a perturbed image, the less weight the instance gets because theoretically any of those patches could have been important. In practice, Kernel-SHAP tends to be computationally much more expensive than LIME but provides somewhat better results.

Integrated Gradients

IG uses the gradient of the model to identify which pixels are important. A property of deep learning is that the training initially focuses on the most important pixels because the error rate can be reduced the most by using their information in the output. Therefore, high gradients are associated with important pixels at the start of training. Unfortunately, neural networks *converge* during training, and during convergence the network keeps the weights corresponding to the important pixels unchanged and focuses on rarer situations. This means that the gradients corresponding to the most important pixels are actually close to zero at the end of training! Therefore, IG needs the gradient not at the end of training, but over the entire training process. However, the only weights that are available in the SavedModel file are the final weights. So, how can IG use the gradient to identify important pixels?

IG is based on the intuition that the model will output the a priori class probability if provided a baseline image that consists of all 0s, all 1s, or random values in the range [0, 1]. The overall gradient change is computed numerically by changing each pixel's value from the baseline value to the actual input in several steps and computing the gradient for each such change. The pixels with the highest gradients integrated over the change from the baseline value to the actual pixel value are then depicted on top of the original image (see Figure 10-6).

Figure 10-6. Integrated Gradients on a panda image (left) and on a fireboat image (right). Images from the IG TensorFlow tutorial (https://oreil.ly/vPhBi).

Choosing an appropriate baseline image is critical when using IG. The explanation is relative to the baseline, so you should not use an all-white or all-black image as a baseline if your training data contains a lot of black (or white) regions that convey meaning in the images. As an example, black areas in X-rays correspond to tissue. You should use a baseline of random pixels in that case. On the other hand, if your training data contains a lot of high-variance patches that convey meaning in the image, you might not want to use random pixels as a baseline. It's worth trying different baselines, as this can significantly affect the quality of your attributions.

The output of IG on two images was shown in Figure 10-6. In the first image, IG identifies the snout and fur texture of the panda's face as the pixels that play the most important part in determining that the image is of a panda. The second image, of a fireboat, shows how IG can be used for troubleshooting. Here, the fireboat is correctly identified as a fireboat, but the method uses the jets of water from the boat as the key feature. This indicates that we may need to collect images of fireboats that are not actively shooting water up in the air.

However, in practice (as we will see shortly), IG tends to pick up on high-information areas in the images regardless of whether that information is used by the model for classifying the specific image.

xRAI

In xRAI, the weights and biases of the trained neural network are used to train an interpretation network. The interpretation network outputs a choice among a family of algebraic expressions (such as Booleans and low-order polynomials) that are well understood. Thus, xRAI aims to find a close approximation to the original trained model from within the family of simple functions. This approximation, rather than the original model, is then interpreted.

The xRAI method combines the benefits of the preprocessing method of LIME and KernelSHAP to find patches in the image with the pixel-level attribution against a baseline image that IG provides (see Figure 10-7). The pixel-level attribution is integrated among all the pixels that form a patch, and these patches are then combined into regions based on having similar levels of integrated gradients. The regions are then removed from the input image and the model is invoked in order to determine how important each region is, and the regions are ordered based on how important they are to the given prediction.

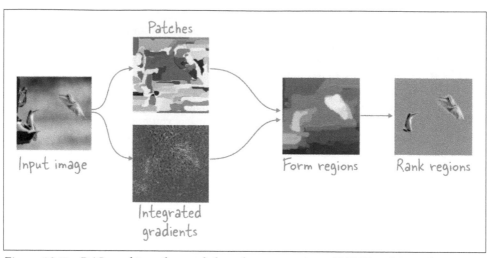

Figure 10-7. xRAI combines the patch-based preprocessing of LIME and KernelSHAP with the pixel-wise attributions of IG and ranks regions based on their effect on the prediction. Image adapted from the Google Cloud documentation (https://oreil.ly/RvZrG).

IG provides pixel-wise attributions. xRAI provides region-based attributions. Both have their uses. In a model identifying diseased regions of an eye (the diabetic retinopathy use case), for example, knowing the specific pixels that caused the diagnosis is very useful, so use IG. IG tends to work best on low-contrast images like X-rays or scientific images taken in a lab.

In natural images where you're detecting the type of animal depicted, for example, region-based attributions are preferred, so use xRAI. We do not recommend using IG on natural images like pictures taken in nature or around the house.

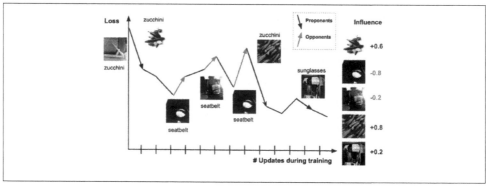

Figure 10-8. Tracin works by identifying key proponents and opponents that impact the training loss on a selected training example. Proponents are associated with a reduction in loss. Image courtesy of the Google AI Blog (https://oreil.ly/OtbBf).

Let's now look at how to get explanations for our flowers' model's predictions using these techniques.

Tracing ML Training for Proponents and Opponents

All the explainability methods covered in the main text are about explaining *predictions* after the model is deployed. Recently, researchers at Google published an interesting paper (*https://arxiv.org/pdf/2002.08484.pdf*) that describes a method called Tracin that can be used to explain the model's behavior on *training examples* during the *training* process.

As shown in Figure 10-8, the underlying idea is to pick a single training example (such as the zucchini image to the left of the y-axis) and look for changes in the loss on that training example as weights are updated. Tracin identifies individual training examples that cause changes in the predicted class of individual training examples or changes in the direction of the loss. Examples that cause reduction in loss (i.e., improve the predictions) are called *proponents*, and those that cause the loss to increase are called *opponents*. Opponents tend to be similar images that belong to another class, and proponents tend to be similar images that belong to the same class as the selected training example. Exceptions to this rule tend to be mislabeled examples and outliers.

Adding Explainability

Because image explainability is associated with individual predictions, we recommend that you use an ML deployment platform that carries out one or all of the explainability techniques mentioned in the previous section for every prediction presented to it. Explainability methods are computationally expensive, and a deployment platform that can distribute and scale the computation can help you do your prediction analysis more efficiently.

In this section, we will demonstrate obtaining explanations using Integrated Gradients and xRAI from a model deployed on Google Cloud's Vertex AI.

 At the time of writing, Azure ML supports SHAP (*https://oreil.ly/wx2D0*), as does Amazon SageMaker Clarify (*https://oreil.ly/MSqhJ*). Conceptually, the services are used similarly even if the syntax is slightly different. Please consult the linked documentation for specifics.

Explainability signatures

The explainability methods all need to invoke the model with perturbed versions of the original image. Let's say that our flowers model has the following export signature:

```
@tf.function(input_signature=[tf.TensorSpec([None,], dtype=tf.string)])
def predict_filename(filenames):
    ...
```

It accepts a filename and returns the predictions for the image data in that file.

In order to provide the Explainable AI (XAI) module the ability to create perturbed versions of the original images and obtain predictions for them, we will need to add two signatures:

- A preprocessing signature, to obtain the image that is input to the model. This method will take one or more filenames as input (like the original exported signature) and produce a 4D tensor of the shape required by the model (the full code is in *09f_explain.ipynb* on GitHub):

```
@tf.function(input_signature=[
             tf.TensorSpec([None,], dtype=tf.string)])
def xai_preprocess(filenames):
    input_images = tf.map_fn(
        preprocess, # preprocessing function from Ch 6
        filenames,
        fn_output_signature=tf.float32
    )
    return {
        'input_images': input_images
    }
```

Note that the return value is a dictionary. The key values of the dictionary (input_images, here) have to match the parameter names in the second signature that is described next so that the two methods can be called one after the other in a third model signature that we will discuss shortly.

- A model signature, to send in the 4D image tensor (XAI will send in perturbed images) and obtain predictions:

```
@tf.function(input_signature=[
        tf.TensorSpec([None, IMG_HEIGHT, IMG_WIDTH, IMG_CHANNELS],
                      dtype=tf.float32)])
def xai_model(input_images):
    batch_pred = model(input_images) # same as model.predict()
    top_prob = tf.math.reduce_max(batch_pred, axis=[1])
    pred_label_index = tf.math.argmax(batch_pred, axis=1)
    pred_label = tf.gather(tf.convert_to_tensor(CLASS_NAMES),
                           pred_label_index)
    return {
```

```
            'probability': top_prob,
            'flower_type_int': pred_label_index,
            'flower_type_str': pred_label
    }
```

This code invokes the model and then pulls out the highest-scoring label and its probability.

Given the preprocessing and model signatures, the original signature (that most clients will use) can be refactored into:

```
@tf.function(input_signature=[tf.TensorSpec([None,], dtype=tf.string)])
def predict_filename(filenames):
    preproc_output = xai_preprocess(filenames)
    return xai_model(preproc_output['input_images'])
```

Now, we save the model with all three export signatures:

```
model.save(MODEL_LOCATION,
           signatures={
               'serving_default': predict_filename,
               'xai_preprocess': xai_preprocess, # input to image
               'xai_model': xai_model # image to output
           })
```

At this point, the model has the signatures it needs to apply XAI, but there is some additional metadata needed in order to compute explanations.

Explanation metadata

Along with the model, we need to supply XAI a baseline image and some other metadata. This takes the form of a JSON file that we can create programmatically using the Explainability SDK open-sourced by Google Cloud.

We start by specifying which exported signature is the one that takes a perturbed image as input, and which of the output keys (probability, flower_type_int, or flower_type_str) needs to be explained:

```
from explainable_ai_sdk.metadata.tf.v2 import SavedModelMetadataBuilder
builder = SavedModelMetadataBuilder(
    MODEL_LOCATION,
    signature_name='xai_model',
    outputs_to_explain=['probability'])
```

Then we create the baseline image that will be used as the starting point for gradients. Common choices here are all zeros (np.zeros), all ones (np.ones), or random noise. Let's do the third option:

```
random_baseline = np.random.rand(IMG_HEIGHT, IMG_WIDTH, 3)
builder.set_image_metadata(
    'input_images',
    input_baselines=[random_baseline.tolist()])
```

Note that we specified the name of the input parameter to the `xai_model()` function, `input_images`.

Finally, we save the metadata file:

```
builder.save_metadata(MODEL_LOCATION)
```

This creates a file named *explanation_metadata.json* that lives along with the Saved-Model files.

Deploying the model

The SavedModel and associated explanation metadata are deployed to Vertex AI as before, but with a couple of extra parameters to do with explainability. To deploy a model version that provides IG explanations, we'd do:

```
gcloud beta ai-platform versions create \
    --origin=$MODEL_LOCATION --model=flowers ig ... \
    --explanation-method integrated-gradients --num-integral-steps 25
```

whereas to get xRAI explanations we'd do:

```
gcloud beta ai-platform versions create \
    --origin=$MODEL_LOCATION --model=flowers xrai ... \
    --explanation-method xrai --num-integral-steps 25
```

The `--num-integral-steps` argument specifies the number of steps between the baseline image and input image for the purposes of numerical integration. The more steps there are, the more accurate (and computationally intensive) the gradient computation is. A value of 25 is typical.

> The explanation response contains an approximation error for each prediction. Check the approximation error for a representative set of inputs, and if this error is too high, increase the number of steps.

For this example, let's employ both image explainability methods—we'll deploy a version that provides IG explanations with the name `ig` and a version that provides xRAI explanations with the name `xrai`.

Either deployed version can be invoked as normal with a request whose payload looks like this:

```
{
    "instances": [
        {
            "filenames": "gs://.../9818247_e2eac18894.jpg"
        },
        {
            "filenames": "gs://.../9853885425_4a82356f1d_m.jpg"
```

```
        },
      ...
    ]
}
```

It returns the label and associated probability for each of the input images:

```
FLOWER_TYPE_INT  FLOWER_TYPE_STR  PROBABILITY
1                dandelion        0.398337
1                dandelion        0.999961
0                daisy            0.994719
4                tulips           0.959007
4                tulips           0.941772
```

The XAI versions can be used for normal serving with no performance impact.

Obtaining explanations

There are three ways to get the explanations. The first is through `gcloud` and the second through the Explainable AI SDK. Both of these end up invoking the third way—a REST API—which we can use directly as well.

We'll look at the `gcloud` method, as it is the simplest and most flexible. We can send in a JSON request and obtain a JSON response using:

```
gcloud beta ai-platform explain --region=$REGION \
    --model=flowers --version=ig \
    --json-request=request.json > response.json
```

To get explanations using IG, we'll deploy this version (`ig`) with the option:

```
--explanation-method integrated-gradients
```

The JSON response contains the attribution image in base64-encoded form. We can decode it using:

```
with open('response.json') as ifp:
    explanations = json.load(ifp)['explanations']
    for expln in explanations:
        b64bytes = (expln['attributions_by_label'][0]
                    ['attributions']['input_images']['b64_jpeg'])
        img_bytes = base64.b64decode(b64bytes)
        img = tf.image.decode_jpeg(img_bytes, channels=3)
        attribution = tf.image.convert_image_dtype(img, tf.float32)
```

The IG results for five images are shown in Figure 10-9. The *10b_explain.ipynb* notebook on GitHub has the necessary plotting code.

Figure 10-9. Integrated Gradients explanation of the flowers model. The input images are in the top row, and the attributions returned by the XAI routine are in the second row.

For the first image, it appears that the model uses the tall white flower, as well as parts of the white pixels in the background, to decide that the image is a daisy. In the second image, the yellow-ish center and white petals are what the model relies on. Worryingly, in the fourth image, the cat seems to be an important part of the determination. Interestingly, the tulips' determination seems to be driven more by the green stalks than the bulb-like flowers. Again, as we will see shortly, this attribution is misleading, and this misleading attribution demonstrates the limitations of the IG approach.

To get xRAI explanations, we invoke `gcloud explain` on the model endpoint for the version we deployed with the name `xrai`. The attributions from xRAI for the same flower images are shown in Figure 10-10.

Figure 10-10. xRAI explanation of the flowers model. The input images are in the top row, and the attributions returned by the XAI routine are in the second row. The bottom row contains the same information as the second row, except that the attribution images have been recolored for easier visualization on the pages of this book.

Recall that xRAI uses the IG approach to identify salient regions, and then invokes the model with perturbed versions of the images to determine how important each of the regions is. It is clear that the attributions from xRAI in Figure 10-10 are much more precise than those obtained with IG in Figure 10-9.

For the first flower image, the model focuses on the tall white flower and only that flower. It is clear that the model has learned to ignore the smaller flowers in the background. And while IG seemed to indicate that the background was important, the xRAI results show that the model discards that information in favor of the most prominent flower in the image. In the second image, the yellow-ish center and white petals are what the model keys off of (IG got this right too). The precision of the xRAI approach is clear for the third image—the model picks up on the narrow band of bright yellow where the petals join the center. That is unique to daisies, and helps it distinguish them from similarly colored dandelions. In the fourth image, we can see that the tulip bulbs are what the model uses for its classification, although the cat confuses its attention. The final classification as tulips seems to be driven by the presence of so many flowers. The IG method led us astray—the stalks are prominent, but it is the bulbs that drive the prediction probability.

IG is useful in certain situations. Had we considered radiology images where pixel-wise attributions (rather than regions) are important, IG would have performed better. However, in images that depict objects, xRAI tends to perform better.

In this section, we have looked at how to add explainability to our prediction services in order to meet the need of decision makers to understand what a machine learning model is relying on. Next, let's look at how no-code tools help democratize ML.

No-Code Computer Vision

The computer vision problems that we have considered so far in this book—image classification, object detection, and image segmentation—are supported out of the box by low-code and no-code machine learning systems. For example, Figure 10-11 shows the starting console for Google Cloud AutoML Vision.

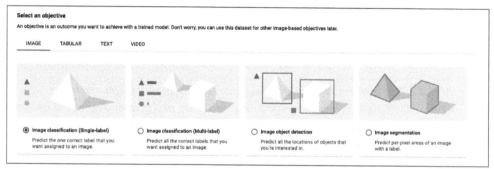

Figure 10-11. Fundamental computer vision problems supported by Google Cloud AutoML Vision, a machine learning tool that you can use without having to write any code.

Other no-code and low-code tools that work on images include Create ML (*https://oreil.ly/Ft1We*) by Apple, DataRobot (*https://oreil.ly/7xXOw*), and H2O (*https://oreil.ly/DHKiK*).

Why Use No-Code?

In this book, we have focused on implementing machine learning models using code. However, it is worth incorporating a no-code tool into your overall workflow.

No-code tools are useful when embarking on a computer vision project for several reasons, including:

Problem viability

Tools such as AutoML serve as a sanity check on the kind of accuracy that you can expect. If the accuracy that is achieved is far from what would be acceptable in context, this allows you to avoid wasting your time on futile ML projects. For example, if identifying a counterfeit ID achieves only 98% precision at the desired recall, you know that you have a problem—wrongly rejecting 2% of your customers might be an unacceptable outcome.

Data quality and quantity

No-code tools provide a check on the quality of your dataset. After data collection, the correct next step in many ML projects is to go out and collect more/better data, not to train an ML model; and the accuracy that you get from a tool like AutoML can help you make that decision. For example, if the confusion matrix the tool produces indicates that the model frequently classifies all flowers in water as lilies, that might be an indication that you need more photographs of water scenes.

Benchmarking

Starting out with a tool like AutoML gives you a benchmark against which you can compare the models that you build.

Many machine learning organizations arm their domain experts with no-code tools so that they can examine problem viability and help collect high-quality data before bringing the problem to the data science team.

In the rest of this section, we'll quickly run through how to use AutoML on the 5-flowers dataset, starting with loading data.

Loading Data

The first step is to load the data into the system. We do that by pointing the tool at the *all_data.csv* file in the Cloud Storage bucket (see Figure 10-12).

Once the data is loaded, we see that there are 3,667 images with 633 daisies, 898 dandelions, and so on (see Figure 10-13). We can verify that all the images are labeled, and correct the labels if necessary. If we had loaded a dataset without labels, we could label the images ourselves in the user interface or farm the task out to a labeling service (labeling services were covered in Chapter 5).

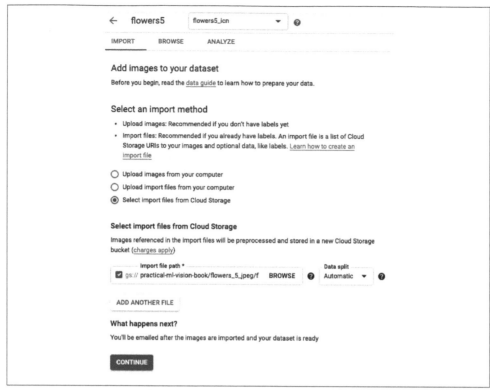

Figure 10-12. Creating a dataset by importing the files from Cloud Storage.

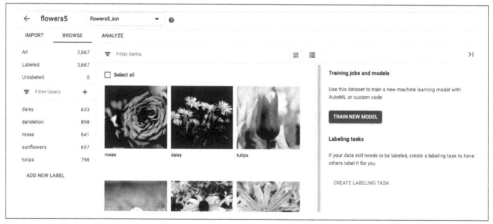

Figure 10-13. After loading the dataset, we can view the images and their labels. This is also an opportunity to add or correct labels if necessary.

Training

Once we are happy with the labels, we can click the Train New Model button to train a new model. This leads us through the set of screens shown in Figure 10-14, where we select the model type, the way to split the dataset, and our training budget. At the time of writing, the 8-hour training budget we specified would have cost about $25.

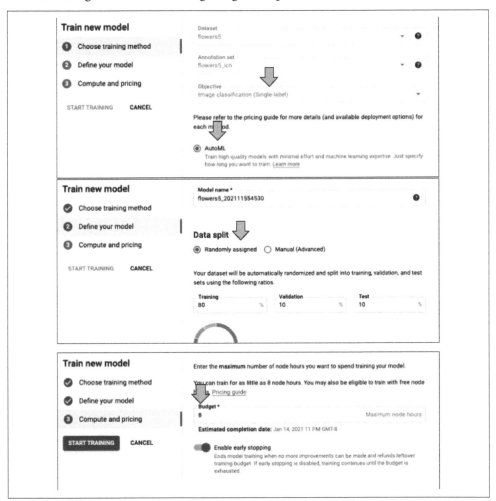

Figure 10-14. User interface screens to launch the training job.

Note that in the last screen we enabled early stopping, so that AutoML can decide to stop early if it doesn't see any more improvement in validation metrics. With this option the training finished in under 30 minutes (see Figure 10-15), meaning that the entire ML training run cost us around $3. The result was 96.4% accuracy, comparable to the accuracy we got with the most sophisticated models we created in Chapter 3 after a lot of tuning and experimentation.

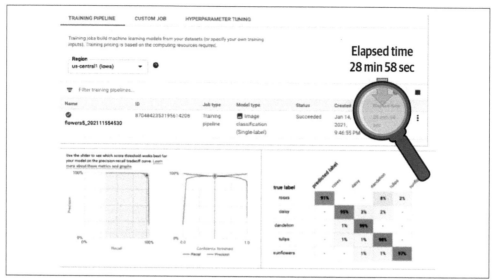

Figure 10-15. AutoML finished training in well under an hour at a cost of less than $3, and it achieved an accuracy of 96.4% on the 5-flowers dataset.

 We should caution you that not all no-code systems are the same— the Google Cloud AutoML (*https://oreil.ly/GvLwR*) system we used in this section performs data preprocessing and augmentation, employs state-of-the-art models, and carries out hyperparameter tuning to build a very accurate model. Other no-code systems might not be as sophisticated: some train only one model (e.g., ResNet50), some train a single model but do hyperparameter tuning, and some others search among a family of models (ResNet18, ResNet50, and EfficientNet). Check the documentation so that you know what you are getting.

Evaluation

The evaluation results indicate that the most misclassifications were roses wrongly identified as tulips. If we were to continue our experimentation, we would examine some of the mistakes (see Figure 10-16) and attempt to gather more images to minimize the false positives and negatives.

Score: 0.376   Score: 0.32   Score: 0.297

Score: 0.243   Score: 0.195   Score: 0.021

Figure 10-16. Examine the false positives and negatives to determine which kinds of examples to collect more of. This can also be an opportunity to remove unrepresentative images from the dataset.

Once we are satisfied with the model's performance, we can deploy it to an endpoint, thus creating a web service through which clients can ask the model to make predictions. We can then send sample requests to the model and obtain predictions from it.

For basic computer vision problems, the ease of use, low cost, and high accuracy of no-code systems are extremely compelling. We recommend that you incorporate these tools as a first step in your computer vision projects.

Summary

In this chapter, we looked at how to operationalize the entire ML process. We used Kubeflow Pipelines for this purpose and took a whirlwind tour of the SDK, creating Docker containers and Kubernetes components and stringing them into a pipeline using data dependencies.

We explored several techniques that allow us to understand what signals the model is relying on when it makes a prediction. We also looked at what no-code computer vision frameworks are capable of, using Google Cloud's AutoML to illustrate the typical steps.

No-code tools are used by domain experts to validate problem viability, while machine learning pipelines are used by ML engineers in deployment, and explainability is used to foster adoption of machine learning models by decision makers. As such, these usually form the bookends of many computer vision projects and are the points at which data scientists interface with other teams.

This concludes the main part of this book, where we have built and deployed an image classification model from end to end. In the remainder of the book, we will focus on advanced architectures and use cases.

## CHAPTER 11

Advanced Vision Problems

So far in this book, we have looked primarily at the problem of classifying an entire image. In Chapter 2 we touched on image regression, and in Chapter 4 we discussed object detection and image segmentation. In this chapter, we will look at more advanced problems that can be solved using computer vision: measurement, counting, pose estimation, and image search.

> The code for this chapter is in the *11_adv_problems* folder of the book's GitHub repository (*https://github.com/GoogleCloudPlatform/ practical-ml-vision-book*). We will provide file names for code samples and notebooks where applicable.

Object Measurement

Sometimes we want to know the measurements of an object within an image (e.g., that a sofa is 180 cm long). While we can simply use pixel-wise regression to measure something like ground precipitation using aerial images of cloud cover, we will need to do something more sophisticated for the object measurement scenario. We can't simply count the number of pixels and infer a size from that, because the same object could be represented by a different number of pixels due to where it is within the image, its rotation, aspect ratio, etc. Let's walk through the four steps needed to measure an object from a photograph of it, following an approach suggested by Imaginea Labs (*https://oreil.ly/FEaPn*).

Reference Object

Suppose we're an online shoe store, and we want to help customers find the best shoe size by using photographs of their footprints. We ask customers to get their feet wet and step onto a paper material, then upload a photo of their footprint like the one shown in Figure 11-1. We can then obtain the appropriate shoe size (based on length and width) and arch type from the footprint using an ML model.

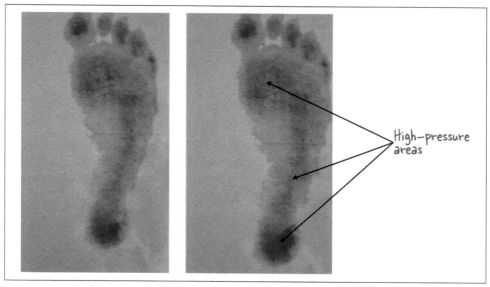

Figure 11-1. Left: Photograph of wet footprint on paper. Right: Photograph of the same footprint taken with the camera a few inches closer to the paper. Identifying the high-pressure areas is helpful to identify the type of arch the person has. Photographs in this section are by the author.

The ML model should be trained using different paper types, different lighting, rotations, flips, etc. to anticipate all of the possible variations of footprint images the model might receive at inference time to predict foot measurements. But an image of the footprint alone is insufficient to create an effective measurement solution, because (as you can see in Figure 11-1) the size of foot in the image will vary depending on factors such as the distance between the camera and the paper.

A simple way to address the scale problem is to include a reference object that virtually all customers should have. Most customers have credit cards, which have standard dimensions, so this can be used as a reference or calibration object to help the model determine the relative size of the foot in the image. As shown in Figure 11-2, we simply ask each customer to place a credit card next to their footprint before taking the photo. Having a reference object simplifies the measurement task to one of comparing the foot against that object.

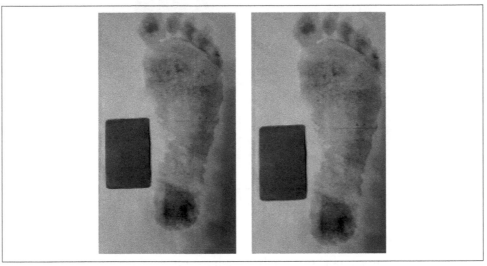

Figure 11-2. Left: Photograph of a credit card next to a wet footprint. Right: Photograph of the same objects, taken with the camera a few inches closer to the paper.

Building our training dataset of different footprints on various backgrounds of course may require some cleaning, such as rotating the images to have all footprints oriented the same way. Otherwise, for some images we would be measuring the projected length and not the true length. As for the reference credit card, we won't perform any corrections before training and will align the generated foot and reference masks at prediction time.

At the beginning of the training we can perform data augmentation, such as rotating, blurring, and changing the brightness, scaling, and contrast, as shown in Figure 11-3. This can help us increase the size of our training dataset as well as teaching the model to be flexible enough to receive many different real-world variations of the data.

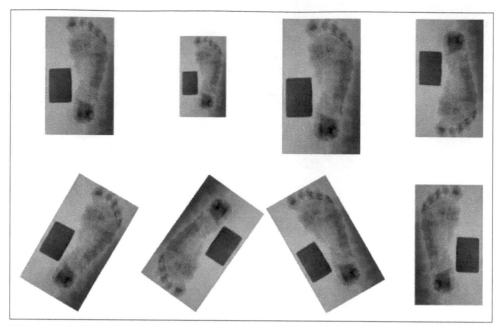

Figure 11-3. Footprint image data augmentation performed at the beginning of training.

Segmentation

The machine learning model first needs to segment out the footprint from the credit card in the image and identify those as the two correct objects extracted. For this we will be using the Mask R-CNN image segmentation model, as discussed in Chapter 4 and depicted in Figure 11-4.

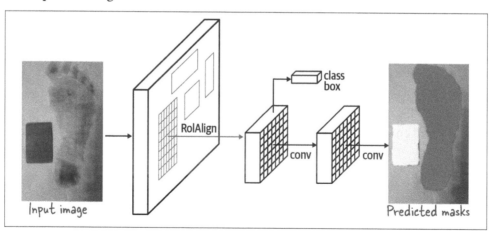

Figure 11-4. The Mask R-CNN architecture. Image adapted from He et al., 2017 (https:// arxiv.org/abs/1703.06870).

Through the mask branch of the architecture we will predict a mask for the footprint and a mask for the credit card, obtaining a result similar to that on the right in Figure 11-4.

Remember our mask branch's output has two channels: one for each object, footprint and credit card. Therefore, we can look at each mask individually, as shown in Figure 11-5.

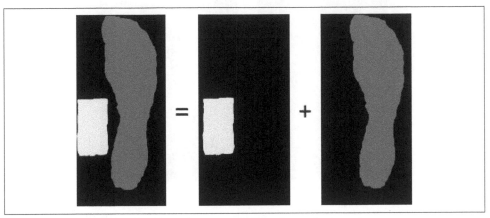

Figure 11-5. Individual masks of footprint and credit card.

Next, we have to align the masks so that we can obtain the correct measurements.

Rotation Correction

Once we have obtained the masks of the footprint and the credit card, they have to be normalized with respect to rotation, for users who may have placed the credit card in slightly different orientations when taking the photograph.

To correct for the rotation, we can use principal component analysis (PCA) on each of the masks to get the *eigenvectors*—the size of the object in the direction of the largest eigenvector, for example, is the length of the object (see Figure 11-6). The eigenvectors obtained from PCA are orthogonal to each other and each subsequent component's eigenvector has a smaller and smaller contribution to the variance.

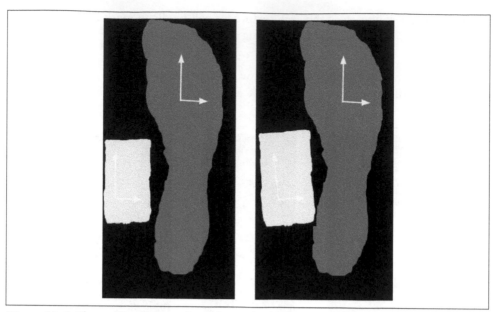

Figure 11-6. The credit card may have been placed in slightly different orientations with respect to the foot. The directions of the two largest eigenvectors in each object are marked by the axes.

Before PCA, the mask dimensions were in a vector space that had dimension axes with respect to the original image, as shown on the left side of Figure 11-6. Using the fact that the eigenvectors are in a different vector space basis after PCA, with the axes now along the direction of greatest variance (as shown on the right in Figure 11-6), we can use the angle between the original coordinate axis and the first eigenvector to determine how much of a rotation correction to make.

Ratio and Measurements

With our rotation-corrected masks, we can now calculate the footprint measurements. We first project our masks onto a two-dimensional space and look along the x- and y-axes. The length is found by measuring the pixel distance between the smallest and largest y-coordinate values, and likewise for the width in the x-dimension. Remember, the measurements for both the footprint and the credit card are in units of pixels, not centimeters or inches.

Next, knowing the precise measurements of the credit card, we can find the ratio between the pixel dimensions and the real dimensions of the card. This ratio can then be applied to the pixel dimensions of the footprint to ascertain its true measurements.

Determining the arch type is slightly more complicated, but it still requires counting in pixels after finding high-pressure areas (see Su et al., 2015 (*https://oreil.ly/AlUIu*), and Figure 11-1). With the correct measurements, as shown in Figure 11-7, our store will be able to find the perfect shoe to fit each customer.

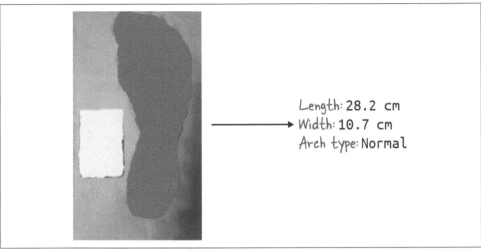

Figure 11-7. We can obtain the final measurements of the PCA-corrected masks using the reference pixel/centimeter ratio.

Counting

Counting the number of objects in an image is a problem with widespread applications, from estimating crowd sizes to identifying the potential yield of a crop from drone imagery. How many berries are in the photograph shown in Figure 11-8?

Figure 11-8. Berries on a plant. Photograph by the author.

Based on the techniques we have covered so far, you might choose one of the following approaches:

1. Train an object detection classifier to detect berries, and count the number of bounding boxes. However, the berries tend to overlap one another, and detection approaches might miss or combine berries.

2. Treat this as a segmentation problem. Find segments that contain berries and then, based on the properties of each cluster (for example, its size), determine the number of berries in each. The problem with this method is that it is not scale-invariant, and will fail if our berries are smaller or larger than typical. Unlike the foot-size measurement scenario discussed in the previous section, a reference object is difficult to incorporate into this problem.

3. Treat this as a regression problem, and estimate the number of berries from the entire image itself. This method has the same scale problems as the segmentation approach and it is difficult to find enough labeled images, although it has been successfully employed in the past for counting crowds (*https://arxiv.org/abs/1703.09393*) and wildlife (*https://oreil.ly/1qdvm*).

There are additional drawbacks to these approaches. For example, the first two methods require us to correctly classify berries, and the regression method ignores location, which we know is a significant source of information about the contents of images.

A better approach is to use density estimation on simulated images. In this section, we will discuss the technique and step through the method.

Density Estimation

For counting in situations like this where the objects are small and overlapping, there is an alternative approach, introduced in a 2010 paper (*https://oreil.ly/EW2J4*) by Victor Lempitsky and Andrew Zisserman, that avoids having to do object detection or segmentation and does not lose the location information. The idea is to teach the network to estimate the *density* of objects (here, berries) in patches of the image.[1]

In order to do density estimation, we need to have labels that indicate density. So, we take the original image and break it into smaller nonoverlapping patches, and we label each patch by the number of berry centers that lie in it, as shown in Figure 11-9. It is this value that the network will learn to estimate. In order to make sure that the total number of berries in the patches equals the number of berries in the image, we make sure to count a berry as being in a patch only if its center point is in the patch.

---

[1] Lempitsky and Zisserman introduced a custom loss function that they call the MESA distance, but the technique works well with good old mean squared error, so that's what we show.

Because some berries may be only partially in a patch, the grid input to the model has to be larger than a patch. The input is shown by the dashed lines. Obviously, this makes the border of the image problematic, but we can simply pad the images as shown on the right in Figure 11-9 to deal with this.

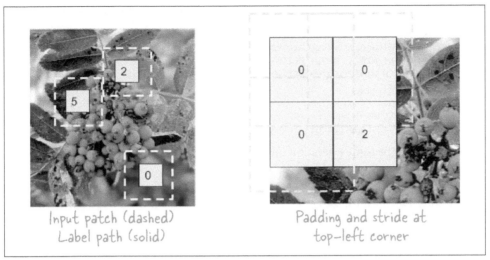

Input patch (dashed)
Label path (solid)

Padding and stride at
top-left corner

Figure 11-9. The model is trained on patches of the original image: the inputs and labels for three such patches are shown in the left panel. The labels consist of the number of berries whose center points lie within the inner square of each patch. The input patches require "same" padding on all sides whereas the label patches consist of valid pixels only.

This method is applicable beyond just counting berries, of course—it tends to work better than the alternatives at estimating crowd sizes, counting cells in biological images, and other such applications where there are lots of objects and some objects may be partially occluded by others. This is just like image regression, except that by using patches we increase the dataset size and teach the model to focus on density.

Extracting Patches

Given an image of berries and a label image consisting of 1s corresponding to the center point of each berry, the easiest way to generate the necessary input and label patches is to employ the TensorFlow function `tf.image.extract_patches()`. This function requires us to pass in a batch of images. If we have only one image, then we can expand the dimension by adding a batch size of 1 using `tf.expand_dims()`. The label image will have only one channel since it is Boolean, so we'll also have to add a depth dimension of 1 (the full code is in *11a_counting.ipynb* on GitHub):

```
def get_patches(img, label, verbose=False):
    img = tf.expand_dims(img, axis=0)
    label = tf.expand_dims(tf.expand_dims(label, axis=0), axis=-1)
```

Now we can call `tf.image.extract_patches()` on the input image. Notice in the following code that we ask for patches of the size of the dashed box (INPUT_WIDTH) but stride by the size of the smaller label patch (PATCH_WIDTH). If the dashed boxes are 64x64 pixels, then each of the boxes will have 64 * 64 * 3 pixel values. These values will be 4D, but we can reshape the patch values to a flattened array for convenience:

```
num_patches = (FULL_IMG_HEIGHT // PATCH_HEIGHT)**2
patches = tf.image.extract_patches(img,
    =[1, INPUT_WIDTH, INPUT_HEIGHT, 1],
    =[1, PATCH_WIDTH, PATCH_HEIGHT, 1],
    =[1, 1, 1, 1],
    ='SAME',
    ='get_patches')
patches = tf.reshape(patches, [num_patches, -1])
```

Next, we repeat the same operation on the label image:

```
labels = tf.image.extract_patches(label,
    =[1, PATCH_WIDTH, PATCH_HEIGHT, 1],
    =[1, PATCH_WIDTH, PATCH_HEIGHT, 1],
    =[1, 1, 1, 1],
    ='VALID',
    ='get_labels')
labels = tf.reshape(labels, [num_patches, -1])
```

There are two key differences in the code for the label patches versus that for the image patches. First, the size of the label patches is the size of the inner box only. Note also the difference in the padding specification. For the input image, we specify pad ding=SAME, asking TensorFlow to pad the input image with zeros and then extract all patches of the larger box size from it (see Figure 11-9). For the label image we ask only for fully valid boxes, so the image will not be padded. This ensures that we get the corresponding outer box of the image for every valid label patch.

The label image will now have 1s corresponding to the centers of all the objects we want to count. We can find the total number of such objects, which we will call the density, by summing up the pixel values of the label patch:

```
# the "density" is the number of points in the label patch
patch_labels = tf.math.reduce_sum(labels, axis=[1], name='calc_density')
```

Simulating Input Images

In their 2017 paper (*https://oreil.ly/CTRLA*) on yield estimation, Maryam Rahnemoor and Clay Sheppard showed that it is not even necessary to have real labeled photographs to train a neural network to count. To train their neural network to count tomatoes on a vine, the authors simply fed it simulated images consisting of red circles on a brown and green background. Because the method requires only simulated data, it is possible to quickly create a large dataset. The resulting trained neural network performed well on actual tomato plants. It is this approach, called *deep simulated learning*, that we show next. Of course, if you actually have labeled data where each berry (or person in a crowd, or antibody in a sample) is marked, you can use that instead.

We will generate a blurred green background, simulate 25–75 "berries," and add them to the image (see Figure 11-10).

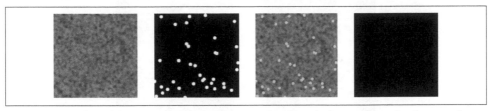

Figure 11-10. Simulating input images for counting "berries" on a green background. The first image is the background, the second the simulated berries, and the third the actual input image.

The key pieces of code are to randomly position a few berries:

```
num_berries = np.random.randint(25, 75)
berry_cx = np.random.randint(0, FULL_IMG_WIDTH, size=num_berries)
berry_cy = np.random.randint(0, FULL_IMG_HEIGHT, size=num_berries)
label = np.zeros([FULL_IMG_WIDTH, FULL_IMG_HEIGHT])
label[berry_cx, berry_cy] = 1
```

At each berry location in the label image, a red circle is drawn:

```
berries = np.zeros([FULL_IMG_WIDTH, FULL_IMG_HEIGHT])
for idx in range(len(berry_cx)):
    rr, cc = draw.circle(berry_cx[idx], berry_cy[idx],
                         radius=10,
                         shape=berries.shape)
    berries[rr, cc] = 1
```

The berries are then added to the green background:

```
img = np.copy(backgr)
img[berries > 0] = [1, 0, 0] # red
```

Once we have an image, we can generate image patches from it and obtain the density by adding up the berry centers that fall within the label patch. A few example patches and the corresponding densities are shown in Figure 11-11.

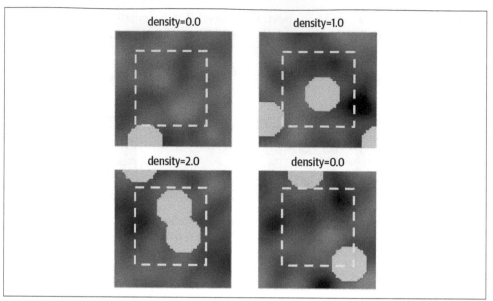

Figure 11-11. A few of the patches and the corresponding densities. Note that the label patch consists only of the center 50% of the input patch, and only red circles whose centers are in the label patch are counted in the density calculation.

Regression

Once we have the patch creation going, we can train a regression model on the patches to predict the density. First, we set up our training and evaluation datasets by generating simulated images:

```
def create_dataset(num_full_images):
    def generate_patches():
        for i in range(num_full_images):
            img, label = generate_image()
            patches, patch_labels = get_patches(img, label)
        for patch, patch_label in zip(patches, patch_labels):
            yield patch, patch_label

    return tf.data.Dataset.from_generator(
            generate_patches,
            (tf.float32, tf.float32), # patch, patch_label
            (tf.TensorShape([INPUT_HEIGHT*INPUT_WIDTH*IMG_CHANNELS]),
             tf.TensorShape([]))
    )
```

We can use any of the models we discussed in Chapter 3. For illustration purposes, let's use a simple ConvNet (the full code is available in *11a_counting.ipynb* on Git-Hub):

```
Model: "sequential"
```

Layer (type)	Output Shape	Param #
reshape (Reshape)	(None, 64, 64, 3)	0
conv2d (Conv2D)	(None, 62, 62, 32)	896
max_pooling2d (MaxPooling2D)	(None, 31, 31, 32)	0
conv2d_1 (Conv2D)	(None, 29, 29, 64)	18496
max_pooling2d_1 (MaxPooling2	(None, 14, 14, 64)	0
conv2d_2 (Conv2D)	(None, 12, 12, 64)	36928
flatten (Flatten)	(None, 9216)	0
dense (Dense)	(None, 64)	589888
dense_1 (Dense)	(None, 1)	65

```
Total params: 646,273
Trainable params: 646,273
Non-trainable params: 0
```

The key aspects to note about the architecture shown here are:

- The output is a single numeric value (density).
- The output node is a linear layer (so that the density can take any numeric value).
- The loss is mean square error.

These aspects make the model a regression model capable of predicting the density.

Prediction

Remember that the model takes a patch and predicts the density of berries in the patch. Given an input image, we have to break it into patches exactly as we did during training and carry out model prediction on all the patches, then sum up the predicted densities, as shown below:

```
def count_berries(model, img):
    num_patches = (FULL_IMG_HEIGHT // PATCH_HEIGHT)**2
    img = tf.expand_dims(img, axis=0)
    patches = tf.image.extract_patches(img,
        sizes=[1, INPUT_WIDTH, INPUT_HEIGHT, 1],
        strides=[1, PATCH_WIDTH, PATCH_HEIGHT, 1],
        rates=[1, 1, 1, 1],
        padding='SAME',
        name='get_patches')
```

```
patches = tf.reshape(patches, [num_patches, -1])
densities = model.predict(patches)
return tf.reduce_sum(densities)
```

Predictions on some independent images are shown in Figure 11-12. As you can see, the predictions are within 10% of the actual numbers.

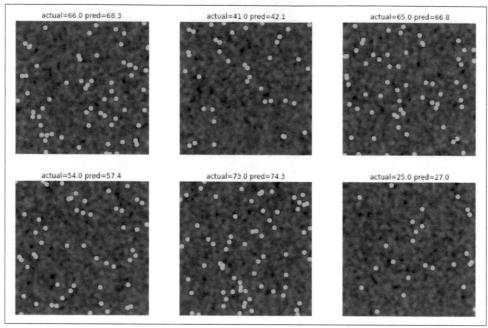

Figure 11-12. Predicted values from the model, compared with the actual number of objects in each image.

When we tried this on the real berry image with which we started this section, however, the estimate was considerably off. Addressing this might require simulating berries of different sizes, not just placing equally sized berries at random positions.

Pose Estimation

There are a variety of situations where we may desire to identify key parts of an object. A very common situation is to identify elbows, knees, face, and so on in order to identify the pose of a person. Therefore, this problem is termed *pose estimation* or *pose detection*. Pose detection can be useful to identify whether a subject is sitting, standing, dancing, or lying down or to provide advice on posture in sports and medical settings.

Given a photograph like the one in Figure 11-13, how can we identify the feet, knees, elbows, and hands in the image?

Figure 11-13. Identifying the relative position of key body parts is useful to provide coaching on improving a player's form. Photograph by the author.

In this section, we will discuss the technique and point you toward an already trained implementation. It is rarely necessary to train a pose estimation model from scratch —instead, you will use the output of an already trained pose estimation model to determine what the subjects in the images are doing.

PersonLab

The state-of-the-art approach was suggested in a 2018 paper (*https://arxiv.org/pdf/ 1803.08225.pdf*) by George Papandreou et al. They called it PersonLab, but the models that implement their approach now go by the name *PoseNet*. Conceptually, Pose-Net consists of the steps depicted in Figure 11-14:

1. Use an object detection model to identify a heatmap of all the points of interest in the skeleton. These typically include the knees, elbows, shoulders, eyes, nose, and so on. For simplicity, we'll refer to these as *joints*. The heatmap is the score that is output from the classification head of the object detection model (i.e., before thresholding).

2. Anchored at each detected joint, identify the most likely location of nearby joints. The offset location of the elbow given a detected wrist is shown in the figure.

3. Use a voting mechanism to detect human poses based on the joints chosen based on steps 1 and 2.

In reality, steps 1 and 2 are carried out simultaneously by means of an object detection model (any of the models discussed in Chapter 4 may be used) that predicts a joint, its location, and the offset to nearby joints.

| Input image | Heatmap of joints | Offsets to nearby joints | Detected human pose |

Figure 11-14. Identifying the relative position of key joints is useful to identify human poses. Image adapted from Papandreou et al., 2018 (https://arxiv.org/pdf/ 1803.08225.pdf).

We need steps 2 and 3 because it is not sufficient to simply run an object detection model to detect the various joints—it is possible that the model will miss some joints and identify spurious joints. That's why the PoseNet model also predicts offsets to nearby joints from the detected joints. For example, if the model detects a wrist, the wrist detection comes with an offset prediction for the location of the elbow joint. This helps in cases where, for some reason, the elbow was not detected. If the elbow was detected, we might now have three candidate locations for that joint—the elbow location from the heatmap and the elbow locations from the offset predictions of the wrist and the shoulder. Given all these candidate locations, a weighted voting mechanism called the Hough transform is used to determine the final location of the joint.

The PoseNet Model

PoseNet implementations are available in TensorFlow for Android (*https://oreil.ly/ rGzZh*) and for the web browser. The TensorFlow JS implementation (*https://oreil.ly/ X1RVj*) runs in a web browser and uses MobileNet or ResNet as the underlying architecture, but continues to refer to itself as PoseNet. An alternate implementation is provided by OpenPose (*https://oreil.ly/EHSMY*).

The TensorFlow JS PoseNet model was trained to identify 17 body parts that include facial features (nose, leftEye, rightEye, leftEar, rightEar) and key limb joints (shoulder, elbow, wrist, hip, knee, and ankle) on both the left and the right side.

To try it out, you'll need to run a local web server—*11b_posenet.html* in the GitHub repository provides details. Load the posenet package and ask it to estimate a single pose (as opposed to an image with multiple people in it):

```
posenet.load().then(function(net) {
    const pose = net.estimateSinglePose(imageElement, {
        flipHorizontal: false
    });
    return pose;
})
```

Note that we ask that the image not be flipped. However, if you are processing selfie images, you might want to flip them horizontally to match the user experience of seeing mirrored images.

We can display the returned value as a JSON element using:

```
document.getElementById('output_json').innerHTML =
    "<pre>" + JSON.stringify(pose, null, 2) + "</pre>";
```

The JSON has the key points identified, along with their positions in the image:

```
{
    "score": 0.5220872163772583,
    "part": "leftEar",
    "position": {
        "x": 342.9179292671411,
        "y": 91.27406275411522
    }
},
```

We can use these to directly annotate the image as shown in Figure 11-15.

Figure 11-15. An annotated image, with the annotations derived from the output of PoseNet. Each of the light gray boxes contains a marker (e.g., rightWrist), and they have been connected by the skeleton.

The accuracy of PoseNet is determined by the accuracy of the underlying classification model (ResNet tends to be both larger and slower but more accurate than MobileNet, for example) and by the size of the output strides—the larger the stride, the larger the patches, so the precision of the output locations suffers.

These factors can be changed when PoseNet is loaded:

```
posenet.load({
    architecture: 'ResNet50',
    outputStride: 32, # default 257
    inputResolution: { width: 500, height: 900 },
    quantBytes: 2
});
```

A smaller output stride results in a more accurate model, at the expense of speed. The input resolution specifies the size the image is resized and padded to before it is fed into the PoseNet model. The larger the value, the more accurate it is, again at the cost of speed.

The MobileNet architecture takes a parameter called `multiplier` that specifies the depth multiplier for convolution operations. The larger the multiplier, the more accurate but slower the model is. The `quantBytes` parameter in ResNet specifies the number of bytes used for weight quantization. Using a value of 4 leads to a higher accuracy and larger models than using 1.

Identifying Multiple Poses

To estimate the poses of multiple people in a single image, we use the same technique outlined in the previous section, with a few additional steps:

1. Use an image segmentation model to identify all the pixels that correspond to persons in the image.

2. Using the combination of joints, identify the most likely location of a specific body part, such as the nose.

3. Using the pixels from the segmentation mask found in step 1, and the likely connections identified in step 2, assign the person pixels to individual persons.

An example is shown in Figure 11-16. Again, any of the image segmentation models discussed in Chapter 4 may be used here.

Figure 11-16. Identifying the poses of multiple people in the image. Adapted from Papandreou et al., 2018 (https://arxiv.org/pdf/1803.08225.pdf).

When running PoseNet, you can ask it to estimate multiple poses using:

```
net.estimateMultiplePoses(image, {
    flipHorizontal: false,
    maxDetections: 5,
    scoreThreshold: 0.5,
    nmsRadius: 20
});
```

The key parameters here are the maximum number of people in the image (`maxDetec tions`), the confidence threshold for a person detection (`scoreThreshold`), and the distance within which two detections should suppress each other (`nmsRadius`, in pixels).

Next, let's look at the problem of supporting image search.

Image Search

eBay uses image search (*https://oreil.ly/JVE2J*) to improve the shopping experience (e.g., find the eyeglasses that a specific celebrity is wearing) and the listing experience (e.g., here are all the relevant technical specifications of this gadget you are trying to sell).

The crux of the problem in both cases is to find the image in the dataset that is most similar to a newly uploaded image. To provide this capability, we can use embeddings. The idea is that two images that are similar to each other will have embeddings that are also close to each other. So, to search for a similar image, we can simply search for a similar embedding.

Distributed Search

To enable searching for similar embeddings, we will have to create a search index of embeddings of the images in our dataset. Suppose we store this embedding index in a large-scale, distributed data warehouse such as Google BigQuery.

If we have embeddings of weather images in the data warehouse, then it becomes easy to search for "similar" weather situations in the past to some scenario in the present. Here's a SQL query (*https://oreil.ly/IxTn1*) that would do it:

```
WITH ref1 AS (
    SELECT time AS ref1_time, ref1_value, ref1_offset
    FROM `ai-analytics-solutions.advdata.wxembed`,
        UNNEST(ref) AS ref1_value WITH OFFSET AS ref1_offset
    WHERE time = '2019-09-20 05:00:00 UTC'
)
SELECT
    time,
    SUM( (ref1_value - ref[OFFSET(ref1_offset)])
        * (ref1_value - ref[OFFSET(ref1_offset)]) ) AS sqdist
FROM ref1, `ai-analytics-solutions.advdata.wxembed`
GROUP BY 1
ORDER By sqdist ASC
LIMIT 5
```

We are computing the Euclidean distance between the embedding at the specified timestamp (`refl1`) and every other embedding, and displaying the closest matches. The result, shown here:

<0xa0>	time	sqdist
0	2019-09-20 05:00:00+00:00	0.000000
1	2019-09-20 06:00:00+00:00	0.519979
2	2019-09-20 04:00:00+00:00	0.546595
3	2019-09-20 07:00:00+00:00	1.001852
4	2019-09-20 03:00:00+00:00	1.387520

makes a lot of sense. The image from the previous/next hour is the most similar, then images from +/− 2 hours, and so on.

Fast Search

In the SQL example in the previous section we searched the entire dataset, and we were able to do it efficiently because BigQuery is a massively scaled cloud data warehouse. A drawback of data warehouses, however, is that they tend to have high latency. We will not be able to get millisecond response times.

For real-time serving, we need to be smarter about how we search for similar embeddings. Scalable Nearest Neighbors (ScaNN) (*https://oreil.ly/1A1t4*), which we use in our next example, does search space pruning and provides an efficient way to find similar vectors.

Let's build a search index of the first hundred images of our 5-flowers dataset (normally, of course, we'd build a much larger dataset, but this is an illustration). We can create MobileNet embeddings by creating a Keras model:

```
layers = [
    hub.KerasLayer(
        "https://.../mobilenet_v2/...",
        input_shape=(IMG_WIDTH, IMG_HEIGHT, IMG_CHANNELS),
        trainable=False,
        name='mobilenet_embedding'),
    tf.keras.layers.Flatten()
]
model = tf.keras.Sequential(layers, name='flowers_embedding')
```

To create an embeddings dataset, we loop through the dataset of flower images and invoke the model's predict() function (the full code is in *11c_scann_search.ipynb* on GitHub):

```
def create_embeddings_dataset(csvfilename):
    ds = (tf.data.TextLineDataset(csvfilename).
        map(decode_csv).batch(BATCH_SIZE))
    dataset_filenames = []
    dataset_embeddings = []
    for filenames, images in ds:
        embeddings = model.predict(images)
        dataset_filenames.extend(
            [f.numpy().decode('utf-8') for f in filenames])
        dataset_embeddings.extend(embeddings)
    dataset_embeddings = tf.convert_to_tensor(dataset_embeddings)
    return dataset_filenames, dataset_embeddings
```

Once we have the training dataset, we can initialize the ScaNN searcher (*https://oreil.ly/zJm5f*), specifying that the distance function to use is the cosine distance (we could also use Euclidean distance):

```
searcher = scann.scann_ops.builder(
    dataset_embeddings,
    NUM_NEIGH, "dot_product").score_ah(2).build()
```

This builds a tree for fast searching.

To search for the neighbors for some images, we obtain their embeddings and invoke the searcher:

```
_, query_embeddings = create_embeddings_dataset(
    "gs://cloud-ml-data/img/flower_photos/eval_set.csv"
)
neighbors, distances = searcher.search_batched(query_embeddings)
```

If you have only one image, call searcher.search().

Some results are shown in Figure 11-17. We are looking for images similar to the first image in each row; the three closest neighbors are shown in the other panels. The results aren't too impressive. What if we used a better approach to create embeddings, rather than using the embeddings from MobileNet that are meant for transfer learning?

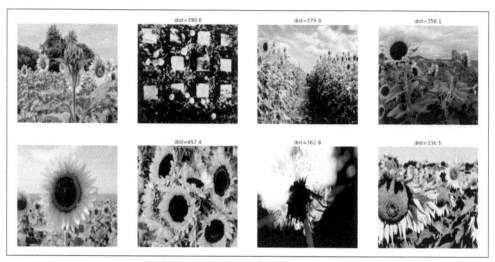

Figure 11-17. Searching for images similar to the first image in each row.

Better Embeddings

In the previous section we used MobileNet embeddings, which are derived from an intermediate bottleneck layer obtained by training a large image classification model. It is possible to use more customized embeddings. For example, when searching for face similarity, embeddings from a model trained to identify and verify faces will perform better than a generic embedding.

To optimize the embeddings for the purposes of facial search, a system called FaceNet (*https://arxiv.org/abs/1503.03832*) uses triplets of matching/nonmatching face patches that are aligned based on facial features. The triplets consist of two matching and one nonmatching face thumbnails. A *triplet loss* function is used that aims to separate the positive pair from the negative one by the maximum possible distance. The thumbnails themselves are tight crops of the face area. The difficulty of the triplets shown to the network increases as the network trains.

Because of the ethical sensitivities that surround facial search and verification, we are not demonstrating an implementation of facial search in our repository or covering this topic any further. Code that implements the FaceNet technique is readily available online (*https://oreil.ly/rRZ9Q*). Please make sure that you use AI responsibly and in a way that doesn't run afoul of governmental, industry, or company policies.

The triplet loss can be used to create embeddings that are clustered together by label such that two images with the same label have their embeddings close together and two images with different labels have their embeddings far apart.

The formal definition of triplet loss uses three images: the anchor image, another image with the same label (so that the second image and the anchor form a positive pair), and a third image with a different label (so that the third image and the anchor form a negative pair). Given three images, the loss of a triplet (a, p, n) is defined such that the distance $d(a, p)$ is pushed toward zero and the distance $d(a, n)$ is at least some margin greater than $d(a, p)$:

$$L - max(d(a, p) - d(a, n) + margin, 0)$$

Given this loss, there are three categories of negatives:

- Hard negatives, which are negatives that are closer to the anchor than the positive
- Easy negatives, which are negatives that are very far away from the anchor
- Semi-hard negatives, which are further away than the positive, but within the margin distance

In the FaceNet paper, Schroff et al. found that focusing on the semi-hard negatives yielded embeddings where images with the same label clustered together and were distinct from images with a different label.

We can improve the embeddings for our flower images by adding a linear layer and then training the model to minimize the triplet loss on those images, focusing on the semi-hard negatives:

```
layers = [
    hub.KerasLayer(
        "https://tfhub.dev/.../mobilenet_v2/feature_vector/4",
        input_shape=(IMG_HEIGHT, IMG_WIDTH, IMG_CHANNELS),
        trainable=False,
        name='mobilenet_embedding'),
    tf.keras.layers.Dense(5, activation=None, name='dense_5'),
    tf.keras.layers.Lambda(lambda x: tf.math.l2_normalize(x, axis=1),
                    name='normalize_embeddings')
]
model = tf.keras.Sequential(layers, name='flowers_embedding')
model.compile(optimizer=tf.keras.optimizers.Adam(0.001),
            loss=tfa.losses.TripletSemiHardLoss())
```

In the preceding code, the architecture ensures that the resulting embedding is of dimension 5 and that the embedding values are normalized.

Note that the definition of the loss means that we have to somehow ensure that each batch contains at least one positive pair. Shuffling and using a large enough batch size tends to work. In the 5-flowers example we used a batch size of 32, but it is a number you have to experiment with. Assuming the k classes are equally distributed, the odds of a batch of size B containing at least one positive pair is:

$$1 - \frac{k-1}{k}^B$$

For 5 classes and a batch size of 32, this works out to 99.9%. 0.1% is not zero, however, so in the ingest pipeline we have to discard batches that don't meet this criterion.

After training this model and plotting the embeddings on a test dataset (the full code is in *11c_scann_search.ipynb* on GitHub), we see that the resulting embeddings cluster with similar labels (see Figure 11-18).

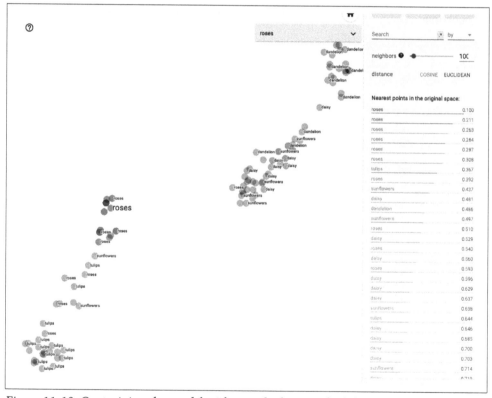

Figure 11-18. On training the model with a triplet loss, we find that images with the same labels cluster together in the embedding space.

This is also apparent in the results obtained when we search for similar images (see Figure 11-19)—the distances are smaller, and the images look much more similar than the ones in Figure 11-17.

Figure 11-19. On training the embedding with a triplet loss, the distances become smaller, and the close-by images are truly similar. Compare with Figure 11-17.

Summary

In this chapter, we explored a variety of use cases that build on the fundamental computer vision techniques. Object measurement can be done using reference objects, masks, and some image correction. Counting can be done through postprocessing of object detections. However, in some situations, a density estimate is better. Pose estimation is done by predicting the likelihood of the different joints at coarse-grained blocks within the image. Image search can be improved by training an embedding with a triplet loss and using a fast search method such as ScaNN.

In the next chapter, we will explore how to generate images, not just process them.

## CHAPTER 12

Image and Text Generation

So far in this book, we have focused on computer vision methods that act on images. In this chapter, we will look at vision methods that can *generate* images. Before we get to image generation, though, we have to learn how to train a model to understand what's in an image so that it knows what to generate. We will also look at the problem of generating text (captions) based on the content of an image.

The code for this chapter is in the *12_generation* folder of the book's GitHub repository (*https://github.com/GoogleCloudPlatform/practical-ml-vision-book*). We will provide file names for code samples and notebooks where applicable.

Image Understanding

It's one thing to know what components are in an image, but it's quite another to actually understand what is happening in the image and to use that information for other tasks. In this section, we will quickly recap embeddings and then look at various methods (autoencoders and variational autoencoders) to encode an image and learn about its properties.

Embeddings

A common problem with deep learning use cases is lack of sufficient data, or data of high enough quality. In Chapter 3 we discussed transfer learning, which provides a way to extract embeddings that were learned from a model trained on a larger dataset, and apply that knowledge to train an effective model on a smaller dataset.

With transfer learning, the embeddings we use were created by training the model on the same task, such as image classification. For instance, suppose we have a ResNet50 model that was trained on the ImageNet dataset, as shown in Figure 12-1.

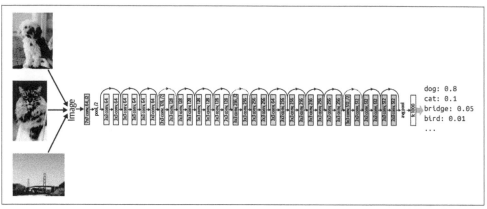

Figure 12-1. Training a ResNet model to classify images.

To extract the learned image embeddings, we would choose one of the model's intermediate layers—usually the last hidden layer—as the numerical representation of the input image (see Figure 12-2).

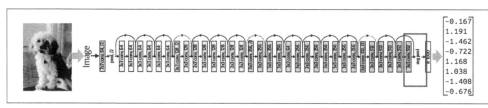

Figure 12-2. Feature extraction from trained ResNet model to obtain image embeddings.

There are two problems with this approach of creating embeddings by training a classification model and using its penultimate layer:

- To create these embeddings, we need a large, labeled dataset of images. In this example, we trained a ResNet50 on ImageNet to get the image embeddings. However, these embeddings will work well only for the types of images found in ImageNet—photographs found on the internet. If you have a different type of image (such as diagrams of machine parts, scanned book pages, architectural drawings, or satellite imagery), the embeddings learned from the ImageNet dataset may not work so well.

- The embeddings reflect the information that is relevant to determining the label of the image. By definition, therefore, many of the details of the input images that are not relevant to this specific classification task may not be captured in the embeddings.

What if you want an embedding that works well for images other than photographs, you don't have a large labeled dataset of such images, and you want to capture as much of the information content in the image as possible?

Auxiliary Learning Tasks

Another way to create embeddings is to use an *auxiliary learning task*. An auxiliary task is a task other than the actual supervised learning problem we are trying to solve. This task should be one for which large amounts of data are readily available. For example, in the case of text classification we can create the text embeddings using an unrelated problem, such as predicting the next word of a sentence, for which there is already copious and readily available training data. The weight values of some intermediate layer can then be extracted from the auxiliary model and used to represent text for various other unrelated tasks. Figure 12-3 shows an example of this kind of text or word embedding where a model is trained to predict the next word in a sentence. Using the words "the cat sat" as input, such a model would be trained to predict the word "on." The input words are first one-hot encoded, but the penultimate layer of the prediction model, if it has four nodes, will learn to represent the input words as a four-dimensional embedding.

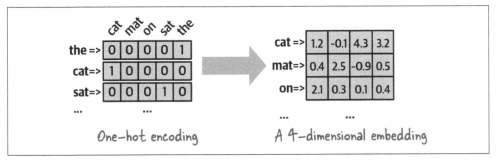

Figure 12-3. Word embeddings created by training a model to predict the next word in a sentence can be used for an unrelated task, such as text classification. The illustration shows the word encoding before (left) and after (right) the auxiliary task.

Autoencoders take advantage of an auxiliary learning task for images, similar to the predict-the-next-word model in the case of text. We'll look at these next.

Autoencoders

A great auxiliary learning task to learn image embeddings is to use autoencoders. With an autoencoder, we take the image data and pass it through a network that bottlenecks it into a smaller internal vector, and then expands it back out into the dimensionality of the original image. When we train the autoencoder, the input image itself functions as its own label. This way we are essentially learning *lossy compression*, or how to recover the original image despite squeezing the information through a constrained network. The hope is that we are squeezing out the noise from the data and learning an efficient map of the signal.

With embeddings that are trained through a supervised task, any information in the inputs that isn't useful or related to the label usually gets pruned out with the noise. On the other hand, with autoencoders, since the "label" is the entire input image, every part of the input is relevant to the output, and therefore hopefully much more of the information is retained from the inputs. Because autoencoders are self-supervised (we don't need a separate step to label the images), we can train on much more data and get a greatly improved encoding.

Typically, the encoder and decoder form an hourglass shape as each progressive layer in the encoder shrinks in dimensionality and each progressive layer in the decoder expands in dimensionality, as seen in Figure 12-4. With the shrinking dimensionality in the encoder and the expanding dimensionality in the decoder, at some point the dimensionality reaches a minimum size at the end of the encoder and the start of the decoder, represented by the two-pixel, single-channel block in the middle of Figure 12-4. This latent vector is a concise representation of the inputs, where the data is being forced through a bottleneck.

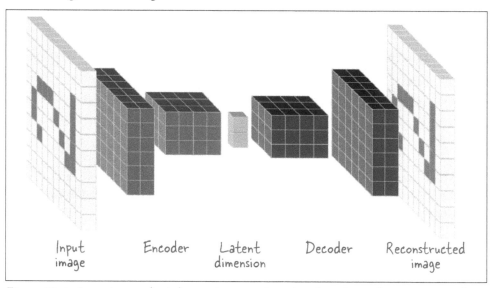

Figure 12-4. An autoencoder takes an image as input and produces the reconstructed image as output.

So, how big should the latent dimension be? As with other types of embeddings, there is a trade-off between compression and expressivity. If the dimensionality of the latent space is too small, there won't be enough expressive power to fully represent the original data—some of the signal will be lost. When this representation is decompressed back to the original size, too much information will be missing to get the desired outputs. Conversely, if the dimensionality of the latent space is too large, then even though there will be ample space to store all of the desired information there will also be space to encode some of the unwanted information (i.e., the noise). The ideal size for the latent dimension is thus something to tune through experimentation. Typical values are 128, 256, or 512, though of course this depends on the sizes of the layers of the encoder and the decoder.

Next we'll look at implementing an autoencoder, starting with its architecture.

Architecture

To simplify our discussion and analysis of the autoencoder architecture, we'll pick a simple dataset of handwritten digits called MNIST (*https://oreil.ly/nia0l*) to apply the autoencoder to (the full code is in *12a_autoencoder.ipynb* on GitHub). The input images are of size 28x28 and consist of a single grayscale channel.

The encoder starts with these 28x28 inputs and then progressively squeezes the information into fewer and fewer dimensions by passing the inputs through convolutional layers to end up at a latent dimension of size 2:

```
encoder = tf.keras.Sequential([
    keras.Input(shape=(28, 28, 1), name="image_input"),
    layers.Conv2D(32, 3, activation="relu", strides=2, padding="same"),
    layers.Conv2D(64, 3, activation="relu", strides=2, padding="same"),
    layers.Flatten(),
    layers.Dense(2) # latent dim
], name="encoder")
```

The decoder will have to reverse these steps using `Conv2DTranspose` layers (also known as deconvolution layers, covered in Chapter 4) wherever the encoder has a `Conv2D` (convolution) layer:

```
decoder = tf.keras.Sequential([
    keras.Input(shape=(latent_dim,), name="d_input"),
    layers.Dense(7 * 7 * 64, activation="relu"),
    layers.Reshape((7, 7, 64)),
    layers.Conv2DTranspose(32, 3, activation="relu",
                           strides=2, padding="same"),
    layers.Conv2DTranspose(1, 3, activation="sigmoid",
                           strides=2, padding="same")
], name="decoder")
```

Once we have the encoder and decoder blocks, we can tie them together to form a model that can be trained.

Reverse Operations for Common Keras Layers

When writing autoencoders, it is helpful to know the "reverse" operations for common Keras layers. The reverse of a `Dense` layer that takes inputs of shape `s1` and produces outputs of shape `s2`:

```
Dense(s2)(x) # x has shape s1
```

is a `Dense` layer that takes `s2`s and produces `s1`s:

```
Dense(s1)(x) # x has shape s2
```

The reverse of a `Flatten` layer will be a `Reshape` layer with the input and output shapes similarly swapped.

The reverse of a `Conv2D` layer is a `Conv2DTranspose` layer. Instead of taking a neighborhood of pixels and downsampling them into one pixel, it expands one pixel into a neighborhood to upsample the image. Keras also has an `Upsampling2D` layer. Upsampling is a cheaper operation since it involves no trainable weights and just repeats the source pixel values, or does bilinear interpolation. On the other hand, `Conv2DTranspose` deconvolves with a kernel, and thus weights, which are learned during model training to get a superior upsampled image.

Training

The model to be trained consists of the encoder and decoder blocks chained together:

```
encoder_inputs = keras.Input(shape=(28, 28, 1))
x = encoder(encoder_inputs)
decoder_output = decoder(x)
autoencoder = keras.Model(encoder_inputs, decoder_output)
```

The model has to be trained to minimize the reconstruction error between the input and output images—for example, we could compute the mean squared error between the input and output images and use that as the loss function. This loss function can be used in backpropagation to calculate the gradients and update the weights of the encoder and decoder subnetworks:

```
autoencoder.compile(optimizer=keras.optimizers.Adam(), loss='mse')
history = autoencoder.fit(mnist_digits, mnist_digits,
                          epochs=30, batch_size=128)
```

Latent vectors

Once the model is trained, we can drop the decoder and use the encoder to convert images into latent vectors:

```
z = encoder.predict(img)
```

If the autoencoder has successfully learned how to reconstruct the image, the latent vectors for similar images will tend to cluster, as shown in Figure 12-5. Notice that the 1s, 2s, and 0s occupy different parts of the latent vector space.

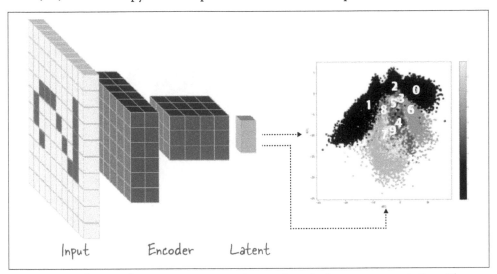

Figure 12-5. The encoder compresses input images into the latent representation. The latent representations for specific digits cluster together. We are able to represent the latent representations as points on a 2D graph because each latent representation is two numbers (x, y).

Because the entire information content of the input image has to flow through the bottleneck layer, the bottleneck layer after training will retain enough information for the decoder to be able to reconstruct a close facsimile of the input image. Therefore, we can train autoencoders for dimensionality reduction. The idea, as in Figure 12-5, is to drop the decoder and use the encoder to convert images into latent vectors. These latent vectors can then be used for downstream tasks such as classification and clustering, and the results may be better than those achieved with classical dimensionality reduction techniques like principal component analysis. If the autoencoder uses nonlinear activations, the encoding can capture nonlinear relationships between the input features, unlike PCA, which is solely a linear method.

A different application might be to use the decoder to turn latent vectors provided not by an encoded image but by a user into generated images, as shown in Figure 12-6.

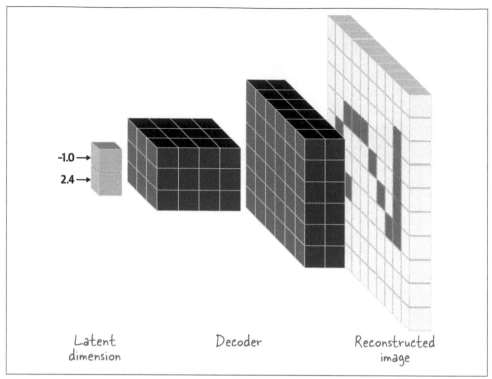

Figure 12-6. *The decoder decompressing a latent representation back into an image.*

While this works tolerably well for the very simple MNIST dataset, it doesn't work in practice on more complex images. Indeed, in Figure 12-7 we can see some of the shortcomings even on the handwritten digits in MNIST—while the digits look realistic in some parts of the latent space, in other places they are unlike any digits that we know. For example, look at the center left of the image, where 2s and 8s have been interpolated into something nonexistent. The reconstructed images are completely meaningless. Notice also that there is a preponderance of 0s and 2s, but not as many 1s as one would expect looking at the overlapping clusters in Figure 12-5. While it will be relatively easy to generate 0s and 2s, it will be quite difficult to generate 1s— we'd have to get the latent vector just right to get a 1 that doesn't look like a 2 or a 5!

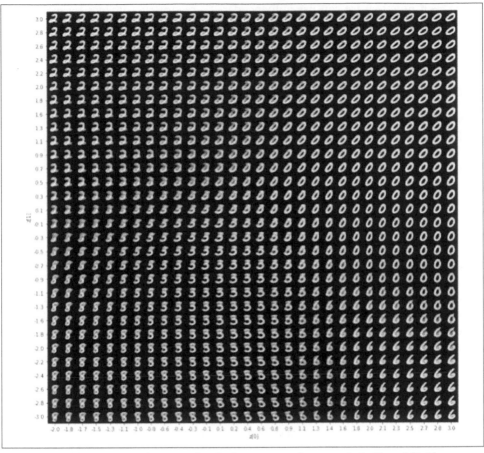

Figure 12-7. Reconstructed images for the latent space between [–2,-3] and [3,3].

What could be the matter? There are vast regions of the latent space (note the white-space in Figure 12-5) that do not correspond to valid digits. The training task does not care about the whitespace at all, but has no incentive for minimizing it. The trained model does a great job when using both the encoder and decoder together, which is the original task we asked the autoencoder to learn. We passed images into the encoder subnetwork, which compressed the data down into vectors (the learned latent representations of those images). We then decompressed those representations with the decoder subnetwork to reconstruct the original images. The encoder has learned a mapping from image to latent space using a highly nonlinear combination of perhaps millions of parameter weights. If we naively try to create our own latent vector, it won't conform to the more nuanced latent space that the encoder has created. Therefore, without the encoder, our randomly chosen latent vector isn't very likely to result in a good encoding that the decoder can use to generate a quality image.

We've seen now that we can use autoencoders to reconstruct images by using their two subnetworks: the encoder and decoder. Furthermore, by dropping the decoder and using only the encoder, we now can encode images nonlinearly into latent vectors that we can then use as embeddings in a different task. However, we've also seen that naively trying the converse of dropping the encoder and using the decoder to generate an image from a user-provided latent vector doesn't work.

If we truly want to use the decoder of an autoencoder-type structure to generate images, then we need to develop a way to organize or regularize the latent space. This can be achieved by mapping points that are close in latent space to points that are close in image space and filling the latent space map so that all points make something sensical rather than creating small islands of reasonable outputs in an ocean of unmapped noise. This way we can generate our own latent vectors, and the decoder will be able to use those to make quality images. This forces us to leave classic autoencoders behind and takes us to the next evolution: the variational autoencoder.

Variational Autoencoders

Without an appropriately organized latent space, there are usually two main problems with using autoencoder-type architectures for image generation. First, if we were to generate two points that are close in the latent space, we would expect the outputs corresponding to those points to be similar to each other after they've been passed through the decoder. For instance, as Figure 12-8 depicts, if we have trained our autoencoder on geometric shapes such as circles, squares, and triangles, if we create two points that are close in the latent space we assume they should both be latent representations of either circles, squares, triangles, or some interpolation in between. However, since the latent space hasn't been explicitly regularized, one of the latent points might generate a triangle whereas the other latent point might generate a circle.

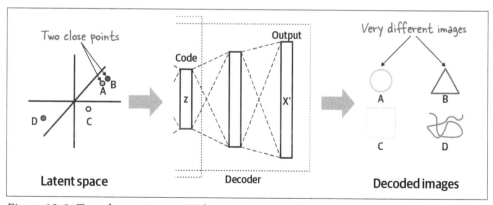

Figure 12-8. Two close points in 3D latent space may be decoded into very different images.

Second, after training an autoencoder for a long time and observing good reconstructions, we would expect that the encoder will have learned where each archetype of our images (for instance, circles or squares in the shapes dataset) best fits within the latent space, creating *n*-dimensional subdomains for each archetype that can overlap with other subdomains. For example, there may be a region of the latent space where the square-type images mostly reside, and another region of the latent space where circle-like images have been organized. Furthermore, where they overlap, we'll get shapes that lie somewhere in between on some square–circle spectrum.

Yet, because the latent space is not explicitly organized in autoencoders, random points in the latent space can return completely meaningless, unrecognizable images after being passed through the decoder, as shown in Figure 12-9. Instead of the imagined vast overlapping spheres of influence, small isolated islands are formed.

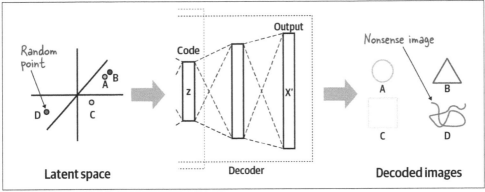

Figure 12-9. A random point in the latent space decoded into a meaningless, nonsense image.

Now, we can't blame autoencoders too much. They are doing exactly what they were designed to do, namely reconstructing their inputs with the goal of minimizing a reconstruction loss function. If having small isolated islands achieves that, then that is what they'll learn to do.

Variational autoencoders (VAEs) were developed in response to classic autoencoders being unable to use their decoders to generate quality images from user-generated latent vectors.

VAEs are generative models that can be used when, instead of just wanting to discriminate between classes, such as in a classification task where we create a decision boundary in a latent space (possibly satisfied with barely separating classes), we want to create *n*-dimensional bubbles that encompass similar training examples. This distinction is visualized in Figure 12-10.

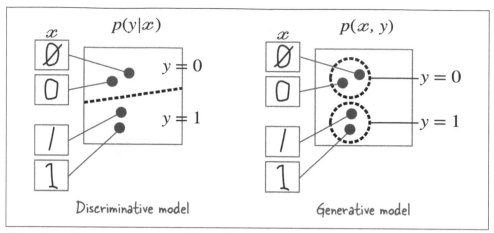

Figure 12-10. Discriminative model conditional versus generative model joint probability distributions.

Discriminative models, including popular image ML models for tasks such as classification and object detection, learn a conditional probability distribution that models the decision boundary between the classes. Generative models, on the other hand, learn a joint probability distribution that explicitly models the distribution of each class. The conditional probability distribution isn't lost—we can still do classification using Bayes' theorem, for example.

Fortunately, most of the architecture of variational autoencoders is the same as that of classic autoencoders: the hourglass shape, reconstruction loss, etc. However, the few additional complexities allow VAEs to do what autoencoders can't: image generation.

This is illustrated in Figure 12-11, which shows that both of our latent space regularity problems have been solved. The first problem of close latent points generating very different decoded images has been fixed, and now we are able to create similar images that smoothly interpolate through the latent space. The second problem of points in the latent space generating meaningless, nonsense images has also been fixed, and now we can generate plausible images. Remember, these images may not actually be exactly like the images the model was trained on, but may be in between some of the main archetypes because of the smooth overlapping regions within the learned organized latent space.

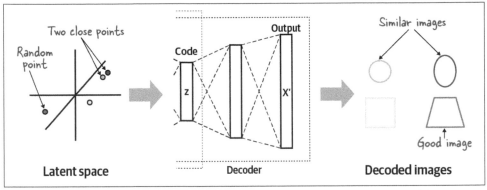

Figure 12-11. Both problems have been solved with an organized, regularized latent space.

Rather than having just a latent vector in between the encoder and decoder networks, which is essentially a point within the latent space, variational autoencoders train the encoder to produce parameters of a probability distribution and make the decoder randomly sample using them. The encoder no longer outputs a vector that describes a point within the latent space, but the parameters of a probability distribution. We can then sample from that distribution and pass those sampled points to our decoder to decompress them back into images.

In practice, the probability distribution is a standard normal distribution. This is because a mean close to zero will help prevent encoded distributions being too far apart and appearing as isolated islands. Also, a covariance close to the identity helps prevent the encoded distributions from being too narrow. The left side of Figure 12-12 shows what we are trying to avoid, with small, isolated distributions surrounded by voids of meaningless nonsense.

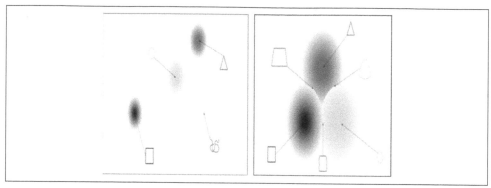

Figure 12-12. What we're trying to avoid (left) and what we're trying to achieve (right). We don't want small, isolated island distributions surrounded by vast voids of nonsense; we want the entire space covered by n-dimensional bubbles, as shown on the right. The goal is to have smoothly overlapping distributions without large gaps.

The image on the right in Figure 12-12 shows smoothly overlapping distributions without large gaps, which is exactly what we want for great image generation. Notice the interpolation where two distributions intersect. There is in fact a smooth gradient encoded over the latent space. For instance, we could start at the deep heart of the triangle distribution and move directly toward the circle distribution. We would begin with a perfect triangle, and with every step we took toward the circle distribution our triangle would get rounder and rounder until we reached the deep heart of the circle distribution, where we would now have a perfect circle.

To be able to sample from these distributions, we need both the mean vector and the covariance matrix. Therefore, the encoder network will output a vector for the distribution's mean and a vector for the distribution's covariance. To simplify things, we assume that these are independent. Therefore, the covariance matrix is diagonal, and we can simply use that instead of having an n^2-long vector of mostly zeros.

Now let's look at how to implement a VAE, starting with its architecture.

Architecture

In TensorFlow, a VAE encoder has the same structure as in a classic autoencoder, except instead of a single latent vector we now have a vector with two components, mean and variance (the full code is in *12b_vae.ipynb* on GitHub):

```
encoder_inputs = keras.Input(shape=(28, 28, 1))
x = layers.Conv2D(
    32, 3, activation="relu", strides=2, padding="same")(encoder_inputs)
x = layers.Conv2D(
    64, 3, activation="relu", strides=2, padding="same")(x)
x = layers.Flatten(name="e_flatten")(x)
z_mean = layers.Dense(latent_dim, name="z_mean")(x) # same as autoencoder
```

However, in addition to the `z_mean`, we need two additional outputs from the encoder. And because our model now has multiple outputs, we can no longer use the Keras Sequential API; instead, we have to use the Functional API. The Keras Functional API is more like standard TensorFlow, where inputs are passed into a layer and the layer's outputs are passed to another layer as its inputs. Any arbitrarily complex directed acyclic graph can be made using the Keras Functional API:

```
z_log_var = layers.Dense(latent_dim, name="z_log_var")(x)
z = Sampling()(z_mean, z_log_var)
encoder = keras.Model(encoder_inputs, [z_mean, z_log_var, z], name="encoder")
```

The sampling layer needs to sample from a normal distribution parameterized by the outputs of our encoder layers rather than using a vector from the final encoder layer as in non-variational autoencoders. The code for the sampling layer in TensorFlow looks like this:

```
class Sampling(tf.keras.layers.Layer):
    """Uses (z_mean, z_log_var) to sample z, the vector encoding a digit.
    """
    def call(self, inputs):
        z_mean, z_log_var = inputs
        batch = tf.shape(input=z_mean)[0]
        dim = tf.shape(input=z_mean)[1]
        epsilon = tf.random.normal(shape=(batch, dim))
        return z_mean + tf.math.exp(x=0.5 * z_log_var) * epsilon
```

The VAE decoder is identical to that in a non-variational autoencoder—it takes the latent vector z produced by the encoder and decodes it into an image (specifically, the reconstruction of the original image input):

```
z_mean, z_log_var, z = encoder(encoder_inputs) # 3 outputs now
decoder_output = decoder(z)
vae = keras.Model(encoder_inputs, decoder_output, name="vae")
```

Loss

A variational autoencoder's loss function contains an image reconstruction term, but we cannot just use the mean squared error (MSE). In addition to the reconstruction error, the loss function also contains a regularization term called the Kullback–Leibler divergence, which is essentially a penalty for the encoder's normal distribution (parameterized by mean μ and standard deviation σ) not being a perfect standard normal distribution (with mean 0 and a standard deviation of identity):

$$L = \left\| x - \widehat{x} \right\|^2 + KL\big(N\big(\mu_x, \sigma_x\big), N(0, I)\big)$$

We therefore modify the encoder loss function as follows:

```
def kl_divergence(z_mean, z_log_var):
    kl_loss = -0.5 * (1 + z_log_var - tf.square(z_mean) -
```

```
                    tf.exp(z_log_var))
    return tf.reduce_mean(tf.reduce_sum(kl_loss, axis=1))
encoder.add_loss(kl_divergence(z_mean, z_log_var))
```

The overall reconstruction loss is the sum of the per-pixel losses:

```
def reconstruction_loss(real, reconstruction):
    return tf.reduce_mean(
        tf.reduce_sum(
            keras.losses.binary_crossentropy(real, reconstruction),
            axis=(1, 2)
        )
    )
vae.compile(optimizer=keras.optimizers.Adam(),
            loss=reconstruction_loss, metrics=["mse"])
```

We then train the encoder/decoder combination with the MNIST images functioning as both the input features and the labels:

```
history = vae.fit(mnist_digits, mnist_digits, epochs=30,
                  batch_size=128)
```

Because the variational encoder has been trained to include the binary cross-entropy in its loss function, it takes into account the separability of the different classes in the images. The resulting latent vectors are more separable, occupy the entire latent space, and are better suited to generation (see Figure 12-13).

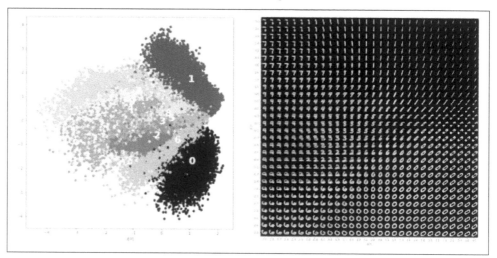

Figure 12-13. Clusters (left) and generated images (right) from a VAE trained on MNIST.

Variational autoencoders are able to create images that look just like their inputs. But what if we want to generate entirely new images? We'll look at image generation next.

Image Generation

Image generation is an important and rapidly growing field that goes well beyond just generating numbers and faces for fun; it has many important use cases for individuals and businesses alike, such as image restoration, image translation, super-resolution, and anomaly detection.

We saw previously how VAEs re-create their inputs; however, they aren't particularly successful at creating entirely new images that are similar to but different from the images in the input dataset. This is especially true if the generated images need to be perceptually real—for example, if, given a dataset of images of tools, we want a model to generate new pictures of tools that have different characteristics than the tools in the training images. In this section, we will discuss methods to generate images in cases like these (GANs, cGANs), and some of the uses (such as translation, super-resolution, etc.) to which image generation can be put.

Generative Adversarial Networks

The type of model most often used for image generation is a *generative adversarial network* (GAN). GANs borrow from game theory by pitting two networks against each other until an equilibrium is reached. The idea is that one network, the *generator*, will constantly try to create better and better reproductions of the real images, while the other network, the *discriminator*, will try to get better and better at detecting the difference between the reproductions and the real images. Ideally, the generator and discriminator will establish a Nash equilibrium so that neither network can completely dominate the other one. If one of the networks does begin to dominate the other, not only will there be no way for the "losing" network to recover, but also this unequal competition will prevent the networks from improving each other.

The training alternates between the two networks, each one becoming better at what it does by being challenged by the other. This continues until convergence, when the generator has become so good at creating realistic fake images that the discriminator is only randomly guessing which images are real (coming from the dataset) and which images are fake (coming from the generator).

The generator and discriminator are both neural networks. Figure 12-14 shows the overall training architecture.

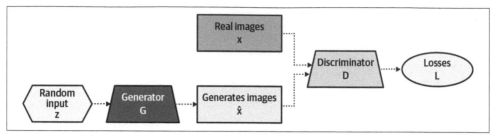

Figure 12-14. The standard GAN architecture, consisting of a generator and a discriminator.

For instance, imagine that a criminal organization wants to create realistic-looking money to deposit at the bank. In this scenario the criminals would be the generator, since they are trying to create realistic fake bills. The bankers would be the discriminator, examining the bills and trying to ensure the bank doesn't accept any counterfeit money.

A typical GAN training would begin with both the generator and the discriminator initialized with random weights. In our scenario that would mean that the counterfeiters have no clue how to generate realistic money: the generated outputs at the beginning simply look like random noise. Likewise, the bankers would begin not knowing the difference between a real and a generated bill, so they would be making terribly ill-informed random guesses as to what is real and what is fake.

The discriminator (the group of bankers) is presented with the first set of legitimate and generated bills, and has to classify them as real or fake. Because the discriminator starts off with random weights, initially it can't "see" easily that one bill is random noise and the other is a good bill. It's updated based on how well (or poorly) it performs, so over many iterations the discriminator will start becoming better at predicting which bills are real and which are generated. While the discriminator's weights are being trained, the generator's weights are frozen. However, the generator (the group of counterfeiters) is also improving during its turns, so it creates a moving target for the discriminator, progressively increasing the difficulty of the discrimination task. It's updated during each iteration based on how well (or not) its bills fooled the discriminator, and while it's being trained the discriminator's weights are frozen.

After many iterations, the generator is beginning to create something resembling real money because the discriminator was getting good at separating real and generated bills. This further pushes the discriminator to get even better at separating the now decent-looking generated bills from the real ones when it is its turn to train.

Eventually, after many iterations of training, the algorithm converges. This happens when the discriminator has lost its ability to separate generated bills from real bills and essentially is randomly guessing.

To see some of the finer details of the GAN training algorithm, we can refer to the pseudocode in Figure 12-15.

Algorithm 1 Minibatch stochastic gradient descent training of generative adversarial nets. The number of steps to apply to the discriminator, k, is a hyperparameter. We used $k = 1$, the least expensive option, in our experiments.

---

for number of training iterations **do**

    for k steps **do**

        • Sample minibatch of m noise samples $\{z^{(1)}, \ldots, z^{(m)}\}$ from noise prior $p_g(z)$.

        • Sample minibatch of m examples $\{x^{(1)}, \ldots, x^{(m)}\}$ from data generating distribution $p_{\text{data}}(x)$.

        • Update the discriminator by ascending its stochastic gradient:

$$\nabla_{\theta_d} \frac{1}{m} \sum_{i=1}^{m} \left[\log D\left(x^{(i)}\right) + \log\left(1 - D\left(G\left(z^{(i)}\right)\right)\right) \right].$$

    end for

    • Sample minibatch of m noise samples $\{z^{(1)}, \ldots, z^{(m)}\}$ from noise prior $p_g(z)$.

    • Update the generator by descending its stochastic gradient:

$$\nabla_{\theta_g} \frac{1}{m} \sum_{i=1}^{m} \log\left(1 - D\left(G\left(z^{(i)}\right)\right)\right).$$

end for

The gradient-based updates can use any standard gradient-based learning rule. We used momentum in our experiments.

Figure 12-15. A vanilla GAN training algorithm. Image from Goodfellow et al., 2014 (https://arxiv.org/pdf/1406.2661.pdf).

As we can see in the first line of the pseudocode, there is an outer for loop over the number of alternating discriminator/generator training iterations. We'll look at each of these updating phases in turn, but first we need to set up our generator and our discriminator.

Creating the networks

Before we do any training, we need to create our networks for the generator and discriminator. In a vanilla GAN, typically this is just a neural network composed of Dense layers.

The generator network takes a random vector of some latent dimension as input and passes it through some (possibly several) Dense layers to generate an image. For this example, we'll be using the MNIST handwritten digit dataset, so our inputs are 28x28 images. LeakyReLU activation functions usually work very well for GAN training because of their nonlinearity, not having vanishing gradient problems while also not losing information for any negative inputs or having the dreaded dying ReLU problem. Alpha is the amount of negative signal we want to leak through where a value of

0 would be the same as a ReLU activation and a value of 1 would be a linear activation. We can see this in the following TensorFlow code:

```
latent_dim = 512
vanilla_generator = tf.keras.Sequential(
    [
        tf.keras.Input(shape=(latent_dim,)),
        tf.keras.layers.Dense(units=256),
        tf.keras.layers.LeakyReLU(alpha=0.2),
        tf.keras.layers.Dense(units=512),
        tf.keras.layers.LeakyReLU(alpha=0.2),
        tf.keras.layers.Dense(units=1024),
        tf.keras.layers.LeakyReLU(alpha=0.2),
        tf.keras.layers.Dense(units=28 * 28 * 1, activation="tanh"),
        tf.keras.layers.Reshape(target_shape=(28, 28, 1))
    ],
    name="vanilla_generator"
)
```

The discriminator network in a vanilla GAN is also made up of Dense layers, but instead of generating images, it takes images as input, as shown here. The outputs are vectors of logits:

```
vanilla_discriminator = tf.keras.Sequential(
    [
        tf.keras.Input(shape=(28, 28, 1)),
        tf.keras.layers.Flatten(),
        tf.keras.layers.Dense(units=1024),
        tf.keras.layers.LeakyReLU(alpha=0.2),
        tf.keras.layers.Dense(units=512),
        tf.keras.layers.LeakyReLU(alpha=0.2),
        tf.keras.layers.Dense(units=256),
        tf.keras.layers.LeakyReLU(alpha=0.2),
        tf.keras.layers.Dense(units=1),
    ],
    name="vanilla_discriminator"
)
```

Discriminator training

Within the outer loop is an inner loop for updating the discriminator. First, we sample a mini-batch of noise, typically random samples from a standard normal distribution. The random noise latent vector is passed through the generator to create generated (fake) images, as shown in Figure 12-16.

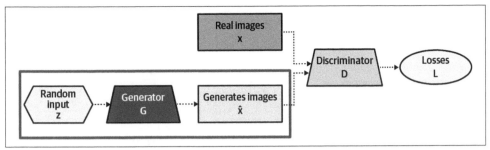

Figure 12-16. The generator creates its first batch of generated images by sampling from the latent space, and passes them to the discriminator.

In TensorFlow, we could for instance sample a batch of random normals using the following code:

```
# Sample random points in the latent space.
random_latent_vectors = tf.random.normal(shape=(batch_size, self.latent_dim))
```

We also sample a mini-batch of examples from our dataset—in our case, real images —as shown in Figure 12-17.

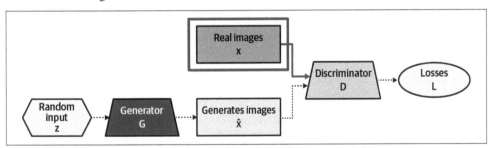

Figure 12-17. We also extract a batch of real images from the training dataset and pass this to the discriminator.

The generated images from the generator and the real images from the dataset are each passed through the discriminator, which makes its predictions. Loss terms for the real images and generated images are then calculated, as shown in Figure 12-18. Losses can take many different forms: binary cross-entropy (BCE), the average of the final activation map, second-order derivative terms, other penalties, etc. In the sample code, we'll be using BCE: the larger the real image loss, the more the discriminator thought that the real images were fake; the larger the generated image loss, the more the discriminator thought that the generated images were real.

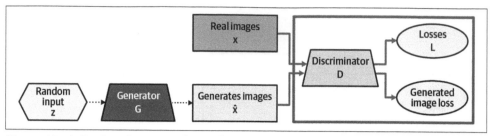

Figure 12-18. Real and generated samples pass through the discriminator to calculate the losses.

We do this in the following TensorFlow code (as usual, the complete code is in *12c_gan.ipynb* on GitHub). We can concatenate our generated and real images together and do the same with the corresponding labels so that we can do one pass through the discriminator:

```
# Generate images from noise.
generated_images = self.generator(inputs=random_latent_vectors)

# Combine generated images with real images.
combined_images = tf.concat(
    values=[generated_images, real_images], axis=0
)

# Create fake and real labels.
fake_labels = tf.zeros(shape=(batch_size, 1))
real_labels = tf.ones(shape=(batch_size, 1))

# Smooth real labels to help with training.
real_labels *= self.one_sided_label_smoothing

# Combine labels to be inline with combined images.
labels = tf.concat(
    values=[fake_labels, real_labels], axis=0
)

# Calculate discriminator loss.
self.loss_fn = tf.keras.losses.BinaryCrossentropy(from_logits=True)
predictions = self.discriminator(inputs=combined_images)
discriminator_loss = self.loss_fn(y_true=labels, y_pred=predictions)
```

We first pass our random latent vectors through the generator to obtain a batch of generated images. This is concatenated with our batch of real images so we have both sets of images together in one tensor.

We then generate our labels. For the generated images we make a vector of 0s, and for the real images a vector of 1s. This is because with our BCE loss we are essentially just doing binary image classification (where the positive class is that of the real images), and therefore we are getting the probability that an image is real. Labeling the real images with 1s and the fake images with 0s encourages the discriminator model to output probabilities as close to 1 as possible for real images and as close to 0 as possible for fake images.

It can be helpful sometimes to add one-sided label smoothing to our real labels, which involves multiplying them by a float constant in the range [0.0, 1.0]. This helps the discriminator avoid becoming overconfident in its predictions based on only a small set of features within the images, which the generator may then exploit (causing it to become good at beating the discriminator but not at image generation).

Since this is a discriminator training step, we use a combination of these losses to calculate the gradients with respect to the discriminator weights and then update the aforementioned weights as shown in Figure 12-19. Remember, during the discriminator training phase the generator's weights are frozen. This way each network gets its own chance to learn, independent of the other.

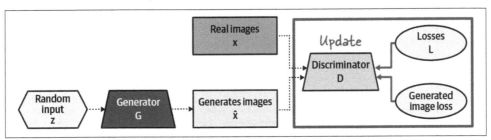

Figure 12-19. Discriminator weights are updated with respect to losses.

In the following code we can see this discriminator update being performed:

```
# Train ONLY the discriminator.
with tf.GradientTape() as tape:
    predictions = self.discriminator(inputs=combined_images)
    discriminator_loss = self.loss_fn(
        y_true=labels, y_pred=predictions
    )

grads = tape.gradient(
    target=discriminator_loss,
    sources=self.discriminator.trainable_weights
)

self.discriminator_optimizer.apply_gradients(
    grads_and_vars=zip(grads, self.discriminator.trainable_weights)
)
```

Generator training

After a few steps of applying gradient updates to the discriminator, it's time to update the generator (this time with the discriminator's weights frozen). We can do this in an inner loop too. This is a simple process where we again take a mini-batch of random samples from our standard normal distribution and pass them through the generator to obtain fake images.

In TensorFlow the code would look like this:

```
# Sample random points in the latent space.
random_latent_vectors = tf.random.normal(shape=(batch_size, self.latent_dim))

# Create labels as if they're real images.
labels = tf.ones(shape=(batch_size, 1))
```

Notice that even though these will be generated images, we will label them as real. Remember, we want to trick the discriminator into thinking our generated images are real. We can provide the generator with the gradients produced by the discriminator on images it was not fooled by. The generator can use these gradients to update its weights so that the next time it can do a better job of fooling the discriminator.

The random inputs pass through the generator as before to create generated images; however, there are no real images needed for generator training, as you can see in Figure 12-20.

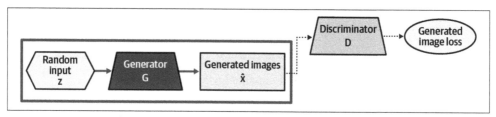

Figure 12-20. We only use generated images for generator training.

The generated images are then passed through the discriminator as before and a generator loss is calculated, as seen in Figure 12-21.

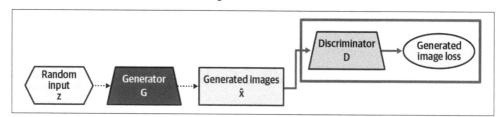

Figure 12-21. Only generated samples pass through the discriminator to calculate the loss.

Notice that no real images from the dataset are used in this phase. The loss is used to update only the generator's weights, as shown in Figure 12-22; even though the discriminator was used in the generator's forward pass, its weights are frozen during this phase so it does not learn anything from this process.

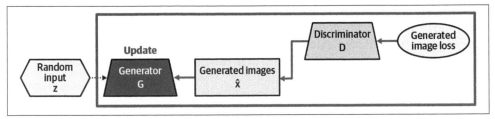

Figure 12-22. The generator's weights are updated with respect to the loss.

Here's the code that performs the generator update:

```
# Train ONLY the generator.
with tf.GradientTape() as tape:
    predictions = self.discriminator(
        inputs=self.generator(inputs=random_latent_vectors)
    )
    generator_loss = self.loss_fn(y_true=labels, y_pred=predictions)

grads = tape.gradient(
    target=generator_loss, sources=self.generator.trainable_weights
)

self.generator_optimizer.apply_gradients(
    grads_and_vars=zip(grads, self.generator.trainable_weights)
)
```

Once this is complete we go back to the discriminator's inner loop, and so on and so forth until convergence.

We can call the following code from our vanilla GAN generator TensorFlow model to see some of the generated images:

```
gan.generator(
    inputs=tf.random.normal(shape=(num_images, latent_dim))
)
```

Of course, if the model hasn't been trained, the images coming out will be random noise (produced by random noise coming in and going through multiple layers of random weights). Figure 12-23 shows what our GAN has learned once training on the MNIST handwritten digit dataset is complete.

Figure 12-23. MNIST digits generated by a vanilla GAN generator.

Distribution changes

GANs definitely have an interesting training procedure compared to more traditional machine learning models. They may even seem a bit mysterious in terms of how they work mathematically to learn the things they do. One way of trying to understand them a little more deeply is to observe the dynamics of the learned distributions of the generator and discriminator as they each try to outdo the other. Figure 12-24 shows how the generator's and discriminator's learned distributions change throughout the GAN training.

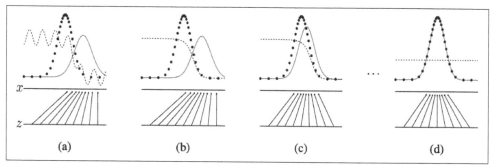

Figure 12-24. Learned distribution evolution during GAN training. The dashed line is the discriminator distribution, the solid line is the generator distribution, and the dotted line is the data generating (true data) distribution. The lower horizontal line is the domain that z is sampled from for the latent space and the upper horizontal line is a portion of the domain of x for the image space. The arrows show how z maps to x by x = G(z). The generator distribution shrinks in regions of low density and expands in regions of high density of the z to x mapping. Image from Goodfellow et al., 2014 (https:// arxiv.org/abs/1406.2661).

In Figure 12-24(a) we can see that the generator is not amazing, but is doing a decent job at generating some of the data distribution. The solid-lined generator distribution overlaps somewhat with the dotted-lined true data distribution (what we're trying to learn to generate from). Likewise, the discriminator does a fairly decent job of classifying real versus fake samples: it shows a strong signal (dashed line) when overlapping the dotted-lined data distribution and to the left of the peak of the generator distribution. The discriminative signal greatly shrinks in the region where the solid-lined generator distribution peaks.

The discriminator is then trained on another batch of real and generated images from the fixed generator within the inner discriminator training loop, over some number of iterations. In Figure 12-24(b) we can see that the dashed-lined discriminator distribution smooths out, and on the right it follows along the dotted-lined data distribution under the solid-lined generator distribution. On the left the distribution is much higher, and closer to the data distribution. Notice that the solid-lined generator distribution does not change at this step since we haven't updated the generator yet.

Figure 12-24(c) shows the results after the generator has been trained for some number of iterations. The performance of the newly updated discriminator helps guide it to shift its network weights and thus fill in some of the gaps it was missing from the data distribution, so it gets better at generating fake samples. We can see this as the solid-lined generator distribution is now much closer to the dotted curve of the data distribution.

Figure 12-24(d) shows the results after many more iterations alternating between training the discriminator and the generator. If both networks have enough capacity, the generator will have converged: its distribution will closely match with the data distribution, and it will be generating great-looking samples. The discriminator has also converged because it is no longer able to tell what is a real sample from the data distribution and what is a generated sample from the generator distribution. Thus, the discriminator's distribution flatlines to random guesses with 50/50 odds, and training of the GAN system is complete.

GAN Improvements

This looks great on paper, and GANs are extremely powerful for image generation—however, in practice they can be extremely hard to train due to hypersensitivity to hyperparameters, unstable training, and many failure modes.

If either network gets too good at its job too fast, then the other network will be unable to keep up, and the generated images will never get to look very realistic. Another problem is mode collapse, where the generator loses most of its diversity in creating images and only generates the same few outputs. This happens when it stumbles upon a generated output that for whatever reason is very good at stumping the discriminator. This can go on for quite some time during training until, by chance, the discriminator finally is able to detect that those few images are generated and not real.

In a GAN, the first network (the generator) has an expanding layer size from its input layer to its output layer. The second network (the discriminator) has a shrinking layer size from its input layer to its output layer. Our vanilla GAN architecture used dense layers, like an autoencoder. However, convolutional layers tend to perform better on tasks involving images.

A *deep convolutional GAN* (DCGAN) is more or less just a vanilla GAN with the dense layers swapped out for convolutional layers. In the following TensorFlow code, we define a DCGAN generator:

```
def create_dcgan_generator(latent_dim):
    dcgan_generator = [
        tf.keras.Input(shape=(latent_dim,)),
        tf.keras.layers.Dense(units=7 * 7 * 256),
        tf.keras.layers.LeakyReLU(alpha=0.2),
        tf.keras.layers.Reshape(target_shape=(7, 7, 256)),
    ] + create_generator_block(
        filters=128, kernel_size=4, strides=2, padding="same", alpha=0.2
```

```
    ) + create_generator_block(
        filters=128, kernel_size=4, strides=2, padding="same", alpha=0.2
    ) + [
        tf.keras.layers.Conv2DTranspose(
            filters=1,
            kernel_size=3,
            strides=1,
            padding="same",
            activation="tanh"
        )
    ]

    return tf.keras.Sequential(
        layers=dcgan_generator, name="dcgan_generator"
    )
```

Our templated generator block then looks like the following:

```
def create_generator_block(filters, kernel_size, strides, padding, alpha):
    return [
        tf.keras.layers.Conv2DTranspose(
            filters=filters,
            kernel_size=kernel_size,
            strides=strides,
            padding=padding
        ),
        tf.keras.layers.BatchNormalization(),
        tf.keras.layers.LeakyReLU(alpha=alpha)
    ]
```

Likewise, we can define a DCGAN discriminator like this:

```
def create_dcgan_discriminator(input_shape):
    dcgan_discriminator = [
        tf.keras.Input(shape=input_shape),
        tf.keras.layers.Conv2D(
            filters=64, kernel_size=3, strides=1, padding="same"
        ),
        tf.keras.layers.LeakyReLU(alpha=0.2)
    ] + create_discriminator_block(
        filters=128, kernel_size=3, strides=2, padding="same", alpha=0.2
    ) + create_discriminator_block(
        filters=128, kernel_size=3, strides=2, padding="same", alpha=0.2
    ) + create_discriminator_block(
        filters=256, kernel_size=3, strides=2, padding="same", alpha=0.2
    ) + [
        tf.keras.layers.Flatten(),
        tf.keras.layers.Dense(units=1)
    ]

    return tf.keras.Sequential(
        layers=dcgan_discriminator, name="dcgan_discriminator"
    )
```

And here's our templated discriminator block:

```
def create_discriminator_block(filters, kernel_size, strides, padding, alpha):
    return [
        tf.keras.layers.Conv2D(
            filters=filters,
            kernel_size=kernel_size,
            strides=strides,
            padding=padding
        ),
        tf.keras.layers.BatchNormalization(),
        tf.keras.layers.LeakyReLU(alpha=alpha)
    ]
```

As you can see, the generator is upsampling the image using `Conv2DTranspose` layers whereas the discriminator is downsampling the image using `Conv2D` layers.

We can then call the trained DCGAN generator to see what it has learned:

```
dcgan.generator(
    inputs=tf.random.normal(shape=(num_images, latent_dim))
)
```

The results are shown in Figure 12-25.

Figure 12-25. Generated MNIST digits produced by the DCGAN generator.

There are many other improvements that can be made to vanilla GANs, such as using different loss terms, gradients, and penalties. Since this is an active area of research, those are beyond the scope of this book.

Conditional GANs

The basic GAN that we discussed previously is trained in a completely unsupervised way on images that we want to learn how to generate. Latent representations, such as a random noise vector, are then used to explore and sample the learned image space. A simple enhancement is to add an external flag to our inputs with a label. For instance, consider the MNIST dataset, which consists of handwritten digits from 0 to 9. Normally, the GAN just learns the distribution of digits, and when the generator is given random noise vectors it generates different digits, as shown in Figure 12-26. However, which digits are generated cannot be controlled.

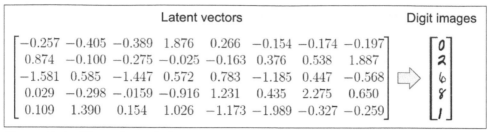

Figure 12-26. Unconditional GAN output.

During training, as with MNIST, we may know the actual label or class designation for each image. That extra information can be included as a feature in our GAN training that can then be used at inference time. With *conditional GANs* (cGANs), image generation can be conditional on the label, so we are able to home in on the specific digit of interest's distribution. Then, at inference time we can create an image of a specific digit by passing in the desired label instead of receiving a random digit, as seen in Figure 12-27.

Latent vectors								Conditional label	Digit images
−0.257	−0.405	−0.389	1.876	0.266	−0.154	−0.174	−0.197	4	4
0.874	−0.100	−0.275	−0.025	−0.163	0.376	0.538	1.887	7	7
−1.581	0.585	−1.447	0.572	0.783	−1.185	0.447	−0.568	5	5
0.029	−0.298	−.0159	−0.916	1.231	0.435	2.275	0.650	1	1
0.109	1.390	0.154	1.026	−1.173	−1.989	−0.327	−0.259	2	2

Figure 12-27. Conditional GAN output.

The cGAN generator. We need to make some changes to our vanilla GAN generator code from earlier so that we can incorporate the label. Essentially, we'll be concatenating our latent vector with a vector representation of our labels, as you can see in the following code:

```
# Create the generator.
def create_label_vectors(labels, num_classes, embedding_dim, dense_units):
    embedded_labels = tf.keras.layers.Embedding(
        input_dim=num_classes, output_dim=embedding_dim
    )(inputs=labels)
    label_vectors = tf.keras.layers.Dense(
        units=dense_units
    )(inputs=embedded_labels)

    return label_vectors
```

Here, we use an `Embedding` layer to transform our integer labels into a dense representation. We'll later be combining the embedding of the label with our typical random noise vector to create a new latent vector that is a mixture of the input latent space and the class labels. We then use a `Dense` layer to further mix the components.

Next, we utilize our standard vanilla GAN generator from before. However, this time we are using the Keras Functional API, as we did for our variational autoencoder earlier, because we now have multiple inputs to our generator model (the latent vector and labels):

```
def standard_vanilla_generator(inputs, output_shape):
    x = tf.keras.layers.Dense(units=64)(inputs=inputs)
    x = tf.keras.layers.LeakyReLU(alpha=0.2)(inputs=x)
    x = tf.keras.layers.Dense(units=128)(inputs=x)
    x = tf.keras.layers.LeakyReLU(alpha=0.2)(inputs=x)
    x = tf.keras.layers.Dense(units=256)(inputs=x)
    x = tf.keras.layers.LeakyReLU(alpha=0.2)(inputs=x)
    x = tf.keras.layers.Dense(
        units=output_shape[0] * output_shape[1] * output_shape[2],
        activation="tanh"
    )(inputs=x)

    outputs = tf.keras.layers.Reshape(target_shape=output_shape)(inputs=x)

    return outputs
```

Now that we have a way to embed our integer labels, we can combine this with our original standard generator to create a vanilla cGAN generator:

```
def create_vanilla_generator(latent_dim, num_classes, output_shape):
    latent_vector = tf.keras.Input(shape=(latent_dim,))

    labels = tf.keras.Input(shape=())
    label_vectors = create_label_vectors(
        labels, num_classes, embedding_dim=50, dense_units=50
    )

    concatenated_inputs = tf.keras.layers.Concatenate(
        axis=-1
    )(inputs=[latent_vector, label_vectors])

    outputs = standard_vanilla_generator(
        inputs=concatenated_inputs, output_shape=output_shape
    )

    return tf.keras.Model(
        inputs=[latent_vector, labels],
        outputs=outputs,
        name="vanilla_generator"
    )
```

Notice we now have two sets of inputs using the Keras Input layer. Remember, this is the main reason we are using the Keras Functional API instead of the Sequential API: it allows us to have an arbitrary number of inputs and outputs, with any type of network connectivity in between. Our first input is the standard latent vector, which is our generated random normal noise. Our second input is the integer labels that we will condition on later, so we can target certain classes of generated images via labels provided at inference time. Since, in this example, we are using MNIST handwritten digits, the labels will be integers between 0 and 9.

Once we've created our dense label vectors, we combine them with our latent vectors using a Keras `Concatenate` layer. Now we have a single tensor of vectors, each of shape `latent_dim + dense_units`. This is our new "latent vector," which gets sent into the standard vanilla GAN generator. This isn't the original latent vector of our original vector space that we sampled random points from, but is now a new higher-dimensional vector space due to the concatenation of the encoded label vector.

This new latent vector helps us target specific classes for generation. The class label is now embedded in the latent vector and therefore will be mapped to a different point in image space than with the original latent vector. Furthermore, given the same latent vector, each label pairing will map to a different point in image space because it is using a different learned mapping due to the different concatenated latent–label vectors. Therefore, when the GAN is trained it learns to map each latent point to a point in image space corresponding to an image belonging to one of the 10 classes.

As we can see at the end of the function, we simply instantiate a Keras `Model` with our two input tensors and output tensor. Looking at the conditional GAN generator's architecture diagram, shown in Figure 12-28, should make clear how we are using the two sets of inputs, the latent vector and the label, to generate images.

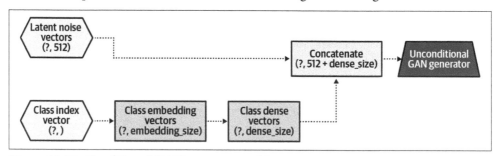

Figure 12-28. Conditional GAN generator architecture.

Now that we've seen the generator, let's take a look at the code for the conditional GAN discriminator.

The cGAN discriminator. For the generator, we created label vectors that we concatenated with our latent vectors. For the discriminator, which has image inputs, we instead convert the labels into images and concatenate the images created from the labels with the input images. This allows the label information to be embedded into our images to help the discriminator differentiate between real and generated images. The label will help warp the latent space to image space mapping such that each input will be associated with its label's bubble within image space. For example, for MNIST, if the model is given the digit 2, the discriminator will generate something within the bubble of 2s in the learned image space.

To accomplish the conditional mapping for the discriminator, we once again pass our integer labels through an Embedding and a Dense layer. However, each example in the batch is now just a vector num_pixels long. Thus, we use a Reshape layer to transform the vector into an image with just one channel. Think of it as a grayscale image representation of our label. In the following code, we can see the labels being embedded into images:

```
def create_label_images(labels, num_classes, embedding_dim, image_shape):
    embedded_labels = tf.keras.layers.Embedding(
        input_dim=num_classes, output_dim=embedding_dim)(inputs=labels)
    num_pixels = image_shape[0] * image_shape[1]
    dense_labels = tf.keras.layers.Dense(
        units=num_pixels)(inputs=embedded_labels)
    label_image = tf.keras.layers.Reshape(
        target_shape=(image_shape[0], image_shape[1], 1))(inputs=dense_labels)

    return label_image
```

As we did for the generator, we will reuse our standard vanilla GAN discriminator from the previous section that maps images into logit vectors that will be used for loss calculations with binary cross-entropy. Here's the code for the standard discriminator, using the Keras Functional API:

```
def standard_vanilla_discriminator(inputs):
    """Returns output of standard vanilla discriminator layers.

    Args:
        inputs: tensor, rank 4 tensor of shape (batch_size, y, x, channels).

    Returns:
        outputs: tensor, rank 4 tensor of shape
            (batch_size, height, width, depth).
    """
    x = tf.keras.layers.Flatten()(inputs=inputs)
    x = tf.keras.layers.Dense(units=256)(inputs=x)
    x = tf.keras.layers.LeakyReLU(alpha=0.2)(inputs=x)
    x = tf.keras.layers.Dense(units=128)(inputs=x)
    x = tf.keras.layers.LeakyReLU(alpha=0.2)(inputs=x)
    x = tf.keras.layers.Dense(units=64)(inputs=x)
    x = tf.keras.layers.LeakyReLU(alpha=0.2)(inputs=x)

    outputs = tf.keras.layers.Dense(units=1)(inputs=x)

    return outputs
```

Now we'll create our conditional GAN discriminator. It has two inputs: the first is the standard image input, and the second is the class labels that the images will be conditioned on. Just like for the generator, we convert our labels into a usable representation to use with our images—namely, into grayscale images—and we use a `Concatenate` layer to combine the input images with the label images. We send those combined images into our standard vanilla GAN discriminator and then instantiate a Keras `Model` using our two inputs, the outputs, and a name for the discriminator `Model`:

```
def create_vanilla_discriminator(image_shape, num_classes):
    """Creates vanilla conditional GAN discriminator model.

    Args:
        image_shape: tuple, the shape of the image without batch dimension.
        num_classes: int, the number of image classes.

    Returns:
        Keras Functional Model.
    """
    images = tf.keras.Input(shape=image_shape)

    labels = tf.keras.Input(shape=())
    label_image = create_label_images(
        labels, num_classes, embedding_dim=50, image_shape=image_shape
    )

    concatenated_inputs = tf.keras.layers.Concatenate(
        axis=-1
    )(inputs=[images, label_image])

    outputs = standard_vanilla_discriminator(inputs=concatenated_inputs)

    return tf.keras.Model(
        inputs=[images, labels],
        outputs=outputs,
        name="vanilla_discriminator"
    )
```

Figure 12-29 shows the full conditional GAN discriminator architecture.

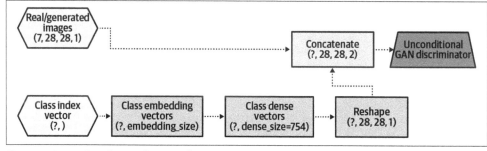

Figure 12-29. Conditional GAN discriminator architecture.

The rest of the conditional GAN training process is virtually the same as the non-conditional GAN training process, except for the fact we now pass in the labels from our dataset to use both for the generator and the discriminator.

Using a `latent_dim` of 512 and training for 30 epochs, we can use our generator to produce images like the ones in Figure 12-30. Note that for each row the label used at inference was the same, hence why the first row is all zeros, the second row is all ones, and so on. This is great! Not only can we generate handwritten digits, but we can specifically generate the digits we want.

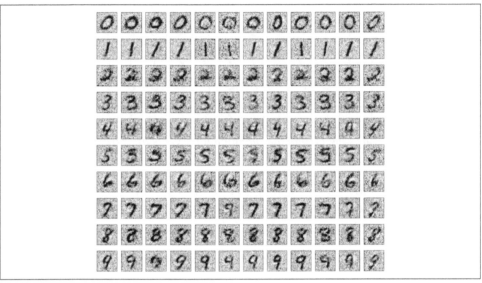

Figure 12-30. Generated digits from the conditional vanilla GAN after training on the MNIST dataset.

We can get even cleaner results if, instead of using our standard vanilla GAN generator and discriminator, we use the DCGAN generator and discriminator shown earlier. Figure 12-31 shows some of the images generated after training the conditional DCGAN model with a `latent_dim` of 512 for 50 epochs.

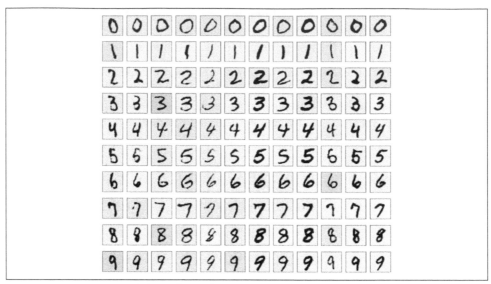

Figure 12-31. Generated digits from the conditional DCGAN after training on the MNIST dataset.

GANs are powerful tools for generating data. We focused on image generation here, but other types of data (such as tabular, time series, and audio data) can also be generated via GANs. However, GANs are a bit finicky and often require the use of the tricks we've covered here, and many more, to improve their quality and stability. Now that you've added GANs as another tool in your toolbox, let's look at some advanced applications that use them.

Image-to-Image Translation

Image generation is one of the simpler applications that GANs are great at. We can also combine and manipulate the essential components of GANs to put them to other uses, many of which are state of the art.

Image-to-image translation is when an image is translated from one (source) domain into another (target) domain. For instance, in Figure 12-32, an image of a horse is translated so that it looks like the horses are zebras. Of course, since finding paired images (e.g., the same scene in winter and summer) can be quite difficult, we can instead create a model architecture that can perform the image-to-image translation using unpaired images. This might not be as performant as a model working with paired images, but it can get very close. In this section we will explore how to perform image translation first if we have unpaired images, the more common situation, and then if we have paired images.

Horse (input) to zebra (output)

Figure 12-32. Results of using CycleGAN to translate an image of horses into an image of zebras. Image from Zhu et al., 2020 (https://arxiv.org/abs/1703.10593v7).

The CycleGAN architecture used to perform the translation in Figure 12-32 takes GANs one step further and has two generators and two discriminators that cycle back and forth, as illustrated in Figure 12-33. Continuing with the previous example, let's say that horse images belong to image domain X, and zebra images belong to image domain Y. Remember, these are unpaired images; therefore, there isn't a matching zebra image for each horse image, and vice versa.

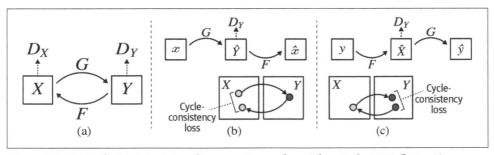

Figure 12-33. CycleGAN training diagram. Image from Zhu et al., 2020 (https://arxiv.org/abs/1703.10593v7).

In Figure 12-33(a), generator G maps image domain X (horses) to image domain Y (zebras) while another generator, F, maps the reverse, Y (zebras) to X (horses). This means that generator G learns weights that map an image of horses, in this example, to an image of zebras, and vice versa for generator F. Discriminator D_X leads generator F to have a great mapping from Y (zebras) to X (horses), while discriminator D_Y leads generator G to have a great mapping from X (horses) to Y (zebras). We then perform cycles to add a little more regularization to the learned mappings, as described in the next panel.

In Figure 12-33(b), the forward cycle consistency loss—X (horses) to Y (zebras) to X (horses)—is from the comparison of an X (horses) domain image mapped to Y (zebras) using generator G and then mapped back to X (horses) using generator F with the original X (horses) image.

Likewise, in Figure 12-33(c), the backward cycle consistency loss—Y (zebras) to X (horses) to Y (zebras)—is from the comparison of a Y (zebras) domain image mapped to X (horses) using generator F and then mapped back to Y (zebras) using generator G with the original Y (zebras) image.

Both the forward and backward cycle consistency loss compare the original image for a domain with the cycled image for that domain so that the network can learn to reduce the difference between them.

By having these multiple networks and ensuring cycle consistency we're able to get impressive results despite having unpaired images, such as when translating between horses and zebras or between summer images and winter images, as in Figure 12-34.

summer Yosemite → winter Yosemite

Figure 12-34. Results of using CycleGAN to translate summer images to winter images. Image from Zhu et al., 2020 (https://arxiv.org/abs/1703.10593v7).

Now, if instead we did have paired examples, then we could take advantage of supervised learning to get even more impressive image-to-image translation results. For instance, as shown in Figure 12-35, an overhead map view of a city can be translated into the satellite view and vice versa.

Figure 12-35. Results of using Pix2Pix to translate a map view to satellite view and vice versa. Image from Isola et al., 2018 (https://arxiv.org/abs/1611.07004).

The Pix2Pix architecture uses paired images to create the forward and reverse mappings between the two domains. We no longer need cycles to perform the image-to-image translation, but instead have a U-Net (previously seen in Chapter 4) with skip connections as our generator and a PatchGAN as our discriminator, which we discuss further next.

The U-Net generator takes a source image and tries to create the target image version, as shown in Figure 12-36. This generated image is compared to the actual paired target image via the L1 loss or MAE, which is then multiplied by lambda to weight the loss term. The generated image (source to target domain) and the input source image then go to the discriminator with labels of all 1s with a binary/sigmoid cross-entropy loss. The weighted sum of these losses is used for the gradient calculation for the generator to encourage the generator to improve its weights for domain translation in order to fool the discriminator. The same is done for the other generator/discriminator set with the source and target domains reversed for the reverse translation.

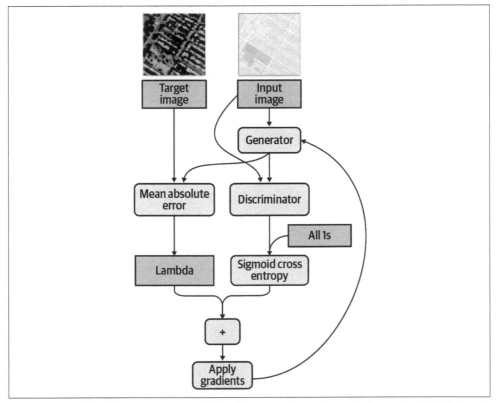

Figure 12-36. Pix2Pix generator training diagram. Image from Isola et al., 2018 (https:// arxiv.org/abs/1611.07004).

The PatchGAN discriminator classifies portions of the input image using smaller-resolution patches. This way each patch is classified as either real or fake using the local information in that patch rather than the entire image. The discriminator is passed two sets of input pairs, concatenated along channels, as shown in Figure 12-37.

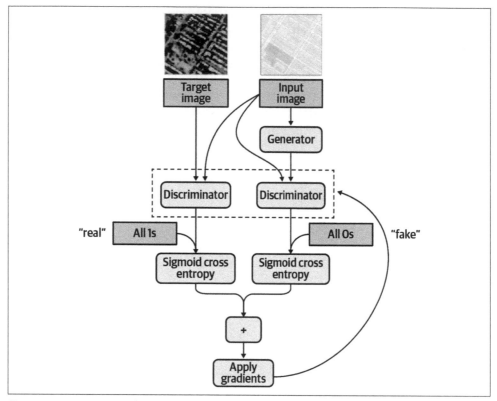

Figure 12-37. Pix2Pix discriminator training diagram. Image from Isola et al., 2018 (https://arxiv.org/abs/1611.07004).

The first pair is made up of the input source image and the generated "source to target" image from the generator, which the discriminator should classify as fake by labeling them with all 0s. The second pair is made up of the input source image with the target image concatenated with it instead of the generated image. This is the real branch and hence this pair is labeled with all 1s. If we think back to simpler image generation this is following the same discriminator training pattern where the generated images are in the fake, all 0 labels branch and the real images we want to generate are in the real, all 1 labels branch. Therefore, the only change compared to image generation is that we are essentially conditioning the discriminator with the input image from the source domain, similar to what we did with conditional GANs.

This can lead to amazing use cases such as Figure 12-38, where hand-drawn objects can be filled in to look like real objects with photographic quality.

Figure 12-38. Results of using Pix2Pix on a drawing to transform it to an image of photographic quality. Image from Isola et al., 2018 (https://arxiv.org/abs/1611.07004).

Just like how we can translate text and speech between languages, we can also translate images between different domains. We can use architectures like CycleGAN with (much more common) datasets of unpaired images, or more specialized architectures like Pix2Pix that can take full advantage of paired image datasets. This is still a very active area of research with many improvements being discovered.

Super-Resolution

For most of the use cases we've seen so far we've been both training and predicting with pristine images. However, we know in reality there can often be many defects in images, such as blur or the resolution being too low. Thankfully, we can modify some of the techniques we've already learned to fix some of those image issues.

Super-resolution is the process of taking a degraded or low-resolution image and upscaling it, transforming it into a corrected, high-resolution image. Super-resolution itself has been around for a long time as part of general image processing, yet it wasn't until more recently that deep learning models were able to produce state-of-the-art results with this technique.

The simplest and oldest methods of super-resolution use various forms of pixel interpolation, such as nearest neighbor or bicubic interpolation. Remember that we're starting with a low-resolution image that, when upscaled, has more pixels than the original image. These pixels need to be filled in through some means, and in a way that looks perceptually correct and doesn't just produce a smoothed, blurry larger image.

Figure 12-39 shows a sample of the results from a 2017 paper (*https://arxiv.org/abs/1609.04802*) by Christian Ledig et al. The original high-resolution image is on the far right. It's from this image that a lower-resolution one is created for the training procedure. On the far left is the bicubic interpolation—it's a quite smooth and blurry recreation of the starting image from a smaller, lower-resolution version of the original. For most applications, this is not of high enough quality.

The second image from the left in Figure 12-39 is an image created by SRResNet, which is a residual convolutional block network. Here, a version of the original image that is low resolution, due to Gaussian noise and downsampling, is passed through 16 residual convolutional blocks. The output is a decent super-resolution image that's fairly close to the original—however, there are some errors and artifacts. The loss function used in SRResNet is the mean squared error between each pixel of the super-resolution output image and the original high-resolution image. Although the model is able to get pretty good results using MSE loss alone, it's not quite enough to encourage the model to make truly photorealistic and perceptually similar images.

Figure 12-39. Super-resolution images. Images from Ledig et al., 2017 (https://arxiv.org/abs/1609.04802).

The third image from the left in Figure 12-39 shows the best (in terms of perceptual quality) results, obtained using a model called SRGAN. The idea to utilize a GAN came from what the SRResNet image was lacking: high perceptual quality, which we can quickly judge by looking at the image. This is due to the MSE reconstruction loss, which aims to minimize the average error of the pixels but doesn't attempt to ensure the individual pixels combine to form a perceptually convincing image.

As we saw earlier, GANs generally have both a generator for creating images and a discriminator to discern whether the images being passed to it are real or generated. Rather than trying to slowly and painfully manually tune models to create convincing images, we can use GANs to do this tuning for us automatically. Figure 12-40 shows the generator and discriminator network architectures of SRGAN.

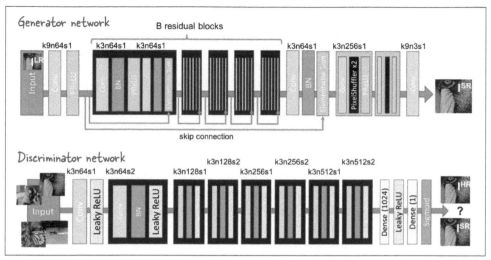

Figure 12-40. SRGAN generator and discriminator architectures. Image from Ledig et al., 2017 (https://arxiv.org/abs/1609.04802).

In the SRGAN generator architecture, we begin by taking a high-resolution (HR) image and applying a Gaussian filter to it, then downsampling the image by some factor. This creates a low-resolution (LR) version of the image, which then gets convolved and passed through several residual blocks, like we saw in Chapter 4 with ResNet. The image is upsampled along the way, since we need to get back to its original size. The network also includes skip connections so that more detail from the earlier layers can condition the later layers and for better gradient backpropagation during the backward pass. After a few more convolutional layers, a super-resolution (SR) image is generated.

The discriminator takes images as input and determines whether they are SR or HR. The input is passed through several convolutional blocks, ending with a dense layer that flattens the intermediate images and finally another dense layer that produces the logits. Just like with a vanilla GAN, these logits are optimized on binary cross-entropy and so the result is a probability that the image is HR or SR, which is the adversarial loss term.

With SRGAN, there is another loss term that is weighted together with the adversarial loss to train the generator. This is the *contextual loss*, or how much of the original content remains within the image. Minimizing the contextual loss will ensure that the output image looks similar to the original image. Typically this is the pixel-wise MSE, but since that is a form of averaging it can create overly smooth textures that don't look realistic. Therefore, SRGAN instead uses what its developers call the *VGG loss*, using the activation feature maps for each of the layers of a pretrained 19-layer VGG network (after each activation, before the respective max-pooling layer). They calculate the VGG loss as the sum of the Euclidean distance between the feature maps of the original HR images and the feature maps of the generated SR images, summing those values across all VGG layers, and then normalizing by the image height and width. The balance of these two loss terms will create images that not only look similar to the input images but also are correctly interpolated so that, perceptually, they look like real images.

Modifying Pictures (Inpainting)

There can be other reasons to fix an image, such as a tear in a photograph or a missing or obscured section, as shown in Figure 12-41(a). This hole-filling is called *inpainting*, where we want to literally paint in the pixels that should be in the empty spot. Typically, to fix such an issue an artist would spend hours or days restoring the image by hand, as shown in Figure 12-41(b), which is a laborious process and unscalable. Thankfully, deep learning with GANs can make scalably fixing images like this a reality—Figure 12-41(c) and (d) show some sample results.

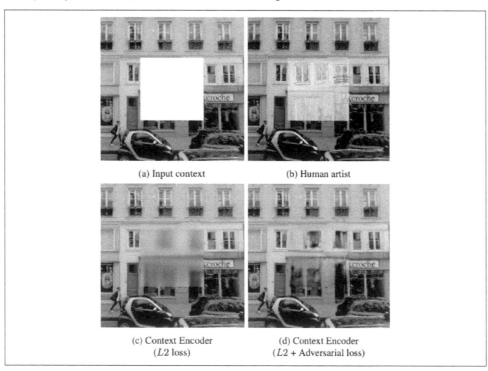

Figure 12-41. Context encoder inpainting results. Image from Pathak et al., 2016 (https://arxiv.org/abs/1604.07379).

Here, unlike with SRGAN, instead of adding noise or a filter and downsampling a high-resolution image for training, we extract an area of pixels and set that region aside. We then pass the remaining image through a simple encoder/decoder network, as shown in Figure 12-42. This forms the generator of the GAN, which we hope will generate content similar to what was in the pixel region we extracted.

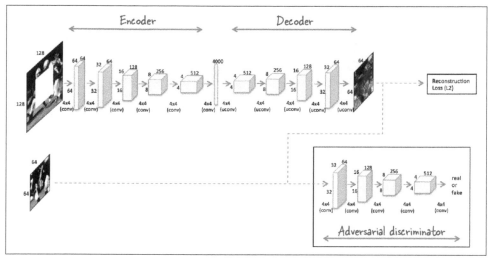

Figure 12-42. Context encoder generator and discriminator architectures. Image from Pathak et al., 2016 (https://arxiv.org/abs/1604.07379).

The discriminator then compares the generated region of pixels with the region we extracted from the original image and tries to determine whether the image was generated or came from the real dataset.

Similar to SRGAN, and for the same reasons, the loss function has two terms: a reconstruction loss and an adversarial loss. The reconstruction loss isn't the typical L2 distance between the extracted image patch and the generated image patch, but rather the normalized masked L2 distance. The loss function applies a mask to the overall image so that we only aggregate the distances of the patch that we reconstructed, and not the border pixels around it. The final loss is the aggregated distance normalized by the number of pixels in the region. Alone, this usually does a decent job of creating a rough outline of the image patch; however, the reconstructed patch is usually lacking high-frequency detail and ends up being blurry due to the averaged pixel-wise error.

The adversarial loss for the generator comes from the discriminator, which helps the generated image patch appear to come from the manifold of natural images and therefore look realistic. These two loss functions can be combined in a weighted sum joint loss.

The extracted image patches don't just have to come from the central region, like in Figure 12-43(a)—in fact, that approach can be detrimental to the training as a result of poor generalization of the learned low-level image features to images without patches extracted. Instead, taking random blocks, as in Figure 12-43(b), or random regions of pixels, as shown in Figure 12-43(c), produces more general features and greatly outperforms the approach of using a central region mask.

Figure 12-43. Different extracted patch region masks. Image from Pathak et al., 2016 (https://arxiv.org/abs/1604.07379).

Anomaly Detection

Anomaly detection is another application that can benefit from the use of GANs—images can be passed to a modified GAN model and flagged as anomalous or not. This can be useful for tasks such as counterfeit currency detection, or looking for tumors in medical scans.

Typically there is a lot more unlabeled data available for deep learning use cases than labeled, and often the process of labeling is extremely laborious and may require deep subject matter expertise. This can make a supervised approach infeasible, which means we need an unsupervised approach.

To perform anomaly detection, we need to learn what "normal" looks like. If we know what normal is, then when an image doesn't fit within that distribution, it may contain anomalies. Therefore, when training anomaly detection models, it is important to train the model only on normal data. Otherwise, if the normal data is contaminated with anomalies, then the model will learn that those anomalies are normal. At inference time, this would lead to actual anomalous images not being correctly flagged, thus generating many more false negatives than may be acceptable.

The standard method of anomaly detection is to first learn how to reconstruct normal images, then learn the distribution of reconstruction errors of normal images, and finally learn a distance threshold where anything above that threshold is flagged as anomalous. There are many different types of models we can use to minimize the reconstruction error between the input image and its reconstruction. For example, using an autoencoder, we can pass normal images through the encoder (which compresses an image down to a more compact representation), possibly through a layer or two in the bottleneck, then through the decoder (which expands the image back to its original representation), and finally generate an image that should be a reconstruction of the original image. The reconstruction is never perfect; there is always some error. Given a large collection of normal images, the reconstruction error will form a distribution of "normal errors." Now, if the network is given an anomalous image—one that it has not seen anything like during training—it will not be able to compress and reconstruct it correctly. The reconstruction error will be way out of the normal error distribution. The image can thus be flagged as an anomalous image.

Taking the anomaly detection use case one step further, we could instead perform *anomaly localization*, where we are flagging individual pixels as anomalous. This is like an unsupervised segmentation task rather than an unsupervised classification task. Each pixel has an error, and this can form a distribution of errors. In an anomalous image, many pixels will exhibit a large error. Reconstructed pixels above a certain distance threshold from their original versions can be flagged as anomalous, as shown in Figure 12-44.

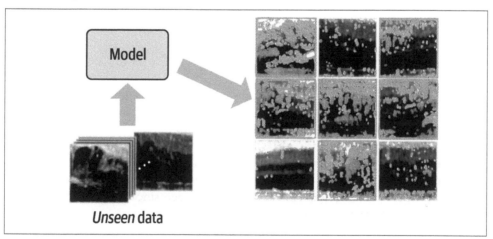

Figure 12-44. *Anomaly localization flags individual pixels as anomalous. Image from Schlegl et al., 2019 (https://oreil.ly/bsOpV).*

However, for many use cases and datasets this isn't the end of the story. With just the autoencoder and reconstruction loss, the model may learn how to map any image to itself instead of learning what normal looks like. Essentially, reconstruction dominates the combined loss equation and therefore the model learns the best way to compress *any* image, rather than learning the "normal" image manifold. For anomaly detection this is very bad because the reconstruction loss for both normal and anomalous images will be similar. Therefore, as with super-resolution and inpainting, using a GAN can help.

This is an active area of research, so there are many competing variations of model architectures, loss functions, training procedures, etc., but they all have several components in common, as seen in Figure 12-45. Typically they consist of a generator and discriminator, sometimes with additional encoder and decoder networks depending on the use case.

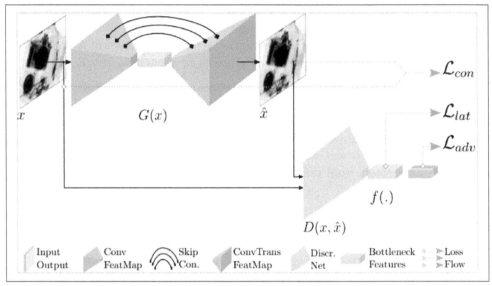

Figure 12-45. Skip-GANomaly architecture, using a U-Net generator (encoder/decoder) with skip connections, discriminator, and multiple loss terms. Image from Akçay et al., 2019 (https://arxiv.org/abs/1901.08954).

The generator can be an autoencoder or U-Net, if the input and output are images, as in Figure 12-45's G, or the generator can just be a decoder that takes as input a user-provided random latent vector. This image autoencoder, since it's part of a GAN, is also sometimes called an adversarial autoencoder.

The discriminator, such as Figure 12-45's D, is used to adversarially train the generator. This is typically an encoder-type network, compressing an image down into a vector of logits to then be used for loss calculations.

As mentioned previously, sometimes there's an additional encoder or multiple generator/discriminator pairs. If the generator is an autoencoder, the additional encoder can be used for regularizing the intermediate bottleneck vector of the generator. If the generator is just a decoder, then the encoder can encode the generator's generated image into a feature vector to reconstruct the noise prior, essentially acting as the inverse of the generator.

As with SRGAN and inpainting, there are usually multiple loss terms: namely a reconstruction loss such as L_{con} and an adversarial loss such as L_{adv} in the example architecture in Figure 12-45. Additionally, there can be other loss terms like Figure 12-45's L_{lat}, which is a latent loss that sums the Euclidean distance between two feature maps in an intermediate layer from the discriminator. The weighted sum of these losses is designed to encourage the desired inference behavior. The adversarial loss ensures that the generator has learned the manifold of normal images.

The three-phase training procedure of image reconstruction, calculating the normal prediction error distribution, and applying the distance threshold will produce different results depending on whether normal or anomalous images are passed through the trained generator. Normal images will look very similar to the original images, so their reconstruction error will be low; therefore, when compared to the learned parameterized error distribution, they will have distances that are below the learned threshold. However, when the generator is passed an anomalous image, the reconstruction will no longer just be slightly worse. Therefore, the anomalies should be painted out, generating what the model thinks the image would look like without anomalies. The generator will essentially hallucinate what it thinks should be there based on its learned normal image manifold. Obviously this should result in a very large error when compared to the original anomalous image, allowing us to correctly flag the anomalous images or pixels for anomaly detection or localization, respectively.

Deepfakes

A popular technique that has recently exploded into the mainstream is the making of so-called *deepfakes*. Deepfakes replace objects or people in existing images or videos with different objects or people. The typical models used to create these deepfake images or videos are autoencoders or, with even better performance, GANs.

One method of creating deepfakes is to create one encoder and two decoders, A and B. Let's say we are trying to swap person X's face with person Y's. First, we distort an image of person X's face and pass that through the encoder to get the embedding, which is then passed through decoder A. This encourages the two networks to learn how to reconstruct person X's face from the noisy version. Next, we pass a warped version of person Y's face through the same encoder, and pass it through decoder B. This encourages these two networks to learn how to reconstruct person Y's face from the noisy version. We repeat this process over and over again until decoder A is great at producing clean images of person X and decoder B is great for person Y. The three networks have learned the essence of the two faces.

At inference time, if we now pass an image of person X through the encoder and then through decoder B, which was trained on the other person (person Y) instead of person X, the networks will think that the input is noisy and "denoise" the image into person Y's face. Adding a discriminator for an adversarial loss can help improve the image quality.

There have been many other advancements in the creation of deepfakes, such as requiring only a single source image (often demonstrated by running the deepfake on a work of art such as the *Mona Lisa*). Remember, though, that to achieve great results, a lot of data is required to sufficiently train the networks.

Deepfakes are something that we need to keep a close eye on due to their possible abuse for political or financial gain—for instance, making a politician appear to say something they never did. There is a lot of active research looking into methods to detect deepfakes.

Image Captioning

So far in this chapter, we have looked at how to represent images (using encoders) and how to generate images from those representations (using decoders). Images are not the only thing worth generating from image representations, though—we might want to generate text based on the content of the images, a problem known as *image captioning*.

Image captioning is an asymmetric transformation problem. The encoder here operates on images, whereas the decoder needs to generate text. A typical approach is to use standard models for the two tasks, as shown in Figure 12-46. For example, we could use the Inception convolutional model to encode images into image embeddings, and a language model (marked by the gray box) for the sequence generation.

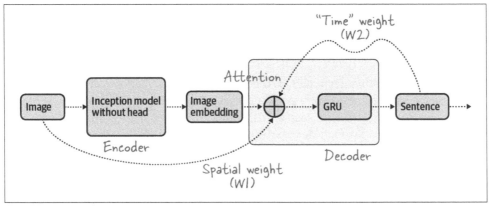

Figure 12-46. High-level image captioning architecture.

There are two important concepts that are necessary to understand what's happening in the language model: attention and gated recurrent units (GRUs).

Attention is important for the model to learn the relationships between specific parts in the image and specific words in the caption. This is accomplished by training the network such that it learns to focus its attention on specific parts of the image for specific words in the output sequence (see Figure 12-47). Therefore, the decoder incorporates a mechanism that *attends* over the image to predict the next word.

A woman is throwing a <u>frisbee</u> in a park.

Figure 12-47. The model learns to predict the next word in the sequence by focusing its attention on the relevant part of the input image. The attention of the network at the time the word "frisbee" is to be predicted is shown in this figure. Image from Xu et al., 2016 (https://arxiv.org/abs/1502.03044v3).

A *GRU cell* is the basic building block of a sequence model. Unlike the image models that we have seen in this book, language models need to remember what words they have already predicted. In order for a language model to take an English input sentence ("I love you") and translate it into French ("Je t'aime"), it is insufficient for the model to translate the sentence word-by-word. Instead, the model needs to have some memory. This is accomplished through a GRU cell that has an input, an output, an input state, and an output state. In order to predict the next word, the state is passed around from step to step, and the output of one step becomes the input to the next.

In this section we will build an end-to-end captioning model, starting with creating the dataset and preprocessing the captions and moving on to building the captioning model, training it, and using it to make predictions.

Dataset

To train a model to predict captions, we need a training dataset that consists of images and captions for those images. The COCO captions dataset (*https://oreil.ly/ t4xr6*) is a large corpus of such captioned images. We will use a version of the COCO dataset that is part of TensorFlow Datasets—this version contains images, bounding boxes, labels, and captions from COCO 2014, split into the subsets defined by Karpathy and Li (2015), and takes care of some data quality issues with the original dataset (for example, some of the images in the original dataset did not have captions).

We can create a training dataset using the following code (the full code is in *02e_image_captioning.ipynb* on GitHub):

```
def get_image_label(example):
    captions = example['captions']['text'] # all the captions
    img_id = example['image/id']
    img = example['image']
    img = tf.image.resize(img, (IMG_WIDTH, IMG_HEIGHT))
    img = tf.keras.applications.inception_v3.preprocess_input(img)
    return {
        'image_tensor': img,
        'image_id': img_id,
        'captions': captions
    }

trainds = load_dataset(...).map(get_image_label)
```

This code applies the `get_image_label()` function to each of the examples that are read. This method pulls out the captions and the image tensor. The images are all different sizes, but we need them to be of shape (299, 299, 3) in order to use the pretrained Inception model. Therefore, we resize each image to the desired size.

Each image has multiple captions. A few example images and the first caption of each are shown in Figure 12-48.

Figure 12-48. A few example images and the first caption for these images from the COCO dataset.

Tokenizing the Captions

Given a caption such as:

```
A toilet and sink in a tiled bathroom.
```

we need to remove punctuation, lowercase it, split into words, remove unusual words, add special start and stop tokens, and pad it to a consistent length:

```
['<start>', 'a', 'toilet', 'and', 'sink', 'in', 'a', 'tiled', 'bathroom', '<end>'
, '<pad>', '<pad>', '<pad>', '<pad>', '<pad>', '<pad>', '<pad>', '<pad>', '<pad>'
, '<pad>', '<pad>', '<pad>', '<pad>', '<pad>', '<pad>', '<pad>', '<pad>', '<pad>'
, '<pad>', '<pad>', '<pad>', '<pad>', '<pad>', '<pad>', '<pad>', '<pad>', '<pad>'
, '<pad>', '<pad>', '<pad>', '<pad>', '<pad>', '<pad>', '<pad>', '<pad>', '<pad>'
, '<pad>', '<pad>', '<pad>']
```

We start by adding the <start> and <end> tokens to each caption string:

```
train_captions = []
for data in trainds:
    str_captions = ["<start> {} <end>".format(
        t.decode('utf-8')) for t in data['captions'].numpy()]
    train_captions.extend(str_captions)
```

Then we use the Keras tokenizer to create the word-to-index lookup table:

```
tokenizer = tf.keras.layers.experimental.preprocessing.TextVectorization(
    max_tokens=VOCAB_SIZE, output_sequence_length=MAX_CAPTION_LEN)
tokenizer.adapt(train_captions)
```

The tokenizer can now be used to do the lookups in both directions:

```
padded = tokenizer(str_captions)
predicted_word = tokenizer.get_vocabulary()[predicted_id]
```

Batching

Each image in the COCO dataset can have up to five captions. So, given an image, we can actually generate up to five feature/label pairs (the image is the feature, the caption is the label). Because of this, creating a batch of training features is not as easy as:

```
trainds.batch(32)
```

since these 32 examples will expand into anywhere from 32 to 32 * 5 potential examples. We need batches to be of consistent size, so we will have to use the training dataset to generate the necessary examples before batching them:

```
def create_batched_ds(trainds, batchsize):
    # generator that does tokenization, padding on the caption strings
    # and yields img, caption
    def generate_image_captions():
        for data in trainds:
            captions = data['captions']
            img_tensor = data['image_tensor']
            str_captions = ["starttoken {} endtoken".format(
                t.decode('utf-8')) for t in captions.numpy()]
            # Pad each vector to the max_length of the captions
            padded = tokenizer(str_captions)
            for caption in padded:
                yield img_tensor, caption # repeat image
    return tf.data.Dataset.from_generator(
        generate_image_captions,
        (tf.float32, tf.int32)).batch(batchsize)
```

Note that we are reading the caption strings, and applying the same processing to each of these strings that we did in the previous section. That was for the purpose of creating the word-to-index lookup tables and computing the maximum caption length over the entire dataset so that captions can be padded to the same length. Here, we simply apply the lookup tables and pad the captions based on what was calculated over the full dataset.

We can then create batches of 193 image/caption pairs by:

```
create_batched_ds(trainds, 193)
```

Captioning Model

The model consists of an image encoder followed by a caption decoder (see Figure 12-46). The caption decoder incorporates an attention mechanism that focuses on different parts of the input image.

Image encoder

The image encoder consists of the pretrained Inception model followed by a `Dense` layer:

```
class ImageEncoder(tf.keras.Model):
    def __init__(self, embedding_dim):
    inception = tf.keras.applications.InceptionV3(
        include_top=False,
        weights='imagenet'
    )
    self.model = tf.keras.Model(inception.input,
                                inception.layers[-1].output)
    self.fc = tf.keras.layers.Dense(embedding_dim)
```

Invoking the image encoder applies the Inception model, flattens the result from the [batch, 8, 8, 2048] that Inception returns to [batch, 64, 2048], and passes it through the `Dense` layer:

```
def call(self, x):
    x = self.model(x)
    x = tf.reshape(x, (x.shape[0], -1, x.shape[3]))
    x = self.fc(x)
    x = tf.nn.relu(x)
    return x
```

Attention mechanism

The attention component is complicated—look at the following description in conjunction with Figure 12-46 and the complete code in *02e_image_captioning.ipynb* on GitHub.

Recall that attention is how the model learns the relationships between specific parts in the image and specific words in the caption. The attention mechanism consists of two sets of weights—W1 is a dense layer meant for the spatial component (`features`, where in the image to focus on), and W2 is a dense layer for the "temporal" component (indicating which word in the input sequence to focus on):

```
attention_hidden_layer = (tf.nn.tanh(self.W1(features) +
                          self.W2(hidden_with_time_axis)))
```

The weighted attention mechanism is applied to the hidden state of the recurrent neural network to compute a score:

```
score = self.V(attention_hidden_layer)
attention_weights = tf.nn.softmax(score, axis=1)
```

V here is a dense layer that has a one output node that is passed through a softmax layer to obtain a final combined weight that adds up to 1 across all the words. The features are weighted by this value, and this is an input to the decoder:

```
context_vector = attention_weights * features
```

This attention mechanism is part of the decoder, which we'll look at next.

Caption decoder

Recall that the decoder needs to have some memory of what it has predicted in the past, and so the state is passed around from step to step, with the output of one step becoming the input to the next. Meanwhile, during training, the caption words are fed into the decoder one word at a time.

The decoder takes the caption words one a time (x in the following listing) and converts each word into its word embedding. The embedding is then concatenated with the context output of the attention mechanism (which specifies where in the image the attention mechanism is currently focused) and passed into a recurrent neural network cell (a GRU cell is used here):

```
x = self.embedding(x)
x = tf.concat([tf.expand_dims(context_vector, 1), x], axis=-1)
output, state = self.gru(x)
```

The output of the GRU cell is then passed through a set of dense layers to obtain the decoder output. The output here would normally be a softmax because the decoder is a multilabel classifier—we need the decoder to tell which of the five thousand words the next word needs to be. However, for reasons that will become apparent in the section on predictions, it is helpful to keep the output as logits.

Putting these pieces together, we have:

```
encoder = ImageEncoder(EMBED_DIM)
decoder = CaptionDecoder(EMBED_DIM, ATTN_UNITS, VOCAB_SIZE)
optimizer = tf.keras.optimizers.Adam()
```

```
loss_object = tf.keras.losses.SparseCategoricalCrossentropy(
    from_logits=True, reduction='none')
```

The loss function of the captioning model is a bit tricky. It's not simply the mean cross-entropy over the entire output, because we need to ignore the padded words. Therefore, we define a loss function that masks out the padded words (which are all zeros) before computing the mean:

```
def loss_function(real, pred):
    mask = tf.math.logical_not(tf.math.equal(real, 0))
    loss_ = loss_object(real, pred)
    mask = tf.cast(mask, dtype=loss_.dtype)
    loss_ *= mask
    return tf.reduce_mean(loss_)
```

Training Loop

Now that our model has been created, we can move on to training it. You might have noticed that we don't have a single Keras model—we have an encoder and a decoder. That is because it is not enough to call `model.fit()` on the entire image and caption —we need to pass in the caption words to the decoder one by one because the decoder needs to learn how to predict the next word in the sequence.

Given an image and a target caption, we initialize the loss and reset the decoder state (so that the decoder doesn't continue with the words of the previous caption):

```
def train_step(img_tensor, target):
    loss = 0
    hidden = decoder.reset_state(batch_size=target.shape[0])
```

The decoder input starts with a special start token:

```
dec_input = ... tokenizer(['starttoken'])...
```

We invoke the decoder and compute the loss by comparing the decoder's output against the next word in the caption:

```
for i in range(1, target.shape[1]):
    predictions, hidden, _ = decoder(dec_input, features, hidden)
    loss += loss_function(target[:, i], predictions)
```

We are adding the *i*th word to the decoder input each time so that the model learns based on the correct caption, not based on whatever the predicted word is:

```
dec_input = tf.expand_dims(target[:, i], 1)
```

This is called *teacher forcing*. Teacher forcing swaps the target word in the input with the predicted word from the last step.

The whole set of operations just described has to be captured for the purpose of computing gradient updates, so we wrap it in a `GradientTape`:

```
with tf.GradientTape() as tape:
    features = encoder(img_tensor)
    for i in range(1, MAX_CAPTION_LENGTH):
        predictions, hidden, _ = decoder(dec_input, features, hidden)
        loss += loss_function(target[:, i], predictions)
        dec_input = tf.expand_dims(target[:, i], 1)
```

We can then update the loss, and apply gradients:

```
total_loss = (loss / MAX_CAPTION_LENGTH)
trainable_variables = \
    encoder.trainable_variables + decoder.trainable_variables
gradients = tape.gradient(loss, trainable_variables)
optimizer.apply_gradients(zip(gradients, trainable_variables))
```

Now that we have defined what happens in a single training step, we can loop through it for the desired number of epochs:

```
batched_ds = create_batched_ds(trainds, BATCH_SIZE)
for epoch in range(EPOCHS):
    total_loss = 0
    num_steps = 0
    for batch, (img_tensor, target) in enumerate(batched_ds):
        batch_loss, t_loss = train_step(img_tensor, target)
        total_loss += t_loss
        num_steps += 1
    # storing the epoch end loss value to plot later
    loss_plot.append(total_loss / num_steps)
```

Prediction

For the purpose of prediction, we are given an image and need to generate a caption. We start the caption string with the token <start> and feed the image and the initial token to the decoder. The decoder returns a set of logits, one for each of the words in our vocabulary.

Now we need to use the logits to get the next word. There are several approaches we could follow:

- A greedy approach where we pick the word with the maximum log-likelihood. This essentially means that we do tf.argmax() on the logits. This is fast but tends to overemphasize uninformative words like "a" and "the."

- A *beam search* method where we pick the top three or five candidates. We will then force the decoder with each of these words, and pick the next word in the sequence. This creates a tree of output sequences, from which the highest-probability sequence is selected. Because this optimizes the probability of the sequence rather than of individual words, it tends to give the best results, but it's computationally quite expensive and can lead to high latencies.

- A probabilistic method where we choose the word in proportion to its likelihood —in TensorFlow, this is achieved using `tf.random.categorical()`. If the word following "crowd" is 70% likely to be "people" and 30% likely to be "watching," then the model chooses "people" with a 70% likelihood, and "watching" with a 30% probability, so that the less likely phrase is also explored. This is a reasonable trade-off that achieves both novelty and speed at the expense of being nonreproducible.

Let's try out the third approach.

We start by applying all the preprocessing to the image, and then send it to the image encoder:

```
def predict_caption(filename):
    attention_plot = np.zeros((max_caption_length, ATTN_FEATURES_SHAPE))
    hidden = decoder.reset_state(batch_size=1)
    img = tf.image.decode_jpeg(tf.io.read_file(filename),
                               channels=IMG_CHANNELS)
    img = tf.image.resize(img, (IMG_WIDTH, IMG_HEIGHT)) # inception size
    img_tensor_val = tf.keras.applications.inception_v3.preprocess_input(img)

    features = encoder(tf.expand_dims(img_tensor_val, axis=0))
```

We then initialize the decoder input with the token `<start>` and invoke the decoder repeatedly until an `<end>` caption is received or the maximum caption length is reached:

```
dec_input = tf.expand_dims([tokenizer(['starttoken'])], 0)
result = []
for i in range(max_caption_length):
    predictions, hidden = decoder(dec_input, features, hidden)
    # draws from log distribution given by predictions
    predicted_id = tf.random.categorical(predictions, 1)[0][0].numpy()
    result.append(tokenizer.vocabulary()[predicted_id])
    if tokenizer.vocabulary()[predicted_id] == 'endtoken':
        return result
    dec_input = tf.expand_dims([predicted_id], 0)

return img, result, attention_plot
```

An example image and captions generated from it are shown in Figure 12-49. The model seems to have captured that this is a group of people on a field playing baseball. However, the model believes that there is a high likelihood that the white line in the center is the median divider of a street, and that this game could have been played on the street. Stopwords (*of, in, and, a,* etc.) are not generated by the model because we removed them from the training dataset. Had we had a larger dataset, we could have tried to generate proper sentences by keeping those stopwords in.

people man group field street large
group man people street large baseball
group standing people man street large
group people man street field large
people man street group field baseball

Figure 12-49. An example image, courtesy of the author, and a few of the captions generated by the model.

At this point, we now have an end-to-end image captioning model. Image captioning is an important way to make sense of a large corpus of images and is starting to find use in a number of applications, such as generating image descriptions for the visually impaired, meeting accessibility requirements in social media, generating audio guides like those used in museums, and performing cross-language annotation of images.

Summary

In this chapter, we looked at how to generate images and text. To generate images, we first create latent representations of images using an autoencoder (or variational autoencoder). A latent vector passed through a trained decoder functions as an image generator. In practice, however, the generated images are too obviously fake. To improve the realism of the generated images, we can use GANs, which use a game theoretic approach to train a pair of neural networks. Finally, we looked at how to implement image captioning by training an image encoder and a text decoder along with an attention mechanism.

Afterword

In 1966, MIT professor Seymour Papert launched a summer project (*https://oreil.ly/AC3Xh*) for his students. The final goal of the project was to name objects in images by matching them with a vocabulary of known objects. He helpfully broke the task down for them into subprojects, and expected the group to be done in a couple of months. It's safe to say that Dr. Papert underestimated the complexity of the problem a little.

We started this book by looking at naive machine learning approaches like fully connected neural networks that do not take advantage of the special characteristics of images. In Chapter 2, trying the naive approaches allowed us to learn how to read in images, and how to train, evaluate, and predict with machine learning models.

Then, in Chapter 3, we introduced many of the innovative concepts—convolutional filters, max-pooling layers, skip connections, modules, squeeze activation, and so on —that enable modern-day machine learning models to work well at extracting information from images. Implementing these models, practically speaking, involves using either a built-in Keras model or a TensorFlow Hub layer. We also covered transfer learning and fine-tuning in detail.

In Chapter 4, we looked at how to use the computer vision models covered in Chapter 3 to solve two more fundamental problems in computer vision: object detection and image segmentation.

The next few chapters of the book covered, in depth, each of the stages involved in creating production computer vision machine learning models:

- In Chapter 5, we covered how to create a dataset in a format that will be efficient for machine learning. We also discussed the options available for label creation and for keeping an independent dataset for model evaluation and hyperparameter tuning.

- In Chapter 6, we did a deep dive into preprocessing and preventing training-serving skew. Preprocessing can be done in the `tf.data` input pipeline, in Keras layers, in `tf.transform`, or using a mix of these methods. We covered both the implementation details and the pros and cons of each approach.

- In Chapter 7, we discussed model training, including how to distribute the training across GPUs and workers.

- In Chapter 8, we explored how to monitor and evaluate models. We also looked at how to carry out sliced evaluations to diagnose unfairness and bias in our models.

- In Chapter 9, we discussed the options available for deploying models. We implemented batch, streaming, and edge prediction. We were able to invoke our models locally, and across the web.

- In Chapter 10, we showed you how to tie together all these steps into a machine learning pipeline. We also tried out a no-code image classification system to take advantage of the ongoing democratization of machine learning.

In Chapter 11, we widened our lens beyond image classification. We looked at how the basic building blocks of computer vision can be used to solve a variety of problems including counting, pose detection, and other use cases. Finally, in Chapter 12, we looked at how to generate images and captions.

Throughout the book, the concepts, models, and processes discussed are accompanied by implementations in GitHub (*https://github.com/GoogleCloudPlatform/practical-ml-vision-book*). We strongly recommend that you not just read this book, but also work through the code and try it out. The best way to learn machine learning is to do it.

Computer vision is at an exciting stage. The underlying technologies work well enough that today, more than 50 years after Dr. Papert posed the problem to his students, we are finally at the point where image classification *can* be a two-month project! We wish you much success in applying this technology to better human lives and hope that it brings you as much joy to use computer vision to solve real-world problems as it has brought us.

Index

Symbols

3D convolution, 189
   (see also Conv3D)
@tf.function annotation, 257, 308

A

absolute loss, 151
abstraction, improving for model prediction
   API, 310
accelerators, 311
   (see also GPUs; TPUs)
   batch prediction performance and, 322
   for edge ML, 324
   on cloud service providers, 312
accuracy, 26, 289
   classification, 290
   defined, 50
   imbalanced datasets and, 66
   plotting, 30
   plotting, 37
activation functions, 22
   defined, 50
   image regression, 31
   introducing in Keras, 35
   LeakyReLU, 403
   None, 31
   nonlinear, adding for hidden layer output,
      34
   nonlinear, sigmoid, ReLU, and elu, 35
activation parameter (convolutional layer), 71
adagrad (adaptive gradients) optimizer, 22
Adam optimizer, 22
   default learning rate, changing, 38
AdamW optimizer, 65

advanced vision problems (see vision problems,
   advanced)
Aequitas Fairness Tree, 200
AlexNet, 75-79
   at a glance, 78
   implementing in Keras, 78
AlexNet paper, 4
Amazon CloudWatch, GPU monitoring on
   AWS, 249
Amazon SageMaker, 268
   Clarify, support for SHAP, 345
anchor boxes, 143-146
anomaly detection, 430-433
anomaly localization, 431
Apache Beam, 319
   batch prediction pipeline, combining with
      REST API approach, 322
   converting JPEG image files to TFRecords,
      202
   pipeline executing on Kubeflow cluster, 335
   pipeline in creating vision dataset, 203
   running code on Google Cloud Dataflow,
      204
   writing pipeline to carry out preprocessing,
      224
Apache Spark, 319
area under the curve (AUC), 27, 50, 293
arrays, 13
   converting to/from tensors, 13
Arthropod Taxonomy Orders Object Detection
   (Arthropods) dataset, 133
attention mechanism (captioning model), 438
audio and video data, 186-189
   Conv3D, use on video, 188

using self-supervised learning, 196
manual, of image data, 189-191
at scale, 191-195
labeling images for multiple tasks, 192
labeling user interface, 192
using labeling services, 195
voting and crowdsourcing, 194
labels, 175
defined, 51
Keras support for two representations, 25
preprocessing in tf.data pipeline, 223
sparse representation for Keras training
model, 28
Lambda layers (Keras), 215
latent vectors, converting images into, 390-394
layers
names of, in pretrained model, 65
per-layer learning rate in pretrained model,
64
in Sequential model, 19
Leaky ReLU, 36, 403
learning rate, 24, 38
defined, 51
differential, 64
schedule, 63
set too high, 63
small value for, 38
LIME (Local Interpretable Model-agnostic
Explanations), 340
linear activation function, 22
Lionbridge labeling service, 195
locations of detected features, 74
logits, 20, 22
defined, 52
loss
binary cross-entropy (BCE), 405
changing to apply penalty on weight values,
39
defined, 52
Huber loss, 158
loss and accuracy curves, 29
on training and validatation datasets training neural network, 37
(see also training)
in SRGAN, 427
training loss, 24
loss functions
captioning model, 440
loss landscape of 56-layer ResNet, 98

variational autoencoder, 399
in YOLO architecture, 137-139
lossy compression, 388

M

machine learning, 2
machine learning engineers, 329
machine learning trends, 329-358, 446
explainability, 339-352
adding explainability, 345-352
ML pipelines, 330-339
automating a run, 338
connecting components, 336-338
containerizing the codebase, 332
creating pipeline to run a component,
335
framework to operationalize, 331
Kubeflow Pipelines cluster, 332
need for pipelines, 331
standard set of steps on, 332
writing a component, 333-336
no-code computer vision, 352-357
evaluation, 356
loading data into the system, 353
training, 355
use cases, 352
machine perception, 9-17
map functions, 15
parallelizing operations, 246
Mask R-CNN, 157, 362
(see also image segmentation)
complete architecture, 166
masks of footprint and credit card (example),
363
ratio and measurements, 364
rotation correction, 363
Matplotlib, imshow function, 14
matrix math, 254
max pooling, 73
mean absolute error (MAE), 298, 423
mean average precision (mAP), 302
mean average recall (mAR), 302
mean squared error (MSE), 32, 298
measurement bias, 198
medical diagnosis, computer vision methods
applied to, 6
metadata
documenting for TensorFlow Records, 245
explanation, 347

creating, 265-267
    shuffling data, 265
    virtual epochs, 266

N

NASNet, 110-113
natural language processing, using computer vision techniques, 187
neural architecture search designs, 110-124
    MobileNet family of architectures, 114-124
    NASNet, 110-113
neural networks, 4
    creating using Keras, 32-49
        early stopping, 41
        hidden layers, 33
        hyperparameter tuning, 42
        learning rate, 37
        regularization, 39
        training the neural network, 36
    depth of, 5
    generator and discriminator in GANs, 401
neurons, 52
NMS (non-maximum suppression), 153-155
no-code computer vision, 352-357
    evaluation results, 356
    loading data, 353
    training the model, 355
    uses of, 352
noise, 29
Noisy Student model, 196
nonlinearity, adding to upsampling steps, 171
Notebooks service on Vertex AI, 332
numpy, 13
    converting image from tensor to array, 14
.numpy function, 252, 309

O

object absence loss, 138
object classification loss, 138
object detection, 131-157, 445
    current research directions, 173
    metadata file for image labels, 191
    metrics for, 299-302
    models, 373
    RetinaNet, 139-157
    using crowdsourcing for labeling, 194
    YOLO architecture, 134-139
object measurement, 359-365
    ratio and measurements, 364

    reference object, 360-362
    rotation correction, 363
odds, 20
104 flowers dataset, 65
one-hot encoding
    defined, 52
    labels, 24, 25
1x1 convolutions, 82
OneDeviceStrategy, 265, 272
online prediction, 311, 312-319
    handling image bytes, 316-319
        adding prediction signature, 317
        exporting signatures, 318
        loading the model, 317
        using base64 encoding, 318
    invoking for batch and stream prediction, 322
    modifying the serving function, 314-316
        changing default signature, 315
        using multiple signatures, 315
    TensorFlow Serving, 312-314
        deploying the model, 312
        making predictions, 313-314
Open Neural Network Exchange (ONNX), 256
opponents and proponents, 345
optical character recognition (OCR), 5
optimizers, 22
    AdamW, 65
    Keras Tuner optimizataion algorithms, 42
overfitting, 29, 39
Oxford Pets dataset, 171

P

padding parameter (convolutional layer), 71
padding, use in image resizing, 215
panoptic segmentation, 173
parallelizing data reads, 246
parse_csvline function, 15
partial derivative of cross-entropy, 23
pass-through parameters, 314
patches, extracting, 368
PatchGAN discriminator, 423
performance
    comparison for image classification architectures, 126
    gains from using Apache Beam batch prediction pipeline with online prediction, 322

numpy array math library, 13
organizing production ML code into packages, 268
wrapping in bash script to forward to ML pipeline component, 334

Q

quality evaluation for models, 303-305
fairness monitoring, 304
sliced evaluations, 303

R

R-CNN, 159
radar, 178
ragged batches, 213
ragged tensors, 222
RandomCrop layer, 229
RandomFlip layer, 228
rank (tensors), 13
raster data, 184
raters, 189
reading data in parallel, 245-248
parallelizing, 245
recall, 26
defined, 52
for imbalanced dataset, 66
receiver operating characteristic (ROC) curve, 27, 292
rectified linear unit (ReLU), 4, 35, 52
recurrent neural networks (RNNs), 189
region proposal networks (RPNs), 157, 158
regions of interest (see ROIs)
regression, 31
counting objects in an image, 366
losses in, 151
metrics for, 298-299
training regression model on patches to predict density, 370
regression loss functions, 32
regularization, 5, 39
defined, 52
dropout in deep neural networks, 45
reinforcement learning, 110
ReLU activation function, 4, 35
advantages and limitations of, 36
remote sensing, 185
Reshape layer, 390, 417
reshaping img tensor, 19
residual blocks, 94

Resizing layer, 213
interpolation options for squashing and stretching images, 214
ResNet, 93-99
quantBytes parameter, 376
residual blocks, 94
ResNet50 architecture, 96
skip connections, 94
summary of, 98
ResNet50 model
pretrained, instantiating, 79
trained on ImageNet dataset to classify images, 386
Responsible AI, 329
(see also bias; explainability of AI models)
REST APIs
combining with Beam batch prediction pipeline, 322
online model predictions served via, 312
RetinaNet, 139-157
anchor boxes, 143-146
architecture, 147-149
feature pyramid networks, 139-143
focal loss (for classification), 149
Mask R-CNN and, 167
non-maximum suppression (NMS), 153-155
other considerations, 155
smooth L1 loss (for box regression), 151
ROIs (regions of interest), 158
assignment to most relevant FPN level, 161
resampling and alignment of the feature maps to, 167
ROI alignment, 162
root mean squared error (RMSE), 298
rotation correction, masks in object measurement, 363

S

satellite images, 179
SavedModel, 256
default signature for serving predictions, 307
deploying as web service on Google Cloud, 312
invoking, 256
saved_model_cli (TensorFlow), 256, 307
saving model state, 255-262
checkpointing, 260-262

TensorFlow model graph output to, 286
training events, monitoring, 287
TensorFlow
  for Android, PoseNet implementations in,
    374
  channels-last ordering, 183
  container creation, base container image
    for, 272
  dataset, 5-flowers dataset, 10
  glob function, 14
  invoking pure Python functionality from,
    252
  Keras model, 19
  Kubeflow Pipelines running on, 331
  making sure Vertex Training is using same
    version of, 271
  mixing resize_with_pad and Keras's Center-
    Crop, 215
  non-maximum suppression, 155
  parallelizing reads of data, 246
  preprocessing as part of tf.data pipeline or
    in Keras layer in the model, 222
  SavedModel format, 256
  tensors, 13
  using image module in preprocessing, 214
TensorFlow Extended (TFX)
  creating CSV reader, 224
  Python APIs on, 332
TensorFlow Hub
  image format used in, 60
  models returning 1D feature vector, 60
  pretrained MobileNet, 58
  pretrained models in, 79
TensorFlow JS PoseNet model, 374
TensorFlow Lite, 324-325
  running, 325
TensorFlow Records (TFRecords), 202-206
  converting JPEG image files to, using
    Apache Beam, 202
  creating using TFRecorder Python package,
    206
  reading, 206-208
  storing images as, 242
TensorFlow Serving, 279
  managed versions on major cloud provid-
    ers, 279
  using in online prediction, 312-314
    deploying the model, 312
tensors

1D, 16
4D, as input/outputs of convolutional layers,
  71
defined, 13, 53
dot product, 67
pred tensor from model.predict, 20
sparse, 208
test datasets, 201
text classification, creating text embeddings,
  387
TextLineDataset, 15
tf.cond function, 253
tf.data API, 15
tf.einsum function, 183
tf.expand_dims function, 367
tf.gather function, 259
tf.image module, 214
  adjusting contrast and brightness of images,
    231
tf.image.extract_patches function, 367
tf.map_fn function, 259
tf.pow function, 253
tf.py_function, using to call pure Python code,
  252
tf.reduce_mean function, 16
tf.reshape function, 19
tf.transform function, 223-226
tf.where function, 253
TF_CONFIG variable, 263
  verifying setup for, 265
threshold (classification metrics), 289, 291
tiles, processing images to form, 238-239
TinyML, 326
tokenizing captions, 436
TPUs, 263, 311
  distribution to, training job submitted to
    Vertex Training, 274
  edge, 325
  sources for, 264
TPUStrategy, 263, 274
  creating, 267
tracing ML training (Tracin), 345
training datasets, 201
  creating for Keras model, 27
training events, monitoring, 287
training loss, 24
training models, 27-32, 330
  autoencoder model, 390
  image preprocessing and, 216-218

About the Authors

Valliappa (Lak) Lakshmanan is the director of analytics and AI solutions at Google Cloud, where he leads a team building cross-industry solutions to business problems. His mission is to democratize machine learning so that it can be done by anyone anywhere.

Martin Görner is a product manager for Keras/TensorFlow focused on improving the developer experience when using state-of-the-art models. He's passionate about science, technology, coding, algorithms, and everything in between.

Ryan Gillard is an AI engineer in Google Cloud's Professional Services organization, where he builds ML models for a wide variety of industries. He started his career as a research scientist in the hospital and healthcare industry. With degrees in neuroscience and physics, he loves working at the intersection of those disciplines exploring intelligence through mathematics.

Colophon

The bird on the cover of *Practical Machine Learning for Computer Vision* is an emerald toucanet (*Aulacorhynchus prasinus*), the smallest species of toucan. Central and South America have large populations from the cloud forests of Costa Rica to Venezuela.

Vibrant green feathers camouflage emerald toucanets in the tropics. Adults typically measure 12–13 inches long, weigh just over 5 ounces, and live 10–11 years in the wild. Their beaks are colorful: yellow on top, a white outline, and red or black on the bottom. They eat fruit and insects, as well as small lizards and the eggs and young of other birds. Groups of about eight will hunt and forage together. Emerald toucanets build their nests by enlarging the nests of smaller birds. The male and female trade off shifts in the nest, incubating, feeding, and cleaning their chicks.

Deforestation has driven emerald toucanets into shade coffee farms. Overall, their population is decreasing. Many of the animals on O'Reilly's covers are endangered; all of them are important to the world.

The cover illustration is by Karen Montgomery, based on a black and white engraving from *Shaw's Zoology*. The cover fonts are Gilroy Semibold and Guardian Sans. The text font is Adobe Minion Pro; the heading font is Adobe Myriad Condensed; and the code font is Dalton Maag's Ubuntu Mono.

Milton Keynes UK
Ingram Content Group UK Ltd.
UKHW032136220824
447251UK00004B/11